Contents

101 Years on Wall Street

An Investor's Almanac

John Dennis Brown

Prentice Hall, Englewood Cliffs, New Jersey 07632

Library of Congress Cataloging-in-Publication Data

Brown, John Dennis
    101 years on Wall Street : an investor's almanac / by John Dennis
  Brown.
      p.   cm.
    Includes bibliographical references and index.
    ISBN 0-13-946013-6
    1. Wall Street--History. 2. Stock-exchange--History.   I. Title.
  II. Title: One hundred one years on Wall Street. III. Title: One
  hundred and one years on Wall Street.
  HG4572.B74 1991
  332.64'273--dc20   90-21454
                                                           CIP

Editorial/production supervision
    and interior design: *Brendan M. Stewart*
Cover design: *Bruce Kenselaar*
Manufacturing buyers: *Kelly Behr* and *Susan Brunke*
Acquisitions editor: *John Willig*

© 1991 by Prentice-Hall, Inc.
A Simon & Schuster Company
Englewood Cliffs, New Jersey 07632

This book can be made available to businesses and
organizations at a special discount when ordered in large
quantities. For more information, please contact: Prentice-
Hall, Inc., Special Sales and Markets, College Division,
Englewood Cliffs, NJ 07632

This publication is designed to provide accurate and
authoritative information in regard to the subject matter
covered. It is sold with the understanding that the
publisher is not engaged in rendering legal, accounting, or
other professional service. If legal advice or other expert
assistance is required, the services of a competent
professional person should be sought.

From a Declaration of Principles Jointly Adopted by a
Committee of the American Bar Association and a Committee of
Publishers and Associations

Printed in the United States of America
10 9 8 7 6 5 4 3 2 1

ISBN 0-13-946013-6

Prentice-Hall International (UK) Limited, *London*
Prentice-Hall of Australia Pty. Limited, *Sydney*
Prentice-Hall Canada Inc., *Toronto*
Prentice-Hall Hispanoamericana, S.A., *Mexico*
Prentice-Hall of India Private Limited, *New Delhi*
Prentice-Hall of Japan, Inc., *Tokyo*
Simon & Schuster Asia Pte. Ltd., *Singapore*
Editora Prentice-Hall do Brasil, Ltda., *Rio de Janeiro*

8 Almanacs   268

9 The D.C. Connection   286

Glossary   294

Abbreviations   300

Index   303

Preface

This book is the production of an addict, drugged by the history and histrionics of the stock market. In self-defense, it has become necessary to retrieve the archives of the past century and assemble them into a single volume.

Stock tables and tales, books and charts threaten my living space. The financial tomes on table, shelf, and mantle are pyramiding, winning a creeping war with a clear view of the TV set. The golfer has become a library rat, searching for vignettes of market legend.

Fortunately, the bulging files, Moody's Manuals, and soaring Xerox bills sum up a fascinating history, offering surprising evidence that the stock market has changed not a whit in the past century. Only its price level. The Dow Jones Industrial Average (DJIA) has gained more than a hundred times since 1896, Dow 28.42 to 3000. Could even a Sherpa, having scaled such a peak, resist a long look back at the upward path?

The market buff, surely no stronger, will see that rascals and scoundrels still abound, as they did in the 1890s. Insiders still profit most, and not only because they know when not to sell. Bear raiders live; they are called program traders.

Every trick and treat on Wall Street has been cloned a hundred times. There have been no significant changes in the market, as opposed to the marketplace. Significant changes have come at the New York Stock Exchange and other important bourses. The demographics of the business have also changed. Individual investors have been elbowed aside by institutional money managers.

Changing more dramatically have been brokerage communications. Instantaneous price reports flash around the world. An electronic track has replaced the glass-domed Western Union ticker. Brokers' desktop minicomputers call up research reports, customer accounts, news, and a wealth of good and bad market recommendations. Picking the winners, however, is as dicey as ever.

The spectacular stock market ascent of the 1980s and the dramatic meltdown of October 1987 encourage a modern conceit that things on Wall Street are either much better or much worse than in the "old days." Not so.

The great bull market of 1982–1990 fell far short of the gains of the 1920s. And the Panic of '87, fortunately, could not match the dismal numbers forged in 1929, save for one horrendous day.

Eight years of Dow activity above the four-digit level do not mean that the game is any easier; adding a zero to the index level hasn't caused the bears to forget their old tricks.

In 1893, when financial backing vanished for the Philadelphia & Reading's merger plans, the railroad and the Rail average were smashed; the average fell 38 percent in just a few months. In the autumn of 1989, a leveraged buy-out of United Airlines lost its financial wings and the stock dived from 294 to 117; the carrier average dropped 29 percent. Banking defections—and every other market fright—have adjusted to the jet age and a stratospheric Dow.

What has changed is breadth, volume, and globalization; all the numbers, if not the percentages, have expanded enormously in the past century. In 1890, only a few score stocks traded on a regular basis at the Exchange and volume for the year would not make up a decent morning's trade today. But prices, on average, were higher then and there were more hundred-dollar stocks.

But I find no indication that lower quotations and a broader selection have brought better or fairer prices than when Benjamin Harrison resided in the White House. The small investors' chances of winning are probably worse than those of their grandfathers, the magic of computers having in some way consistently increased commissions at the retail level. In the meantime, stocks poorly chosen act as indifferently as ever.

Pools, corners, and manipulations continue, if disguised semantically. Junk bonds were not invented yesterday by Drexel Burnham. They were perfected over a century ago by greedy railroad promoters. J. P. Morgan advanced the Street's sophistication in 1901 when his U.S. Steel promotion floated a record amount of watered stock and junk bonds. He also did pioneer work in "green mail," ransoming control of the Louisville & Nashville Railroad.

What all those stock tables and tales, books and charts illustrate is an endless repetition of psychological patterns, frenzied speculations followed by panic, and desperate credit crunches. Both the highs and lows always magnify the facts. The restless market has not changed and the long climb to Dow 3000 was never easy.

Each decade has offered two or three splendid opportunities to make serious money in the stock market. And approximately the same number of opportunities to be financially blind-sided. The patterns will continue.

This 101-year stock market retrospect illustrates many other valuable lessons that will remain unchanged by time. As Justice Oliver Wendell Holmes, Jr., wrote in a 1921 decision, "A page of history is worth a volume of logic."

Introduction

Consider this marvelous contemporary description of the bullish merger mania that swept Wall Street in the early 1900s:

> Market and intrinsic values parted company. The business of commission houses swelled beyond all precedent, and weary clerks toiled to midnight adjusting accounts of lawyers, grocers, physicians, waiters, chorus singers and clergymen who were learning to acquire wealth without labor. . . .
>
> Florists, jewellers, perfumers, restaurateurs, modistes and vendors of automobiles rejoiced in the collateral prosperity secured to them by the boom in stocks.[1]

So it was in 1901. And 1929, and 1987, among other years. More is found in this volume on each of those years, and on every other year, bull and bear, since 1890.

A retrospect for each market year helps sort out the legends from the facts. The worst year in stock market history was 1931—not 1929 or 1932. And 1915, when America was armorer to a world at war, was the best. The Dow's gain then was triple the best year of the 1980s.

Longer sequences, bull and bear markets, are covered in Chapters 3 and 4. Panics, those swift and brutal purges that strike like a tornado in the night, are collected in the section on bear markets while "buying panics" are detailed in the previous section.

A Monthly Almanac forecasts September dangers and Christmas joys in a study of the 101-year record for each month. Election market sequences and decennial patterns are also noted.

Stock market statistics are gathered later in the book. The figures may be insufficient for some and too detailed for others, but salient points are capsuled in best and worst of series listings.

One can easily locate the largest volume day of 1899 or the worst market month of 1932 as well as the annual changes and ranges for the three most important Dow Jones averages.

The book's gauge for market change is the Dow Jones Industrial Average, except where otherwise noted. It may not be the best gauge, but it is the "Market" to the public and the best documented of all.

A short history of the Dow raises questions about the many substitutions in the list. Such giants as General Electric and General Motors were exiled for years, only to recover their Dow citizenship with little or no explanation. Hopefully, the *Wall Street Journal* archives will at some time reveal the secrets of the revolving door membership qualifications.

The "Outside Market," the former Curb Exchange that is now the American Stock Exchange, gets attention, though statistical records prior to the move indoors in 1921 are unreliable. Tokyo, the world's largest stock market and London, the world's broadest marketplace, are also sketched.

Throughout the book, stock prices and index levels have been rounded off, except when the figures have serious historic or mathematical importance. Major price movements—not always seen as major bull or bear markets—are tabulated, for market students often differ in their interpretations.

Percentage changes for the indices are stressed in statistical tabulations. That is the only way to equate fluctuations at the Dow 28 level, the low of 1896, with Dow 3000, the high of 1990.

1

Lessons from
the Past

HISTORY 101: DOW 28 TO DOW 2800

A history of the stock market teaches many lessons. Learning them is the problem.

The simplest lesson is that we are in a secular bull market. Ignored by the press on May 23, 1990, was the fact that the Dow Jones Industrial Average had on the previous day passed a monumental milestone. The average's close, 2852, marked an advance of 100 times from its historical low of 28.48 in August 1896.

In July 1990, at 3000, the Industrials were up over 1400% from the 197.46 low of July 1950, so a large gain has come in modern times.

Another lesson learned but herein ignored involves the danger of committing any long term forecast to print, where it can be harpooned by latter day chroniclers. The eminent Yale economist, Professor Irving Fisher, remains the most famous victim of the forecasting quicksands.

In August 1914, writing a special war feature for the *New York Times*, he commented that he saw little future for investment stocks during the conflict. In 1915, the Dow Industrial Average would enjoy its biggest advance of the century. In 1929, the unfortunate professor, finally converted to the bull side, opined that the stock market had reached a lofty "new plateau." Within weeks, the crash had written bear history.

The lessons from a 101 year retrospect are, however, so seductive that they demand formulation as to themes and patterns and as to the timing with which they might cast themselves for the balance of this century.

Generalities come first. Great price movements in the 1990s will plagiarize the bull-bear scripts of the past, but there'll be new stars and staging. Since the 1880s, nearly every decade has witnessed a Dow doubler, a bullish sequence or sequences which put the Industrials up at least 100 percent from an important low. Expect another before 2000. Don't expect 1989's final Dow level of 2753 to be doubled. But do expect a 100 percent gain from the first major low of the decade.

In the two decades of restraint during the past century—the 1960s and 1970s—the market compensated by offering a multiplicity of bull markets; there were three in each period. For the record, the best advance sequence in the 1960s amounted to 80 percent, while the best gain in the 1970s equaled 76 percent. Again, these measurements are only for the best segment, or segments, of the decade. The overall gain for the roller-coaster 1970s was but 38 Dow points, less than 0.5 percent.

A bear market will come in the 1990s, probably a pair of them. In the olden days, bear market declines of 40 percent to 49 percent were common, but modern investors have been lucky. There has been only one slump of that magnitude since the start of World War II; that was in 1973–1974. We don't expect a return of the bad old days, but setbacks in the 1990s will come more swiftly in a pattern similar to the price breaks of the late 1980s.

There will be no "new era." And price and value will continue to part company at market extremes. Price vaults over value at crests and value over prices at troughs, sometimes with alarming speed.

For instance, the innovative retailer, Gap, one of the big NYSE winners in the 1980s was valued at 78 in the summer of 1987. In October, the shares traded at 16, though earnings were at a record level and would rise further in 1988 and 1989. Sanity and reason depart the market in periods of great stress, when even the good news is held hostage to fear.

Gathering in the past suggests some specifics in time and probabilities. Decades ago, a highly successful trader at the Chicago Board of Trade "passed" and among his papers were found secret grain trading formulas—timing forecasts drawn from historical patterns. The secrets lived on as "The Voice From the Tomb." Similar secrets lie hidden in the archives of the stock market.

THE VOICE FROM THE TOMB: BULLISH FOR THE 1990S

Like the voice from the tomb, the stock market's record of the past 101 years holds ethereal warnings and promises for the 1990s. On balance, they are very optimistic. Every decade since the 1870s, save the dismal 1930s, has seen an advancing stock level and new peaks for corporate earnings.

The 1990s should not differ. Expect record earnings and a record price level for the Dow, once the quicksands of the decade's early years are passed.

The dramatic advance of the 1980s does not mean that the end is near in terms of the final high for the market.

A lag and lurch pattern can be identified on three occasions in this century. In each case, a secular period of broad consolidation was followed by a vigorous lurch ahead. In terms of both price and time, the previous surges out of a very broad horizontal consolidation into new high ground have extended far beyond the initial bullish leg.

When the industrial demands of World War I broke the 12-Stock Dow Average out of the 40–103 range which had bound it since 1897, that index was pushed up near the 160 level by late autumn of 1916. The revised, 20-Stock Average adopted at that time confuses the picture, but both averages pushed on to new highs in 1919. The terrible deflation that followed devastated the market but was not the end of the longer bullish episode, for the Dow reversed and rose to the historic heights of 1929.

In the 1950s the market broke the chains of depression psychology, and the appreciation of stocks, as reflected in their price-earnings ratios, was greatly expanded. Sharply higher share prices were seen in the next decade also. In 1982, the market, after losing an early round to inflation and a 20 percent prime rate, broke the reins which had restrained it since the mid-1960s. Prices, earnings, and dividends expanded rapidly, as they had in the Eisenhower years.

The large expansion of profits, dividends, and stock prices in the 1950s—the Dow was up 243 percent versus 178 percent in the 1980s—did not deter further substantial gains in the 1960s. And the vigorous restructuring of American industry in the 1980s promises further stock market improvement in the 1990s. Inflation, which undermined shares in the late 1960s, will be the wild card.

If the Dow should match the peak performance of the 1960s, when it rose 47 percent above the best level of 1959, then the average will move modestly above 4000 before the beginning of the twenty-first century. But, in line with historical patterns, patient investors should expect to be rewarded with more attractive buying opportunities than those afforded at the record levels of 1990.

When to Buy

The most profitable time for the purchase of stock in the 1990s will be in the early years of the decade, whenever the recession so long forecasted reaches black proportions. The eight years of economic expansion during the 1980s set a peacetime record and its life expectations were short in 1990. Perennial recession alarmists, like the stopped clock, would finally be right.

The market low for the ten-year period leading into the twenty-first century should come no later than 1993. This rationale is based on a study of the decennial patterns of stock prices (Chapter 8). It reveals that the Industrials' low in every decade has come in the early years: 1903, 1914, 1921, 1932, 1942, 1950, 1962, 1974, and 1982. Rather special circumstances such as World War I and Watergate/OPEC delayed the pattern in 1914 and 1974.

Otherwise the lows of 1913 and 1970 would have improved the record of early readings.

When to Sell

On the basis of the decennial record, expect the decade's high in either 1997 or 1999. Over the past century the Dow's decade peaks have been recorded in the following late years: 1899, 1907, 1919, 1929, 1937, 1946, 1959, 1966, and 1989. The S&P 500 and the NYSE index made their decade highs in 1968, not 1966.

The 1973 Dow high was a notable exception, but not for the market. Most of the broad-based market indices registered their ten-year tops in 1979. Smoke-stack stocks did the Dow "in" during the late 1970s.

Expect 1999 to be a double-strong "sell" year. Not only will it mark a decade's turn, with the anticipated usual hype like the alliterate "Soaring Sixties," but the applause for opportunities in the twenty-first century will have reached deafening proportions by that time. Industrial stock prices witnessed a major peak just before the beginning of the twentieth century, topping in September 1899.

George Lindsay's long-term timing studies, originally published in the "George Lindsay Opinion" and updated in the mid-1980s by *The Advisor,* call for an important market top in the fall of 1997, and a second, possibly superior high in 1999.

From a fundamental standpoint, portfolios should be liquidated if the Dow Jones price-earnings (PE) ratio approaches 20 times earnings in a maturing advance. In depression troughs and early recovery periods, a high ratio is not a valid danger signal.

The last time the Dow's PE ratio moved into never-never land was in the summer of 1987, a lovely time for a farewell to equities. At the August peak, the Dow had ballooned to 21.6 times trailing earnings. In 1972, the Dow ratio was only 15.2X, but the anointed "Nifty Fifty," so favored by institutions, was appraised at infinity. In December 1961 a record was established which still stands. The Dow reached 22.9X earnings; a seven-month bear panic was about to begin.

At the end of the 1950s, the ratio was 19.8 and trouble lay just a week away. In 1937, the market turned down from a 19.3 reading and in 1929 from 19.1. Twenty times earnings, history proves, is too rich a price for the Dow.

A "Perfect" Selling Rule

Selling stocks at the beginning of a recession is a perfect rule. Unfortunately, the event is not on real time. The official timer for the business cycle is the nonprofit National Bureau of Economic Research and their pronouncements are ex post facto handicapped since it usually takes two quarters of lowered output of goods and services to trigger the alarm. By then, the market has usually slumped. Such a scenario seemed probable in early 1991.

The Stocks to Buy

The great market performers of the past 70 years have been those innovative companies which offered products to make peoples' lives easier, more enjoyable or healthier, if not necessarily better.

The auto, motion picture, radio, and cable-TV industries all spawned sensational market performers. Xerography, fast food, instant pictures, chain stores, cigarettes, drugs, and computers built other marvelous leaders. Look for new products or companies that seem to offer prospects for an easier, more enjoyable life at home or work—or even on the jogging path, where the trendy Reeboks or Nikes might have been discovered. Also, be alert for technological breakthroughs in energy and environmental cleanup. A clean environment gets everybody's vote, but the big players over the past decade have already been rewarded with splendid gains. Their dominance will continue but more spectacular action will come from some of the niche companies and new technology. Clean water makers will do well.

Biotechnology has enormous promise, but many of the stocks are priced as if they had already packaged a combination nostrum for AIDS and cancer. Patient health investors will prosper with the veteran drug companies.

Retailing's Lure

Wall Street has always had a soft spot for innovative retail players. Sears, Roebuck (Sears), Woolworth, the Great Atlantic & Pacific, Federated Stores, Allied Stores and Wal-Mart, to name just a few, have enjoyed spectacular moves over the past 80 years. Home Shopping scored a sensational success in the 1980s before it crashed and burned.

Retailers were the top market group during the 1980s. Circuit City Stores, Limited, and Dillard Department Stores were among the NYSE's top performers, up between 3,823 percent and 8,265 percent. Toys 'R Us and Home Depot were other notables in a group which was not the consensus favorite in 1979. Toys 'R Us, for example, sold at five times earnings in 1980.

Rewards to successful retailers have always been rich, though the stocks lack the mystique of the high techs. On the other hand, IBM's gain in the 1980s was but 50 percent; it was a serious laggard.

Don't expect retailing sizzle to fully repeat in the 1990s, but anticipate that Wall Street will discover new favorites. A trendy newcomer will dominate the malls in the 1990s. Watch for it. The stock will receive top billing even if group appreciation is lower than in the 1980s.

For the Lazy Investor

Expect the dominant, successful giants of the past to roll on. Who will catch up with Coca-Cola, Procter & Gamble, Johnson & Johnson, General Electric, Minnesota Mining, Boeing, and Disney? The lazy investor can build a solid portfolio of such household names, accumulating them during the early 1990s.

"Far Out"

Shearson Lehman Hutton's imaginative 224-page "look back" from the year 2000 fantasizes a possible Dow 9500 in the 1990s. The estimate captures the "far out" award for long-term forecasts.

If Shearson is correct, there will be so many glorious winners that selection will not be all that important. But if some lesser reward—say Dow 4000—is the final top, then selection will become more vital. A march to 4000 would equal a percentage gain much smaller than that of the 1980s.

Investors will gain insight on the future from the next recession. Expect that the bigger winners of the decade's bull move will come from those industries and companies showing superior relative performance in the troubling decline. This excludes defensive-type stocks which offer a haven in hard times but lose their superior strength when "action" capital comes flooding back into the market.

BULLISH PASSAGES IN THE 1990S

Whatever the final market results in the 1990s, expect that at least two major buying opportunities will be presented. Every decade since the 1860s, save for the 1920s, has witnessed two major troughs.

The anatomy of the bull in the 1990s will resemble that of its predecessors, though bullish patterns and durations lack the ragged consistency displayed by most bear markets. They do last longer; gravity works speedy change in the price of shares, once they tilt downward. And they are generally more rotational in leadership. Stampedes are rare, though less so now that institutions run in a pack.

Their genesis is more easily recognized than that of bear markets. Expect them, in the 1990s, to be midwifed by a perception of easier credit and a startling expansion of volume to the upside. August 1982 was a classic, high-volume "V" turn sparked by a drastic downturn in interest rates.

Duration

Super-long bull markets have been rare. There have been only four since 1890, lasting from 73 months (1896–1902) to 96 months (1921–1929). Table 1-1 details 25 major Dow advances; not all rate as full-fledged bull moves.

Longish intervals, 38 to 56 months, have also been rare with only four since McKinley was elected to the White House in 1896. The last was February 1978 to April 1981.

More typical episodes have lasted from 21 to 32 months. The years between 1966 and 1976 recorded three in that range, and the 1957–1960 advance of 27 months was almost exactly at the timing midpoint.

Expect such nominal time spans during the 1990s. The stretched run of

TABLE 1-1 GAINS AND DURATION OF MAJOR ADVANCES

		Leading Dow average Percentage gains			
Years	Gain (%)	Years	Gain (%)	Years	Gain (%)
1921–1929	497	1907–1909	90	1900–1901	48
1932–1937	372	1962–1966	86	1893–1895*	47
1982–1987	250	1917–1919	81	1978–1981	38
1949–1956	222	1974–1976	76	1888–1890*	35
1896–1899	173	1987–1990	73	1966–1968	32
1903–1906	144	1970–1973	67	1890–1892*	30
1942–1946	129	1957–1960	63	1960–1961	30
1914–1916	112	1938–1938	60	1911–1912	29
				1939–1939	28

		Duration (Months + Days)			
Years	Duration	Years	Duration	Years	Duration
1921–1929	96m + 11d	1970–1973	31m + 17d	1917–1919	22m + 16d
1949–1956	81m + 25d	1914–1916	27m + 23d	1974–1976	21m + 16d
1982–1987	60m + 14d	1957–1960	26m + 15d	1987–1990	20m + 28d
1932–1937	56m + 3d	1903–1906	26m + 11d	1890–1892*	15dm + 26d
1942–1946	49m + 2d	1888–1890*	26m + 3d	1960–1961	13m + 19d
1962–1966	43m + 15d	1966–1968	25m + 27d	1911–1912	12m + 6d
1978–1981	38m + 0d	1893–1895*	25m + 10d	1900–1901	8m + 25d
1896–1899	36m + 29d	1907–1909	24m + 5d	1938–1938	7m + 13d
				1939–1939	5m + 5d

* Dow 20-Stock Average

the 1980s should not be a restraining influence. Super-long advances of 1896–1902 and 1949–1956 were followed by new highs in the next cycle. The bearish excesses of the post-1929 period delayed a new high for 25 years, however.

At a minimum, expect the DJIA to advance in at least six years during the 1990s, as it has in every decade since 1910, save for the 1930s.

Percentage of Gain

There is little gain commonality among bull moves. Take away the four supergainers—advances of over 200 percent—and the percentages drop sharply. Only four others gained over 100 percent and all from rather extreme lows, as in 1942.

Since World War II, there have been two superadvances and eight other important moves. Three of those were dwarf bulls, with advances of 30 percent to 38 percent. Four were in the plus 63 percent to 86 percent range. We expect this latter standard as a minimum during the 1990s. Table 1-1 shows the extent of gains in major advances.

The Passing

The passing of a bull market, unlike its birth, is usually lingering and confusing to investors and technicians alike. Deceitful tops often appear in place long before the true peak, as occurred in 1971 and 1984.

While a popular fancy endows the bull finale with a high volume, church steeple top, that formation is more common to individual stocks. The 1929 top remains the most infamous steeple, but the turns in 1919 and 1973 were equally swift.

Multiple tops have been more common. A so-called triple top in 1956–1957 stretched over 15 months with the Dow nicking the 520 level on three widely separated occasions. Well-formed double tops were recorded in 1937 and 1946, among other years. In 1906, a stretched top lasted from January until December. But the volatile 24-hour international market now in place suggests that the price tops of the 1990s will blow off more rapidly than in the past.

If church steeple formations have been an exception, peak volume frenzy at the market's major highs has been an absolute rarity. Not since 1916 have NYSE volume and the leading index topped out together. Volume peaks precede price peaks. In the 1921–1929 advance, monthly volume topped in November 1928. The 1987 activity high was in January; the Dow's peak came in August.

By reputation, the end of the bull markets of the 1990s will signal an impending depression. But none came in the aftermath of the 1962 Kennedy Panic. A gaggle of economists honked for a recession after the stunning meltdown of 1987, but there was none. Instead, earnings and dividends went to a record high the following year.

The Common Denominator

A common denominator for all bull markets is a total capitulation by the bears late in the game. In the summer of 1987, they finally ran up the white flag and surrendered en masse to Robert Prechter's long-touted target of Dow 3500. Bullish consensus then killed all.

Also common to the terminal bull is the "madness of crowds," usually focused on those stocks which have already scored enormous gains. Tales and visions of easy wealth, rumors of coups, pools, and secret machinations infect the senses.

In 1973, it was an institutional dementia. In 1968, it was "hot" new issues and as sorry a bag of trash as ever topped out a market—franchisors, conglomerates, and computer lessors. Oils in 1919, coppers in 1906, and the newly formed industrial trusts of 1901–1902 were previous siren groups.

In 1929, the scandalous investment trusts were the final madness, while in 1987 a merger mania seized speculators. The dread virus of greed, part gold rush fever and part Tulip Mania, has ended every bull market.

Other Anticipations

Expect that major peaks will be accompanied by a record number of stock splits, increased dividends, and brilliant earnings announcements. Such overwhelming good news is coincident and not an indicator of another leg of a long advance.

Remember that the patterns and durations of bull markets vary greatly, much more so than those of bear markets. The bullish adventures of the 1990s will differ from those of the 1980s, or those of the 1970s.

One absolute will remain. Price will outrun earnings, which is the key to really enormous stock market profits. In the extremely solid 1949–1956 advance, the Dow earnings increased by 42 percent and the composite dividend by 55 percent. But the Industrials' gain amounted to 222 percent as the price-earnings multiple for the average more than doubled.

BEARISH PASSAGES IN THE 1990S ───────────────────────────

Expect market joy to be more transient in the 1990s than in the last decade, with a return to more frequent bear episodes. In the 14 years from 1942 until 1956, there was one bear market. In the next 14 years, five. In 12 years from 1978 to 1990, there was but one bear market, plus one record panic. Expect a more two-sided market. The bear-beast is not endangered, just hibernating.

Duration

The 1990s should not bring any long bearish episodes, just more volatile moves, thanks to the globalization of markets. Since 1942, only one bear market has lasted over 18 months, the 1973–1974 production. Some earlier, secular types dragged on for years, as in 1937–1942. That long decline, however, can be divided into three distinct segments. The three bear markets encompassed in the early 1960s averaged only 160 trading days.

It doesn't take a grizzly to shred a pretty good stock portfolio, however. Dozens of quality stocks will be cut in half in even a minor bear market, as in 1960.

Percentage of Loss

Major bear markets have been amazingly consistent in their damage, 1929–1932 being a nasty exception, with the Dow down 89 percent. The uniformity of loss in severe declines can be seen in Table 1-2 with an average loss of 45 percent for eight major bear markets, excluding 1929-1932.

A major depression would cut the Dow by that amount again. But with a caring and cooperative Fed, one shouldn't expect it. There has been only one

---

TABLE 1-2   LOSSES AND DURATION OF MAJOR DECLINES

Leading Dow average — Percentage declines

Years	Loss %	Years	Loss %	Years	Loss %
1929–1932	89	1968–1970	36	1912–1914	24
1937–1938	49	1895–1896*	34	1981–1982	24
1906–1907	49	1899–1900	32	1946–1949	24
1919–1921	47	1909–1911	27	1938–1939	23
1901–1903	46	1961–1962	27	1956–1957	19
1973–1974	45	1976–1978	27	1960–1960	17
1892–1893	43*	1890–1890*	26		
1939–1942	40	1966–1966	25	1990–?	?
1916–1917	40				
1987–1987	36				

Duration (Months + Days)

Years	Duration	Years	Duration	Years	Duration
1946–1949	36m + 16d	1956–1957	18m + 17d	1960–1960	9m + 21d
1929–1932	34m + 6d	1968–1970	17m + 24d	1966–1966	7m + 29d
1939–1942	31m + 17d	1976–1978	17m + 8d	1961–1962	6m + 14d
1901–1903	28m + 24d	1892–1893*	16m + 23d	1890–1890*	6m + 5d
1909–1911	22m + 7d	1981–1982	15m + 17d	1938–1939	4m + 28d
1912–1914	22m + 1d	1916–1917	12m + 29d	1987–1987	1m + 25d
1906–1907	21m + 28d	1937–1938	12m + 22d		
1919–1921	21m + 22d	1899–1900	12m + 20d		
1973–1974	22m + 26d	1895–1896*	11m + 5d	1990–?	?

* Dow 20-Stock Average

such blow since World War II. Seven other declines since then posted losses between 17 percent and 27 percent, though the 17 percent intra-year figure for 1960 lacks serious bear credentials, despite an economic recession.

Dow 2000 should provide psychological support in the 1990s, just as 1000 was a psychological lid between 1966 and 1982. A decline to 2000 would mark a loss of 33 percent from the 3000 level of mid-1990, a nasty slide but not a killer wave.

The Passing

Individual stocks frequently end their bearish sequences in a frenzy of activity. And bear markets, by reputation, do also. But the greatest bear of all time ended with a low volume whimper in early July 1932. Activity in the previous month had been the lowest since 1924. The historic World War II bottom, the last below Dow 100, came in a week of very light trading.

Spike or "V" type turns remain common, seen in 1893 and 1896 as well as in 1970, 1978, and 1982. In many instances, however, a double bottom has been formed even after a sharp turn. October 1962 brought the Cuban missile crisis and a good second low after the bear bottom of June. In December 1974 the Dow dipped slightly under the low figure of early October. The wild gyrations of 1932 saw the Dow at 41 in July, 80 in September and then a frightening retreat back below 50 intra-day in February, 1933.

The market will not await a recession's end before turning. It anticipates, ordinarily by many months. In 1970, the recession did not end until November 1, by which time the Dow was already up 20 percent from its crisis low of May. Similar market anticipations were seen in December 1974 and August 1982.

The great panic of 1907 was followed in 1908 by a severe economic contraction, but the battered Dow gained a startling 47% in that latter year.

The widespread recession alarms of recent years should moderate the first downturn of the 1990s. History's worst market crashes have spun down out of clear air turbulence.

A Common Denominator

Panic and fear have been the common denominators at the crisis stage of bear markets. In the olden days, commercial panic, clearing house certificates and padlocked banks routinely heightened investors' alarm, but federal safety nets have reduced those financial threats.

The last 90 to 120 days of every bear market have witnessed a brutal acceleration of the Dow's decline, a frightening downward tilt in the chart slope. By early March 1932, the Dow was down nearly 77 percent from its 1929 peak. In the next four months, the loss was 53.5 percent—more than any other bear sequence—as the Industrials plunged from 89 to 41 with frightening speed.

A bear market in 1937–1938 was most severe, though it lasted but 12 months. But the decline in the final month of March was paralyzing, cutting 24 percent from a a market which had already suffered a nasty haircut.

In 1970, the April–May percentage hit on the Dow was over 20 percent, equalling the damage in the first 15 months of the decline from the 1968 peak. Watergate and tight money pushed the market into crisis in the summer of 1974. In mid-June, at 852, the Dow was at the same level as the 1973 year end. By early October, the average had fallen to 585, a 31 percent smash in about three-and-one-half months.

Under such conditions, stocks can be proven "cheap;" Disney, for example was under 17 in 1974 versus a peak at 122 the previous year. But will the cheap get even cheaper? Fear and razor-thin equities in margin accounts make good judgment impossible.

Someone, of course, always buys at those cheap prices. Insiders used to turn the markets. In recent decades, it has been institutional buying, for most have cash reserves and the strengthening knowledge that on the next day and every other day of the year, there will be additional funds rolling in. Mutual funds, unfortunately, are occasional victims of their shareholders' cash demands, being forced to liquidate fund portfolios near the market bottom.

Bear market reversals in the 1990s will be vitalized by frantic institutional buying volume. Peer pressures will suck the chips out of the money funds and T-bill caches, as they did in the dramatic turn of August 1982.

Neither Bull nor Bear

The stock market spends only about 60 percent of its time in a pure bullish or bearish mode. The remainder of its time is spent in reversing the primary thrust, by secondary reactions, for example, or in sideways action.

The 1921–1929 advance lasted for 96 months. In that long ascent the Dow advanced in 56 months, declined in 27, and moved sideways—less than a 1 percent monthly change—on 13 occasions. In 40 of 96 months, the Dow was out of phase or neutral to the major trend, or about 42 percent of the time.

Expect some lengthy consolidations lasting months during the 1990s. In the past they have lasted as long as a year, as in 1943–1944, or even longer—July 1947 to June 1949. A long, sideways formation with an upward tilt occupied the last three quarters of 1986, just prior to the explosive advance of the following January.

In 1901–1902, although already in a bear mode, the Industrials traded in a long line formation, roughly Dow 62–68, for nearly a year. They were able to avert trouble because of the new highs for the divergent Rails. But global markets of the 1990s will surely reduce the duration of consolidation patterns.

Warnings for the 1990s

The return of a virulent inflation could crush the optimism visualized for the 1990s. Certainly it makes it nearly impossible to forecast a logical level for the Dow eight or ten years out. Timing is much easier to forecast than price. As the decade moves on, probable price levels can be estimated. But how to forecast the nation's course of inflation and debt a half-dozen years ahead?

If one were guaranteed Dow earnings of $250 five years out, then how high the Dow? How would the earnings be esteemed? At 20 times that figure, a ratio seen at some giddy peaks in the past? Or at something near seven times, the depressed ratio of 1979, 1974, and 1948–1949? The difference in Dow value would be more than *3,000 points, 1750 to 5000!*

Inflation's course will play a large part in the appraisal of the market. Alan Greenspan, like previous Chairmen of the Federal Reserve Board, is determined to keep inflation at bay. His success should secure the "Nifty Nineties."

A failure—or his replacement by a political hack—will deflate the strong price-earnings ratios developed in the late 1980s and rework the optimism of "the voice from the tomb" into the "Nasty Nineties." Inflation will also determine the course of the bond market.

Perceived fears of the 1990s will be well discounted on Wall Street. It is the unexpected that will most quickly shatter prices. The market lived with the dangerous "cold war" for decades, with only occasional shocks, as in October, 1962. In 1989–1990, the war threat seemed to disappear and the market prospered with the democratization of Eastern Europe and hopes for a "peace dividend."

Thus it came to pass that the market was unprepared for the Persian Gulf events of August, 1990. Other Saddam-like surprises will blindside the market during the 1990s decade, but they are impossible to predict.

About the Bond Market

Over the centuries, the bond market has been free of most of the gyrations suffered by stocks. An occasional financial crisis—1893, 1907, 1921—pushed bond markets down to a handsome yield basis. But between 1890 and 1965, 6 percent was about as handsome as it got.

Decades of free spending and inflation finally whipped the U.S. bond market into unparalleled volatility in the early 1980s. A lot of hurt was dished out to bondholders who learned that a "triple A" rating would not protect against loss of half, or more, of one's principal.

Thus, several low-coupon AT&T bonds fell as low as 35, or $350 for a thousand-dollar par bond. Bond prices became as volatile and dangerous as stock prices.

If a reduction in inflation has reduced some of the dangers of owning bonds, volatility will remain high by the standards of any decade of the past century, save for the 1980s. Early 1990 was indicative.

In late December 1989, long Treasury bonds were selling to yield 7.85 percent and the experts' consensus was for a 7 percent yield before 8 percent, meaning that bond prices would advance sharply. Unfortunately consensus kills bonds as well as stocks.

March T-bond futures, priced well above par just before Christmas 1989, fell by $8,000 a contract by Valentine's Day. Paper losses on real governments amounted to about $80 a bond, or 8 percent in just a few weeks. "Safe paper" had lost nearly as much as the Dow in the surprising winter rout.

Expect such financial violence to continue. The world is linked in 24-hour trading systems, and untoward jiggles in the German bond market or Japanese currency can cause adversity for bond owners.

Clipping coupons is no longer a genteel occupation.

Investors who can't live with bond volatility should opt for CDs and money market instruments.

Bond funds offer diversification but no guarantees against rising yields. And distressed investors have learned that such closed-end offerings frequently sell at a discount to net asset value, regardless of quality. Another seamy bit of knowledge gained by fund investors is that the "enhancement" of bond fund yields by such sophisticated management techniques as options and futures hedging never equals the computer's needled model. The only sure success secret for bond investors is a rising bond market.

Institutional types, S&Ls, and pension managers learned in 1989–1990 that junk bonds were aptly named and deserved a yield of about 6 percent more than governments, not the stingy premium at which they had been so adroitly merchandised by Drexel Burnham Lambert and others.

Fortunately, few individuals were involved with the junk as a direct investment. As for the institutional money managers, the money, after all, was not theirs.

The final reckoning of the junk bond collapse of early 1990 will cause further after shocks. Many bonds not labeled "junk" will default in the next financial crisis; hundreds of companies have leveraged their operations to the hilt with increased debt.

Such foolishness buried the railroads a century ago and it will smash many industrials in the 1990s. There is reason to think that the next corporate debt crisis will be funereal for many firms. Thirty percent of all corporate cash flow, say the experts, is now devoted to interest payments.

Beware Bulgarian Fund #3

Single-country mutual funds like the Thai Fund and the Spanish Fund were among the startling winners in the stock race of 1989. Perestroika expanded Wall Street's horizons and at the beginning of the 1990s, the potential for economic makeovers in Eastern Europe was most beguiling.

The employment of funds in those backwater areas, it was said, would make investors rich. Or, at least, the underwriters. The minefields of language, currency, and cultural barriers in Eastern Europe were seen to pose only minimum problems, though foreign investment has proven a treacherous art, even for large English investments in American rails a century ago.

Fads overdone become Wall Street croppers, burying the tardy groupies. The racy success of early offerings—double-knits, solar power, franchising—always encourages a great outpouring of new adventures; latter-day promoters simply Xerox pioneer prospectuses and substitute new names for the originals.

Beware Bulgarian Fund #3. The fad will be over by the time Wall Street gets into serial financing for the Balkans.

Avoid Yesterday's Heroes

Don't buy the last cycle's heroes during the next recession. Hottest issues in the 1960s were the "go-go" stocks. Many disappeared from the stock tables in the next decade. Winnebago and Bausch Lomb would be the big winners for buyers at 1970s' trough, not the hot dogs of 1968.

In the 1970s, the oils, oil service shares, and golds were the biggest winners. Their collapse in the mid-1980s was classic. Radio Corporation and the other high flyers of the 1920s were good names to buy in 1932—like every other survivor—but the biggest heroes of 1929 did not repeat in 1932–1937.

A look back at other heated favorites shows the same problems. Oils, coppers, and steels, along with many other groups, have all struggled for years—at one time or another—to recapture past glories. The market can move any group swiftly higher, save for one with an enormous overhang of disenchanted investors, all anxious to sell once they can "get even."

2

Yearly Retrospects: 1890–1990

<u>1890</u> Why 1890?

It was not an important historical year nor was it an extravagant market year. It lacks the easy credentials of 1900's entrée into the twentieth century. And it is not posted simply to round out a 101-year odyssey.

The year 1890 leads off because it provides the first full year of statistics for a Dow Jones average which can be tracked into the 1990s. The index, the 20-Stock Average, can be traced directly to today's Transportation average, allowing for an occasional change of equipment. The year provides a natural beginning for a study of the major price movements of the Dow averages.

One should not presume that a Victorian innocence inhibited Wall Street a century ago. A free-spirited banditry ruled the New York Stock Exchange (NYSE) and it would continue for decades, barely sanitized by the Securities & Exchange Commission.

Pools, corners, and manipulations were common, as they had been since the Exchange was formally organized in 1817. Investor information was pretty much confined to insiders and corporate news was most generally revealed by rumor or market action. The most reliable statistics on the Street were from the railroads. And the most reliable journal of record was the weekly *Commercial & Financial Chronicle*, 44 pages in its first issue of 1890. *The Wall Street Journal* was a four-page daily.

The *Chronicle,* in its statistical review of 1889, published January 4, 1890, carried prices for 117 active issues, of which 81 were rails. A few industrial trusts, large business combinations, were listed but not trusted. Sniffed the *Chronicle,* ". . . it makes a vast difference whether a stock of the Vanderbilt sort is selling at 120 or a Trust certificate of unknown capitalization and unknown earning capacity."[1]

Heading the *Chronicle's* annual stock tabulation was the Atchison, Topeka & Santa Fe, which opened 1890's first day of trading at 33. Eleven of the active rail common stocks were priced over 100.

The 20-Stock Average (18 rails and two "industrials"—Western Union and Pacific Mail) opened at 72.06. This is the average tracked until the beginning of the separate Dow Industrial and Rail indices in 1896.

The decade got off to an excellent start, with various rail indices rising to their best level since the early 1880s. The New York, New Haven & Hartford, highest-priced active stock at the Exchange, touched 270. But it was to be a year of first-half strength, second-half weakness and panic.

The period's first stock market panic—and there would be many—was caused by a credit crisis in Argentina, of all places. The problems there forced London's great merchant bank, the House of Baring, into suspension as the massive government and rail credits which it had financed in the South American country crumbled. The Bank of England was forced to the rescue.

Baring Brothers, founded before the Revolution, had close and historic business ties with New York, and the cables of crisis from London pushed the New York exchange into a late autumn slump. The British were large holders of American securities and when London values were strained, New York could look for selling cables on American paper prior to its opening.

Aggravating the Rails' second-half slide was the Sherman Silver Purchase Act, passed in July; it had made the dollar suspect. Stringent money and a very poor grain crop combined to do further damage.

In each month after June, the leading index suffered lower highs and lows and the bear market was already well under way when it culminated in the Baring Crisis of early December. The six-month loss of about 26 percent would be typical of mini-bear markets for the next 100 years.

Individual issues, to be sure, were treated more drastically. The agricultural roads—the "Grangers"—were hard hit by the poor crop prospects. The Chicago, Milwaukee & St. Paul, then popularly known as the "St. Paul" and later as the "Milwaukee," fell from 80 to 44 while the Illinois Central was a 35-point loser from its peak at 120.

Serious erosion in the market had started in October. Unsettling news about the "gaucho speculations" brought London selling and in New York, the bullish schemes of Henry Villard in his controlled Northern Pacific and North American shares turned sour in November, after a strong Democratic showing in the off-election year.

Bear raiders took the Northern Pacific down from 28 on November 3 to 17

---

[1]The *Commercial & Financial Chronicle,* New York January 4, 1890, p. 30, col. 1.

a few days later and North American was slashed from 34 to 7 in the same period. On November 15 the hard news about Baring became public; a new low gave way to a sharp rally in late November. That was followed by a final low for the 20-stock index in early December.

Pricing had been no better at two rival exchanges—the outdoors, curbstone market (later the New York Curb Exchange) or the Consolidated Stock & Petroleum Exchange, housed in its own imposing building.

The nouveau industrial stocks had received their first severe testing. Edison General Electric, the "electric trust," tumbled from 119 to 65. Sugar Refineries, "the sugar trust," melted away from 79 to 48 within three months. It would be re-named American Sugar Refining in 1891.

The six-month decline remains one of only three intra-year bear markets; the others occurred in 1960 and 1966.

1890 20-Stocks First 72.06. High 78.38 Jne 4. Low 58.10 Dec 8. Close 61.96, −14.1%.

1891 American grain farmers and the railroads would be doubly blessed in 1891. A wheat crop without parallel would find a huge wheat-flour export demand, with record grain tonnage moving to tidewater in the last few months of the year.

The size of crops and exports were vital factors in rail traffic and the nation's economy a century ago. Crop conditions and export potential were given broad coverage in the financial press. Thus, the agricultural events of August would swiftly reverse an uninspired market.

The London Panic of late 1890 had been brutal, but soon ended. By the end of January 1891, the Bank of England had reduced its interest rate twice and repaid the emergency gold loan from France.

Easier rates helped confidence in the United States, but business dragged. Iron production, a key industrial gauge, fell heavily with first-half output down 25 percent from the same period of 1890. By late July, the Rail average had slumped back to the closing level of 1890.

Then, it suddenly became known that Russian farmers were facing a complete crop failure, proving that the communists only inherited the problems of farming in those northern latitudes. France also would have a disastrous harvest.

In early August, the Czar's ukase banned the export of rye, an embargo to be followed later by one on wheat. America's record bounty of the plains would have no problem finding a profitable market.

Rails rallied enthusiastically. Granger roads, whose car-loadings would shoot up, were coveted regardless of quality. The Minneapolis & St. Louis more than doubled, 8 to 18, between July and August. Iowa Central moved from 6 to 16 during the fall, the M-K-T from 8 to 21. The Atchison, which had advanced from 25 to 47, peaked in September, but most carriers remained firm into the year-end, as dividend hikes were widely anticipated.

"Miscellaneous stocks," issues other than the railroads, did well also. American Cotton Oil, 17 in July, doubled. Chicago Gas jumped from 42 to 72. But the large repatriation of gold to London early in the year barely nudged Homestake Mining, the nation's largest gold producer. It moved up only two points, to 13. In the fall, the huge grain exports returned bullion and pushed the United States into its best trade balance in ten years.

1891 20-Stocks First 62.75. High 73.25 Dec 28. Low 61.50 Jly 30. Close 72.88, +17.6%.

1892 By the early 1890s, a few industrial stocks had found a home at the NYSE, but the list was slim and fairly well confined to the trusts formed in the previous few years—sugar, lead, tobacco, cotton oil, and so forth.

So traders were happy to find several new industrials introduced to the Exchange in 1892. Their names would be around a long time: General Electric (succeeding Edison General Electric) and U.S. Rubber. Colorado Coal (Fuel) & Iron, to be a speculative leader for decades, also joined the listings.

The year started out with great speculative volume in the rails. Activity was centered in the coal roads as Angus McLeod and the Philadelphia & Reading Railroad hatched a plot to monopolize anthracite production and transportation. The Reading would lease the New Jersey Central and Lehigh Valley roads and manage the Lackawanna's coal business.

Such a combination, it was hoped, would "enhance the price of coal by monopoly" and thus bring great fortunes to shareholders and coalers. In the January–February period, Central of Jersey ran from 112 to 145 and Delaware, Lackawanna from 69 to 84. The Reading did even better, advancing from 19 to 33 by February 11, when it set a trading volume record. Total activity soared to 1,447,000 shares at the Exchange, also a record.

But within a month, the market had topped and the stocks trended raggedly lower for the balance of the year. Crops were reduced and the Granger railroads put on the defensive. Investment rails, like the New York Central, whose range was a narrow 108–119, were quiet, while the Richmond Terminal and associates slipped into a friendly receivership. The Richmond system, a labyrinth across the Old South boasted over 8,000 miles of tracks, second only to the Atchison.

Autumn slippage in the pools of the Distillers Trust and the New York & New England railroad hurt the market, but General Electric, listed in the summer, was solid enough, with a range of 104–120.

The year had been marked by growing political and labor unrest, including the bitter, bloody strike at Carnegie Steel's Homestead, Pennsylvania, works. Populist leaders were demanding Federal ownership of the railroads, telegraph, and telephone companies along with an income tax and unlimited silver coinage.

Bulls were further offended when Grover Cleveland was returned to the White House, after a four-year sabbatical, along with a Democratic Congress, only the second since the Civil War. Prices slipped lower, recording an unusual Christmas low.

The year 1892 can be remembered as a watershed year in historical minutia. The western frontier was passing and in Coffeyville, Kansas, one of the nineteenth century's last "badman" legends passed as the Dalton gang was wiped out in an attempted bank heist. In Massachusetts, the Duryea brothers opened a lane into the twentieth century, patenting the first gasoline engine.

1892 20-Stock First 73.45. High 75.68 Mar 4. Low 66.86 Dec 23. Close 68.10, −6.6%.

1893

The last great mercantile and credit crisis of the nineteenth century smashed the market in 1893. During the summer, the casualty list included a fast-swelling list of banks, insurance companies, and brokers. Cash currency commanded a premium of 5 percent over certified checks.

Saddest event of the year, however, was the long roll call of railroad failures and receiverships, a listing which included many of the great names of rail history along with the perennial cripples, like the Erie.

The Reading suffered the first major derailment. Burdened by enormous interest charges and bank debt, the rail-coal monopoly went into receivership in February. Some said that the Reading failure came because it had taken control of the New York & New England Railroad, which Drexel-Morgan had coveted for the New Haven. A banking squeeze, vengeful or not, did the Reading in. Its shares, 33 a year earlier, would fall to 6 in the summer panic.

Trustification, as would be proven many times in the next ten years, came easier than trust profits.

In May, the National Cordage sham collapsed. James R. Keene, who had helped manipulate the stock to 74, had liquidated his position before the trap was sprung. The shares, 69 in April and 57 early in May, collapsed to 10 in the latter month.

The nation, at the same time, suffered from a growing currency crisis, originating in the Sherman Silver Act of 1890 and driven by a growing foreign distrust of dollar holdings. Heavy foreign selling of securities encouraged the efflux of gold and the Treasury's bullion holdings fell dramatically.

Commercial and banking failures increased. The New York Clearing House was forced to issue loan certificates, whereby banks short of ready cash could deposit other collateral with the clearing house, receiving in return the loan certificates. These could be used for interbank clearances and even found ready acceptance among private citizens.

In the meantime, rail traffic had collapsed. At the Union Pacific, earnings estimates dived in June. "Bottom dropped out of west bound transcontinental traffic," was the wire to headquarters.[2]

-----

[2]Maury Klein, *Union Pacific, Birth of a Railroad, 1862–1893* (Garden City, NY: Doubleday & Company, Inc., 1987), p. 655.

The bear market climaxed on July 26 as the Erie bit the receiver's bullet for the third time; the 20-Stock Average closed at 43.47, down 39 percent from the January high. Encouraged by bargain prices, European buying, and the probability of a repeal of the Sherman Act, the market then mounted a spectacular rally. American Sugar, 135 in February and 62 in July, traveled back to 106. Chicago Gas, 95 in January, had been smashed to 39 in July but recovered to 70. Distillers & Cattle Feeding, always a pool favorite, was lifted up from 12 to 35 in the rally of early fall.

The speculative rails, however, continued to fall, even though the Silver Act would be finally repealed in November, by which time the action was fully discounted. The Union Pacific went under the gavel in October and the Atchison and then the New York & New England would, in December, join the other 72 roads meeting in the nation's courthouses because of 1893 receivership or bankruptcy. The market sagged sharply in December on the unexpected news of the Atchison default.

1893 20-Stocks First 67.65. High 70.87 Jan 21. Low 43.47 Jly 26. Close 51.35, −24.6%.

1894 Depression gripped the nation in 1894, but the stock market panic and distress liquidation of 1893 had already anticipated and discounted most of the year's problems, one of which remained the demands of the Silverites.

The silver clamor rose again, as farm prices fell to disaster levels. Wheat, $1.16 per bushel in the export boom of 1891, dropped to 50 cents. Corn, 40 cents a bushel in early 1893, sold for about 20 cents at Chicago. Free and unlimited coinage of silver was seen as the inflationary prescription for low crop prices.

The bargain stock prices of July 1893 had been erased by the fierce autumn rally, and share fluctuations in 1894 were restricted. U.S. Rubber, which had fallen to 17 during the 1893 crash, had closed the year at 43. Its 1894 range would be but 12 points: 33–45.

During the summer, the rails were nearly paralyzed as a result of the sympathy strike by the American Railway Union on behalf of the Pullman strikers. The year's best rally came in August, when the three-month strike ended. Action in the industrial trusts, often manipulated, was more volatile than that of the rails.

American Sugar Refining spun up from 76 to 110. Several senators, it was later determined, had their hand in the sugar bowl and had slyly added duties on the importation of both raw and refined sugar to a new tariff reduction bill. Other, more honest Democrats did force through general cuts in customs duties. Such loss of revenue to the federal government necessitated an income tax, to Wall Street's sorrow.

Another poor crop year curtailed the market's August enthusiasm and many rails, including the Baltimore & Ohio, the nation's oldest road, cut their dividends. The B&O fell from 82 in April to 58 in December. Meanwhile, J. P.

Morgan, having successfully reorganized the Richmond Terminal system, brought the 1892 rail casualty out under a new flag, the Southern Railway.

Though stock indices ended the year near their lows, they had at least survived a period of terrible depression, one which saw grain prices at their lowest average level in the history of the country, and unemployment and labor unrest at a new peak. Over 640 banks had failed.

If stock prices had been apathetic, volume at 49 million shares, about half of what it had been ten years earlier, was even more so.

1894 20-Stocks First 50.73. High 57.60 Aug 27. Low 50.73 Jan 2. Close 51.06, −0.6%.

1895

Market technicians were little noted in 1895. But if identified, they would have been confused. Following the passive year of 1894 the 20-Stock Average in March an 18-month low but quickly reversed with a dazzling rally which pushed the index to a two-year high in September. Another reverse then took place and autumn erosion led to the year's most startling action—the December Venezuelan panic—and a new 1895 low. Such multiple whipsaws have been rare, particularly within a one-year span.

The December shock came when President Cleveland astonished the natives and England by launching a missile message to Whitehall which seemed to threaten war on our largest creditor. The underlying cause had been a border dispute between England and Venezuela, which caused Cleveland to chime the Monroe Doctrine.

Weakness in early 1895 had been caused by a perennial gold crisis. But a Morgan syndicate had swapped gold for 30-year 4 percent government bonds and saved the Treasury and sound money concepts, for a time.

The market's response, a 31 percent rally between March and September, was ahead of business conditions; the Atchison, in reorganization had risen from 4 in January to 24. A portion of the summer push sprang from a Supreme Court decision voiding the income tax clause of the 1894 tariff.

By 1895, September had already earned a bad market reputation. So it should have been no surprise when the Labor Day week rolled the market over from its peak on September 4. Prices slid during the fall despite good crop production, with a loss of about 10 percent for the Rails.

The Dow crashed in December, down nearly 15 percent in the third week alone when it suffered a climatic loss of 8.5 percent on December 20. Not until 1931 would the Rail average again take such a beating.

Coming on top of the autumn stumble, the fierce panic saw many stocks cut in half from their September highs. General Electric, a leader earlier in the year, spun down from 42 to 21, losing 12 points in the crisis selling. Other leading issues losing 50 percent included the St. Louis Southwestern (Cotton Belt), National Lead, and the Missouri, Kansas & Texas (Katy).

Southern Rail found that Morgan's cloak did not deceive the bear and the stock dropped from 15 to 7. The Reading lost 80 percent of its value in three months. But December's presidential bluster was quickly gone, along with the foreign crisis, and the Rails, after touching a new low for the year, firmed and ended 1895 on the plus side.

1895 20-Stocks First 50.52. High 63.77 Sep 4. Low 48.56 Dec 21. Close, 52.23, +2.3%.

1896   The vexing whipsaw action of 1895 was replaced in 1896 by something rather worse, another extension of the bear scenario which had been in place since 1892. In the process, most rail indices would plunge to their lowest level since 1885. For other averages, it was the lowest point since 1878.

Market pricing started well. Cleveland's war buffoonery was quickly forgotten and a large sale of government bonds for gold put the Treasury's gold reserve problems to rest for a few months.

But rails were shocked when the historic Baltimore & Ohio went into receivership in the early spring. The road was the largest corporation in Maryland and its debt and shares were heavily owned by the City of Baltimore and Hopkins University. The stock, 44 in January, plunged to 13 in March.

The "silver problem" revived in the summer. William Jennings Bryan, the fire-brand silver advocate, was nominated as the Democratic candidate for the White House. He mesmerized his Chicago convention with his "Cross of Gold" speech and the threat of further currency chaos swayed the market to panic, as gold again emigrated from the country. Political parties split badly. There were "silver Republicans" and "gold Democrats," but Bryan's strength peaked too early, in August.

It was at this time that the newly created Dow Jones Industrial Average recorded its all-time low, 28.48, having lost 30 percent of its value in about two months. (Its first reading was at 40.94 on May 26, 1896.) National Lead and General Electric both lost about 50 percent of their value in the drop from April levels and Colorado Fuel was hurt worse, 34 to 14.

Rails were badly wounded, and some quality issues, relatively unaffected by the terrible rail crisis of 1893, dropped below their worst level of that year. The August collapse was compounded by the failure of the Moore brothers in Chicago. "Heedless speculation" in a pair of industrials, New York Biscuit and Diamond Match, was their undoing. The Chicago Stock Exchange would be padlocked until November, but the "silver panic" was ended.

By late August, the hysteria of the Silverites had become a handicap, and the merits of sound money, both in the nation and in Mark Hanna's GOP campaign coffers, more apparent.

An excellent and predictive rally got under way and carried through the election, though a short panic in call money pushed the rate to 127 percent on October 21. Call money, which could be "called" in at any time, was lent to brokers to finance their inventory of securities or to aid them in financing their customer margin accounts. Just before the election, nervous investors were backed up at the New York Subtreasury's gold window, seeking insurance against a surprise Bryan victory.

William McKinley captured the election and stocks topped out within a few days, having discounted the GOP victory in the swift rally of autumn.

It had been a wild year. Chicago Gas fell from 71 in May to 45 in August but reached 79 in November. American Cotton Oil's roller-coaster went from 19 to 8 to 18. Southern Pacific preferred was routed from 33 to 16 and back to 33, all within seven months.

The 1896 election had not laid the silver question to rest. Bryan would be the Democratic nominee for President again in 1900 and 1908. But a growing prosperity, lowered unemployment, a strong trade balance, and much higher farm prices during the next few years would sap silver's appeal.

1896 20 Stock First 51.83. High 56.79 Feb 24. Low 41.82 Aug 8. Close 51.33, −1.7%.

1897

The year 1897 was the first full year in which we have the advantage of a complete Dow Jones Industrial Average along with the older, Rail average.

Both made a hesitant start but rallied vigorously after mid-April and recorded their annual highs in September. Doubts then set in. There had been many false starts since 1893 and the "Cuban" problem cooled enthusiasm, as rioting in Havana and Spanish belligerency over the island's future continued.

Some of the spring hesitancy had been caused by the Trans-Missouri Rate Case. The Supreme Court verdict broadened the Sherman Anti-Trust Act's scope and ruled against the railroad rate pools. Lows for the year were seen in April, at the time of an outbreak of a war between Greece and Turkey.

Summer strength was stirred by a Supreme Court decision, which inhibited the rate powers of the Interstate Commerce Commission, and a new GOP tariff. Big volume flowed into the Street; second-half activity was more than double that of the first six months at the NYSE. Rails were particularly favored; their earnings along with those of the iron companies were improving rapidly.

Voting trust certificates for the Northern Pacific doubled in value, 11 to 22, and shares of the New York Susquehanna tripled. The Missouri Pacific, 14 in April, reached 40 in September. American Sugar's stock price benefitted from new sugar duties. The company had been wise enough to stockpile quantities of the commodity before the new tariff went into effect. The stock surged from 110 to 160. National Lead doubled.

Urban and interurban rails—known as the electrics versus the steam railroads—captured the attention of promoters, politicians and manipulaters. Metropolitan Street Railway, a consolidation of practically all the street railways of Manhattan Island, was a favorite. Its stock, at par in October, reached 132 in December, despite an easier market. Overcoming the handicap of a 20 percent stock dividend, the shares were then bulled to 172 by February 1898.

An improving attitude in late autumn resulted from the splendid grain crops and a huge demand from Europe, which had suffered a poor harvest. Wheat advanced to its best level since 1891.

The prospect of enhanced gold reserves also buoyed spirits as Alaska enjoyed its first real boom. Thirty thousand Americans rushed to the Klondike where gold had been discovered the previous autumn. The news had not reached the West Coast until the early summer of 1897.

After the disappointing depression of the mid-decade, new hope for trade, a stable currency, and business finally seemed to assure the nation that prosperity was, indeed, just around the corner.

1897 DJIA First 40.74. High 55.82. Sep 10. Low 38.49 Apr 19. Close 49.41 +22.2%.

1898 The second year of the McKinley administration treated the market, foreign trade, and the nation with equal kindness. America's first foreign war in a half-century was quickly turned into an overwhelming victory.

War against Spain began in April and ended in July. Both averages made their lows in the spring, following weeks of moderate pressure caused by the sinking of the battleship *Maine* in Havana harbor on February 15.

Trustification, the formation of giant industrial combinations with, some said, an intent of monopoly, had been comatose since the depression of 1893, but prosperity quickly revived it. The trust boom would last until 1903.

Federal Steel, which would itself be consolidated into U.S. Steel in 1901, paved the way with a huge $100-million amalgamation. Included were five steel companies, enormous iron ore reserves and an assortment of rails and lake steamship firms. National Biscuit, Union Carbide, and Otis Elevator were also trusted in the same year, along with the English-controlled American Thread Company, which would become the first U.S. industrial to be listed at the London Stock Exchange. For the first time, speculative interest converged on the industrial shares.

The bull market gained great momentum in June. Rail earnings were improving and a huge spring wheat crop would push results for the northwest carriers—the Northern Pacific, St. Paul, Great Northern and Canadian Pacific—sharply ahead. The Northern Pacific more than doubled from 19 to 44.

Industrial weakness of early spring was strongly reversed. Colorado Fuel, which had fallen from 27 to 17, would reach 33 by the year end. The new trusts benefitted from a great deal of floor muscle later in the year. Federal Steel, 29 in October, reached 52 by the year end, and National Biscuit climbed from 31 to 53 in the same period. The oldies were not forgotten, however. U.S. Rubber more than tripled, from 14 to 48. N.Y. Air Brake was the year's most sensational pool performer; only 14 in April, it reached 120 in September, fell back to 89, and then rebounded to 120 in December.

A strong GOP showing in the off-year elections boomed the market at the year-end and the Rails ended December at their peak price for the year, while the Industrials were less than one-half point below their August high.

1898 DJIA First 49.31. High 60.97 Aug 26. Low 42.00 Mar 25. Close 60.52, +22.5%.

1899

Domestic trade, foreign commerce, and the flotation of industrial undertakings were all at a record level in 1899. In the first two months of the year, industrial combinations representing a capitalization of over $1.1 billion were promoted—an amount far exceeding the figure for all of 1898.

Speculative frenzy reached the high point of the decade. Pools and manipulations were everywhere. January set the tone when 13 trading days registered volume of over 1 million shares. There had been none in the previous two years.

Prices boomed until May, when the death of ex-Governor Flowers, a leading bull in the industrial sector, cut short the "Flower Market." His machinations had helped push N.Y. Air Brake from 14 to 200 and the shares were at 185 on the day of his death. The next day, the stock wilted to 135, compounding the grief of his followers.

But the excitement of many new trust manipulations helped the market recover quickly and both averages advanced to their yearly highs in September. All of the trusts were overcapitalized, and many would quickly falter.

But some of the Trust Class of '99 survived famously, in one form or another, for nearly a century. American Car & Foundry, Borden, Electric Boat (General Dynamics), Republic Steel, Union Bag, and United Fruit are among them.

Amalgamated Copper gained control of the Anaconda Montana property and amalgamated it with other mines in the year's largest consolidation. The initial underwriting was rigged as were most of the stock's moves over the next eight years. Rockefeller interests controlled the company.

The Industrials peaked in the post-Labor Day session. Labor threats, high money rates, and the prospect for war in the Transvaal then eroded the market. War came on October 12 in South Africa and Britain's dismal fortunes were duly reported to the world by a pair of most famous war correspondents—Winston Churchill and Richard Harding Davis.

A war crisis led to London selling and panic in the bloated industrial sector. In December, the Dow lost 23 percent in a two-week period. A sharp fall on December 18 of 8.7 percent would stand as its record loss for 30 years.

The trusts and manipulations paid the piper during the autumn malaise. American Malting, a new combination, fell from 34 to 7. International Paper lost nearly 50 points from its high at 66. International Silver, another 1899 beginner, dropped from 36 to 10 within three months while John W. Gates' American Steel & Wire, a 1899 re-trustification, was knocked down from 72 to 32.

In December, both averages fell below their 1898 closes, but improved war news brought a sharp rally late in the month, allowing the indices to end moderately higher for the year. But for many new issues, the major price rewards of trustification had already been recorded. It would take 17 years for International Paper to recover its lost ground.

Despite the Great Train Wrecks of 1893 and the depression years of 1894 and 1895, the Dow Rails had managed a 25 percent gain for the decade. Their market dominance was not yet challenged by the new industrial trusts, for it was only in the last 18 months of the decade that the nouveau Dow group had gained a solid speculative following.

1899 DJIA First 60.41. High 77.61 Sep 5. Low 58.27 Dec 18. Close 66.08, +9.2%.

1900 "McKinley Prosperity" spread across the nation at the beginning of the twentieth century and business cashed in. AT&T's subscriber base gained 27 percent in the year and rail earnings were at the best level since 1883. Standard of Jersey increased its dividend from $33 to $48 and the shares climbed to 825. The shares traded at the Curb and would not transfer to the NYSE until 1920.

Two old neighbors on St. Paul's Summit Avenue wrapped up one of the nation's biggest real estate deals. James J. Hill's Northern Pacific sold Frederick G. Weyerhaeuser's lumber group 900,000 acres of the rail's huge land grant timber holdings at $6 per acre.

Rails far outnumbered all other groups at the NYSE, but the *Commercial & Financial Chronicle* also carried listings under three other headings: Express, Coal & Mining, and Various. Gas companies, old-line trusts, and tobaccos were prominent among the "Various." Two Mexican railway systems and two Canadian carriers, including the popular Canadian Pacific, made up the active foreign listings.

Though investors approved of the GOP verities such as a high tariff and sound money—the nation returned to a formal gold standard in May—stocks failed to match business gains. Some 60,000 U.S. troops were tied down in the Philippines searching for the rebel, Aguinaldo. Others helped face the Boxer Rebellion in Peking.

Fears of populism and free silver were revived by the Democratic nomination of William Jennings Bryan and many speculative issues were hard hit. Republic Steel dropped from 28 to 9 and U.S. Rubber lost more than half its value, 44 to 21. The summer rally was nearly invisible; each month, January to September, saw a new low.

In that latter month, the Galveston Hurricane laid 8,000 to rest along with a few insurance companies, but the Industrials ended their minor bear market a few days later. It had lasted exactly one year. The Rails, meanwhile, had fallen by less than 13 percent.

A frenzied buying panic seized the market after McKinley's re-election.

Colorado Fuel & Iron, 29 in September, leaped up to 57. Also in November, the nation's first auto show debuted in New York; it offered a full menu of power: 19 gas cars, 7 steamers, 6 electrics, and a pair of hybrids.

General Electric was the muscle in pushing the Industrials higher for the year, following the earlier stresses typical of the decennial "0" years. The bullish enthusiasm of the election period boosted the Industrials 34 percent off the September low. General Electric doubled its dividend, as sales leaped over $25 million, and the stock touched 200. It was the growth leader of the new "electric age," and the highest-priced Industrial issue.

Heated demand for speculative rails boomed the entire market in the last quarter. Erie 2nd preferred nearly tripled between September and the year-end, as did the Cotton Belt. The Katy almost doubled, while the St. Louis & San Francisco ran up from 9 to 25. None of those stocks were in the Rail average, but the quality lines had also benefitted; the average ended the year on its absolute high.

1900 DJIA First 68.13. High 71.04 Dec 27. Low 52.96 Sep 24. Close 70.71, +7.0%

1901 America's first billion dollar corporation, U.S. Steel, was formed in early 1901, put together in a lightning thrust by J. P. Morgan. In capitalization, assets, and sales and with 168,000 employees, it immediately dwarfed every other company in the world.

It brought together Andrew Carnegie's efficient plants, along with hundreds of other domestic ironworks. For the most part, they were already neatly packaged in established consolidations. Morgan made U.S. Steel a "trust of trusts" by joining together American Steel & Wire Co., with its 29 concerns, the American Sheet Steel Co., with 26 concerns, and eight other huge organizations.

Following hard on a series of rail mergers and raids, the Steel trustification spurred great speculation. "Announcement of the steel merger . . . inflamed the public imagination . . . and all classes and conditions of men came tumbling into the market intent upon doubling their money in a day," wrote Edmund Clarence Stedman.[3] The narcotic spell of a bull market was no different in 1901 than in 1929 or 1987.

In April a frenzy of trading and speculation swept the Rail group. Rumors of mergers and consolidations drove prices and volume to record levels with Union Pacific trading a record 650,000 shares on one day.

The wildest days lay ahead, however, as Edward H. Harriman, the Union Pacific, and Kuhn, Loeb & Co. battled James J. Hill, the Great Northern, and J. P. Morgan for control of the Northern Pacific. The Northern Pacific had just gained control of the Chicago, Burlington & Quincy, a line which Harriman

---

[3]Edmund Clarence Stedman, Editor, and others. *The New York Stock Exchange: Its History, Its Contribution to National Prosperity, and Its Relation to American Finance at the Outset of the Twentieth Century,* New York. Mail and Express Job Print, 1905, p. 397.

also coveted for its strategic connection into Chicago. Harriman's secretive buying of Northern Pacific shares was shortly revealed as the stock, below 100 in April, rushed up to 160.

Short sellers swarmed to the attack, but Morgan was determined to save control of the Northern Pacific and ordered 150,000 common shares bought at the market, there being 800,000 shares (half voting preferred) outstanding. The price exploded to 1000 as desperate shorts rushed to cover. "Giants of Wall Street in Fierce Battle for Mastery, Precipitate Crash that Brings Ruin to Hordes of Pygmies" was the banner head on the *New York Herald,* May 9.

Good stocks were heedlessly sacrificed by the shorts to cover losses in the Northern Pacific. From a high of 88 on May 7, the Santa Fe was cut to 43 on May 9. U.S. Steel lost more, percentagewise, 53 to 24. Harriman's Union Pacific was smashed from 131 to 76. But the enormous losses were just half of a classic yo-yo pattern. On May 10, a huge reflex rally occupied the market. Steel rallied back to 45 and the Union Pacific to 112. The advance for the Rails, 6.5 percent, would stand as their largest daily gain until 1931.

The Dow also moved higher and reached a mini-bull peak in June. A strike against U.S. Steel and the September assassination of President Mc-Kinley kept the Industrial group under pressure for the balance of the year. Republic Steel fell from 24 to 12 and Amalgamated Copper from 130 to 61 between June and September. The Rails, diverging, ended the year with a modest gain. Between May and December the Frisco was a 22–57 winner and the Erie 2nd preferred tripled to 75.

General Electric continued as a vigorous exception to general weakness among the trusts. Its January low was 184 and the year's high came in December at 290. Unfortunately, its strength couldn't help the Industrials. Schnectady's pride had been ousted from the average, replaced by the likes of the manipulated Amalgamated Copper.

If U.S. Steel and the Northern Pacific carnage were the primary business headlines of the year, there was at least one other story of equal importance— oil. An enormous wildcat well, 100,000 barrels a day, blew in just south of Beaumont, Texas, on January 10. Spindletop, as it was called, would spawn three petroleum giants—Gulf, Texaco, and Sun.

1901 DJIA First 70.44. High 78.26 Jne 17. Low 61.52 Dec 24. Close 64.56, −8.7%.

1902

Excited by the magnificent success and syndicate profits of the U.S. Steel trust, whose sales in 1902—its first full year—would reach $561 million, investment bankers and promoters rushed to enroll investors in a fresh series of trust adventures. Like 1899, 1902 would be a vintage year for trust promotion, as measured by the number of amalgamations.

The largest and most successful effort was Morgan's International Harvester underwriting, the profits from which would carry the banking firm through the perilous days of 1903. Other industrial groupings failed to find any trust magic, however; the American Witch Hazel trust, several barrel trusts, a grass twine combine, and the American Talking Scale trust fell almost immediately on hard times.

The year 1902 was the sixth strong year for the Rails, despite Attorney General Knox's March suit against the Northern Securities Company, the holding company into which the great antagonists of the Northern Pacific battle had placed their shares. Knox also filed against the "beef trust," the loose consortium of Chicago meat packers. A great anthracite coal strike, which started in May, lasted for months and was only settled when the President brought acute pressure on Morgan and the intransigent rail chiefs (who controlled the mines) to arrange a settlement.

Many eastern railroads reached their highest level in several decades and the Santa Fe rose to a record 94; it had been 19 at the turn of the century. The Sault Ste. Marie, 15 in 1901, did even better, soaring to 84.

The Industrials remained flat during the first nine months of the year, despite modest Rail enthusiasm. National Lead, a Dow member, made it from 16 to 32, though the leading coppers were under pressure. Anaconda fell from 36 to 20. U.S. Steel lost one third of its value, falling as low as 30 in December. Its $10.74 earnings and $4 dividend were viewed skeptically by investors.

In September, the Rails peaked, concluding their six-year advance and tight money pushed prices lower during the autumn. A bankers' pool helped pull the market back together for a superior Christmas rally.

The annual change for the Dow, barely one-quarter point, remains a mini-record.

1902 DJIA First 64.32. High 68.44 Apr 24. Low 59.57 Dec 15. Close 64.29, −0.4%.

1903 Undigested securities or, as some said, "indigestible securities," did the 1903 market in. The problem was most acute at the house of J. P. Morgan. In a rare miscalculation, the firm had welded together a North Atlantic shipping trust, the shares of which no one was interested in buying. Some shares were still in syndicate hands three years later.

Trade figures and agricultural statistics were generally good for the year along with rail traffic and construction. But it was a bear year for the Street, the Dow losing over a third of its value between mid-February and the year's low in November.

It became famous as the "Rich Man's Panic." The trust barons found their huge paper profits, built on watered stock, swiftly dewatered. The Tin Can Trust—American Can—lost 90 percent of its value and U.S. Rubber, the Rubber Trust, shrunk from 44 to 8. Declines in each case are measured from their trust-boom peak.

Short selling then being in the natural scheme of things, Morgan's favorite stock, U.S. Steel, was attacked by old and new enemies, including Edward Harriman. The company was seen as fundamentally weak and dropped from 40 to 10, as the steel trade fell apart. By November, the company had shut down 25 percent of its plants. The bloated dividend, halved in October, would be eliminated in January 1904.

Transit lines were roughly treated, but the steam roads held together and the coal lines resisted strongly. Carriers hoped that the new Elkins Act, providing for fines against both givers and receivers of freight rebates would halt the granting of special favors to big shippers.

Though there was a large decline for the Dow, the year lacks stature among the great market recessions. There was no commercial panic and no financial crisis beyond that suffered by innocents trapped in the overcapitalized trusts.

The year is perhaps best remembered as a symbolic beginning of the auto and air age. Henry Ford, having failed twice before, launched into production with his third automobile company, while long-distance motoring took a 3,000-mile step forward as a pioneer Packard completed the first transcontinental run, a 52-day ordeal from San Francisco to New York.

In December, the Wright brothers, in a non-media event—there were only five spectators—got their plane launched and airborne at Kitty Hawk. The flight lasted all of 20 seconds.

1903 DJIA First 64.60. High 67.70 Feb 16. Low 42.15 Nov 9. Close 49.11, −23.6%.

1904 The market struggled all through the first half of 1904 to recover from the shocking trust collapse of 1903. The dividend elimination by U.S. Steel in January staggered investors who just two years previously had seen the giant combination as a tower of industrial strength.

The Russian-Japanese war, which broke out in January and March's antitrust decision against Northern Securities cooled bullish hopes which had been revived after the bear market low of the previous November. At the end of June, both averages were about where they had been at year-end. Fortunately, there had been few new stock promotions. Investment bankers were still bagged with a great overhang from 1903 and the level of new offerings was the lowest since 1885.

A rapid change of sentiment occurred in the second half. A huge rail construction continued, with 5,900 miles laid during the year, and it supported a great improvement in steel demand.

Colorada Fuel & Iron benefitted, advancing from 26 to 58, while U.S. Steel was up nearly fourfold from an all-time low in May. U.S. Rubber and U.S. Cast Iron both tripled, as did the St. Louis & San Francisco.

The coppers were an exceptionally strong group, beginning a superior advance to the 1906–1907 highs. Copper Range gained from 38 to 75, cresting over the 1902 top. International Paper had a strong recovery, 10 to 26, and smokeless tobacco enjoyed an early success with American Snuff, a 90 to 170 winner.

Both averages reached their highs in December; the Industrials had advanced by 50 percent from the June low, encouraged by a revival of the iron trade.

1904 DJIA First 47.38. High 73.23 Dec 5. Low 46.41 Mar 12 Close 69.61, +41.7%.

1905 In 1905, for the first time in the century, the Rail average lost relative strength to the Industrials. Its gain for the year was only about half that of the junior average.

Rather ominously, many leading carriers failed to match their 1902 highs, even after the Rail average crossed its previous record peak of that year. The New Haven, which had reached 255 in 1902, peaked at 216, while the Pennsylvania, 85 in 1902, topped at 74. Like many other important rails, both issues recorded their 1903–1906 bull market high in late 1905.

In the meantime, the steels and metals which dominated the 12-Stock Dow Industrial Average were enjoying a huge boom. American Smelting was a leader of the list, boosted by a bull pool. The shares reached 170, double the year's low and 124 points over the worst mark of 1904. Anaconda jumped from 25 to 74. The wily pool operator, James R. Keene, was active in National Lead and the trust's share moved from 24 to 90.

U.S. Steel, near 8 in 1904, reached 43 while American Locomotive, performing better than most of its railroad customers, moved from 33 to 76.

Stocks were strong despite a long investigation into insurance graft, rebates, and illegal speculations with insurance funds. The stench from the investigation of the packing trust offended customers as far removed as the Prussian quartermasters and Swift & Co.'s stock had a high for the year at 114 versus 177 in 1902. It would never recover its former investment stature.

Excited volume in November led to great year-end strength with the market, on November 26, leaping up on a rare gap in what *The Wall Street Journal* called one "of the wildest openings in years," with the tape five to seven minutes late. Copper prices reached 18 cents and there were high hopes for Anaconda, since the Rothchilds had bought 247,000 shares from the Hearst estate. The shares would be removed as an immediate overhang on the American market by being placed with long-term investors in Europe.

Great volume and manipulation were evident in December. It was described by *The Wall Street Journal* as "A great stock speculation that has carried to dizzy heights, in certain specialities, chiefly industrial, though it has been controlled by powerful and skillful hands . . . the action of the market is wonderful, indeed."[4]

1905 DJIA First 70.39. High 96.56 Dec 29. Low 68.76 Jan 25. Close 96.20, +38.2%.

---

[4]*The Wall Street Journal,* New York, Dec 19, 1905, sec. 1, p. 1, col. 1.

<u>1906</u> A lust for copper drove the Dow to a high-volume, speculative peak in January 1906. Anaconda, it appeared, truly owned the richest hill on earth—or would, once the conflicting claims could be bought out.

The years of 1906 and 1907 would be the glory years for the coppers. Later markets would seek their El Dorados in oil, uranium, or gold, even in the air waves or as in 1933 in whiskey. But for two years, coppers were the speculative kingpins and in January 1906, they helped ram the Industrial average over 100 for the first time. American Smelting and Amalgamated Copper were Dow members and five other of the 12 issues were involved in the metals trade.

January's excitement and huge volume had already begun to lag by late spring when the great San Francisco earthquake and fire ravaged that city on April 18–19. The market held decently at first, but as additional news of the tragedy spread (E. F. Hutton's private wire to New York was commandeered by the army to help maintain communications out of the west), the market began a slide to the Dow 85 level, down 17 percent from the record January peak of 103.00.

Fire and casualty companies were stressed and several hundred millions in stocks and bonds had to be liquidated by the insurance firms as they struggled to honor the unparalleled claims in San Francisco.

In August, the "Harriman Market" brought the Rail average roaring back as he (and his controlled roads) poured millions into rail securities seeking, it was rumored, a true transcontinental route. The funds had come from the dissolution of the Northern Securities Company. Huge acquisitions were made in the Illinois Central (29.6 percent control), the Baltimore & Ohio, and the St. Joe and Grand Island. Lesser amounts of the Atchison, the St. Paul, and the North Western were purchased.

Despite the initiation of antitrust suits against Standard of Jersey and American Tobacco (neither of which would be settled until 1911), the market was well supported throughout the autumn. Charts show that the averages constructed a long-extended top, a formation which would not be repeated until 1937. Many rails, in 1906, achieved price levels which would never again be challenged. Northern Pacific was among them. American Telephone & Telegraph, impacted by tight money, could only advance to 145, far below its 1902 peak of 186.

In December, Harriman's followers pushed the Rails higher again to within a point of the January peak, while the Dow lagged a bit, and properly. Not until 1915 would the Industrials' earnings improve on the 1906 figure.

1906 DJIA First 95.00. High 103.00 Jan 19, Low 85.18 Jly 13. Close 94.35, −1.9%.

<u>1907</u> The autumn panic of 1907 was the worst since 1893. And the last great mercantile and commercial crisis of the era, one played out with classic excesses.

An enormous copper corner failed. "Trust companies," masquerading as commercial banks, were cut loose to bankruptcy by their rivals and the New

York Clearing House. A record spate of new issues glutted the Street. Call money reached 125 percent during the autumn crisis.

Rails were under siege from state legislatures and Alabama even cancelled the Southern Railway's franchise. A dividend cut helped drop its shares from 34 to 10. Judge Kenesaw Landis, a later czar of baseball, showed his iron glove early on fining Indiana Standard $29 million for illegal rebates, an extraordinary sum for the day. His decision, in early August, helped fold the market.

Stocks had never really recovered from a startling setback in March, and there was no help to be had from Europe, beset by its own problems. British Consols sold at their lowest level since 1848 and there was heavy liquidation of American railroad securities by London.

In the early fall, copper prices were smashed from a nominal 25 cents per lb. to about 13 cents and within weeks a Curb corner in copper shares also collapsed. Banking repercussions mushroomed. A run in New York spread to other eastern cities and westward to Pittsburgh, where Westinghouse Electric went to the wall and the city's stock exchange was forced to close.

J. P. Morgan was called in once again. His bankers' consortium, large deposit credits from the Treasury, and gold from England helped pull the city back together. But not before the clearing house had been authorized to issue $100 million in clearing house certificates—a fallback to the crisis methods of 1873, 1883, and 1893.

Before the Morgan rescue was completed in mid-November, enormous damage had been done to the market, banking, and employment. Coppers were routed; Calumet & Hecla, paying a dividend of $70, was smashed from 1000 to 535. Anaconda from 76 to 25. Bethlehem Steel laid off 7,000 workers.

The Erie lost over two-thirds of its value and the Delaware & Hudson, Missouri Pacific, and C&O saw their prices halved. Steels were slashed, Colorado Fuel & Iron falling from 54 to 14 while U.S. Steel was cut from 50 to 22, where its price was Morgan-supported. Steel's earnings, despite the fall slump, would be a remarkable $15.61 per share.

Other industrial trusts again, as in 1903, proved they were no less immune to hard times than other corporate organizations. U.S. Cast Iron was broken from 50 to 17, Corn Products from 25 to 8.

The year marked the Dow's worst decline of the century—until 1931. Yet the index held above the 1903 low. The Rails' decline below the worst 1903 level was a hint of longer-term troubles.

1907   First 94.25.   High 96.37 Jan 7.   Low 53.00 Nov 15.   Close 58.75, −37.7%.

1908 "In trade and mercantile affairs," noted the *Commercial & Financial Chronicle* in its review of 1908, "the year was one of intense depression, relieved only by a partial recovery the latter part of the year."[5]

---

[5]The *Commercial & Financial Chronicle,* New York, January 2, 1909, p. 5, col. 1.

But the stock market, which had been completely liquidated in the great panic of 1907, diverged from fundamentals and moved briskly higher. The year remains an unheralded bull hero. The 47 percent advance for the Industrials has not been matched in the years since 1933 and was the second largest gainer between 1897 and 1928. The numerous dividend cuts and omissions during the year proved to have been discounted in the panic of 1907. Dow earnings were halved, to $4.15, but that too was in the market.

Many advances were sensational. Allis-Chalmers, which in January dipped below its worst 1907 figure, tripled. Erie did the same, 12 to 36. The Chicago & Alton, a rumored merger candidate, soared from 10 to 69 while the Denver & Rio Grande was a 14–41 winner. General Electric, 90 in 1907, reached 163. Reversal of the fine on Indiana Standard aided sentiment.

The market advance came despite legislation adverse to business along with political attacks on wealth and capital. In July, the GOP's nomination of William H. Taft for the presidency increased the market's vigor. He seemed attractive as he lacked the "explosive utterances and wrathful denunciations" of "Teddy" Roosevelt, which had so often appalled business leaders.

The steel stocks maintained market leadership in a year which witnessed the formation of General Motors and production of Henry Ford's first Model T. When William Jennings Bryan whiffed on his third strike at the White House, Wall Street's post-election celebration saw the year's top prices. U.S. Steel reached 59, though $4.05 earnings were only about a quarter of those of 1907. Investors who were bagged by Morgan's mystique and Keene's manipulations in 1901 were finally marginal winners.

Coppers struggled with lost luster, meanwhile, but United Fruit had a splendid year and more than doubled its dividend to $18. The rich bounty was viewed with skepticism, however, and the stock topped at 148. Union Pacific was a Rail leader, though the carriers lacked the Industrials' steam. The Northern Pacific, 233 in 1906 and 101 in 1907, could only recover to 158.

The year 1908 was much like 1975 would be. A stock market collapse in the preceding year had discounted all of the bad news and shares would mount an exceptional rebound, ignoring greatly depressed industrial conditions.

If the panic of 1907 was forgotten by the market in 1908, its banking lessons were not. The Morgan-backed Aldrich-Vreeland Act was passed to help provide more liquidity in times of commercial crisis. It would be of great assistance to the nation in the opening days of World War I, as the FRB did not formally begin operations until November of 1914.

1908 DJIA open 59.61. High 88.38 Nov 13. Low 58.62 Feb 13. Close 86.15, +46.6%.

1909

Business activity enjoyed a strong revival in 1909, encouraged by another high-tariff act, while the stock market rode through a tumultuous year, boosted by a great number of pools and manipulations.

James R. Keene formed two pool groups in the same stock and promoted the Columbus Hocking Coal & Iron into a silk purse, 22 to 92. The shares would hit 10 in 1910. The Chicago Rock Island, also a later case study for the Pujo Committee investigation, astounded a holiday audience on December 27 by running up 31 points to 81 within minutes. A brokerage firm, it seems, had split a 40,000-share market order between 20 brokers. The firm, the NYSE admitted later, had been a bit shortsighted, as had been the speculator. Rock Island shares were back to 23 by the following July.

There were other, more solid stock moves during the year. Edward Harriman's crown jewel, the Union Pacific, advanced to 219, up from a panic low of 100 in 1907 and 38 in 1899. U.S. Steel continued its great strength, reaching 95 after a sloppy spring when price cuts threatened the industry. Rumors, later proven correct, of a huge "melon cutting" by Wells Fargo, pushed the stock up to 670; it had been 250 in 1908.

AT&T, on an acquisition spree, paid $25 million in September for the Western Union stake in New York Telephone and then, later in the year, bought control of Western Union without a nod to the antitrust forces.

In November, the Industrials almost reached their 1906 peak, even though earnings were far below the 1906 figure. Since the turn of the century, the Dow had gained about 50 percent, a modest figure considering the great economic advances of the period. The great industrial trusts formed with such excitement in the 1900–1903 period had been handicapped by the huge over-capitalizations extracted in their formation. The "watered" stock, or amount issued in excess of tangible assets, had been enormous in every case, about $700 million in the case of the steel trust alone.

Among the decade's best performers had been the western rails; their watered capital had been squeezed out in the great reorganizations of the 1890s. The coal roads had also prospered in the first decade of the new century along with various specialties, such as American Smelting and National Biscuit.

For most corporations, 1909 was the last strong year until the war boom of 1915. Not until then would the Dow exceed its twin peaks of 1906 and 1909. For the Rails, it would be a much longer wait. Fundamental problems, government wartime operations, and a balky Interstate Commerce Commission would keep the index below its 1906–1909 highs until 1927.

1909 DJIA First 86.27. High 100.53 Nov 19 Low 79.91 Feb 23. Close 99.05, +15.0%.

1910 The market staggered coming out of the gate in 1910 and never recovered. Both Dow averages gapped down in a sharply lower opening, and the gaps were not closed for years. It would be a typically difficult "0" year, as 1890 and 1900 had been. The brutal January collapse of the bull pools in Columbus Hocking Coal & Iron ended winter's rally hopes; the Hocking shares fell from 91 to 22 within days. A long period of business dullness, which would only end with World War I, was about to begin.

Halley's Comet passed without stock exchange tremor on April 19, but there was concern about the earth's encounter with its tail and stocks again turned sharply lower. The worst slump of the year pushed prices steadily down until late July.

The ICC, not Halley, was the real culprit. Railroads had planned for rate increases in June, but an injunction blocked the hike and insurgent Republicans and a Democratic coalition voted the ICC power to stay rate advances by as long as 10-months. No workable standards were set and rates and classifications were left to be decided according to the particular biases of the individual members. The carrier index fell below the panic level of 1907 and the Wabash, Railroad, a perennial cripple, dropped heavily. The Union Pacific slumped from 205 to 152.

It was not only the ICC and its rate rulings that injured rail holders. A speculative syndicate seeking a transcontinental rail route had gathered in vast holdings of connecting lines from the Eastern Seaboard to the Pacific, starting with the Lehigh Valley and ending with the Western Pacific. Included among other lines were the Wabash and the Chicago, Rock Island.

As railroad prices eroded, the British-Canadian group's margin position became stressed and the forced liquidation fed upon itself. Finally, Kuhn, Loeb took over the syndicate position, bringing a halt to the Rails' bear market. "The Harriman bankers," the *New York Times* dryly reported in early August, "relieved them of a too heavy burden of stock."[6]

Selling also appeared from London, where a speculative boom in rubber plantations had suddenly lost backing. A retrogression in business came mostly during the second half, though the Dow's strong first-half earnings helped the average show a better bottom line for the year. Sears, a new mercantile giant, hiked its annual payout from $4.50 to $7 and the shares traded up to 190 in November, after a 120 low in October.

Standard Oil of Jersey, still paying a $40 dividend, slipped badly, struck down by antitrust worries and mounting crude oil stocks. Continental buyers had learned to shy away from the obvious monopoly risks in the American market, and U.S. Steel was under mild pressure all year, dropping from 91 to 61. Colorado Fuel was cut from 53 to 23 and the Denver Rio Grande lost by the same score.

The Texas Company, born shortly after Spindletop, was finally listed at the NYSE. It had a tentative start, with a 134–144 range in the final third of the year.

Just when the market had began to gather strength, with ten consecutive advancing days in October, the autumn rally was aborted by the Democrats' congressional victory in November, their first since 1894. The major averages both ended the year on a weak note, well below the October rally tops.

1910   First 98.34.   High Jan 3 98.34.   Low 73.62 Jly 26.   Close 81.36, −17.9%.

---

[6]*The New York Times,* August 7, 1910, pt. 5, p. 7, col. 7.

1911 The antitrust wave reached its high-water mark in 1911, at least in terms of courthouse victories and media coverage. Standard Oil of New Jersey and American Tobacco were both ordered dissolved in May. In October, the Justice Department, capping months of rumors, filed suit against the nation's largest corporation, U.S. Steel.

The May decrees were market non-events; the cases had been festering for years and the resolution discounted. Indeed, stockholders of the two "dissolved firms" would fare quite well. The sum of the parts would be valued for much more than the whole, a recurrent sales theme for brokers ever since.

Jersey would distribute shares in over 30 companies on a pro-rata basis, including stock in such jewels as Atlantic Refining, Standard of California (Chevron), and Standard of Indiana (Amoco).

The tobacco company would distribute shares in American Snuff, R. J. Reynolds (RJR), and British-American Tobacco, among others.

Dow earnings for 1911 sagged, but the disappointment had been well discounted by the sharp first-half slide of 1910, and the September low for the Industrials was essentially a trap for tardy bears. The low was barely a point beneath that of 1910 and the market quickly reversed. Rails, meanwhile, had diverged, holding well above their 1910 low.

General Motors joined the elite at the NYSE, though its early days were not rousing. First listed in August, the stock's range for the year was 52–35, the high coming in the summer. A few unique stocks such as Commonwealth Edison, Canadian Pacific, and Sears registered record highs in 1911, as they had in the two previous years.

For the Wabash Railroad it was another black year. Despite its 1905 receivership and reorganization, it had managed to dig another financial pit, acquiring the Wheeling & Lake Erie, and a debt it could not handle. The shares, at 18 in March, slid to 6 in December when directors threw in the towel.

In September, when the year's market low had been registered, France and Germany had appeared near war, with German troops massed at the French border. By November, the two had conveniently compromised their African claims. Germany would recognize France's Morocco protectorate and France ceded about 100,000 square miles of the French Congo to Berlin. The tidy arrangement helped the European bourses recover their balance and the Dow gained about 12 percent in the autumn rally. U.S. Steel's antitrust suit, filed in late October, had been discounted and hurt for but a day.

As it turned out, 1911 was a very dull year. Volume was at the lowest level yet seen. During the year, curbstone brokers formally organized into the New York Curb Market Association and named a president.

1911 DJIA First 82.11. High 87.06 Jne 19. Low 72.94 Sep 25. Close 81.68, +0.4%.

1912 Bedeviled by the Pujo "Money Trust" investigation, widespread labor problems including a strike by 25,000 textile workers at American Woolen, and heavy gold exports, the Dow average still managed to stagger up to a mini-bull high in the fall of 1912. The peak, however, was well below the tops of 1906 and 1909, despite improving earnings.

The market was turned back first by the outbreak of a Balkan War, which caused investment chaos in Europe, and second by the election of the "radical" Woodrow Wilson. He took advantage of the GOP split where Roosevelt and his "Bull Moose" party received more votes than the incumbent, Taft, and the regular GOP machine.

Market highs were made in the early autumn; it would be three years before the Dow could recover its peak. The Rails' timetable would be delayed 15 years.

Volume and excitement were both curtailed during the year; the Rails' gain to 116.84 from 116.83 in 1911 remains a mini-record of sorts. Texas Company proved a disappointment, falling to 74 in active trade, down from a 144 high after its introduction at the Exchange in 1910. A few quality rails, like Norfolk & Western and the Louisville & Nashville (L&N), overcame the general lethargy and rose to record highs.

Food stocks became intensely popular. Quaker Oats, 100 in 1907, rose to 397 and National Biscuit was also favored. Bethlehem Steel and U.S. Rubber reached new highs. American Can, a longtime disappointment despite its trust label, raced from 11 to 47 between February and October.

Marine historians remember the year best for the tragic loss of the "unsinkable" White Star liner, *Titanic,* in April (it was part of Morgan's steamship trust). Western historians will recall that the year finally brought statehood to the last of the "original 48," New Mexico and Arizona, while business historians focus on Parcel Post authorization, which helped Sears climb nearly 100 points from its 1911 low to 221. It was a great catalyst to the growth of its booming catalogue business in rural areas.

While stock splits and large stock dividends had become popular in 1910–1911, very high-priced issues continued plentiful and popular. One could count more than 80 common stock issues at the NYSE priced at over 100, including a score over 200.

Many stocks at both major exchanges traded near 300. American Tobacco, American Express, and the Lackawanna were among them. Calumet & Hecla was near 600. Standard of Indiana, a Curb stock, declared a 2,900 percent stock dividend—surely a record—and spurted from 4,000 to 7,000 within weeks.

This predominance of high-priced stocks contrasts sharply with modern conditions. Most listed corporations, encouraged by the NYSE, strive to keep shares more modestly priced by frequent splits and stock payouts.

1912 DJIA First 82.36. High 94.15 Sep 30. Low 80.15 Feb 10. Close 87.87, +7.6%.

1913 A stillness fell over the stock exchange in 1913. It was almost as if the market sensed the end of an era. Deteriorating business conditions were matched by a strange apathy. Volume at the NYSE was the lowest since 1897. There was not a single million-share day, for the first time since 1898.

A new banking era began late in the year with the approval of the Carter-Owen bill, which would establish the Federal Reserve system. It was historically fitting, for J. Pierpont Morgan, who had for decades been the lender of last resort, passed away in the same year, dying in Rome in April. His death, it was said, had been hastened by the Pujo hearings.

Both Dow averages crested in early January and then sank steadily into the summer months. Europe's bourses were kept in turmoil by the Balkan Wars and the highest money rates, on average, since 1875. In St. Petersburg, however, a frenzy of speculation boomed the new-issue market. Banks, sugars, and steels were especially popular and the French and Germans were both heavy investors.

Business, like the stock exchange, was slow on the eve of World War I. By November, U.S. Steel's backlog was half that of a year earlier. Bethlehem Steel slipped to 25, as did General Motors; that level would be their low for the decade. Studebaker had a disastrous fall from 50 to 13.

Rails, often abused by the greed and cupidity of their directors, continued to suffer. The St. Louis & San Francisco failed; its rail construction had been a bonanza for insiders. But rising industry costs also pinched. State taxes had doubled since 1907 and rate relief was at best a 12-month bureaucratic nightmare.

The Missouri Pacific was cut from 44 to 21, while the corrupt and faltering New Haven crashed to 65. It had been a $255 stock in 1902, adored by widows and orphans for its dependable dividend.

October brought the first general tariff reductions since the Civil War. Since customs duties provided about two-thirds of federal revenues, the act also forced the introduction of an income tax, for those earning over $4,000.

In November, the Justice Department opened a new front against one of the most ineffectual "monopolies," American Can. The Tin Can Trust had been one of the original candidates for trustification into U.S. Steel, but fortunately for that trust, it had not been included since it endured years of poor results. In 1916, the Supreme Court would rule against dissolution.

A Justice Department victory was recorded, however, in 1913. The Union Pacific, which had acquired control of the Southern Pacific in 1901, was finally forced to divest its holdings in its southern rival. Edward Harriman had not lived to see this defeat, having died in 1909.

Throughout the year, Europe remained a steady seller of American shares. Many of their long-favored rails were driven to the lowest level since 1907, or even 1900, by a combination of that liquidation and the carriers' earnings squeeze.

1913 DJIA First 88.42. High 88.57 Jan 9. Low 72.11 Jne 11. Close 78.78, −10.3%.

1914 World War I began in July 1914. The NYSE immediately shuttered and would remain closed until December. Yet, within a year, New York would replace London as the world's financial hub. That was the most important financial event of the century for Wall Street.

The initial war reaction at the world's bourses was panic and a drumroll of closures. On Monday, July 27, Vienna, Brussels, Budapest, and Paris closed. On Tuesday, the Canadian exchanges closed. Amsterdam, Berlin, and St. Petersburg shut down on Wednesday with Rome and Edinburgh following on Thursday and London and New York on Friday. Other U.S. exchanges followed the NYSE action and would remain closed.

During the week of July 27–30, prices had collapsed at the Exchange. Foreign selling and bear raids smashed prices. General Motors fell by 39 points. The surprise, perhaps, was that an event so long anticipated should precipitate such a shock wave. On Friday, minutes before the opening bell, the NYSE Board of Governors voted the closure. It was a defensive move; the floor was swamped with selling orders from around the world.

War had threatened the world for the first six months of 1914, yet the Dow, at the end of June stood slightly higher than at the year end. The June collapse of the old-line dry goods house, H. B. Claflin, had more immediate impact on the market than the assassination in Sarajevo on June 28 of Archduke Ferdinand, Crown Prince of Austria.

The *Commercial & Financial Chronicle,* in its issue of July 4, wrote, "The assassination . . . has impressed . . . not least of all because of the surprisingly small degree of consternation with which the world at large received the news."[7]

Consternation did follow in late July when Austria declared war on Serbia and investors of the world frantically sought to convert their stock and balances to cash. On Saturday, Germany declared war on Russia and invaded France on Sunday without benefit of formalities.

On August 3, in New York, immediately rose questions as to how emergency sales of stock might be made and what the duration of the shut-down might be. Exchange authorities quickly arranged for trades to be made through its Clearing House, but only with required approval of the Committee of Five, an ominously named group which had been given emergency powers. Trades could only be made at minimum prices, or higher; that floor was usually the close of July 30. No one hazarded a guess about the length of the "holiday."

Thus, trade was forced into the street where a "gutter" or "illegal" (the Exchange's adjective) market sprang up. Trade was at much lower than mandated levels and increasingly so throughout the autumn. Depressing war news and a stunning series of dividend cuts, climaxed by late October negative action by U.S. Steel, forced the black market prices of popular stocks sharply lower. Steel was driven down to 38 versus its closing level at 51 on July 30. Only such "reliable" war stocks as the sugars traded at large premiums to the minimum levels.

---

[7]The *Commercial & Financial Chronicle,* New York, July 4, 1914, p. 9, col. 2.

The official Dow low for the war years was registered July 30; the "real," if unofficial low, came in the street market in the last week of October.

Despite the continued bans in New York, some regional exchanges began trading in October and the New York Curb officially reopened in November. Trading was light.

When the Exchange reopened on December 12, still with minimum pricing, world perceptions had changed. U.S. paper, stocks, bonds, and currency, were seen as preferable to any European counterpart. Enthusiastic buying developed for those shares seen as war beneficiaries.

General Motors, an extreme example, traded as high as 85 versus its 55 low on July 30. The Dow closed the historic Saturday session at 74.56, more than 4 percent above the July 30 figure.

The Rails, beset by their own unique problems, also rallied, but then slipped below their July close later in December.

1914 DJIA First 78.59. High 83.43 Mar 20. Low 71.42 Jly 30. Close 74.73, −5.1%.

1915   The unemployment and depression of 1914 reversed swiftly into a boom of historic proportions in 1915. The Dow's annual gain of nearly 82 percent has never been challenged. It was, of course, the most successful of all the decennial "5" years, whose perfect record of advances is still continued.

America was officially neutral and a supplier to both warring parties. Business activity, which had never fully recovered from the panic of 1907, exploded. Farm dreams came true. A record wheat crop—the first over 1 billion bushels—was harvested and then merchandised at marvelous prices.

The steel industry enjoyed a dramatic reversal after a winter pause. In January, U.S. Steel omitted its dividend and the minimum NYSE trading price for the shares (the minimum-price rule stayed in effect until April 1) had to be cut and cut again, before all the disappointed sellers could be accommodated. The final low was 38, in February; the stock would double by August.

Bethlehem Steel, however, had no need for an upset price. It would be the lead bull in the great war boom. Its shares, 46 in January, hit 246 in July, 346 in August, and 600 in October. Commodity stocks and coppers were other natural war "plays." South Porto Rico Sugar, 28 early in the year climbed to 164 and then went on to 240 in 1916; "Puerto Rico" was a 1959 name change. Inspiration Copper nearly tripled, 17 to 47.

General Motors was a dazzling new star. It had traded at 55 in July 1914, and 82 in February but reached 558 in December, several months after William C. Durant had recaptured control from the bankers.

During the year, Germany's submarine campaign, which included the sinking of the Cunarder *Lusitania,* and widespread German spy activities in the United States gradually forced American opinion into the Allies' corner. The 15.6 percent decline which came in the aftermath of the May 7 loss of the

Lusitania was the only serious Dow setback during the entire year. In early June, Secretary of State William Jennings Bryan, the three-time Democratic presidential nominee, resigned, objecting to bellicose notes to Germany, but by late July, the Dow had reached an important new high.

Increasing military backlogs strengthened the year-end view that 1916 would be another strong business period. The nation's rails were already operating near capacity, but fixed rates and rising inflation restrained their 1915 index gain to 22 percent.

1915 DJIA First 54.63. High 99.21 Dec 27. Low 54.22 Feb 24. Close 99.15, +81.7%.[8]

1916 Tremendous fundamentals, possibly the best in history, propelled the 1916 market upward. Individual issues exploded in dazzling moves. But, when the year was over, the leading Dow averages were both modestly lower.

It remained, however, a brilliant bull market for American economic statistics. An enormous, favorable trade balance ran at about six times the prewar figures. Gold poured into the country and the dollar soared against the currencies of both war belligerents, the Allies and the Central Powers.

The Dow's earnings, which had finally risen above the 1906 record in the previous year, advanced by 134 percent to $24.64. The bottom-line figure would not be exceeded until 1950! U.S. Industrial Alcohol, 15 in 1915, reached 171, while Central Leather was bulled from 33 to 123 in the same period. In November, when the Dow reached its record 110.15 peak, volume at the NYSE expanded to 36 million shares, third highest month of the century. Throughout the year, the war economy dominated the market. Pancho Villa's raid into New Mexico in March and General Pershing's pursuit of him into Mexico were ignored on the floor.

But a sudden peace scare in December plunged the Dow 18 percent and brought accusations of insider trading against shorts who were believed to have benefitted from leaks of President Wilson's peace feelers. The shorts included Bernard Baruch, the friend of many presidents. Within a few months, he would be named war production czar.

The peace scare abruptly turned into a war scare on December 21 when Secretary of State Robert Lansing stated that the United States was being drawn into the war. The Industrials dropped over 5 percent on huge volume, a 15-year high.

Thus, the market came to close lower for the year, despite the giant moves by many "war babies," along with General Motors, which was still in the civilian business. General Motors had reached an astounding price of 850 in late autumn, up from 55 on the black war day of July 30, 1914.

---

[8]The Dow average figures at the end of this annual review are for the new 20-Stock Average, adopted by Dow Jones in 1916 and computed back to July 1914.

A huge amount of speculative hurt was dealt in the last three weeks of 1916. Crucible Steel, 96 in November, crashed to 50 in December. War, not peace, had become overnight the serious market threat. And, though few would have believed it, both averages had already recorded their wartime highs.

1916 DJIA First 98.81. High 110.15 Nov 21. Low 84.96 Apr 22. Close 95.00, −4.2%.

1917 The winds of war chilled the stock market all through 1917, though American troops would not be involved in fighting until November. Conscription, inflation, an excess profits tax, and increased Washington interference in business kept the market off balance. Bethlehem Steel, 700 in 1916, would split 3:1 and sell down to 199, basis the old stock.

Germany torpedoed prices on January 31 when Berlin's ambassador delivered a note to the State Department warning that submarine attacks on neutral and belligerent shipping would begin the following day. The Dow had a nasty drop of 7.2 percent on February 1 and fell further the following session. On February 3, the U.S. liner *Housatonic* was sunk by a German submarine and the president informed Congress that the United States would sever diplomatic relations.

Tensions escalated so sharply that President Wilson, though re-elected on a peace platform, was forced in April to ask Congress for a declaration of war. It passed, though 50 Representatives and five Senators opposed it.

The market had by now discounted both peace and war and by mid-June the Dow was nearly back to 100, four points above the close of 1916. But armorer to Europe, business found, was better than armorer to a warring America. Profits were constricted by price rulings, increased taxes, railroad congestion, and raw material priorities. During the last half of the year, monotonous if light selling forced the Industrials to a new low in each month, even as the United States geared up for battle.

In December, the federal government took over the nation's railroads and the carriers' index fell to its lowest level since 1898. "War babies," curiously, were also under pressure. Secondary coppers went to the slag heap and secondary rails did no better. Minneapolis & St. Louis fell from 32 to 7 while many quality carriers lost about 50 percent of their value, as did General Motors.

U.S. Steel, which had made a late wartime high at 137 early in the year, dropped to 80 as the 13-month bear move wound down on low volume.

The Rails had been treated most harshly, losing about 33 percent at their worst mark, 70.75, just before Christmas. The average had stood at 89.41 on July 30, 1914.

1917 DJIA First 96.15. High 99.18 Jan 3. Low 65.95 Dec 19. Close 74.38, −21.7%.

1918 Neither prospects for victory nor the armistice of November could create more than temporary enthusiasm in the 1918 market. Volume fell sharply for the second year in a row, with the Exchange's tally being barely higher than in 1900.

For a brief winter period, "Heatless Mondays" cut the Exchange's work back down to a five-day week, but there was no crowding, as activity slowed during the first four months of the year, stalled by German successes in the Somme and Flanders.

Summer pricing was flat, but prices improved modestly in the early fall. Peace came swiftly after the surrender of Bulgaria and though the armistice did not come until November 11, the final defeat of the Central Powers had been fully discounted by mid-October, when the Dow reached its high for the year. A brief recession set in, which would end early in 1919.

The war's fourth and final Liberty Loan Drive began in late September. Over half the adult population had participated, swayed not only by patriotism but the work of such admired entertainers as Douglas Fairbanks. For many citizens, it was their first adventure in securities and laid a base for the enormous expansion of stock and bond activity in the 1920s.

Speculative stock fever was cooled during 1918 by government controls, increased taxes, material shortages, and federal administration of the railroads. Business, nevertheless, was booming and when peace came many were unprepared. War orders were quickly cancelled and the general level of business activity fell sharply along with the Dow. At Thanksgiving, the index was at its lowest level since June, when Belleau Wood was proving such a difficult engagement for the Allies.

Steels were sold down. Retailers and the auto stocks, on the other hand, saw brighter days ahead. Sears, 134 in June, climbed to a high of 186 in December. Detroit, squeezed for steel late in the war by Baruch's War Industries Board, anticipated a peacetime auto boom and General Motors, which had fallen to 74 in 1917 (adjusted for split), reached 164.

Rails were notably unenthusiastic at the year end as privatization hopes were handcuffed by liberal protagonists beating the drums for government ownership. The federal railroad administration would not release the carriers until the spring of 1920.

AT&T was luckier, in a way. The Post Office Department had taken over its operations in July, but the system would be privatized again in 1919. Still, increasing interest rates and the government operation had knocked its shares down to 90. They had been 114 on July 30, 1914 and 135 in 1916, with both levels carrying the same $8 annual dividend.

The carrier index at the end of 1918 was down 6 percent from its pre-war level, despite the lines having had more traffic than they could handle for four years.

1918 DJIA First 76.68. High 89.07 Oct 18. Low 73.38 Jan 15. Close 82.20, +10.5%.

1919

For the first two months of 1919, the stock market was puzzled by its peacetime role. Traders could remember the somber market experienced before the events of 1914 when the Dow bogged down in the 79–86 range.

But leaping domestic demands, along with requirements for rebuilding Europe, stirred business—and a spiraling rate of inflation. It would be a big year for oils. Peace demands, projected to fall, rose in startling fashion. Drilling and promotions boomed and the shares with them. Texaco reached 345, triple its low of 1916. Mexican Petroleum, which owned a fabulous concession in Mexico, gushed up to 264, a 100-point gain during the year. Its low in 1918 had been 79.

General Motors resumed its strong leadership, racing up to 407 late in the year from a January low at 119. An awkwardly named company, Computing-Tabulating-Recording Corp., scored its first serious advance, moving up to 64 from a low of 30 in the previous year. It would become better known in later years as International Business Machines.

Scandals, corners, and manipulations were common. In October, near the market peak, volume reached 37 million shares, the highest since January 1906. The Dow reached a record high, but not the faltering Rails. Pennsylvania Railroad, for example, barely managed 48. It had peaked at 85 in 1902 and 74 in 1905. Like the other Rails, it was a victim of a secular bear market.

A string of major strikes in the autumn—750,000 steel and mining workers were out—compounded by a sudden mushrooming of interest rates in November finally stopped the market dead in its tracks. The Fed raised the discount rate to 4.75 percent on November 4 from the 4 percent level in effect for two years and call money shot up to a weekly average of 14.9 percent from 5.5 percent at the end of October.

That was all for the market. It had formed a rare "spike" top, appearing almost like a steeple top in charts of the period. There was no look back, no second chance. The Dow had reached an all-time high November 3, but fell 12 percent by the month end. The high would stay in place until the beginning of the "Coolidge Market," almost exactly five years later.

1919 DJIA First 82.60. High 119.62 Nov 3. Low 79.15 Feb 8. Close 107.23, +30.5%.

1920

Bloated stocks, commodities, and inventories were summarily excised in 1920 as super-inflation turned within months into the worst deflation since the post-Civil War period. The violent reversal from boom and wild inflation into recession and deflation would be repeated in 1981–82.

The commodity darlings of 1919 were quickly forsaken, giving up in most cases all of their war and postwar gains. American Beet Sugar turned bitter with a drop from 104 to 33, and Central Leather's performance was slightly worse, 105 to 30.

Crowded auto showrooms became lonely. Pierce Arrow tumbled from 83 to 15. General Motors, which split 10:1, foundered despite enormous insider buying from its president, William C. Durant. Near the end of the year, he was forced from the executive suite for the second time; the Du Pont interest was enlarged. The shares were smashed down from 410 to 128, basis the old stock.

Despite the debris of deflation, a number of bull pools and corners had braved the trend early in the year. Durant had effected a corner in the "old," pre-split GM shares, but the Exchange arranged a truce. The president of Stutz achieved the last pure, classic corner at the Exchange, squeezing the shares of the Indiana automaker from 100 to 724 within weeks. Unfortunately, the profits didn't stick.

Every area of the market, save for the privatized Rails, was deflated. Atlantic Refining, the highest-priced issue at the Exchange, was cut down from 1570 to 890. A buyers' strike melted retailers' prices and May Department Stores dropped from 138 to 65. Sears' catalogue magic was no protection from consumer wrath; the stock fell from 243 to 84.

In June, the Federal Reserve Board nailed the longs, pushing the discount rate to 7 percent. Stocks collapsed. Tight money spread, along with an autumn depression. A show of market strength in mid-September was shattered by a monstrous bomb explosion just outside J. P. Morgan & Co; 30 were killed.

General Motors's December sales were barely a quarter of what they had been in June. Ford laid off 40,000 just before Christmas, closing its Highland Park plant as the market staggered to its low for the year.

Once again, the "0" year had turned out badly for the bulls. Excluding the 1930s, the year remains the second worst in Dow history, after 1907, with the index losing 32.9 percent. Even the election victory of Harding, returning the GOP to the White House after eight years of Democratic rule, could not rally the market for a single day.

1920 DJIA First 108.76. High 109.88 Jan 3. Low 66.75 Dec 21. Close 71.95, −32.9%.

1921 In January 1921, General Motors sold barely 6,000 cars versus 46,852 in the best month of 1920. Despite later improvement, passenger unit sales would be down 41 percent for the year. Annual truck sales fell a startling 84 percent and the auto industry, for the first time in its brief history, knew depression. General Motors posted a loss for the year. The next one would not show until 1980.

Detroit was not the only depression victim. Corporate profits collapsed and the Dow ended up with red ink for its composite earnings, a historical first. Henry Ford barely saved his company, bailing out of his major problem of a huge inventory by shipping all assembled cars to dealers, draft bills of lading attached. A few agencies went to the wall, but Ford Motors survived and rumors of a distress public offering were scotched.

Commodity prices were halved or quartered from the post-war highs and the sick stocks of 1920 got sicker. Porto Rico Sugar, which had tripped from 155 to 70 in 1920, crashed to 26. Sears, which had fallen from 243 to 85, continued its slide to 54. Studebaker was a notable exception to the bear trend, holding above its low of 1920 and rising to 93 from a winter low of 43. It was to be an early bull market leader.

It was a dangerous first quarter for business, over-extended in inventory and debt. But in April, the Fed relented, cutting the discount rate to 6 percent. Two more cuts by September turned the tide with the Dow making its final low—a double bottom against that of June—in August. That summer scene would be repeated in 1982.

By autumn of 1921, business and optimism had both enjoyed a minor revival. Oils recovered strongly, along with the building stocks. Mid-Continent Petroleum doubled and Otis Elevator rose from 87 to 148. Retailers and auto suppliers were also popular. May Department Stores raced up from 66 to 114 and Firestone bounced from 50 to 90.

Unfortunately, the Rails ended the year with a modest loss. That was not too bad, considering the trauma of June, when the average had registered its lowest level since 1898.

One of the few bullish surprises of 1921 had been the vote of confidence shown by American Telephone; it increased its annual dividend basis to $9 from $8. System revenues were up 10 percent despite the recession. The shares had touched a January low at 96, but rose to 120 in November.

It had been one of the outstanding opportunities to purchase the stock of American Telephone for important capital gains. Declining interest rates and the euphoria of the coming bull market would drive the shares to 310 in 1929, even though there would be no further dividend increase for decades.

The year of 1921 also provided a rare chance to buy bonds in front of a huge secular advance. For both American Telephone and bond buyers, the last such golden opportunity had been in 1907.

1921 DJIA First 72.67. High 81.50 Dec 15. Low 63.90 Aug 24. Close 81.10, +12.7%.

1922 The great business and stock market boom of the 1920s laid its foundation in 1922. Automobile sales soared by nearly 60 percent—a gain unmatched since, except during the 1946–1947 release from war restrictions. Construction also rose to a record.

Bulls enjoyed a splendid roll. The Industrial average managed to reach a higher high in 14 of 15 months, starting in August 1921. Business confidence was strong and the Dow's composite dividend was raised by 31 percent, though leaving it well short of the war years' payout.

General Motors suffered a relative lapse as its sales increase lagged the industry percentages. The dividend was cut and, alarmingly, the stock fell to an all-time low at 8¼. Studebaker, on the other hand, sped up to 142; its late 1920 bear low had been 38.

Rail revenues suffered from rail and coal strikes, but retailers enjoyed a boom. Woolworth, no dime stock, moved up from 137 to 223. Montgomery Ward doubled to 25.

Volume and excitement peaked in the spring, just before a long coal strike got under way, but the Dow struggled higher into the autumn. *Radio* was about to become a household word, spurred by the first commercial program and President Harding's broadcast from the Francis Scott Key memorial, a presidential radio first. Other air addicts got a glimpse of the future when Lt. James H. Doolittle spanned the continent in an army bomber in less than a day. But Radio Corporation and Wright Aeronautical, brilliant winners later in the decade, were unexploited, selling at lows of 3 and 6, respectively, during the year.

Mushrooming auto sales stirred interest in the oils. Standard of Indiana was a 60-135 winner at the Curb. but Vacuum Oil (Mobil) was the price leader, as it pushed up from 299 to 710. The Secretary of the Interior, bribed with a strong box full of bonds, leased the Navy's Teapot Dome oil reserves to one of Harry Sinclair's oil companies; the scandal would rock Washington a bit later.

An enormous construction boom boosted the building stocks and U.S. Cast Iron Pipe, a venerable and certifiable trust, jumped from 16 to 39.

Prospects for large Democratic gains at the off-election topped the market in October, but the year's gain was still the best peacetime effort since 1908.

1922 DJIA First 78.91. High 103.43 Oct 14. Low 78.59 Jan 10. Close 98.73, +21.7%.

1923   In the long-term Dow chart of the 1920s, the 1923 slippage appears as a mere pause in the great bull market. And so it was, unless one were caught in one of the few really bad stock spills.

The Dow suffered an intra-year correction of under 19 percent between March and October. The meager decline testifies to the secular strength of the market, as there was plenty of bad news.

Belgian and French troops reoccupied the Ruhr. War debt talks collapsed. The White House was scandal ridden. The discount rate was hiked. President Harding died suddenly and somewhat mysteriously, though that was a nonevent at the Exchange.

All the bad news, however, didn't keep auto sales from setting a record for the second straight year. There were, amazingly, 63 percent more cars on the road than in 1920. The Dow's earnings, despite an economic slump late in the year, were up 52 percent.

Concerns over Detroit's 1924 prospects gave the rubber stocks a solid pounding and Goodrich fell from 41 to 17. General Motors, still in the teens, lost only four points, but the manipulated Durant Motors hit the rail and skidded from 84 to 21.

Speculators had a fertile field. Jesse Livermore and the chief storekeeper of Piggly-Wiggly attempted a corner in the grocery chain's shares and the

NYSE responded by having the stock delisted. Lawsuits followed. Houston Oil continued a roller-coaster saga: 41 in 1921 to 92 the following year to 41 in 1923. A succession of giant oil discoveries during the decade would blunt every effort to turn the energy stocks into dependable market leaders.

Marlin Oil, later Continental (Conoco), was slashed from 60 to 18. Sinclair Consolidated, a heavy in the Teapot Dome scandal, went from 39 to 16. Speculative rails were also tripped, many losing half their value.

Some market students see the 1923 action as a mini-bear market, but there was great underlying strength. The Dow's year end level, coming only two months after the October low, showed a loss of barely three points from that of 1922. Growth companies like American Telephone and American Tobacco both gained about a million new customers during the year, and their stocks were very firm. Cigarette output was up over 20 percent.

IBM felt the market's tremor and tumbled from 84 to 67 within six months, yet reversed to close at an all-time high of 97 at the year end.

The brief summer slump for the market had seen volume fall sharply. The Rails had encouraged bulls by reversing their downward course in August; their low came on August 4, the first market day after the death of President Harding, who was succeeded by Vice-President Coolidge.

1923 DJIA First 98.77. High 105.38 Mar 20. Low 85.76 Oct 27. Close 95.52, −3.3%.

1924

Calvin Coolidge left one important mark on financial history. He was the first president to avoid the indignity of a losing year on Wall Street during a four-year administration. And after presiding over the great boom of 1924–1928, he cleverly chose "not to run" in 1928, leaving the 1929 tin can tied to the coattails of his successor, Herbert Hoover.

The great "Coolidge Market" got underway in the fourth quarter of 1924 as his election helped frame a perfect market ending to the year. The DJIA finished on December 31 at its yearly high and the Rails were just a point beneath their peak of December 18.

Earlier in the year, a slow steel and auto demand had kept the bulls at bay; passenger car sales fell for the second time in the decade. But enormous construction demands fueled the economy. Cement and building stocks prospered, along with the plumbers. Crane leaped from 30 to 60.

Booming utility demands helped ram General Electric from 194 to 322 and Sears, planning to expand from catalogue sales to retailing, more than doubled its low of 1923. Radio stocks were suddenly growth anointed; there were 2.5 million receivers in American homes versus but 5,000 in 1920. RCA started a long upward wave, advancing from 19 to 67. It had gone through a 1:4 reverse split; each owner of 100 shares was left with a certificate for only 25 shares. Curb pools bloated prices for secondary radio issues Dubilier and Thompson.

Du Pont commenced production of cellophane, but the shares did little. Its enormous holding of General Motors was temporarily disappointing as Motors' sales fell by 19 percent. General Motors also used a 1:4 reverse split to force its share price higher; it was an unique action for a class stock.

Walter P. Chrysler's reorganized Maxwell Motors was a star, however, long before Jack Benny's humor would feature the marquee. Maxwell sales were up about 25 percent in a slow year for Detroit and the shares revved up from 10 to 40.

Western rails helped their index to a healthy gain, a move which did not fully reflect some startling advances in the southwestern carriers. The Katy more than tripled to 34 between May and November. The St. Louis & San Francisco and the Missouri Pacific equaled that advance.

Oil stocks, pressured by crude pricing, were quiet, though Standard of Ohio was an exception, pushing up 102 points to 190.

The year end was a very special period at the Exchange, as two important milestones were passed. In November, monthly volume of 42.8 million shares broke the old record of April 1901. In December, the Dow surmounted its record peak of 1919. The events were seen as portending much greater achievements in the coming years.

1924 DJIA First 95.65. High 120.51 Dec 31. Low 88.33 May 20. Close 120.51, +26.2%.

1925 A brilliant Detroit sales recovery with auto-truck production up 16 percent fired the stock market to a record high in 1925. The psychological problems just over Dow 120 were finally cleared in May, and the Industrials reached a top at 159, nearly 30 points above the peak of 1919.

It was another brilliant success for the "5" year in the decennial sequence; each of those years since 1885 had witnessed a strong market advance.

General Motors, whose unit sales gained 42 percent, was the quality leader and advanced from 65 to 150. Other popular auto names outdid General Motors in investor popularity. Dillon, Read bought out the Dodge brothers for $146 million in cash, the largest such deal in history. Nash won top-dollar price, rising to 448 while Hudson Motor won the stock car race with a gain of 311 percent to 140.

With competition so heated, Henry Ford allowed that his cars, previously all black, would be offered in a "rainbow" of colors—green, gray, and maroon.

Tire shares benefitted enormously from Detroit's resurgence. General Tire was the premium leader in a ride from 233 to 415. Increasing gasoline and fuel demands helped firm oils. Humble, one of the great crude producers (and a Jersey subsidiary), was up over 100 percent, 42 to 95.

Retailers were firm. Montgomery Ward doubled and Woolworth did almost as well, 112 to 220. Chain stores were immensely popular, save with small-town merchants.

The enormous construction boom, which had begun in 1921, finally reached its peak, as measured by building permits. Giant Portland Cement, 2 in 1924, jumped to 42. U.S. Gypsum advanced from 112 to 208 during the year.

Earnings for the Dow reached a peacetime high, up nearly 50 percent from 1924. The only tricky passage of the year came in November, when the Federal Reserve upped the discount rate to 4 percent, causing great if only temporary alarm.

For the Rails, it was also a satisfying year. The average closed over 100 for the first time since 1917. Unfortunately, the index at 112.93 was no higher than it had been in April 1901.

1925 DJIA First 121.25. High 159.39 Nov 6. Low 115.00 Mar 30. Close 156.66, +30.0%.

1926 The first shocking correction of the great 1921–1929 advance hit the "Coolidge Market" in February 1926. Frenzied volume, great complacency, and a record margin debt had already sounded warnings, and a drastic decline began in February.

The *Commercial & Financial Chronicle* fired a broadside. Easy money and other evils, it seemed, ". . . had promoted a speculation . . . which in magnitude and daring and sheer recklessness has no counterpart in this country and probably no counterpart in the entire history of the human race."[9]

Which left little editorial ammo for 1929.

The six-week selling frenzy ripped about 17 percent from the Industrials' level, and would prove to be the most severe correction of the entire 1921–1929 period. It was at this time that General Motors began to demonstrate its powerful market leadership. The firm would push 1926 sales to more than $1 billion, only the second company to reach that figure. U.S. Steel had done it first, 10 years earlier. Knocked down to 113 in the bear attack, Motors quickly reversed and by August had reached 225, nearly 76 points above its 1925 high. Motors' many stock distributions to its shareholders in the 1926–1929 period obscure its superior advance. In 1926, a 50 percent stock dividend was paid and that was followed by a 2:1 split in 1927. In January 1929, a 2.5:1 split was distributed. A patient owner ended up with 750 shares for each 1925 count of 100 and a 92 price versus an adjusted 15.

Many secondary autos began to feel the pressure of the financial and productive superiority of the major producers at this time and recorded their stock highs for the decade in the 1925–1926 winter months. Hudson, 140 in late 1925 and 123 in January, fell to 41 in October; its peak price in 1929 would be 94. Chrysler was not immune. It lost half its value in the first quarter but would drive on to much higher levels in the next several years.

Specialty stocks continued to be popular. Butterick, the venerable pattern maker, moved from 18 to 71. Warner Brothers proved real show-biz, advancing from 12 to 70.

Earnings and volume dipped slightly for the year, which was generally

---

[9]The *Commercial & Financial Chronicle,* New York, March 6, 1926, p. 1209, col. 1.

one of consolidation following the violence of the first quarter, where problems had been tipped by a record schedule of underwritings, overtaking the old mark set in 1919.

In the fall of 1926, real estate suffered a 1929-type crash early on. Millions were lost in Florida when massive land speculations, often in underwater or "wetlands" lots, were collapsed by a monstrous September hurricane.

1926 DJIA First 158.54. High 166.64 Aug 14. Low 135.20 Mar 30. Close 157.20, +0.3%.

1927   Sidetracked for 21 years, the Dow Rail Average finally switched back to the main stem in 1927 and overcame its historic high from January 1906. The Western Maryland shot up from 14 to 68 between January and June; the Chicago Great Western went from 9 to 23 in the same period.

Bolstered by a newly strong partner, the Industrials recorded another stunning performance and in December, sped past the Dow 200 milestone with ease, despite the travails previously suffered at Dow 100. Sixty years later, the average, thwarted for years at the 1000 level, would find 2000 an equally easy mark to overcome.

Auto sales lagged, however, as buyers delayed, awaiting a look at Henry Ford's new Model A. But General Motors, aided by the great popularity of the Pontiac, improved its position with unit sales up nearly 27 percent. A modest business slump slowed U.S. Steel production and suddenly the steel trust was No. 2 in sales, for the first time in history. General Motors had grabbed the top spot.

"New" names came to the front. International Harvester climbed all year, 135 to 256. Johns-Manville moved from 57 to 127; Alcoa from 68 to 145. Macy & Co. was a strong retailer, with a jump from 124 to 244. The attraction of "artificial silk," or rayon, ran Celanese from 44 to 117.

Wright Aero's Whirlwind engine moved Charles Lindbergh and the *Spirit of St. Louis* from Long Island to France without a hitch in late May and the air age on the Exchange floor revved up immediately. Wright's shares flew from 25 to 94.

Many specialty stocks outdid the Dow. Vulcan Detinning, with pool assistance, made it from 17 to 80 between January and August. Texas Pacific Land Trust rose from 15 to 40 within six months. The increasing popularity of electric refrigeration helped Kelvinator rise from 6 to 38.

The public, meantime, was beginning to appreciate the Exchange game and volume rose 29 percent, breaking the 1925 record as the Dow swept through a 50-point range for the first time in history. Bulls' enthusiasm was unaffected by the landing of U.S. Marines in Nicaragua and China during the year. American Telephone & Telegraph was aggressively innovative during 1927. In addition to opening commercial telephone service between New York and London, the firm made a successful demonstration of television, connecting New York and Washington, where Secretary of Commerce Herbert Hoover anchored the show.

1927 DJIA First 155.16. High 202.40 Dec 31. Low 152.73 Jan 25. Close 202.40, +28.8%.

1928 An irresistible speculative addiction swept Wall Street in 1928. Every volume record at the NYSE—daily, weekly, monthly—was broken again and again. The year's activity jumped by 60 percent over 1927.

Street dealers accommodated the new stock junkies with pools, manipulations, and an orgy of stock offerings. And, best of all, with higher prices. Radio Corporation was a real fix, being levitated from 85 to 420. Warner Brothers celebrated talking pictures and an Al Jolson contract with a long run from 13 to 138. Chrysler bought Dodge Brothers from Dillon, Read for $170 million in stock. Everybody was happy, as the shares boomed—55 to 141.

Three discount rate hikes in the first seven months brought back memories of 1919–1920, however, and the major average was only nervously higher, despite individual pyrotechnics. But tremendous excitement built up in August and the market drove upwards to a 299 level intraday on Thanksgiving Eve, being cheered mightily by Herbert Hoover's election to the White House. Many energy stocks, along with other commodity-type issues, made their bull market highs during the autumn.

General Motors continued as a great market leader, advancing from 130 in January to 225 in November; it had split 2:1 in 1927. Aircraft production doubled during the year, to 4,216 planes, and Wright Aero continued its non-stop flight to 289, up more than 200 points from January. Walt Disney recognized the trend and released his first Mickey Mouse cartoon—"Plane Crazy." So did Dow Jones. They regrouped the Dow average into a 30-stock index during the autumn, increasing the peerage by 50 percent. Wright was included in the new postings, along with other swingers like Radio and Victor Talking Machine.

Detroit stocks were having a good year, but the pride of Moline, Illinois, outdid the autos. John Deere & Co., which had ploughed up from 70 to 250 in 1927, added another 350 points, reaching 600. International Harvester climbed to 395, up 170 from its February low.

The peak monthly volume for the entire 1921–1929 bull market was registered in November. With the Industrials at 296 on Thanksgiving Eve, Dow 350 by Christmas seemed a sensible target. Instead, a vicious post-holiday bear raid shattered the market. Bears were assisted by some new Fed ploys and a verbal shot at speculators by Treasury Secretary Mellon.

Radio Corporation, 403 on Wednesday, December 5, closed at 298 on Saturday and had plenty of company on the downside. The panic's low came in that short session, and its half-day volume record would never be broken.

Buyers swarmed in on Monday, and bullish forces swept the bad Fed news under the carpet. It was a reasonable "correction," they claimed, and one which had only erased the "shoe clerks," along with any store owners who couldn't meet margin on a three-day 100-point break in a stock like Radio.

On December 31, the market closed on its absolute high of the year, Dow 300.00. It was a memorable, round number. No year-end close would approach the level until 1953.

The 300 level already had its skeptics. *Barron's* would point out in its first issue of 1929 that stock prices at the year end were already "discounting the exceptional prosperity anticipated for 1929." The Dow was at 18 times earnings. Chain stores were ardently admired; many, like W. T. Grant sold at 30X earnings, as did General Electric. Even utilities were idolized. Consolidated Edison sold at 24 times earnings at its best 1928 level and AT&T at nearly 17.5X. Such heated approbation would increase before the bull market tapped out.

1928 DJIA First 203.55. High 300.00 Dec 31. Low 191.33 Feb 20. Close 300.00, up 48.2%.

1929   The year 1929 remains the gauge of stock market doom. Its autumn collapse cost the Dow more than 49 percent. In a similar time span of great violence in 1987, the Industrials dropped "only" 36 percent.

The earlier period has been immortalized in song, cartoons, movies, plays, and, by myth, even in skydiver stats. Richard Whitney's famous bid "205 for 10,000 Steel," on one of the worst days of October, was also the stuff of legend. But halting the panic was like trying to catch a cannonball. U.S. Steel shares plunged down to 150, the bear pools having outpowered Morgan's banking syndicate, for whom Whitney had acted.

Opportunities, of course, had abounded early in the year. Dozens of issues gained 100 points or more. Alcoa was quite splendid, rising from 146 to 540 between January and September. But many other issues, including such disparate Dow names as American Sugar, Chrysler, Goodrich, and International Nickel had, by the end of January, already recorded their bull market peak.

Despite frightening volatility in the spring, occasioned by rumblings at the Fed, there was no severe test of nerves, like that of December 1928, until October. Yet, on June 1, the Dow was at 299, fractionally below its 1928 close.

Scores of stocks had been badly hammered in the violent spring fluctuations. Chrysler had fallen from 135 to 65. White Sewing Machine was down 75 percent. Losses for Inspiration Copper, Schulte Retail Stores, and Ward Baking were all over 40 percent. Case Threshing Machine, a pool favorite, had seen 216 points sliced away in a drop from 509 to 293.

Even measured by the Industrials, the fabled advance of 1929 was just an extraordinary "summer rally," as can be seen in Figure 2-1.

During the giddy days of summer, the Dow shot up from 300 to 381. Brokerage offices were jammed. For the affluent, floating boardrooms would ease the boredom of shuffleboard on the premier North Atlantic runs. Mike Meehan, whose firm held more NYSE memberships than any other, opened a

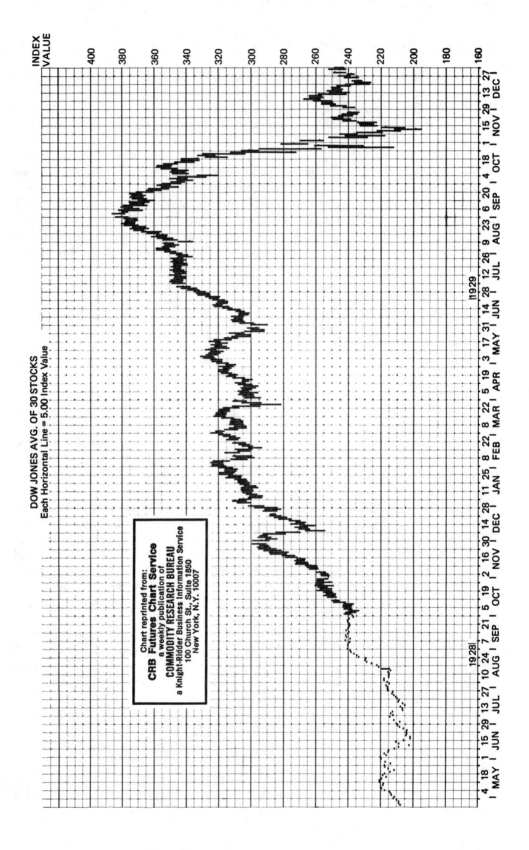

DOW JONES AVG. OF 30 STOCKS
Each Horizontal Line = 5.00 Index Value

INDEX VALUE

400
380
360
340
320
300
280
260
240
220
200
180
160

1928|

4 18 | 1 15 29 | 13 27 | 10 24 | 7 21 | 5 | 2 16 30 | 14 28 | 11 25 | 8 22 | 8 22 | 5 19 | 3 17 31 | 14 28 | 12 26 | 9 23 | 6 20 | 4 18 | 1 15 29 | 13 27
I MAY | JUN | JUL | AUG | SEP | OCT | NOV | DEC | JAN | FEB | MAR | APR | MAY | JUN | JUL | AUG | SEP | OCT | NOV | DEC

|1929|

brokerage office on the *Berengaria* in August—two brokers, two wireless operators and a board marker.

And while market warning signs abounded, most players wanted "one more hand." After all, Meehan's Radio manipulations had gained $4,924,078 for a blue-ribbon pool within about three weeks in March.

All of the pool manipulations in 1929 were not in the fancies. Over 100 pools were effected by NYSE members during the year and included such Dow Jones blue chips as American Tobacco, Chrysler, Goodrich, National Cash Register, and Union Carbide. One group which had missed the summer excitement was the motors. Auto sales in 1929 had not kept pace with the Dow, being barely higher than in 1928. General Motors earnings would be lower for the year and the stock had topped in March—a warning unrecognized at the time. The "General Motors Bellwether Theory" would develop later.

Sensitive to the public's enormous appetite for stocks, Wall Street expanded its bill of fare, cooking up nearly $12 billion in new shares for sale. Well over $2.3 billion of that was in investment trust paper. Hundreds of funds were promoted, many of them highly leveraged.

This "professional management" would be the last great sales cliche of the 1920s. By the record, it worked only as long as the market kept going up. United Founders, a flagship of one group, with assets of over $300 million, saw its stock fall from $75 to 75 cents during the next few years.

By the end of the summer, stock prices, margin debt, and speculative fever were all at record levels, as were price-earnings ratios. Banks, a cozy part of pools, and investment underwritings, were seen as the best "play" on the great securities boom, since brokerage firms were not publicly owned. National City was valued at over 100 times earnings, and ratios of 50X were common for the money-center banks.

Despite the lofty level of stocks, there was a good feeling about the "new era." Cars were more affordable. A radio in every room seemed probable. TV was rumored to be just around the corner. Commercial air transportation was coming of age and movies were talking.

The good feeling started to end shortly after September 3 when the 1921–1929 bull market had crested at Dow 381.17. A panic arrived in October and the collapse of prices over the next few weeks remains awesome. Morgan's $240 million banking pool was drained. Auburn Auto careened from 514 to 120. Alcoa from 540 to 180. Advance Rumely, a former pool favorite that had peaked at 105 in May, traded down to 7. Wright Aero, 299 in February, plummeted to 60.

Even American Telephone, whose $9 dividend was not even yet suspect, was abandoned. It fell from 310 on September 19 to 197, a shattering experience for its conservative holders. It did recover, however, to close higher for the year, along with such other investment favorites as American Can, General Electric, and Jersey. But higher "for the year" still meant enormous losses from summer's bloated prices.

The bearish convulsions had not been sparked by any specific bad business news. Rather, the financial press remained full of splendid earnings reports, extra dividends, stock splits, and glowing forecasts. The Dow earnings for the year would be $19.94 versus $15.76 in 1928 and the composite dividend, at $12.75, would be up 45 percent from the previous year.

Individual stocks were priced less realistically. Burroughs Adding Machine was valued at 42 times earnings. Chase Bank, Radio Corporation, and Montgomery Ward were all at ratios of 60X or more. Utility holding companies were priced like fancy growth stocks: Columbia Gas, Commonwealth & Southern, and National Power & Light were all awarded a PE ratio in the mid-forties.

The autumn smash was perhaps most sobering for the electric & gas companies. They had been presumed to insure relatively more safety than the industrial sector of the market, but their autumn anguish was worse than that of the other averages. The Dow Utilities fell by 55 percent; Brooklyn Union Gas was a 249 to 100 victim within weeks.

The agony of the 1929 panic ended November 13 with the Dow at 199. What lay ahead, after a deceitful recovery into April, was worse—a depthless world depression.

Despite the shattering 1929 losses, the decade of the 1920s finished with the Industrial average up 132 percent from the level of December 1919 when it stood at 107.

1929 DJIA First 307.01. High 381.17 Sep 3. Low 198.69 Nov 13. Close 248.48, −17.2%.

1930 Stock market panic gave way to world depression in 1930, but only after a sensational final running of the bulls.

The smash of 1929 dropped the Dow from 381 to 199. The largest bear market rally in history then pushed the average back to 294 in April. It was a terrible trap for the bulls, seducing many who had avoided the October panic back into the market, though the rally was frothy and artificial.

The *Commercial & Financial Chronicle* found the trend suspect three weeks before it was all over, "The advance in prices on the Stock Exchange, under more or less manipulation, has been gradually gaining momentum," with the push coming from "the mass of bank credit and idle funds available for the prosecution of speculative operations . . ."[10]

Hollywood stars led the 1930 advance. Loew's, Paramount, and Warner Brothers all topped their best levels of 1929. Warner Brothers, which had fallen to 30 in November, made a huge run back to 80, 15 points above the 1929 peak. Many solid blue chips accomplished startling rallies. AT&T, 193 in the fall rose briskly to 274. John Deere surged to a record high. General Electric, which had split 4:1, rose from an adjusted crash low at 42 to 95.

Huge volume gave the spring advance some authenticity. Exchange activity in April was over 111 million shares, larger than any 1929 month, save October.

---

[10]The *Commercial & Financial Chronicle*, New York, March 29, 1930, p. 2084, col. 1.

But trade and industry lagged the rally. Europe was already gripped by crisis. Japan's principal export, silk, fell victim to the depression and an early April selling panic forced the Tokyo Stock Exchange to close for a day.

In June, the Hawley-Smoot tariff bill was signed by the president, over the objections of dozens of foreign countries and a rare consensus of American economists. Over 1,000 of that routinely splintered fraternity had signed a petition opposing the new bill.

The "beggar thy neighbor" trade policy wiped out what little hope was left on Wall Street and the Dow plunged by 23 percent during a three-week period in June. From that oversold position, a summer rally did develop, but it ended abruptly in September. In October, the Dow dropped below the worst level of 1929 and the final blow came in December, when the Bank of New York with 60 branches failed. The Dow lost nearly 16 percent in 12 trading days.

Rather incredible damage was done during the year, though the bear market would not end for another 18 months. Aluminium (Alcan), 232 in the spring, was axed to 58. Technicolor, a "hot" new issue earlier in the year at 85, developed into a $7 disaster by the year end.

Wright Aero, one of the superjets of the previous three years, was shot down from 60 to 11, at which point it had already lost 93 percent of its peak 1929 value, after adjusting for a 2:1 split.

1930 DJIA First 244.20. High 294.07 Apr 17. Low 157.51 Dec 16. Close 164.58, −33.8%.

1931 While 1929 got the headlines, the worst year in American stock market history was 1931. As the "Year of the Bear" in every world bourse and at New York, the year's loss of 53 percent remains a record for the Dow. It exceeded the two-year damage of the very severe 1973–1974 crash. Even worse damage was done the Rails. Their loss of 65.2 percent remains a record one-year assault on any Dow Jones average.

At the beginning of the year, there was some hope, if only because 1929 and 1930 had been so bad. The *Commercial & Financial Chronicle* commented January 3, 1931, ". . . the future essayist will probably find (1930) to have been the most dismal year in the mercantile and financial history of the United States."[11]

For a time, the venerable publication appeared correct. The Dow, which would have three classic bear market rallies during the year, punched up from a December 1930 low at 158 to a February peak of 194, a 23 percent gain.

But business was bad and getting worse. Enormous unemployment threatened the nation's political stability. Bank failures averaged nearly 200 per month. The Veterans' Bonus briefly helped market sentiment in the winter, but in March, the Dow plunged as new European trade barriers were erected.

---

[11]The *Commercial & Financial Chronicle*, New York, April 1, 1981, p. 1, col. 1.

The bears kept pounding through the year, causing NYSE, federal, and media investigations into short selling. Margin accounts were fatal to longs. A. O. Smith, a Curb favorite which had sold at 250 the previous year, was taken down from 192 to 33. Warner Brothers lost box-office appeal. The stock, 80 in 1930, fell to 2. Alcoa was chopped from 224 to 48. Even Auburn, artificially posted to 296 in April, gave up, falling back to 85.

A swift four-week rally in June advanced the Dow 28 percent on hopes for a moratorium on war debts. The summer rally was already over. In September, England abandoned the gold standard. Europe's exchanges shut down and the Dow suffered its worst month in history, losing nearly 31 percent—far worse than the October losses of 1929 and 1987.

Shorts covered heavily after the gold crisis and helped the Dow to a sizzling advance of 36 percent between early October and November 9. It was but one of many vicious short-covering rallies which accompanied the long bear market.

On November 10, the bears returned to pummel the market again, increasing their bearish position in 12 of the next 14 reporting sessions (short sales were required to be computed daily). On November 21, in an extraordinary example of bearish confidence, day-trade shorts executed over 10 percent of all sales at the Exchange.

That pessimism was extreme, but the market was so fundamentally weak that consensus won, with the Dow falling to a new low at 74 in mid-December. November's rally high would stand until May 1935.

1931 DJIA First 169.84. High 194.36 Feb 24. Low 73.79 Dec 17. Close 77.90, −52.7%.

1932 For bull and bear alike, 1932 was the most savage year in stock market history. No complete bear market, save for that of which 1932 was a part, has ever punished the Dow as severely as did the four-month decline from March 8 to July 8. The Dow lost 53.6 percent of its value in that brief period.

And few bull attacks have ever equaled the rocket performance of summer when the Rails tripled within eight weeks and the Utility average doubled.

In the spring, a numbing fact had become clear. Despite having lost a hundred or so points in the 1929–1931 slash, many stocks were still vulnerable to percentage losses of huge proportions. Santa Fe, after two years of damage, fell from 94 to 18 between January and June. American Smelting and Goodyear each saw their prices cut by 80 percent. General Electric and Westinghouse both lost two thirds of their early 1932 value.

While most stocks, in and out of the Dow, had made their low by the end of June, the Industrial average, warped by a few bad losers, did not come to its 1929–1932 bear end until July 8. Volume that Friday was very low, 720,000 shares at the NYSE.

The worst days for the economy still lay ahead, but the averages were about to enjoy an explosive ascent, even though it seemed to lack any specific motivation except hope. The Industrials nearly doubled in the period from July 8 until the first week of September, yet lagged the even more sensational upturn of the Rails and Utilities.

Spectacular fivefold increases were common. Southern Pacific steamed up from 7 to 38, a pattern almost exactly matched by the L&N. Some speculative rails did better. Goodyear and United Aircraft, both Dow members, were also up by a factor of five. Despite the severity of the depression, new hope unearthed old funds. Volume in early September peaked at over 5 million shares. The bull party was already over, however.

Election concerns stymied the market and then, after a brief inflation celebration of Roosevelt's victory, the market drifted lower, stressed by numerous bank failures. But the summer miracle lingers in the record book. August's 68 percent gain for the Rails, for example, remains a record never touched by any index.

1932 DJIA First 74.62. High 88.78 Mar 8. Low 41.22 Jly 8. Close 59.93, −23.1%.

1933 A winter of despair was followed by a summer of frenzied hope in 1933. Never has the psyche of the market experienced such a tumultuous reversal. In February a wave of bank closings and bank "holidays" pushed the Dow back below 50, intra-day, and economic confidence was further impaired by shaky cooperation during the transition period from the Hoover to Roosevelt White House.

In the predawn hours of Saturday, March 3, both New York and Illinois, by some strange coincidence, proclaimed bank holidays. President Roosevelt, taking office on that day, followed suit on Sunday by proclaiming a national holiday and calling the Congress into a special session.

The stock exchange shuttered, not to reopen until March 15, by which time some approved banks were operating. When trading resumed, fear was gone, and the Dow closed at 62.10 versus 53.84 on March 3. The "daily" advance, 15.3 percent, remains the largest in history. The next 100 days were packed with excitement, booming hope, myriad new alphabetical government agencies, and a roaring bull advance.

Everyone knew prices were cheap and suddenly there was a fear that they would get no cheaper. An enormous speculation burst upon the market. Monthly volume at the NYSE in both June and July exceeded any monthly figures ever recorded, save for October 1929.

Rail debt and preferred issues were suddenly coveted. St. Louis & San Francisco preferred leaped from 1 to 9. Seaboard Airline 6 percent bonds jumped from $20 to $310. Chrysler zipped from 8 to 58. The frenzy of hope doubled the Dow's value in just over four months, a bullish pace never matched before or since.

Prohibition was on its way out and the most toasted groups were the distillery and container stocks. Anchor-Hocking ran from 7 to 37; National Distillers, 17 to 125. On July 18, the party abruptly ended. An enormous four-day hangover dropped the Dow nearly 19 percent. American Commercial Alcohol, beneficiary of a "whiskey pool" on the way up, was cut from 90 to 29 within the week.

Business teetered and FDR, having removed the nation from the gold standard in April, mounted a deliberate inflation plan, seeking to raise commodity prices. He racheted the price of gold higher, on a near-daily basis, from the old figure at $20.67.

Thus, Homestake, like the other golds, could ignore the autumn's dragging market, which hurt the Rails more than the Industrials. The legendary South Dakota producer reached 373 in the year's last quarter, up from a low of 145 in January.

For the Industrials, the year's gain ranks second only to that of 1915. The February–July advance marked the only time in its history that the Dow managed an intra-year gain of 100 percent—50.16 to 108.67.

1933 DJIA First 59.29. High 108.67 Jly 18. Low 50.16 Feb 27. Close 99.90, +66.7%.

1934

By 1934, if not before, the political honeymoon was over for FDR's new administration. The unrealistic business hopes of the "100 Days" would end in the fall slump of 1934.

Increased federal bureaucracy and spending, the National Recovery Act (NRA), even a pair of securities acts could not guarantee prosperity nor a strong stock market. The Dow made a miniscule new high in February, above that of September 1933, but the Rails failed to confirm.

The balance of the year comprised a choppy consolidation for the Industrials. Gulf Oil, for example, had moved from 24 in 1933 to a February top at 77. Its drop back to 50 amounted to a 50 percent correction. Chrysler which had exploded from 7 to 58 in 1933 fell to 29.

Meanwhile, it was a primary bear market for the Rails, one which would not end until the spring of 1935. By September 1934, the decline already amounted to about 42 percent. In 1933, Baltimore & Ohio had rolled from 8 to 38; it slid back to 13 in 1934 and would hit 7½ the following year.

There were a few solid Dow winners around, however, like American Can and Woolworth. And, in a great individual advance, Philip Morris overcame its 1929 high. Homestake added more riches to the pockets of the true believers by rising to 435 following FDR's final fixing of gold at $35. Homestake would remain the highest-priced issue at the NYSE until its split in 1937.

By the end of the year, the economy had turned and even commodity prices were creeping higher. Despite the Rails' negative action, the Dow ended slightly plus for the year, having overcome the nasty correction which had peeled off about 23 percent of its value between February and July.

Volume at the NYSE had suffered a record contraction, falling by over 50 percent from the 1933 level.

1934 DJIA First 100.36. High 110.74 Feb 5. Low 85.51 Jly 26. Close, 104.04, +4.1%.

_____

1935 Detroit drove the stock market back into the right lane in 1935. Even with unemployment in the high teens, auto sales climbed by 52 percent in the year, returning some fundamental prosperity to the economy and the market.

Auto leadership, however, came after a dismal first quarter. The Utility average had dropped beneath its low of 1932 and rail bankruptcies were the worst since 1893.

But late spring brought a stunning increase in industrial strength as the motors, steels, and industrial suppliers suddenly boomed. Timken Roller Bearing, which had earned $1.45 in 1934 put $3.10 on the bottom line in 1935 and the shares rolled up from 28 to 72. Square D moved from 7 to 44.

Many steels doubled and the farm equipments were strong. Allis-Chalmers rose from a first-quarter low at 12 to 38 in October, as its red ink suddenly disappeared. Chrysler sped up from 30 to 90 in about the same period. Coca-Cola brought back boom-time memories with a 4:1 split—a rarity during the depression years. Its earnings and price were well above the 1929 peak.

Wrangles between business and the administration continued and FDR's National Recovery Act was ruled unconstitutional. Banking confidence had, at least, been restored by the FDIC and the bitter weeding out process. Bank suspensions totaled only 34 versus 4,000 in 1933.

Where possible, dividends were generally, if not generously, increased. General Motors, one of the rare corporations to have maintained some payout through the harsh depression years, upped its dividend to $2.26 from $1.50. Among the Rails, Union Pacific was a bright spot. It earned and paid a $3 dividend in 1933 and in every following year of the 1930s.

The battered Utilities, after their bad first-quarter slide, reversed to gain 66 percent in 1935; the mark remains their best record.

1935 DJIA First 104.51. High 148.44 Nov 19. Low 96.71 Mar 14. Close 144.13, +38.5%.

_____

1936 Big employment gains, big auto gains, and big confidence gains boomed the market in 1936. Drawbacks like big union gains, mushrooming work stoppages, and Hitler's reoccupation of the Rhineland were largely ignored. FDR's re-election helped push the Dow to its 1936 peak.

Even the rails showed vital signs, and the Dow Rail index posted composite earnings of $3.71 after four years of red ink. Earnings for the Industrials were up 59 percent for the year. Big Steel reversed four years of deficits and Texaco earned $4.10 versus $1.84 in 1935. Jones & Laughlin ran up from 30 to 100 during the year.

Chrysler, with a strong balance sheet and earnings more than double the previous peak of 1928, voted an astounding dividend melon, paying $12 versus $2 in the previous year. The stock rose to 139, a remarkable comeback from the survival low of 5 in 1932. Buying the shares for the big payout, a "dividend play," did not work. Purchasers hiked their income but would wait 15 years to recapture the principal paid out to acquire the shares.

Large speculative volume—though far short of 1933—reentered the market, and January's NYSE activity would not be matched until 1951. In February, margin requirements, for the first time under the new federal regulations, were increased to 55 percent.

A sharp break in April set up a strong summer and the Dow posted higher readings in each month from May through November. The Rails, after three years, finally topped their July 1933 recovery peak. But not the Utilities.

Homestake reached a glittery high at 554, an amazing depression success story. Its dividend was $56, just about what the shares had been worth ten years earlier.

At the year-end, consumer consensus was that the travails of the depression years were finally finished. Employment, retail and auto sales, and confidence had all registered recovery highs. For the Dow, it was the best year-end close since 1929, and the average seemed poised to advance over 200.

1936 DJIA First 144.13. High 184.90 Nov 17. Low 143.11 Jan 6. Close 179.90, +24.8%.

1937 Just when America thought the deep, dirty depression days were gone forever, they returned with a vengeance. The Dow lost 33 percent of its value in 1937. The August–November panic loss was 40 percent, equal to that of a severe bear market. But a year-end rally cut the damage, despite the sinking of the U.S. gunboat *Panay* by Japanese bombers while the ship was in Chinese waters.

Early on, an overwhelming enthusiasm for steels had topped out the 1932–1937 advance. Big Steel ran to 127 in March, up 47 points from the November high. Bethlehem Steel, which had lost money in four of the previous five years, rose quickly to 106.

Metals and the rubbers were also strong, the latter group despite the fact that the major autos topped in late 1936. A few overachievers even overcame the 1929 heights. Coca-Cola's great popularity continued and it tripled its 1930 high. Many container issues, along with Phillips Petroleum, National Lead, and even a few Rails were among those reaching record levels. They were really a very special group, since the 1937 Dow top was only about half the 1929 peak.

Temporarily ignored in the year's early enthusiasm were tightening manuevers by the Fed, mushrooming sit-down strikes and, later, a growing uneasiness with the presidency. Despite enormous personal popularity, FDR had stirred up a two-party hornet's nest with his proposal to pack the Supreme Court.

Stocks staggered through the summer. Japan invaded China. The Dow finally worked up, on low volume, to a double-top on August 14, just four points below the March peak. On September 1, both Dow averages opened below their worst levels of the previous day, creating a nasty downside gap. A severe economic and market panic followed. The August–November drop was something less than the autumn collapse of 1929, but larger than that of 1987. A margin reduction to 50 percent on November 1 failed to halt the break.

Industrial production faded faster than in 1930. U.S. Steel plummeted to 49—a 71 point loss in the autumn rout. Crucible did worse, percentagewise, 82 to 21. Alcoa dropped 105 points from 177. Unemployment increased by two million, astonishing the New Deal economists.

While 1937 was only the third worst year of the 1930s, losing 32.8 percent for the Dow, no year since that decade has even equaled the bearish bronze performance of 1937.

1937 DJIA First 178.52. High 194.40 Mar 10. Low 113.64 Nov 24. Close 120.85, −32.8%.

1938   The second great depression of the 1930s lasted for one year. Frightened by its solid, black credentials, bureaucrats awarded the crisis a facelift. In Washingtonese, it became a "recession."

There would be no label change for the bear slide which accompanied the crisis. Though short, it remains the second worst in history, ending on March 31; Hitler's Austrian anchluss provided the final push down. The economic depression would end two months months later.

Great volatility and abrupt direction changes ruled the market all year. The Rails were lucky to escape with painful volatility. Class I rails suffered their second largest deficit in history and the industry's dividends were halved. Yet, the average ended a bit higher for the year. The spring low, 19.00, was the era's final hit on the carriers. Their average would triple during the war years; the Dow Industrials would "only" double during the same period.

Peace advocates were vocal in 1938, but large orders began to pour into the defense industry. Douglas Aircraft flew up from 31 to 81. Its 21-seat DC-3 would become the industry's leader and the California firm produced 410 aircraft in 1938; sales over $28 million were nearly triple the 1936 figure.

Lockheed performed better, however, advancing from 6 to 38, and aviation bugs got a further lift when Howard Hughes circled the world in record time. Chrysler, having lost 100 points in the bear market, bounced from 35 to 89 within a few months and Anheuser-Busch, even then No. 1 in suds, moved to 250 before splitting 5:1.

At the end of September the Munich agreement seemed to promise peace and that illusion spurred the market up to its mini-bull peak in November. The Rails gained 44 percent in the final six weeks of the seven-month advance.

1938 DJIA First 120.57. High 158.41 Nov 12. Low 98.95 Mar 31. Close 154.76, +28.1%

1939

When World War I broke out, there were only sellers about and every bourse in the world was forced to close. At the outbreak of World War II in September 1939, there were no bears. London closed briefly, but every other exchange from Europe to New York to Tokyo recorded sharply higher prices following Germany's surprise invasion of Poland on September 1.

The year had opened on a firm note, but Germany's march on Czechoslovakia brought the Dow crashing down to a mini-bear market low in early April. It was not a "mini" for many stocks. Steels and rubbers were sold heavily, Alleghany-Ludlum and Goodrich both losing 50 percent from their autumn highs of 1938.

A classic reversal in April turned the market quickly higher and the boom in war orders and rail traffic kept prices moving ahead. When war came on September 1, a buyers' panic swept stock prices nearly straight up for eight days. Speculators chased the great winners of 1915, anticipating a repeat. Bethlehem Steel, the greatest stock of that earlier era, as it had advanced from 46 to 600 within one year, was a choice of proven merit. The war madness swept it up from near 50 to 100. But Hitler would be dead before most of the coveted "war babies" would show a profit for the September speculators.

War issues, but not the war issues of 1915, would be the big beneficiaries of the coming conflict. Railroad car and locomotive building companies, like American Car & Foundry, mostly doubled in September, along with such obvious war choices as Interlake Iron and Calumet & Hecla.

Wall Street's fever peaked September 12, ending the third in a string of volatile, miniature moves for the Dow, all completed within 18 months. The winds of war had swirled sporadically along the Street, as well as in Washington.

Though September's hottest favorites faded quickly, drugs, airlines, and leading rails held strongly into the year end. Pan-American's new Clipper service to Europe helped it double in the last few months.

By the year-end, the intense high-volume excitement of September had long faded, though the Dow was still higher than its level when war broke out. Du Pont, Cluett Peabody (Arrow shirts), and Sears, among other diverse issues, had exceeded their best level of 1929. Hundreds of quality issues, including U.S. Steel, General Motors, and AT&T, were far below their closes of 1929.

Not surprisingly, the 1930s remain the only decade in a century during which the leading market average lost ground. The Dow's 1930–1939 loss was nearly 40 percent, in a drop from 248 to 150. Earnings had been halved to $9.11

for the select group. The Dow dividend, $6.11, was less than that of 1925, even somewhat lower than the $6.21 paid out in the war boom year of 1916.

1939 DJIA First 153.64. High 155.92 Sep 12. Low 121.44 Apr 8. Close 150.24 −2.9%

1940

In May 1940, "sitzkrieg" turned to blitzkrieg and the Nazis swept the Allies from Western Europe. The stock market collapsed in what would be the worst panic of World War II, much worse than that which followed Pearl Harbor.

During the winter and early spring, the Industrials had constructed a classic "line" formation, a long horizontal movement which had been bounded on the top by Dow 152 and on the bottom by 145. On May 9, the average had closed mid-range, at 148.

The German blitz forced the British to the beaches at Dunkerque and the Industrials suffered a frightful fall from their "shelf," losing nearly 25 percent within a few weeks to a low at 112. Volume of nearly 4 million shares on May 21, when the Dow dropped 6.8 percent, would stand as the most active day of the decade.

Many issues were convulsed from a year's high in April to an annual low in May. General Motors was one, ranging from 56 to 37. Not a few stocks compressed both their 1940 high and low into the month of May. Atlantic Refining, Baldwin Locomotive, and Norfolk & Western were among them. American Hawaiian Steamship also foundered, 51 to 23 within three weeks.

By early June, British troops safely off the beaches, the panic ended. Stocks moved erratically higher, but on low volume. Their movement was largely dominated by war news, of which little was good. Losses to U-boats were fearful and in August, Britain was besieged from the skies.

Throughout the year, the Bank of England continued as a dogged seller of American securities. England had already dug deeply into her currency and gold reserves to finance the purchase of arms and munitions. Over $335 million in American shares requisitioned for sterling from private owners in Britain had been liquidated by November, 1940.

War stocks generally already had more business than they could efficiently handle, but that fact was already known and appreciated by the market. Revenues for many would increase tenfold during the war, or even more; But profit and share gains would be restricted. United Aircraft sales pushed from $52 million to $734 million between 1939 and 1943 and earnings increased by 50 percent. But the stock fell from 51 to 24 in the same period.

Nylons, a minor currency in post-war Europe, were introduced by du Pont in May with little impact on the stock. FDR's third-term election in November left the GOP sulking once again, but after a one-day setback, the market quickly recovered to a post-blitzkrieg high. That level, Dow 138, would not be exceeded until the final defeat of the Afrika Korps in May 1943.

The Rails' loss for 1940 was slightly less than that of the Industrials, even though 109 roads operating over 77,000 miles were in either bankruptcy or receivership. The total amounted to about one-third of the country's mileage.

1940 DJIA First 151.43. High 152.80 Jan 3. Low 111.84 Jne 10. Close 131.13, −12.7%.

1941

By late 1941, the stock market knew that war was coming. It just didn't know how or when the bad news would arrive. So, Sunday, December 7, 1941, FDR's "shocking day of infamy," had only modest impact, as compared with the disastrous panic which followed the 1940 Nazi blitzkrieg.

The Dow Industrials, 116.60 on the Saturday before Pearl Harbor, lost only four points on December 8 and 8.8 percent in December's liquidation.

Stocks had been in a mild if stubborn downtrend since the fall of 1940. Foreign selling and great indecision on the part of traders—1941 volume was the lowest since 1918—kept rallies restrained all year despite busy factories where demand was boosted by Lend-Lease.

Even the defense issues fell during the year as prospects for U.S. war involvement increased. Bethlehem Steel lost nearly 45 percent during the year. Automobile stocks were equally disappointing. But the Pearl Harbor lows for that group would stand as their wartime worst level, despite the fact that 1941 earnings would be a wartime best. Chrysler's 1941 earnings would not be exceeded until 1948.

Rails were disappointing, though the industry's most extravagant earnings increases lay just around the curve, in 1942. Union Pacific slumped from 86 to 48.

When the Nazis turned on Russia, June 22, the year's best rally was already underway, but it quickly stagnated. In October, two U.S. destroyers were torpedoed by U-boats and war seemed inevitable, what with Japan's aggressive military expansion in the Far East.

Only the oils, of major groups, were strong all year. Their index topped in December but then they too were impacted by the new war in the Pacific. Superior Oil, along with the other crude producers, like Skelly, had large earnings increases. Superior, a great finder of oil, would never integrate into refining and marketing; for decades it would be a stock proxy for crude demand.

Earnings for 1941, $11.64, would be the best of all the war years for the Dow. The average price-earnings ratio was the lowest since 1925.

1941 DJIA First 130.57. High 133.59 Jan 10. Low 106.34 Dec 23. Close 110.96, −15.4%.

1942

The blackest days of World War II came in the spring of 1942 and were mirrored by a sullen stock market. Yet there was no panic in the Street. There was not a single million-share day during the period.

Japanese and German victories seemed unending, and their forces invincible. But, for some reason, the Industrials, on April 28, just quit going down. The market was sold out; volume on that Tuesday was but 313,000 shares. On the following day, the Utility average recorded its all-time low, 10.58. American Telephone was a very weak stock; its president warned that new taxes might force a dividend cut.

Every section of the market had been pounded, save for the motors, that group having bottomed in the previous December. Many rails, at the low of the year, sold for about one times earnings. New York Central, a venerable survivor of a century of rail wars, traded below 8, where its price barely exceeded its 1942 earnings, which would be $7.61.

On May 26, the Dow suffered its last close below the 100 level, and in early June, the Battle of Midway marked a turning point for the war in the Pacific, though such was not absolutely clear at the time. The market, in any event, did not celebrate. Guadalcanal and other torments lay ahead. Stocks finally moved grudgingly higher in the fourth quarter, encouraged by Allied landings in North Africa and Stalingrad's stubborn defenses.

War news had dominated trading during the year, but a few groups, including the airlines, were showing independent strength. American Airlines flew from 25 to 59 while Pan-Am and United both doubled their lows of the spring. Most of the rubber stocks also doubled; Goodyear bounced up from 10 to 27, where it was valued at about five times earnings.

In December, technicians were pleased to see a sudden bloom of volume with a half-dozen days when activity topped one million shares. The Street could use it. Annual volume turned out to be the second lowest full-year figure of the century, the worst since 1913, and a NYSE membership sold for $17,000, the lowest price since 1897.

Rail earnings were quite extraordinary in relation to share prices. The Baltimore & Ohio earned $16.77 in a year in which its common stock price ranged only from 2⅝ to 4⅛. Illinois Central earned $17.52 and the stock sold as low as 6.

For such beleaguered roads the earnings were earmarked, not for common dividends, but for defaulted bond interest, tardy repayment of debt maturities, and arrears on preferred stock.

U.S. railroad net income in 1942 was four times that of 1940 and seven times that of 1939. It translated into the most incredible figures ever seen for any Dow average.

The Dow Rails earned $14.10 in 1942. At the year-end, the price-earnings ratio, with the index at 27.39, was 1.9X. At the year's low, the ratio had been 1.65X. Lower earnings (because of taxes), and a higher esteem for those earnings would put the PE ratio at 10X by 1945.

1942 DJIA First 112.77. High 119.71 Dec 26. Low 92.92 Apr 28. Close 119.40, +7.6%.

1943 War news improved so rapidly through 1943 that in July, when Allied troops successfully invaded Sicily, the market would begin to worry about the economics of peace.

In January, President Roosevelt had sailed on the *U.S.S. Iowa* for the Casablanca conference and the news seemed to improve dramatically thereafter.

In early February, the Nazis surrendered at Stalingrad and, during the spring, the Bismarck Sea victory, the Japanese evacuation of Guadalcanal, and the final surrender of Rommel's desert forces cheered the market.

Stock prices at the time closely followed victory's course. Upside volume made a notable return to the Exchange in March when nearly 37 million shares traded, the largest figure since September 1939. The Industrials reached 142 in May, a strong advance from the subpar level just one year earlier, but trading activity and momentum suddenly slackened.

The invasion of Sicily and, in September, Italy, left the market unmoved. Buying evaporated, victory on Germany's perimeters being already discounted. In October, volume was cut to less than 40 percent of the March number.

Victory's dimly seen outline left the aircrafts mostly lower for the year. Glenn L. Martin and many others failed their 1942 peak and Martin's top price, 26, was far below the 48 level seen in 1940. Rails and metals were soft during the second half. International Nickel slipped from 37 in the spring to 25 in November.

Excess profits taxes restrained any price mushroom for the Rails. Atlantic Coast Lines earned $21.23 per share when federal taxes were double its net income. Debt reduction took precedence over dividends and the 1943 low was 24.

Secondary automobile shares prospered, but General Motors and Chrysler could not overcome their 1939–1940 highs. Studebaker and Hudson both returned to a dividend basis, having found defense work more dependable than yearly model changes.

IBM struggled up to 81, from a 1942 low at 50, but still lagged all its yearly peaks of 1935–1940. Its reported earnings, $4.05, were at the low end of a ten-year range between $4.01 and $4.86, though sales had increased sevenfold.

Despite tremendous Allied successes during the last nine months of the year, the Dow ended the fourth quarter within a point of its value at the end of March.

If victory was closer, so was the economic enigma of peace.

1943 DJIA First 119.43. High 145.82 Jly 14. Low 119.26 Jan 8. Close, 135.89 +13.8%.

1944 At the end of May 1944, the Dow was exactly where it had been one year earlier, despite building military successes. But within a week, the consolidation would be resolved to the upside. D-Day was the spark.

Rome fell June 5. The Allies landed in Normandy June 6. Within the month, the Japanese mainland would come under serious B-29 attacks and the

Imperial Navy would lose three desperately needed carriers in the Battle of the Philippine Sea.

Huge June volume doubled the April–May total and many consumer stocks were brilliant leaders. Decca Records, 5 in 1942, spun up to 41. Universal Pictures had increased nearly fivefold in the same period. Gimbel's and Spiegel, Inc. both doubled during the year.

Even the Rails, whose traffic curve was flattening, were strong in the last few months of the year. The Nazi death rattle at December's Battle of the Bulge failed to slow the advance.

Mostly, the war issues and oils failed the bulls. The 1944 highs for Crucible Steel and United Aircraft, for example, were lower than in each of the previous five years. Jersey, Standard of Cal, and Standard of Indiana all lagged their best prices of 1943.

It was a great year for the Allies and for the Industrials. Neither one, however, had quite recovered its position of September, 1939. The stock of Bethlehem Steel, whose sales had increased from $414 million in 1939 to a war peak of $1.9 billion, was at 1944's best price fractionally lower than in September 1939. The Industrials were several points below the best level of that same month. FDR's re-election saw the Dow 13 points over the 1940 election day level.

The Rails had done better. At the year-end, they were up over 44 percent—their second best advance since 1890. The gain had advanced them well above their best level of 1939.

1944 DJIA First 135.92. High 152.53 Dec 16. Low 134.22 Feb 7. Close 152.32 +12.1%.

1945   Meat, gasoline, shoes, and canned goods, among other consumer items, had been rationed by the government during World War II. Dealers rationed liquor. Purchasers of two bottles of Southern Comfort and one rum were allowed to buy a no-name fifth of bourbon.

By 1945, the public was parched for nylons, steaks, cars, scotch, and a full tank. With the war's final verdict virtually assured, stock traders switched into consumer goods in 1945. "War babies" were passé. Retailers and liquors led the list. Gimbel Brothers tripled during the year and Allied Stores advanced from 20 to 48. Schenley shot up from 20 to 87.

With military air transport priorites likely to disappear, investors could read a superior airline flight plan. Trans World Air (TWA) flew from 26 to 79.

Germany was obviously going down and after the invasion of Okinawa in April and the B-29 fire bomb raids over Japan, that island's fate also seemed doomed. But Hiroshima saw stock prices no higher than on May 9, V-E Day. Not until late August did the boom begin. Then, even the aircrafts joined the new advance. The Rail average had gone through a sort of reverse victory celebration, a summer slump, but shortly after V.J. Day, the index revived and pushed up 26 percent to the December high.

Consumer and luxury stocks never wavered. Hunt Foods tripled. Warner

Brothers, 7 in March, moved up to 18 late in the year. Gold mining had been shut down by the government in 1942 and suddenly the prospects for renewed operations seemed bright. Homestake, 23 shortly after the federal edict, raced up in 1945 from 42 to a summer peak at 61.

Events of tremendous importance—the death of President Roosevelt, V.E. Day and the atom bombs—had small market impact. But stocks gathered great strength after the Japanese surrender, unlike the reaction at the end of World War I, and the excitement would continue until May 1946.

If there was an anomaly in the market, it was in the jaded approach to the major automakers, whose prospects were perfectly brilliant. General Motors' gain was only 16 points, from 62 to 78. Auto buffs focused on the secondary issues, betting that the enormous, pent-up auto demand would make even the likes of Kaiser Auto, Tucker, Hudson, and Packard rich. But it would be a very short lap for all but the Big Three.

In December, the Dow finally exceeded its 1937 high, climbing to the best level since October 1930. It was the fourth consecutive year for the Industrials to advance and the seventh consecutive gain for the decennial "5" year.

1945 DJIA First 152.58. High 195.82 Dec 11. Low 151.35 Jan 24. Close 192.91, +26.6%.

1946

A depression, the Cassandras said, followed every war. For a time, in late 1946, the perils of peace seemed severe, indeed, as panic and pessimism swept the Street.

During the first five months of the year, however, the victory celebration of late 1945 had continued at a rowdy pace. So rowdy that the Federal Reserve Board raised margins to 100 percent—the only time in history that full coverage has been required across the board. But the January action failed to seriously temper the market's excitement and the Dow roared on to its bull market high in May at 212.50.

During the buoyant spring, consumer stocks expanded on their great 1945 prosperity. In most cases, chart patterns added a church steeple top to a previous long advance. Decca Records had increased tenfold since 1942. In early 1946, it recorded a further 50 percent markup.

Speculative enthusiasm and volume waned during a summer consolidation and in the session following Labor Day, the leading averages opened with large down-gaps, a repeat of the 1937 action. The market fell rapidly to a panic low in early October. Speculative types who survived the stock action found themselves hammered again that month as a large cotton corner collapsed.

Business had slowed dramatically. War contracts had been cut savagely during the previous year, but vast dislocations continued to plague industry. Steel shortages, parts shortages, strikes, and a rail embargo caused many plant shutdowns.

Rail traffic collapsed and airline traffic fell short of expectations. The

Nickel Plate, 75 in late 1945, was knocked down to 26. New York Central fell from 36 to 14. United Airlines, 63 in December of 1945, fell to 20. Retailers were liquidated, Marshall Field dropping from 58 to 30. The golds were not spared.

After a few weeks of liquidation, the motors and chemicals began to resist. Many, including General Motors and Allied Chemical, made their post-war low in October 1946, not in the summer of 1949.

Neither the Industrials or the Rails would ever suffer an annual close below the final level of 1946.

1946 DJIA First 191.66. High 212.50 May 29. Low 163.12 Oct 9. Close 177.20 −8.1%.

1947 During the post-war years, the market gave no quarter to bad earnings and no credit to record earnings. The latter were adjudged a creation of war-induced shortages and were given a savage price-earnings haircut. Investors' mindset was focused on a depression.

In 1947, all of Bristol Myers' Bufferins couldn't stop the headache when earnings fell from $4.89 to $2.67 and the stock plummeted from 63 to 32. Philip Morris increased earnings from $2.04 to $2.60 (they would rise to $5.84 the following year) but the shares dropped from 71 in 1946 to 25.

On February 1, the Fed cut margin requirements to 75 percent. Specula-tors ignored the courtesy and by mid-May, the Dow was down to 163.21, less than one-tenth point from the October low. It might have been worse, but the proposal of Representative Sabbath, to put more federal control over the mar-ket failed to gather a clan. He wanted to tax all short sales five percent.

The best rally of the year followed, based on hopes for a tax cut and the passage of the Taft-Hartley bill over the president's veto. A peak in July was the end of the bulls' hopes and the market moved choppily for the balance of the year.

A few groups posted their post-war lows during the year, the oils, air-crafts, and rails among them. Autos continued relatively firm; Chrysler, which split 2:1, moved from 43 to 69. Coal issues regained strength, with Pittston jumping from 17 to 39 in the last half. Union Pacific, 55 in late 1946, pushed back up to 82 within two points of its 1946 peak.

Investors were a stubbornly bearish lot in 1947. The Dow earnings boomed up 38 percent and would rise another 23 percent in the following year. But buyers refused the bait, the Dow gaining but 2 percent. Even popular General Electric had a rare fall from grace. It more than doubled its earnings, yet closed lower for the year. Earnings would rise again in 1948.

1947 DJIA First 176.39. High 186.85 Jly 24. Low 163.21 May 17. Close 181.16, +2.2%.

1948 A 20-year record for the Dow was broken in 1948 as the Index's earnings finally exceeded those of 1929. They totaled $23.07 versus $19.94 in 1929. Unfortunately, the celebration was blind-sided late in the year by President Harry Truman's surprise reelection and the Dow ended with a small loss.

Earlier in the year, investors had nibbled at stocks, and volume, which had declined since 1945, would gain 19 percent at the NYSE. Rails were up 58 percent from the 1947 low. For a time, the market seemed on a rumble. It ignored the heat of inflation, the Berlin airlift, recurrent labor problems, and the return of credit controls, pushing above the 190 level last seen in August 1946 time after time. Many groups, like the tobaccos, retailers, drugs, air transports, and utilities, had already completed their bear cycle.

Oils were standouts. A severe winter and increased crude pricing pushed their earnings to record levels and shareholders were rewarded, though not handsomely. Superior Oil saw earnings explode from $11.51 to $35.26. At the year's peak, the stock was valued at 6.6X earnings. Sinclair doubled in 1948; Richfield Oil was a bigger winner, 18 to 48.

Many airlines, having suffered huge profit and equity losses, reached bear market lows. United, 63 in 1945, made its turn just below 10, as did TWA, which had flown to 79 in the last year of the war. Traffic growth had been tremendous, but equipment and servicing costs had gone up even faster.

Rails again prospered. The Kansas City Southern doubled during the year and the mercurial Nickel Plate did better. The shares had sold at 19 in 1947, but bloomed to 92 in 1948 as earnings more than doubled to $39. There would be no dividend, however; preferred stock arrears totaled $68.50 per share, a hangover from the 1930s.

Post-election jitters gave the American market a sloppy year-end. Steels and autos suffered severely, Truman not being seen as a "smoke-stack" man. Still, both Rails and Utilities ended the year slightly higher.

1948 DJIA First 181.04. High 193.16 Jne 15. Low 165.39 Mar 16. Close 177.30, −2.1%.

1949 The nation's investors had become so traumatized by a depression mindset by 1949 that even *Life* magazine, in an unlikely feature published in March, pointed out the pathetic level of stock prices as measured against fundamentals like earnings, dividends, and cash in the till.

But neither *Life* nor the FRB, which lowered margin requirements on March 30, could curb the growing rift between value and price. The market sank lower in June when both the leading averages posted their bear market lows amidst great pessimism on the part of Dow theorists. For the Industrials, it was in reality an unique three-year triple bottom: 163.12 in 1946, 163.21 in 1947, and 161.60 in 1949. That picture would be clearer later on, to be sure.

Price-earnings ratios, nevertheless, spoke of enormous bargains. Multiples of two or less were not uncommon. Rails, in particular, suffered such disaffection. Nickel Plate and Illinois Central were among such "cheapies." The latter, which had earned $14.60 in 1948, sold below 23. Farm equipment maker Minneapolis-Moline earned $7.20 but sold at 10. Chrysler and Jones & Laughlin were priced at less than three times their 1949 earnings.

General Motors, International Paper, Safeway, and Atlantic Refining were seen as more valuable, worth between three and four times earnings at their lows of 1949. All were rare bargains by any historical measurement.

Save for Chrysler, every stock noted in the bargain list would earn more in 1950 than 1949. Chrysler's net would slip only from $15.19 to $14.69.

Both averages reversed quickly from June's bear trap and by October, the Dow had again crossed 190, despite a mammoth steel strike. After Christmas, the average finally reached 200 again, on increasing volume. The autumn strength had been accompanied by extraordinary odd-lot liquidation.

On September 3, 1949, the Dow had stood at less than half the level seen 20 years earlier, despite higher earnings. During the 1940s, the Dow's bottom line had increased 110 percent over the 1949 level; the average was up a third. Giant economic strides had been studiously ignored by the market since 1946.

The depression trauma had been broken. Stocks have seldom been so cheaply valued, but were unwanted. NYSE volume fell below that of 1906.

One of the rare investment opportunities in the post-war world went almost unnoticed during the year. In Japan, General Douglas MacArthur authorized the stock exchanges to reopen and in both Osaka and Tokyo traders were swamped with enthusiastic domestic volume.

The gains of the next few decades in the Japanese market are difficult to translate, given the enormous advance in both stock prices and the value of the yen, but stock certificates "Made in Japan" were the cheapest in the world.

1949 DJIA First 175.03. High 200.52 Dec 30. Low 161.60 Jne 13. Close 200.13, +12.9%.

1950 By the time the skeptics were finally convinced, in 1950, that peace and prosperity were a great parlay, war in Korea temporarily halted a great new bull campaign.

Reborn bulls had pushed the Dow sharply higher in the spring of 1950, overcoming the 1946 peak of 212.50 with no difficulty. Then, in late June, the sudden shock of the Korean War scuttled the market. The largest volume since the opening days of World War II pushed stocks sharply lower, the Dow falling from 224 on June 23 to a July low at 197. U.S. troops had arrived in Korea on July 1.

"War brides" again became a vogue among stock pickers. Steels, coppers, rails, and aircrafts were avidly gathered. Glenn L. Martin doubled. Copper Range rose from 12 to 41, enjoying a vigorous demand from both peace and war industries. The Dow's earnings mushroomed to $30.70 for the year, up from $23.54, leaving shares still cheaply valued.

There were pockets of weakness, of course. Gold followers remembered the mining restrictions of World War II and Homestake fell from 50 to 32. Coca-Cola, which had boasted an elitest PE multiple for years, became more common when 1950 earnings fell to $7.41 from $8.76. In a very strong market, the stock dropped from 165 to 113, the low coming in December.

Early victories for the United Nations forces in Korea pushed the Dow to a new high in the fall, aided by GOP gains at the mid-term election. But when Chinese forces became involved at the Yalu River in late November, prices were cut back sharply. But both lead indices rallied strongly in late December to close just short of the yearly highs.

The gains had all come in the last six months, both averages having been minus for the year in early July. It was an auspicious start for the second half-century. The travails near the Dow 200 mark—the high area of 1931, 1937, and the post-war years, had finally been surmounted.

1950 DJIA First 198.89. High 235.47 Nov 24. Low 196.81 Jan 13. Close 235.41, +17.6%.

1951   Eight years of advancing earnings for the Dow finally came to a halt in 1951, as the bottom line dropped to $26.59 from $30.70. But, for long-term bulls, the game had only begun.

Speculation heated up in January, despite a margin increase to 75 percent. Volume for the month, over 70 million, was the highest since July 1933. It was a runaway for the Rail average, up nearly 35 percent by early February from the Yalu River low just two months earlier.

The Peking connection made the war's conduct more complicated and in April, General Douglas MacArthur, who wanted to bomb north of the Yalu, was cashiered as Supreme Commander. The stock market, which had little stomach for war with China, and her possible Russian ally, pushed up to a new high at 263 in May. Peace talks would start in July.

Oils displayed extreme strength all year, Superior rose to 570, up a couple hundred points from the year's low. CBS aired the first commercial color telecast, but such innovation was priced at only 7X earnings for the broadcaster. AT&T added its millionth stockholder, but the shares traded a few points below the 1901 high, when the dividend was $7.50, not the famous $9 rate voted in each year since 1921.

Inflation, labor disputes, construction bans, and a hodgepodge of price ceilings kept the market from ever really flying. The year's industrial peak came in September at 276 and speculation and volume dwindled through the balance of the year. The cigarette makers, almost alone, had continued in a bearish posture, but they would soon be joined by others.

Many industries such as steels, farm equipments, chemicals, and drugs registered highs which would stand for several years. Parke, Davis would not equal its 1951 peak until 1958.

Automobile issues showed great technical promise, resisting the fright of a sizeable earnings decline—nearly 40 percent for General Motors—plus dividend reductions. In the case of Motors, the consolidation period would be rewarded with a tripling of its price by 1955.

1951 DJIA First 239.92. High 276.37 Sep 13. Low 238.99 Jan 3. Close 269.23, +14.4%.

1952   A resurgent enthusiasm for new wheels and the auto shares, along with allied stocks, helped the Dow to its fourth yearly advance in 1952. It was not much, up but 8 percent, but it would have been nothing without Detroit's success.

For Chrysler, a return to popularity meant that its shares, at 98 up from 68, were finally valued at over 10 times earnings, which were $9.04. Only three years before, on $15 earnings, the stock had been priced below 50. Perceptions of a depression looming over the horizon had changed and even Studebaker bested its 1946 high.

After early winter strength—Amerada rose from 142 to 235—the oils retreated and the drug issues were sharply lower for the year. The Rails, however, turned in a big earnings increase and made their high in December at 113, having gained 174 percent since the 1949 low. It was their first rise over 100 since 1931 and the long-haul western lines were leaders.

If the market was trendless most of the year, there were plenty of reasons. Dow earnings would fall slightly. The Korean peace talks dragged interminably. President Truman seized, if unsuccessfully, the steel mills. Volume at the NYSE fell for the second year and was 36 percent below the 1950 level, not entirely because the Exchange, in a nod to modern times, eliminated Saturday sessions.

During the year, many tobaccos and motion pictures made their unique bear market lows. American Tobacco slipped to 54, down from 101 in 1946.

In November, General Dwight D. Eisenhower was elected president, the first Republican to serve in 20 years. The trendless market charged up to the year's peak at 292 on December 30, helped enormously by great holiday strength in General Motors and Chrysler.

1952 DJIA First 269.86. High 292.00 Dec 30. Low 256.35 May 1. Close 291.90, +8.4%.

1953   The joy of stocks had become a little too routine by early 1953 and the bulls, for the first time since the Korean War surprise, took a breather; the Dow wound up with its first 10 percent correction of the period.

Autos were the nervous leaders on the downside. Studebaker, which had taken years to climb from 11 to 29, skidded badly and would continue down to 10 in the spring of 1954. Chrysler plunged from 98 to 58 in about the same period.

Rotational strength continued, however. Foods and grocery chains were firm. American Can, International Paper, and General Electric all marched to record highs late in the year, even as the tobaccos turned weak again.

The year had started on a strong note, however brief. The Dow's 294 on January 5 was a high which would stay in place for 13 months. Some see the January–September intra-year dip of 1953 as a mini-bear market. But a big speculative volume continued at the ASE and Toronto markets in cheap mining shares.

Both Industrials and Rails dragged lower, however, despite the suspension of all wartime wage and price controls and a reduction of the margin requirement to 50 percent. The Korean Armistice was signed in late July, but a weak set of Rails weighed on the market into September.

The Rails, which lost 20 percent in their mini-downdraft from December 1952 to September proved that stingy price-earnings ratios were not dead. Illinois Central fell to 33, though its earnings for the year were $9.30.

Although oil share prices were generally weak, rich west Texas discoveries attracted large exploration and drilling programs. The brothers Liedtke and one George Bush founded Zapata Petroleum Corporation, which would in 1963 become the Pennzoil Co.

In September, both Dow averages scored their lows. A few days later, the Street's investment bankers beat an antitrust rap, after spending over $5 billion in lawyer fees. When the year ended with only modest losses, and the Dow at barely 10X earnings, brokers sensed that the joy of stocks still had plenty of life. The mild 1953 correction had cost the Industrials only 13 percent.

The year left one NYSE volume milestone in the record book. Friday, October 9, was the last day to ever register volume of less than 1 million shares—only 900,000 shares traded.

1953 DJIA First 292.14. High 293.79 Jan 5. Low 255.49 Sept 14. Close 280.90, −3.8%.

1954

It had taken 25 years, but one ghost of 1929 was finally exorcised in November 1954, when the Dow Industrials surpassed the 1929 high. There was no technical resistance at the old top of 381.17. Margin calls, depressions, two wars, and time had long since liquidated stagnant holdings.

The advancing market of the previous years had been orderly, but now a new intensity of excitement gripped the Street. Boardrooms were crowded. Margin debt, one measure of public involvement, increased all through the year. Mutual fund ownership, which had steadily increased since 1949, boomed.

Bullish joys were broad and almost without limit. Armco Steel, Disney, Douglas, Columbia Broadcasting, and Sperry were among the diverse issues that doubled.

An awkwardly named little firm by the name of Haloid showed large promise by moving from 32 to 96. The company, it seemed, manufactured photographic paper, a niche growth industry, and had paid dividends since 1928. A few years later, at much higher prices, Haloid would add a new and equally awkward name becoming, for a while, Haloid-Xerox.

Rails and Utilities had an excellent year, but lagged far below their 1929 tops; the Utility average ended 1954 at half its peak level of 1929. Rather extreme strength pushed the carriers up in the last half of the year. New York Central gained 50 percent in the last two months. Baltimore & Ohio ran from 19 to 40 during a longer surge. The second-half push on the Rails gave them their second best year in history, up 55 percent. After a poor fundamental year, they were anticipating increased earnings and payout in 1955.

The bull market, judged long in the tooth only a year earlier, had developed an exciting new vigor and easily overwhelmed the modest recession in place at the year's beginning. A bout of severe profit in early December was viewed as only a normal correction. Senator Prescott Bush of Connecticut, a former investment banker whose son had skipped the Street to search for oil in west Texas, said that he "saw no cause for alarm." Right on. The Dow did not even pause at 400, closing at the year's high. Excluding 1933, the year's gain remains the best since 1928.

1954 DJIA First 282.89. High 404.39 Dec 31. Low 279.87 Jan 11. Close 404.39, +44.0%.

1955   Market veterans best remember 1955 as the year "Ike" had his heart attack. Thirty-six holes of golf in Denver's mile-high atmosphere did the president and the market in. At the NYSE, it was the biggest dollar loss since 1929. Volume was the highest since 1933 and the Dow lost nearly 32 points in the first-day shock. The collapse came from an absolute high, 487.45.

In market lore, the September 26th incident will be most remembered, but the economy and stocks had a splendid year, despite the brutal pause. The inflation rate was actually a negative figure and equities responded with high volume and great excitement, despite two margin hikes. The increase in profits for the S&P 500 list was at a record pace. By November, the steel industry was operating at 98.8 percent of capacity. A 3:1 stock split boosted General Motors.

Aluminums were strong, Reynolds moving from 22 to 60. Venezuelan Petroleum, whose earnings were mushrooming, advanced from 25 to 96. Du Pont zoomed nearly 100 points, from a low of 157 to 250. Hertz, newly popular, nearly doubled and airlines boomed, with Eastern, 22 in 1954, reaching 58.

In November, "Ike" returned to the White House and the market moved swiftly higher. Paradoxically, a leading group all year, the autos, suddenly lost momentum, despite record output of nearly 8 million passenger cars. General Motors, 59 in 1954, topped at 162 in November, and then slumped 17 percent in December. It would prove to be an ominous divergence from the market. As in 1929, 1937, and 1946, the early General Motors peak would prove a leading indicator of trouble for the Dow, which would not top until April 1956.

1955 DJIA First 408.89. High 488.40 Dec 30. Low 388.20 Jan 17. Close 488.40, +20.8%

1956 By 1956, speculative excesses had begun to fan over the six-year bull market. Volume at the American Stock Exchange, where low-priced oil and Canadian mining plays proved very seductive, had doubled since 1950 while NYSE activity was up only 24 percent.

Margin debt had increased by May 1956 to a peak more than five times that at the end of 1948. Investors were aggressively and successfully pursued. Mutual fund accounts had climbed by 189 percent since 1948.

Though the autos, along with many other groups, had made apparent tops in 1955, there were few fears on the Street. The Dow surged over the 500 milestone without effort and reached its 1949–1956 bull market high, 521.05 on April 6. The Dow would touch 521 again in August and in July 1957 before the bear really took over. It was a rare triple-top. A broader gauge, the NYSE index, would not reach its final high until the summer of 1957.

A rotating top made exit easy for the bulls. Retailers and chemicals, among others, had peaked in 1955. Sears had celebrated a 3:1 split at 41 in 1955. By late 1956, it was 28. Aircrafts' long flight ended in late 1956. The office equipments did not halt until 1957. In the meantime, new favorites like Lukens Steel, the largest plate maker, rose from 14 to 61 in 1956.

Ford proved a disappointment to its new public shareholders. The largest underwriting in history, 10.2 million shares, had been sold at 64½ in January by the Ford Foundation, after being vastly oversubscribed. But in a poor auto climate, the stock fell to 52 during the summer.

Eisenhower's ileitis attack created a one-day, high-volume drop in June, but it was not like the heart attack episode. In the last half of 1956, the market gamely held on in the face of frightening foreign news and higher interest rates. In July, Egypt seized the Suez Canal. Russian tanks smashed Hungarian freedom fighters in October. British, French, and Israeli forces zeroed in on Egypt in November.

In the same month, Eisenhower won a smashing presidential victory, but his great personal popularity could not help the GOP to gain control of either house, a great rarity in presidential years. The disappointment brought a quick market decline.

By a small miracle—the Rails had diverged sharply to the downside—the Dow closed higher for the year; it had intensely worked the 465–520 range for months. Speculative rails had been hurt badly. The New Haven, 39 in 1955, fell to 12 in 1956 and would tumble further, to 5, in the next year.

1956 DJIA First 485.78. High 521.05 Apr 6. Low 462.35 Jan 23. Close 499.47, +2.3%.

1957 When the Russians launched Sputnik I, October 4, 1957, it was the ego-smash of the decade for Americanism. And an apt excuse for a small panic. Tight money worries had already begun to outweigh the anticipation of record corporate earnings. Not a few investment Brahmins deserted common stocks entirely, as dividend yields slipped below those of AAA bonds.

In early August, the Dow was still over 500, near its record 521 high. But the market eroded in September and Sputnik's shocking success cost the Industrials 10 points initially and then pushed the market straight down to a close at 419.79 on October 22.

Eisenhower's decision to stump the country on economic, missile, and defense policies reversed the market in a one-day 180 percent turn. The Dow opened October 23 with an a huge upside gap, never filled. It was "the most vigorous rally of a generation," according to *The Wall Street Journal.*

If the bear move had been mini, it was so time-compressed after July's third effort at surpassing the 520 area that it seemed most violent. Pittston, 84 in the summer, would fall to 45 in October. The loss would not be recovered for ten years. Delta Airlines fell from 40 to 14. Kaiser was a particularly soft aluminum, 70 to 22. Crucible Steel suffered from its historic volatility and dropped from a record high of 40 to 16.

For the Rails, the bear business was more serious. It was their worst yearly decline in history, save for the multiple bloodbaths of the 1930s. Amazingly, the average, at 96 in December was back to its level of early 1901. Delaware, Lackawanna, a $300 stock a half-century earlier, was smashed from a 26 to 6 without a rally.

Sputnik II and the president's mild stroke halted the late October recovery. On December 6, America's space try, the Vanguard rocket, broached and plunged the Dow back to 426. A successful flight by an Atlas ICBM later in the month spared the market from further space humiliations.

During the year, the social issues involved in September's school confrontation in Little Rock, Arkansas has caused more market turmoil than the classic Du Pont antitrust decision of June. In that case, ruling some 35 years after the fact, the Supreme Court declared Du Pont's "massive" (23 percent) ownership of General Motors to be in violation of antitrust laws. Du Pont would finally divest its General Motors shares in 1962.

1957 DJIA First 496.03. High 520.77 Jly 12. Low 419.79 Oct 22. Close 435.69, −12.8%.

1958 Sandwiched between the great bull markets of the early 1950s and 1960s, the intense buying panic of 1958–1959 has never received its proper credit.

The year started slowly. Explorer I, the U.S. rebuttal to Sputnik, flew on January 31 without any lift for the market. Two cuts in the discount rate and a reduction in the margin rates were nonevents. In May, at 455, the Dow was barely higher than it had been four years previously. In June, the unemployment rate, at 7.7 percent, was at its highest level since the 1930s.

But a heady excitement about important new or newly improved technical products was about to launch historic market runs. Hoary leaders were shunted aside. Haloid-Xerox, Texas Instruments, Fairchild Camera, Polaroid, Aerojet-General were the new breed of market force. IBM, already a dazzling high-wire artist, passed out more thrills, advancing from 300 to 552 during the year.

Texas Instruments tripled, from 27 to 86; it was but a small percentage portion of its large 1957–1959 gain from 16 to 194. Beginning in March, each month's Dow close was above that of the preceding period and the recently spavined Rails rolled out their largest yearly gain in history, up 61 percent.

A buying panic got underway in July, just after U.S. Marines were invited into Lebanon. In September, the 1956 Dow high was erased. In October, monthly volume at the NYSE broke all records since 1933. Two margin increases, the second to 90 percent, did nothing to slow the advance. It wasn't all glamorous new products either. A&P shares pushed up from 24 to 59 in 1958 and went on to 88 the next year, after adjusting all figures for the firm's 10:1 split.

While traders shunned many aircraft stocks in favor of exciting new missile technology, Boeing flew higher, 34–58 between February and October, borne on the wings of its new "707s." Earnings for the Dow were down for the year, but the players didn't care. The year's advance was the second best since 1935.

1958 DJIA First 439.27. High 583.65 Dec 31. Low 436.89 Feb 25. Close 583.65, +34.0%.

1959   In early 1959, even when stocks were easing, the market showed great strength. In March, when the Dow suffered its first losing month in a year, the drop was less than two points. The precipitous advances of the last half of 1958 continued into late summer. Milestone 600 on the Dow was easily exceeded in February.

A host of corporate copycats sought to profit on the fascination for the new product market. But the big winners of 1958 continued to dominate the new high list, though a few veterans, like the oils, turned easy early in the year. Standard of Cal eroded from 62 to 46 during the year. Airlines also peaked early.

Treasury gold stocks were dropping sharply, but the mining shares were surprisingly restrained, Homestake only able to advance from 40 to 49. Many group charts show a sharp peaking at mid-summer, when a mammouth steel strike which would be the longest in history got underway.

The Rail average topped at about this time, as did the NYSE index. The S&P high came in the first week of August, just before the discount rate was upped to 4 percent, its highest level since 1930.

Stock splits and rumors of splits excited the market during the entire year. AT&T finally rewarded its shareholders with a small payout increase and a 3:1 division. That ended the famous $9 dividend, paid since 1921. The shares which had been 160 in 1957 rose to 267 in 1959, before adjusting for the split.

Dow Chemical, Eastman Kodak, and General Electric helped to pump up the Industrials to a record high on December 31. It was typical of the holiday success of the decade. In six years, the Dow had closed at its very high, or within a point thereof, on the final day of trading.

During the decade, there had been great rotational strength. The defense and "war babies" were strong early on, followed by the motors. Extreme strength was visited on the technology, missile, and office equipment issues in 1958 and 1959. IBM was up more than tenfold during the decade.

Late starter (1955) Texas Instruments had done better in less time, soaring from 5 to 194. It would reach 256 in 1960. The decade remains the best in stock market history: the Dow gained 239 percent. Share prices had advanced much faster than fundamentals. Earnings for the Dow were up "only" 46 percent during the ten years; dividends had increased by 63 percent.

Risks had also increased, as the volatility of the next decade would prove. The Dow's price-earnings ratio of 1949, 8.5X at the year end, had increased to 19.8X in 1959. The rich dividend return of 1949, 6.4 percent, had been reduced to a dangerous level at 3.05 percent.

1959 DJIA First 587.59. High 679.36 Dec 31. Low 574.46 Feb 9. Close 679.36, +16.4%.

1960   Hyperbole rewarded, the Dow took two short steps in the direction of the "Soaring Sixties," reaching a record high, 685.57, on the year's second day. But stocks quickly twisted to the downside leading to a spring low on May 1, when it was learned that an American U-2 spy plane had been shot down over Russia.

Fortunately, the strong rotational leadership of the previous few years was maintained in 1960, which accounts for the mildness of the nine-month, mini-bear market. It was a rarity, falling all within one calendar year.

Oils, autos, and steels were weak. Stainless steel maker, Allegheny-Ludlum, 61 in 1959 fell to 34. But drugs, Hollywood types, and the office equipments ignored the bearish scenario. The mild recession which began in April was salved in August by a discount cut; margin requirements had already been reduced. But on September 1, the Pennsylvania Railroad, for the first time in its 114-year history, was completely shut down by a strike.

In the post-Labor Day session, the Dow fell sharply and continued to the year's low at 566 in October. John F. Kennedy won the presidential election in a squeaker, but it had little market impact.

Some coming market giants of the decade put on a great preview in 1960, despite the year's negative trend. Haloid-Xerox, still an OTC stock, climbed from a low of 27 to 74 bid at the year end. IBM, 407 early on, pushed up to a record 600 in December. The Utilities were strong all year, ending plus 14 percent, a great relative divergence from the Rails, which were down by 15 percent.

Though the Dow also closed lower for the year, its composite dividend was higher, as it would be in every year of the decade, save for 1967.

1960 DJIA First 679.06. High 685.47 Jan 5. Low 566.05 Oct 25. Close 615.89, −9.3%.

1961 The most speculative year between 1958 and 1968 caused a great market overheating in 1961. In the first quarter, the bowling stock craze, which had begun in 1957, finally peaked, American Machine & Foundry having increased nearly 30 times. For the bowlers, the Soaring Sixties and Seventies were already over. Brunswick would not overcome its 1961 high of 75 for 25 years.

Though the bowlers split the scene early, there were plenty of new players. TV issues replaced the bowlers as recreational favorites. Zenith rose from 32 to 83, Magnavox from 15 to 38. Manipulations helped push the new-issue market into a frenzy. But there were plenty of blue chip names on the line. American Tobacco reached 112; it had sold at 45 in 1959 on earnings not much below those of 1961. Telephone, after nearly three decades of an unchanged dividend, found that shareholders appreciated modest increases and raised its payout for the third time in three years.

Casualty stocks were embraced and there was a great demand for names like Aetna and Travelers; the latter rose from 92 to 171. Ford finally earned its 1956 underwriting buyers a profit, advancing from 64 to 118 during the year. Annual volume at the NYSE exceeded 1 billion shares for the first time since 1929 and at the ASE, where some bad habits still hung on from the old Curb days, heated speculation pushed the year's activity up by 71 percent. The April fiasco at the Bay of Pigs had been quickly forgotten and in May, the Dow easily passed another important milestone, 700, aided by Alan B. Shepard's historic space flight.

A lightning construction job in August, the Berlin Wall, couldn't halt the market, but gains were limited over the rest of the year. The Rails topped in October and the Dow, with very weak technicals, in December. Dow composite earnings of $31.91 had become richly priced, with the veteran index selling at nearly 23 times earnings, a record in any bull market year.

By coincidence, the December decision to send direct military support to Vietnam coincided closely with the bull market top. But no one anticipated the impact that beginning would have on inflation, taxes, interest costs, and social unrest during the balance of the decade.

1961 DJIA First 610.25. High 734.91 Dec 13. Low 610.25 Jan 3. Close 731.14, +18.7%.

1962 The huge volume of 1961 had kept brokers so busy that some of them forgot the rules. On January 5, 1962, the SEC accused the American Stock Exchange of "manifold and prolonged abuses by specialists and other brokers." The president of the ASE had beat the Feds to the door, resigning in December.

The abuses of the previous period would be a festering sore for months, but the hard hit on the market came from the April confrontation between President Kennedy and the steel industry over price increases. Harsh words and intense administration pressure forced the industry to back track, but the White House was suddenly perceived as antibusiness.

Stocks entered a violent downphase in late April, and it would continue until the final week of May, when the Dow, on the 25th, suffered its worst point loss since 1929 on large volume. Confidence during the month had been eroded by SEC hearings and revelation of insider leaks from an important market letter. Merrill Lynch Vice-President Donald T. Regan testified that his company had "goofed" in promoting Aquafilter stock in 1961; the shares had fallen from 6 to 1 within months.

Steel issues were crushed, Big Steel falling from a 1961 top at 91 to 38. But the entire list was badly hurt, for various reasons. Cancer fears cut American Tobacco's price in half, and the pricey enthusiasm of 1961 led to other fearsome drops. Reynolds Metals, Richardson Merrill, and Sperry Rand, among many others, lost over 60 percent from the late 1961 tops. IBM held better in percentage terms, but its 607 to 300 drop was eyecatching.

Although the "Kennedy Panic" ended in May, the Dow eroded further, to a late June low at 536. Booming auto sales sparked an excellent rally into autumn when the potentially lethal Cuban missile crisis jammed the index sharply lower. A number of groups, including the rubbers and tobaccos, made their bear market lows in October. Firestone had fallen about 23 percent below its worst June figure.

The resolution of the missile crisis brought a great buying surge and the November advance, up 10.1 percent, was the Dow's best month since September 1939. General Motors, boosted by record auto sales, led the strong rally into December and gave an indication of good things to come by closing higher for the year, despite the Dow's 11 percent slump.

1962 DJIA First 724.71. High 726.01 Jan 3. Low 535.76 Jne 26. Close 652.10, −10.8%.

1963 On Friday, November 22, 1963, the NYSE halted trading at 2:07. It was only its third emergency closing in history and was caused by the panic which had swept the market on news of the assassination and death of President John F. Kennedy.

In the final seven minutes of trading, volume had run over 2 million shares. Polaroid had lost 16 points before being suspended from activity. Xerox, IBM, Control Data, RCA, and several dozen other volatile issues were also shut down. Continued emergency conditions were widely forecast and the Exchange would opt to remain closed on Monday.

At the reopening Tuesday, it was quickly apparent that Wall Street's Camelot would continue under Lyndon Baines Johnson's banner; a buyers' panic swept prices steeply higher in the third largest gain in history. The Dow would march on to a record high in the first week of December.

For the entire year, the market had focused on broadly higher earnings. Bottom line for the Dow increased 13 percent for the year to $41.21 and individual issues outperformed the index. Chrysler, hiked its earnings to $4.35 from $1.81 and celebrated with a pair of 2:1 splits within eight months. The stock was a 18–50 winner. Oil companies, for the most part, pushed earnings above the 1956 record figures. Superior Oil, which had sold as low as 885 in 1960, rose from 1045 to 1559.

Some of the great leaders of the 1950s continued their power play. Xerox, which had split, rose from 29 to 87. Both airlines and rails did well. American and Northwest Airlines doubled. An efficient new mail-order house, New Process, grabbed headlines as it raced from 33 to 102.

In mid-July, the discount rate was hiked to 3.5 percent, the first increase since 1960, and in early November margin requirements were shoved up to 70 percent. Neither action had any market impact. Nor did a 25 percent increase in the cost of postage. The Department hiked the first-class mail cost to five cents.

Lyndon Johnson's succession to the White House encouraged a surprising enthusiasm among bulls. At the year end, they were pointing toward Dow 800, only 37 points away and both the Rails and Utilities were finally within sighting distance of the lost peaks of 1929.

Volume, 1.146 billion shares, had finally exceeded the 1929 figure of 1.125 billion and was almost exactly double the figure of 1954.

1963 DJIA First 646.79. High 767.21 Dec 18. Low 646.79 Jan 2. Close 762.95, +17.0%.

1964 In 1964 the Dow Jones Rail Average celebrated the thirty-fifth anniversary of the 1929 crest by finally overcoming its peak level of that infamous autumn. The Utility average did likewise. Both were ten years tardy; the Industrials had broken above their 1929 high in 1954.

Though the Rails' percentage gain in each year from 1963 through 1965 was superior to that of the Industrials, the latter group remained the true market leader. In February, the Dow easily passed milestone 800. A consensus view for higher earnings was confirmed as corporate management, in a show of great confidence, raised the Dow's composite dividend rate by over 33 percent during the year, from $23.41 to $31.24, the biggest percentage hike since 1936.

Breadth was good. Oils continued their solid uptrend, along with the drillers. J. Ray McDermott rose from 22 to 40. General Motors breached 100, up from 1962's 45. Specialty stocks got new attention. Sunshine Mining, the historic Idaho miner, reaped the benefit of higher bullion prices and made the vociferous silver bugs happy by advancing from 10 to 36. But its advance paled beside that of Rollins Broadcasting, which jumped from 14 to 80, despite trailing earnings of less than $1. Merck received a nice second-half push, 34 to 51. Communications Satellite (Comsat) was a hot new issue, zipping from 20 to 72.

Texas Gulf Sulphur insiders, as it would turn out later, got early word of a huge copper strike at Timmons, Ontario, and were greatly enriched when public players pushed the shares up to 65 from the year's low at 21.

Vietnam continued to heat and in August, the Tonkin Gulf attack on a U.S. destroyer put the market briefly lower. The year's high came shortly after LBJ's election, but then rumors of a Fed discount hike, which materialized on November 24, temporarily cooled the bulls. Monthly and annual volume records were broken during the year and 6-million share days—always a great curiosity except in times of huge stress—became common.

1964 DJIA First 766.08. High 891.71 Nov 18. Low 766.08 Jan 2. Close 874.13, +14.6%.

1965 In the record book, 1965 was another great year. The Dow ended up nearly 11 percent, closing on its very high, December 31. There were, however, serious defections from the bull cause during the year. The Utilities, out of their 35-year post-1929 dungeon for only ten months, peaked in April. They had, over the previous years, become coveted for growth, not dividends, becoming richly overpriced. No one would have guessed it, but the 1965 top would stand for 20 years.

In the autumn, General Motors climbed to 113¾ and then balked, a disappointing divergence with the lead average. Amazingly, 1965's top would not be challenged in either the 1970s or the 1980s.

Other important backsliders included such important groups as the banks, chemicals, international oils, and retailers.

During the summer, the Industrials lost nearly 100 points from Dow 940. It was the first 10 percent setback for the index since 1962. Vietnam, inflation, and large Treasury gold losses were among the reasons. But the most important influence was a warning of FRB Chairman Martin about perilous similarities between 1929 and 1965. It led to a June price smash.

If there were defectors from the bull cause, there was fearsome excitement among the winners. Defense and space demands kept the aircraft and electronics soaring. Fairchild Camera was sensational, 27 to 165. Motorola added 109 points from 63. United Aircraft, 25 in 1964 and 50 in early 1965, reached 90. Admiral Corporation soared from 8 in 1965 to 67 in early 1966.

Pan-American was on its last great climb. It more than doubled, 25 to 56, between the summer and year end. One of the great investment opportunities of the year, however, was ground-locked and almost unnoticed, save for fast-food addicts. Paine Webber brought McDonald Corporation public at $22.50. Shares would increase tenfold by the end of the decade.

At the year-end, the Dow was vulnerable. Its dividend yield was a puny 2.95 percent, the lowest ending figure in history. Treasury gold stocks had fallen to a 26-year low. The Consumer Price Index was rolling higher and the dollar was increasingly suspect. Military personnel in Vietnam totaled nearly 190,000, up about tenfold during the year.

1965 DJIA First 869.78. High 969.26 Dec 31. Low 840.59 Jne 28. Close 969.26, +10.9%

1966   The all-time high-water mark for the Dow Jones Industrial Average, adjusted for inflation, came in January 1966. Dow 3000 in 1990 would not approach the 1966 level when weighted by the Consumer Price Index. M. C. Horsey's rare chart of the adjusted Dow can be found in Chapter 3 of the book in the retrospect of the 1966–1968 bull market.

Adjusted or not, the Dow did fulfill one dream in 1966 when the average kissed the 1000 level, intraday. There were several near misses at a close over 1000, but the feat would be delayed until November 1972.

Some market students view 1966 as the top of a long secular bull market which began in the worst war days of 1942. But even by the short span, 1962–1966, there had been rich rewards. Northwest Air flew up from 12 to 126 in that period and Delta did better. The Milwaukee railroad was a 7–75 winner, Chrysler, 9 to 61. A final bull peak, 995.15, was reached on February 9. Money was tightening and the "General Motors" bellwether warning was in effect; General Motors had topped in 1965. Another smokestack stock was in more serious trouble; U.S. Steel had been unable to top its best 1959 mark.

For the third time in the decade, an ultra-short bear market would wreak havoc. The Dow would lose 25 percent by October in another intra-year mini-bear like that of 1960. Individual issues were tormented by frightening drops. The Milwaukee, a volatile issue for a century, backed down from 75 to 26 between April and October. Motorola, the TV-electronic favorite, was smashed from 234 to 92. Douglas Air got a bad press when it was revealed that insiders had hit the silk before news of bad earnings; the shares fell from 112 to 30.

Increasing Vietnam bombings, including the first Hanoi strike, tighter credit, and talk of higher taxes to help cure inflation were the rationales for the long-delayed correction. On October 7, the decline ended at 744, a nasty fall from February's 995 level. A strong GOP showing in the off-year election boosted the Dow to 821 in November. California's Ronald Reagan was among eight new Republicans governors elected to office. But tax selling and Detroit sales worries pinned the Dow back at the end of the year. The year's decline had been the worst since 1937.

In nine of twelve months, the Dow had lost ground, its worst record in a century, save for 1920 which was a ten-month loser. The year 1966 also stands in the record book as the last year in which odd-lot traders, historically net buyers of stock, ended up as purchasers. They have been heavy net sellers in every year since.

1966 DJIA First 968.54. High 995.15 Feb 9. Low 744.32 Oct 7. Close 785.69, −18.9%.

1967   The year 1967 was a vintage year for speculators. About 45 percent of all issues listed at the NYSE would gain 50 percent or more. The low for the year came on the first day of trading and by the end of the month, the Dow had recorded a record monthly point increase.

However rusty they might be, bankers had not forgotten how to lower interest rates and on January 26, for the first time since 1960, the prime was reduced. In March, monthly volume set a record and in August, the NYSE was forced to close early on nine occasions so that cage sections could catch up with their huge backlog.

Huge speculative profits were chalked, despite further commitments in Vietnam, black riots, war riots, and new troubles in the Mid-East. Computer types were idolized. Memorex skipped from 62 to 226 and Control Data revived with a move with 34 to 166. Some lesser names increased tenfold.

Sadly, the speculative rampage was ended for some. Ling-Temco-Vought, 26 in late 1966, wheeled up to a record 170 in August. In 1970, the shares would fall to 7. Boeing hit 112; its 1970 low would be 12. Air transports peaked. Northwest Air, which had sold for less than 4, adjusted in 1960, topped at 135.

Excluding office equipments (Burroughs moved from 91 to 192), the blue chip market ruled little better than firm. General Motors recovered just about half of its 1966 loss. Big Steel's 1967 range was a 77 to 88 and the last price was 78.

In November, the banks regrouped and raised the prime, adding to the late fall uncertainties. Foreign bankers were checking gold out of the Treasury vaults by the ton and U.S. holdings fell to a 30-year low. Antiwar demonstrations had unsettled the market in October and the Rails scored a disastrous record. Starting on October 3, they fell for 24 of 25 days.

But the speculative fever would not break even when the FRB raised reserve requirements. The NYSE raised requirements, too, to 100 percent initial margin on nearly a score of forgettable stocks. But Big Board losses were well recovered by December, except for the Utilities, where relative weakness continued.

Volume at the NYSE during the year had jumped by over 630 million shares to 2.530 billion. The two billion milestone came 38 years after the one billion share milestone in 1929.

1967 DJIA First 786.41. High 943.08 Sep 25. Low 786.41 Jan 3. Close 905.11, +15.24

1968

The year 1968 was the most speculative market year since 1929, and no where more so than at the ASE. Volume there reached a record high as a percentage of trade at the NYSE. Turnover was 65.5 percent versus 24 percent at the Board, a level not seen at either Exchange since the 1930s. It was super "go-go" at the ASE; the gain for its price change index in the 1966–1968 period was six times that of the Dow. The change of 1968, plus 33 percent, was only about half that of 1967, but dwarfed the Dow gain.

The pace of business became so torrid that the Street couldn't handle it. To the amusement of critics, the Board was forced, first, to shorten its trading hours and then, in June, to enforce a union dream—the four-day week. Brokers could play golf on Wednesday without guilt.

While many speculative issues, at both exchanges, were winners by 20 times in the 1966–1968 run, some of the Street's senior citizens, past world leaders, lagged. Blue chips like Du Pont, Jersey, U.S. Steel, General Motors, AT&T, and General Electric failed to meet their 1966 highs. Speculators had been drawn to the likes of University Computing, which ripped up from 3 to 186 in the 1966-1968 period.

Though 1967 had been marked by speculative hysteria, 1968 moved off to a poor start. Inflation, the *Pueblo* incident, and U.S. troops in Cambodia were reasons enough. Then, on March 15, the London gold pool collapsed. The world's lust for gold had been aroused by its dischantment with the dollar and the pool could no longer contain the $35 price. The FRB was forced to hike the discount rate and the daily London gold fixing was suspended until April 1. It reopened at a disappointing $37.70, but later in the year would reach $41.90.

On March 31, LBJ revealed that he would not be a candidate for re-election and also announced that he would de-escalate Vietnam bombings. The market responded with a higher gap opening and an advance of nearly 4 percent. The bull was back.

Forgettable names like International Industries (a pancake house), Mohawk Data, and Zimmer Homes took the spotlight; they were only representative of the scores of franchisers, computer firms, and mobile home manufactures which seemed to promise overnight wealth. Zimmer Homes made it from 8 to 55 during the year. International Industries tripled, from 18 to 58.

It was the year of the conglomerate and they were idolized much as the great trusts had been at the beginning of the century. Over 4,000 corporate mergers and acquisitions were made during the year. James Ling continued to gather in great batches of such disparates as Braniff, Jones & Laughlin, Computer Technology, Okonite, General Felt, Wilson Sporting Goods, National Car Rental, and Chance Vought.

Quality was pretty much forgotten, though Chrysler and many oils advanced to record highs late in the year, despite two increases in margin requirements, the second to 90 percent. The fever for gold brought renewed buying to the mining shares and Dome Mines, 38 in 1967, moved up to 88.

A slim cut in the discount rate in August helped the autumn action, but not the Democrats, and in the November election Richard Nixon won the White

House. Three prime rate increases in November and December cooled passions and the Dow, in a contra-seasonal move, sold off sharply at the year end. Despite the year's volatility, the Dow's gain was small.

1968 DJIA First 906.84. High 985.21 Dec 3. Low 825.13 Mar 21. Close 943.75, +4.3%

1969

Not satisfied with three swift prime-rate increases at the end of 1968, bankers, a rather unsentimental lot, greeted the New Year, 1969, with yet another hike to 7 percent, the highest level since 1921. Between the credit crunch and inflation, the market was headed for tough times, though earnings would hold up well.

Despite stringent money, the Dow dug in and traded up to the year's high in May, though the regulated Rails and Utilities were eroding. In June, the sixth increase in the prime within six months—a nasty 1 percent pop to 8.5 percent—re-enforced the bearish message and the Dow fell sharply to 802 in July. Neil Armstrong's "moon walk" was of no earthly help.

Aircrafts, which had generally topped in 1967, continued their steep dive. By the year end, United Aircraft had dropped to 39 from an early-year high at 81. Conglomerates stuck together for awhile, but holders were unnerved when an antitrust suit was filed against Ling-Temco, even though the Dallas firm was already self-destructing because of its enormous debt.

Continued Mid-East tensions and rumors of wage-price controls roiled the market. Gold shares were liquidated when bullion prices failed to match the bugs' lofty hopes. London Gold, $43.83 in March, had fallen to $35.00 by December. Homestake was a 46–16 loser. Notwithstanding the market, drugs had an outstanding year, as did the office equipments. National Cash Register was a 108–162 winner and closed the year at 161. Disney ignored the bear trend with a run from 70 to 135 while McDonald's ended at 43, up from a low of 24.

Pancake franchisors, mobile-home parts makers, and computer leasing, or conglomerates thereof, were finding it tough to make real money. But some stock prices levitated even when the companies were brain-dead. National Student Marketing went to 72 and was 58 in December. By May, after a 2:1 split, the shares had fallen below 1. It would be worth less than 2. Four Seasons Nursing, up from 6 to 91 in a big 1968–1969 run, sold at 84 in December 1969, and fifty cents in the late spring of 1970.

Smoke-stack stocks also were hurt. In December, U.S. Steel hit its lowest price since 1955 and the market got no help from a scheduled reduction in the income tax surcharge. Utilities had been struck with their worst loss since 1931.

The advance-decline ratio for all common stocks at the Exchange was nearly 1:5, the ratio being much worse than in 1966, though the Dow's loss in the earlier year had been larger. The figure displayed an ominous weakness in the breadth of the market.

Despite the decade's shabby ending—the Dow's final gain for the period was only 18 percent—there had been some brilliant moves by individual stocks. Perhaps none was more celebrated than that of Xerox which, on an adjusted basis advanced from a price of less than 2 in early 1960 to a peak of 115 in 1969. Its sales, $37 million in 1960, would near $1.5 billion in 1970.

1969 DJIA First 947.73. High 968.85 May 14. Low 769.93 Dec 17. Close 800.36, −15.2%.

1970 During the first six months of 1970, everything that could go wrong for the market went wrong, save for slight and belated cuts in margins and the prime. In March, the prime was dropped to 8.5 percent, but the action did not placate the market. The rate had been 6.25 percent in November 1968.

Record trade and budget deficits, auto cutbacks, a mail strike, student riots, inflation, the invasion of Cambodia, and the Kent State tragedy brought about a great malaise. Gold refused to do its thing, falling to $34.75, below the old managed price of $35. Many of the most hyped issues of 1967–1969 lost 90 percent of value, measured from the peaks.

Quality's dramatic losses came mostly in 1970. Xerox, 115 in January, bottomed at 65 in August, making its low at about the same time as IBM, a 387–220 loser in that period. January's highs had been a record for both. Allied Chemical fell to its lowest level since 1942; du Pont to a 16-year low.

On May 26, following three weeks of panic during which the Dow had peeled off 100 points, the average closed 631.16. On the following day, it gained 31.04 points, the largest point gain in history and the biggest percentage advance since the beginning of World War II. The average was back over 700 by month end.

The panic was over, if not the bad news. In June, Penn-Central bankrupted and Chrysler was rumored in trouble. Goodbody & Co. failed in the fall and many other brokerage firms were in trouble, buried in paperwork and bad trading positions.

General Motors was struck and the war flared again. But four straight prime cuts set the bankers to handing out clock-radios with consumer loans and speculators revived quickly. Champion Homes, a leader in the mobile-home industry, made it from 8 to 31 by year end. It was helped, along with others, by 12 consecutive daily advances by the Dow Industrials during November.

The traditional Christmas rally appeared and, surprisingly, the Dow which had been in desperate shape in May was able to close higher for the year, though that gain was deceiving. There had only been 744 advances at the Board versus 1,010 declines.

University Computing, a former darling which had sold at 107 in December, 1969, fell as low as 13 and closed at 22. The ten most active issues at the ASE were all lower for the year.

The litter of brokerage house problems during the year—McDonnell & Co., Dempsey-Tegler, and Goodbody plus other rumored scandals—resulted in a tardy law to safeguard the assets (but not the market values) for clients of troubled firms. President Nixon signed the Security Investor Protection Act into law in December. It set up a nonprofit corporation, the SIPC, which acts in a somewhat similar fashion to the Federal Deposit Insurance Corporation.

1970 DJIA First 809.20. High 842.00 Dec 29. Low 631.16 May 26. Close 838.92, +4.8%.

1971 By April 1971, the market's psyche had turned 180° from the position of the previous spring, much as in 1932–1933. Despair had given way to a speculative fever. The Transportation average had already doubled the 1970 low, given strong help from its new members, the airlines and truckers. Volume at the NYSE would leap to another record, passing the 3 billion milestone for a total of 3.8 billion, up nearly 1 billion shares from the 1970 level.

Five consecutive discount rate hikes had done their job, but that was all there was. The course of interest rates shifted abruptly upward and four prime increases between April and August dampened enthusiasm, to the dismay of the new stockholders of Merrill Lynch, which had gone public in June.

A few maladjusted issues even fell back beneath their 1970 lows—Alcoa, American Can, and American Smelting—just to pick some "A's" from the Dow average. Memorex, 173 in 1969, stumbled to 19, two-dozen points below its 1970 low. Steels and motors, hampered by huge imports, struggled. The oil service stocks, like Schlumberger and Halliburton, were solid winners; Schlumberger tripled its 1970 low to 156. The oils mostly turned weak late in the year, Superior dropping from 221 to 138 within four months.

A few new names repeated 1968's sizzling performance. Ponderosa Systems, a self-service steak house, climbed from 8 to 74; it had been 3 in 1970 and would be below 4 again in 1974. Levitz Furniture and New Process, the mail-order house, scored stunning successes but were topped by Winnebago, plus 471 percent for the year, and Bausch & Lomb, up 271 percent.

The most important market news of the year came in mid-August when President Nixon announced a freeze on wage and prices for three months and closed the gold window. The Treasury would no longer redeem foreign central banks' dollar holdings for gold. For bullion prices, it was a non-event.

But investors welcomed any attack on inflation. The Dow gained a record 32.93 points on record volume of 31.7 million shares. But second thoughts soon cast doubts on the program's prospects and the market fell back sharply to a new low, below 800, in November.

Then the interest rate yo-yo spun around once again. A pair of discount rate cuts and a margin reduction heartened the bulls. A straight-up rally pushed the Dow temporarily back over 900, with the average closing about where it had been at mid-February.

The gain for the Transports, up 42 percent, was its best since 1958.

1971 DJIA First 830.57. High 950.82 Apr 28. Low 797.97 Nov 23. Close 890.20 +6.1%

1972

Dow 1000, a tough psychological milestone, was finally topped in November 1972. It came after months of technical complexities which left advisers, although never confused, at frequent polar differences.

The breadth of the market had peaked in 1971, a disturbing indicator. And the carriers peaked in April 1972, as it would turn out. A choppy summer gave way to a new Dow surge in October, and Nixon's re-election furnished the bulls vigor to overcome the citadel at 1000. But the Transports slumped and ended lower for the year, a bearish divergence.

The market was in trouble at the end of 1972, despite a four-digit Dow. It involved the peerage of quality growth. The scams and hoopla of 1967–1968 were gone. But institutions were bonkers over "growth stocks," seen as the new elitism and cheap at any price. The new peerage was known as the "Nifty Fifty," and they had reached extravagant PE levels during the year.

There was no legal limit to the multiple an instition might pay for the anointed. Not even 100 times earnings. Automatic Data Processing sold at a price of 100 versus earnings of 95 cents. Polaroid, no stranger to colorful projections, earned only $1.30 but the shares were pushed to 150. Names like Disney, McDonald's, MGIC, Bausch & Lomb, and International Flavors sold at over 70 times earnings. A multiple of 50 for growth stocks was run of the Street, though IBM commanded a PE of only 39.

There was some hype about a shortage of quality growth issues; some feared they would all be locked up in institutional vaults. Investors were saved from the threat by some early unlocks. Curtiss Wright's license for a rotary engine had been worth a run from 13 to 59, but the Wankel lost compression and the shares fell back to 27. Levitz Furniture, an enormous 1970–1972 winner, found it necessary to uncook the books and the stock lost its cachet; it was battered from 60 to 18.

Despite such failures, the glamours outperformed the Dow by about 4:1 during the year. The "Nifty Fifty" theorem had been half-proven. To whom the Fifty would be sold, since they were already over-owned by the institutions, was a question as yet unanswered.

1972 DJIA First 889.30. High 1036.27 Dec 11. Low 889.15 Jan 26. Close 1020.02, +14.6%.

1973

In the winter of 1973, the economic news fell from admirable to abominable in near record time and the stock market followed suit. Bulls enjoyed eight marvelous trading days, as the Dow rushed up to a record of 1051.70 on January 11. That was all. The figure would not be seen again until 1982.

A sharp drop put the Dow below 1000 at the month end. The monthly reversal was a warning sign for fans of the January barometer. In February, the prime rate was raised; there would be 15 more advances by early fall.

In April, the Chicago Board of Trade introduced equities option trading.

This new "investment opportunity" has proven a rich lode for market letters, fund strategists, and "how to get rich" scribes. Insiders have found the options an ideal means to leverage up their knowledge.

Agricultural prices were soaring, spurred by Russian buying and a classic inflation demand for commodities. The inflation rate would double that of 1972. No one outside the United States wanted dollars and many Americans connived to switch their Washingtons for illegal gold or more admirable currencies. In March, world currency markets had to shut down temporarily. The dollar had been officially devalued again. In May, gold leap-frogged the $100 level and by June had traded at $127, doubling the early January level.

"New Watergate Revelations," a standing head, was a summer banner and by August, the Dow had lost 200 points, at 852. The gloom was heavy enough to spark a fierce move back to 987; it was the grandest bear market rally since 1929–1930.

Unbelievably, the autumn news steadily worsened. The Yom Kippur war, the Arab oil embargo, the resignation of Vice-President Agnew, impeachment talk, and a half-dozen Watergate sentences battered the hopes of speculators.

Energy and gold issues, of course, did well. Superior Oil raced from 201 to 338 within two months. Homestake rose from a low of 23 to 71 in late December. Those who postponed selling for tax reasons could have gotten 99 in January.

The two-tier market was being leveled, meanwhile. Avon, valued at 140, or 65 times earnings early in the year, was seen as worth only 24 times earnings later on, despite a better bottom line. The declining rate of appreciation left the cosmetics stock at 57.

Extreme London weakness helped push the Dow to 788 in December, but a superior rally gave investors year-end hope, despite long gas lines. Unfortunately, the worst days of crisis for Nixon, the country, and stocks lay ahead.

1973 DJIA First 1031.68 High 1051.70 Jan 11. Low 788.31 Dec 5. Close 850.86, −16.6%

1974   The 1974 market was the worst disaster since the 1930s. Early on, the Dow put on a brave show and was above its 1973 close in early June. But other averages and market indicators were pointing toward lower prices.

Inflation, driven by the huge price increases for crude oil, encouraged the collapse, though the 1972–1973 two-tier price system had driven many growth equities to unsustainable levels. Blue chips like Kodak and General Electric lost over 45 percent of their value in 1974 and were off 60 percent from their bull market highs.

Dozens of lesser stocks lost 95 percent of their value. An unrelenting liquidation punished the mortgage companies. Small stock investors, who had been introduced to real estate leverage through the popular REITs, found that institutional gloss, once removed, was of little value. Thus, the Chase Manhattan (mortgage/realty) shares crashed from 70 to 4.

The period from early June until October 4 was frightful, with the Dow tumbling from 860 to 584. Soaring interest rates and Watergate were bad enough, but gas lines were awful. The Watergate tapes finally did the president in, but even Nixon's resignation, August 9, could not staunch the flood of selling.

Polaroid, 150 in 1972 and 89 in early 1974, wound up at 14. Even the oils gave way. Superior Oil, whose earnings had risen from $1.27 in 1972 to over $15 in 1974, was smashed from 304 to 134 late in the year.

Gold bugs were also vexed by the bearish tide. Though gold would approach $200 by the year end, when U.S. citizens would finally be legally allowed its charms, Homestake fell from 70 to 29 within a few weeks in late summer. Fund liquidation and an adviser sell signal were blamed.

Great Western Sugar was the extreme exception to the panic liquidation. Takeover rumors pushed it up nearly 600 percent, helped by a huge increase in raw sugar prices. Other sugar equities trailed Great Western higher, hopeful of more merger sweet-talks.

The October crisis point, Dow 585, was followed by high-level volume during the fourth quarter as investors strove to calculate the impact of lower interest rates. Most averages had seen their bottom in October, but several weak Dow players pulled that index to a new low in early December. The year's loss was the worst since 1937 and left the Dow totally unappreciated, priced at but 6.2 times its trailing earnings, and at the lowest level since the 1962 Cuban missile crisis.

IBM had lost nearly $11.6 billion in market value in a 32 percent fall from 247. It could have been worse; both Coca-Cola and Xerox were down by 58 percent during the year.

1974 DJIA First 855.32. High 891.66 Mar 13. Low 577.60 Dec 6. Close 616.24, −27.6%

1975 An enormous reflex rally shot the market up in January 1975 for the best monthly gain since 1939. Record volume of over 32 million shares on January 27 helped the Dow leap-frog the troublesome heights at 675 which had blocked rallies the previous autumn. The Dow ended January at 704, up from 616.

Four cuts in the prime rate during the month were catalysts which inspired the huge institutional buying surge. Though the country was caught in the worst recession since the 1930s, the fire sale prices of 1974 had discounted most of the problems, and ten additional prime reductions before mid-June helped convince the skeptics.

The market's course was up through mid-July, for a gain of 53 percent from the December low, and then sideways to lower. During the first six months of 1975, the torrid advance had pushed more 820 stocks at the NYSE up by 50 percent or more.

Retailers remained strong all year and Dayton-Hudson was exceptional. Earnings of $1.57 in 1974 had gained no respect and the shares sold at 7 in

January 1975. It was a true bargain. Earnings doubled during the year and the stock shot up to 28. Data General also quadrupled, with earnings up 50 percent. Some growth issues recovered lost mystique; Disney and Automatic Data Processing tripled their 1974 lows. Digital Equipment ran from 45 to 141.

In the last half of the year, banks turned weak and lower gold prices pressured the metal shares. Xerox was another disappointment, slumping to a new 1974–1975 low, after writing off its mainframe computer business. Its former market magic would not be copied again.

Though some sectors of the country were indifferent, at best, to New York City's financial crisis of early fall, its impact blunted the market until it was finally shaken off by promises of federal aid. The market recovered a nice balance late in the year, led by the autos. General Motors traded at 59 in December, up from 29 just a year earlier.

In 1974, the stock market collapse had virtually discounted the end of the world. So the market could easily ignore the large 1975 drop in the Dow's earnings, from $99.04 to $75.66. The year's gain was the second best since 1933. London's FT Index was more spectacular; it doubled in 39 trading days.

Stock brokers had another reason to remember the year. "May Day" had brought the end of fixed commissions. Institutions would drive their rates down to a few cents per share, blighting the outlook for the wire houses. Individuals would discover commissions to be a two-tier market from which they would not generally benefit.

1975 DJIA First 632.04. High 881.81 Jly 15. Low 632.04 Jan 2. Close 852.41, +38.3%.

1976 Cloning 1975's great winter performance, the Dow set an all-time January advance record in 1976, gaining nearly 15 percent in an institutional buying panic. A year earlier, daily volume over 32 million had set a record. Eighteen trading days in the 1976 January–February trading period would see NYSE activity above that level.

Having started from 852, the Dow rushed up to a 1003 close in early March. Market veterans visualized much better things ahead, as the motors had taken over a strong leadership, based on an explosive auto demand. GM earnings, but $3.27 in 1974, tripled to $10.08. Ford's bottom-line improvement was even better.

But if Dow 1000 was easily achieved, it was not easily improved upon. The year's high came in September, at 1014.79, but that was only five points better than the late March peak. Many stocks, however, would continue their winning ways through the balance of the year. A pair of Houston energy stocks did rather well, Houston Oil & Mineral climbing from 11 to 48 and Mitchell Energy from 12 to 40.

Such gains underperformed the year's biggest winner, however. Gambling issues were torrid and Resorts International "B" was up nearly 750 percent. Teledyne, which continued to shrink its capital base, moved from 22 to

81, while Cummins Engine, the leading diesel engine maker, outperformed its automotive rivals, rising from 20 to 47. It would reach 59 early in 1977.

If stocks were generally firm into the year end, a few groups lagged, having registered important cyclical highs in the first quarter. Many chemicals and drugs were among them. Dow Chemical fell from 57 to 38, Merck from 82 to 63 in a year which saw the Dow end up 17 percent. Pricey growth stocks also yielded late in 1976, though the election of Jimmy Carter to the White House had been discounted.

In December, the prime fell back to 6 percent and the Industrials scratched out a yearly close over 1000 for the second time in history. It was, as it would turn out, a gift only for the Christmas season. The closing level would not be improved until 1981.

1976 DJIA First 858.71. High 1014.79 Sep 21. Low 858.71 Jan 2. Close 1004.65, +17.9.

1977 Beset by budget and trade deficits, the dollar turned cripple in 1977 and, incredibly, lost ground even to the Mexican peso. The Consumer Price Index rate of change was inching higher, after declining for two years, and gold, which had fallen to $100 in 1976, was marching upward.

A half-dozen increases in the prime rate, starting in May, kept both stocks and bonds under pressure.

Despite such travails, the "market," as opposed to the Dow, held on stubbornly. The advance-decline line did not top until July and both the AMEX index and that of the OTC stocks ended the year higher, despite decisive losses by the lead Dow averages.

The Industrials in November closed at the 800 level, having dropped more than 200 points. The traditional year-end rally improved the index only modestly.

The closely watched steels were downside leaders all year. Bethlehem Steel, which showed a loss for the first time since 1938, plunged from 40 to 18. Chemicals, autos, and banks were also poor performers. There were few really strong major groups, but many low-priced specialties like Itek, Church's Fried Chicken, Triangle Pacific, Technicolor, and the perennial phoenix, Storage Technology, did well. Cargo containers were strong; Interway nearly tripled. Small explorers and oil services were firm but could not match a new high-tech flyer, Data Terminal, a 16–66 winner.

The year was basically dull, as NYSE statistics prove. Over 500 issues showed price changes of less than 10 percent. Among the swingers—issues gaining or losing 50 percent or more—there were 97 up big but only 11 bad losers, despite generally lower earnings and a lower Dow index.

1977 DJIA First 995.75. High 999.75 Jan 3. Low 800.85 Nov 2. Close 831.17, −17.3%

1978 For the second year in a row, in 1978, the "market" performed creditably while the Dow disappointed. Five members of the index lost between 29 percent and 36 percent of their value. Allied Chemical was the worst of the lot, but Chrysler, Johns-Manville, Minnesota Mining, and Sears gave the loss portfolio a diversified look.

Sears was an unique disaster. The growth mystique, which had pushed it to 30 times earnings in 1972, was gone, and the shares fell to 20, seven times earnings, where they traded at the lowest level since 1963 despite a record bottom line.

Though the Industrials fell 26 points during the year, the NYSE index, the S&P 500, and the ASE all advanced. There were more advances than declines for the year at the NYSE. Gambling issues continued their winning ways and Boeing jetted from 25 to 76 as earnings estimates expanded.

The year had begun badly. The discount rate was upped and the Dow crumbled from 831 to 776 in the first seven trading sessions. By the end of February the average was at 742, the lowest level since February 1975. Even the oils were routed.

Cable-TV shares and the energy service companies pretty much ignored the mess and for some bona fide growth stocks, 1978 was the last chance to shop at cheap prices. Merck dropped to 47, about 12 times earnings. When it had last sold at that price in 1974, it was valued at 19 times earnings.

It was a year of extraordinary price swings for the Dow, from 831 at the end of 1977 to 742 in February, to 907 in August and back down to 785 in November. European buying, fortunately, was encouraged by the weak dollar.

The confusing Dow chart pattern was seen by some as part of a secular consolidation pattern, promising much higher prices once the price formation was resolved. The *Advisor* headlined its November 10 issue "1800–2300 For the Dow" and went on to declare "We view this long consolidation as forming a continuation type diamond pattern promising much higher prices.... Major bull markets have shown a remarkable pattern of quadrupling or quintupling the level of the previous bear market lows.... The super-bull market which will emanate should quadruple the low of December 6, 1974 at 557.60. That would put the Dow Jones Industrial Average at 2310.40."[12]

A final top of 2888 could be projected by quintupling the 1974 low.

In the end, the 14 increases in the prime rate between May and the year end were too much. The Fed raised the discount rate twice in October and the second jump, a full 1 percent, convinced the Street that Washington was serious. Despite broad market strength, the Dow struggled to hold 800 as the year ended.

1978 DJIA First 817.74. High 907.74 Sep 8. Low 742.12 Feb 28. Close 805.01, −3.1%.

---

[12] The *Advisor,* Houston, Vol IV, No. 21, November 10, 1978, p.1,2,3.

1979 Frustrated bulls finally urged the Dow a bit higher in 1979. It was a remarkable achievement in view of ballooning interest rates, a Federal Reserve credit squeeze, seizure of the Iranian hostages, and long gasoline lines. Sadly, the year's close at 839 still left the average lower than it had been 15 years previously, when it ended 1964 at 874.

Gold and silver were seen as more desirable than most stocks. "Collectibles," some of dubious merit, were widely hyped to investors. At the London gold fix, the metal advanced swiftly throughout the year, crossing $300 in July, $400 in October, and $500 at the year's closing fix. Silver did better in percentage terms and was reflected in the price of Hecla. The historic northwestern miner led all other gainers at the NYSE for the year, advancing 800 percent.

Gasoline lines focused attention on the energy stocks and the boom in the speculative oils and mines at the American Stock Exchange pushed its index up 63 percent for the year. Dome Petroleum was a 20–49 winner, while at the NYSE, Louisiana Land jumped from 22 to 55.

Several events in October substantiated the view that huge volatility often struck in the tenth month. A $1 billion IBM bond offering was eagerly hawked by prestige underwriters, headed by Merrill Lynch and Salomon. Unfortunately, Paul Volcker and the Fed then engineered the infamous "Saturday Night Massacre," and the weekend credit crunch drowned the bond market. Before the underwriters could wriggle out they had lost a record $10 million in what looked like a cinch deal.

The Dow, in the meantime, suffered one of those rare and frightening sequences wherein it reverses from the area of the year's high to the year's low within just a few weeks—in 1979, from October 5 to the low November 7. The swift turn reminded veterans of the savage reversals of 1929, 1937, and 1940.

Fortunately, the market was uninflated and no further damage could be wrought. Even Russia's invasion of Afghanistan in the last week of the year had little impact.

During the decade of the 1970s, the Dow's earnings had more than doubled. But inflation's grasp made the numbers suspect and the major average had gained only 38 points, less than 5 percent. However, a merger wave was heating up which would add a new bullish leverage to the market in the 1980s. In the final week of 1979, Exxon concluded its ill-considered buy-out of Reliance Electric for the staggering sum of $1.2 billion, a merger record. A decade later, the Reliance deal would fall near the bottom of a historic list of the 100 biggest mergers.

1979 DJIA First 811.42. High 897.61. Oct 5. Low 796.67 Nov 7. Close 838.74, +4.2%.

1980 Unparalleled violence swept the financial markets in 1980. The prime, 20 percent in January, fell to 10.75 percent in July, and then soared to 21.5 percent in December. Bonds were more volatile than the stock indices, even though the Dow's yearly range, 730–1009 intraday, measured the span of the previous four years.

Currency markets suffered huge fluctuations, as did all commodities. OPEC fixed crude prices at $26 in January and Saudi Arabia, normally a price dove, hawked its quota at a $2 premium over other Gulf prices.

Inflation, Afghanistan, Iran, and Bunker Hunt drove the precious metals market into a winter convulsion. On January 21, the London gold fix was $850 and $1,000 seemed a reasonable target. By April, the price had fallen to $485, only to recover to $720 in September when the Iran-Iraq war broke out.

The stock market, which had benefitted from heated speculation early in the winter, found itself embroiled in the metals' panic. Silver fell from $50 to $11 within weeks and a rumored $1 billion in margin calls put some of the Street's leading houses against the wall, along with a lot of margin accounts.

On March 27, the Dow collapsed to an intraday low at 730, down from 904 in January. Panic affected every area of the market. Aircraft makers McDonnell Douglas and Lockheed were both halved in price. Superior Oil was smashed from 176 to 119 within four weeks, though it would subsequently recover to 251. The aircrafts also recovered strongly.

The DJIA staggered through April, but by July had reached a new high for the year. In November, driven by strong oil issues and the GOP victory, it hit 1000. It was not a year for short pockets. Dome Mines, in an exaggerated sense, reflected the trading violence of the year. Because of its large holdings of Dome Petroleum, it seemed the perfect parlay—gold and crude oil. The shares traded at 36 in November 1979, touched 79 in early March, fell to 48 in late March, and shot up to 133 in September. In December, the stock dropped to 80.

Enormous gains were run up in the 1979–1980 period by speculative oils and the oil service companies. Reading & Bates, the Tulsa drilling contractor, advanced from 9 to 60. Mitchell Energy went from 6 to 60. But like the gold mining shares, many energy issues including names like Louisiana Land, Occidental Petroleum, Schlumberger, Amerada-Hess, Hughes Tool, and McDermott would record their best prices of the decade in 1980.

Ronald Reagan's election pushed the market swiftly higher in late November to its final top, just over 1000. For many issues and some indices, the bull market was already over, though the Dow would creep to a new peak in April.

1980 DJIA First 824.57. High 1000.17 Nov 20. Low 759.13 Apr 21. Close 963.99, +14.9%.

1981 Consensus kills trends in the stock market and at the beginning of 1981, the consensus mania was for crude at $50 per barrel and a big oil portfolio. But oils would be the most surprising victims of the 1981 decline, the broadest since 1974 at the NYSE.

Bulls had but a few days to savor the strong 1981 start when newsletter writer Joe Granville's "abandon all hope" message sparked a giant sell-off on record volume of 93 million. But the market recovered its balance and drove to a bull market high of 1024.05 on April 27. By which time Standard of Ohio, despite enormous Alaskan reserves and estimated earnings of $8, had mysteriously slumped to 45 from a 92 high in late 1980.

The Dow's rather lonely strength in April was cut short by six quick interest rate hikes and a clear-cut Dow theory sell signal. Concerns about the budget deficit and the success of President Reagan's economic plans were other excuses for the growing weakness, which would gain momentum through September. Sohio fell further to 36. Arco dropped from 55 to 22, Halliburton from 86 to 44. Conoco, however, proved that oil was indeed cheap on the Street. Its shares pushed up from 48 to 92 in late summer, as Du Pont won control of the company in a bidding war.

Gold, like oil, was under pressure all year and the London gold fix slid to a close below $400. Western Deep, the rich Kaffir, was sliced from 85 to 30, and Homestake from 88 to 36.

International Harvester, which had joined the Dow in 1925, was the list's worst performer, falling from 26 to 6 under the impact of huge losses. IBM, in a heretical performance, fell to 9 times earnings, its lowest evaluation in decades.

There were a few strong divergences during the year. Boeing and McDonnell Douglas lost 50 percent of their value, but Lockheed doubled. General Motors, a market leader at 58 in April, fell to 34; Chrysler, collapsed to an all-time low—3. Cascading interest rates in the last quarter balanced worries about earnings. The average closed 15 points lower than it had in 1971, though its dividend of $56.32 exceeded the earnings posted in that earlier year.

1981 DJIA First 972.78. High 1024.05 Apr 27. Low 824.01 Sep 25. Close 875.00, −9.2%.

1982 On August 12, 1982, the Dow Industrials closed at 776.92, almost exactly where they had been in January 1964. The average had been locked in a trading range of 578–1052 for 18 years.

The vise was about to be broken, starting with the most stunning bear market reversal since 1932. Interest rates were suddenly seen as near their bottom, at least by Salomon Brothers' swami, Henry Kaufman. The stock market exploded. There had never been a 100-million share day at the Exchange, but 133 million shares traded on August 18, and there would be 24 more days over 100 million shares before Christmas.

By early September, the Dow had reached 930; in November it touched 1065, topping the peak of early 1973. For the year, the advance was the second best since 1958—all accomplished in the last four and one-half months. The August–December 294-point range exceeded the total Dow range for 1976–1981. Good news and good stock prices had been badly missed during the first seven months of the year. Argentina had invaded the Falklands and Israel invaded Lebanon. Unemployment was worse than in 1974 and some experts foresaw a return to a 20 percent prime. The top, however, would be 17 percent, reached in April.

The rate forecasters had reckoned without the deflation which had been a stranger to the economy since the 1930s. Gold fell to $297. Commodity prices were in a state of collapse. Crude consistently sold at a discount to posted prices. By November, the prime had fallen to 11.5 percent and the Dow celebrated on November 3 with a record 43 point gain on 137 million shares.

Pressured prices of early summer soared. Chrysler, a Detroit phoenix, was a new leader; it advanced from 3½ to 17¾. Federal National Mortgage, a pure interest rate play, quadrupled. Ford raced from 17 to 42. Oils rallied valiantly, but in most cases ended the year lower, though far above their worst levels. Exxon had provided a splendid investment opportunity during the summer, dropping to 25, where it was priced at about five times earnings and with a lofty yield of 12 percent. Even the mining shares boomed again, gold having rallied from $297 to $481 in less than 80 days. Homestake astonished the new gold deflationists by leaping from 17 to 56.

Earnings for the Dow for the year were badly warped by massive write-offs and restructuring. Bethlehem Steel's bottom line was the worst, minus $33.42. Thus, Dow composite earnings of but $9.15 were an anomaly, along with the PE ratio of 114X.

1982 DJIA First 882.52. High 1070.55 Dec 27. Low 776.92 Aug 12. Close 1046.54, +19.6%.

1983 Finally free of the psychological overhang at 1000, the Dow easily gained an additional 200 points in the first half of 1983 before suffering a modest correction. The market benefitted from great fundamental news.

First, a January OPEC meeting broke up in disarray, indicating flat to lower crude pricing. Gold's collapse from the $510 level in February indicated that inflationary fears could be laid to rest. And for the first time since 1966, the interest rate market was so stable that there was no discount rate change throughout the entire year. The rate was locked at 8.5 percent.

The prospect for better earnings, lower inflation, and interest rate stability encouraged investors to bid stocks higher, both in price and PE ratios. Thus, IBM which had sold at less than 10 times earnings in 1982 scored a big advance to 134, where it was valued at over 14 times earnings.

Speculative money was in the market big and spec stocks outdid the Dow. High techs were favored. The Street, responsive to the fad, brought more than $12 billion in new public offerings during the year, a figure about ten times the amount of 1982. Rate stability made the thrifts an easy sale and the number of publicly owned savings and loans doubled during the year. Not all were in Texas, either.

Market problems there were, but they were mostly confined to individual issues. Grenada and the Russian "kill" on the Korean airliner were largely ignored. But Texas Instruments hit an air pocket in April, plunging from 158 to 107 within a few days on bad earnings. Mary Kay Cosmetics emulated Avon of a decade before, dropping from 45 to 13. Tandy was nearly halved and secondary airlines suffered enormously from rate wars.

The popularity of Chrysler and Lee Iacocca continued. The stock ran to 36, ten times its price of early 1982. General Motors, with earnings of $11.84, rose to 80, up from 29 the previous year. The year's record volume of 21.6 billion shares, about double the 1980 level, aided the brokerage shares; Merrill Lynch rose to 56, and the figure would stand as its high throughout the decade. Late in the fall, speculative and unlisted issues faltered badly, but the DJIA loss was minimal.

Speculators who needed another option "hit" got the chance. Stock index trading had been introduced in 1982 and stock index options were added as a new fix for the venturesome. The sale of "naked" stock puts would, in 1987, prove somewhat more treacherous than pork belly trading.

1983 DJIA First 1027.04. High 1287.20 Nov 29. Low 1027.04 Jan 3. Close 1258.64, +20.3%

1984

Lengthy consolidation periods have occurred in every long-playing bull market. The sideways movement has often continued for about 12 months and has served as a period of rotational correction without severe technical damage to the market.

The calendar year of 1984 was merely correctional for the Dow, though other more extended indices suffered through private bear markets. Both the NASDAQ and ASE averages sold down sharply. But then, both had doubled between August 1982 and June 1983. The OTC index lost 32 percent in its 1983–1984 decline, a more-than-mini bear market. On the other hand, the Dow, at its correction low, was off only 15.5 percent, and the seven most active issues for the year at the NYSE were all winners.

Big stocks were helped by big buy-outs and group sympathy to such largesse. The big target stocks in 1984 were the oils. Chevron took over Gulf in the biggest deal in history, $13.3 billion. Texaco shanghaied Getty in a merger costing $10 billion plus the shocking alienation of affection judgment which awarded Pennzoil $11 billion against Texaco. And Mobil grabbed the famous oil finder, Superior.

There were many other excitements and headlines, of course. "Ma Bell" breathed her maternal last at a price of 63½, splitting into many "Baby Bells." The government, if not the householder, had finally won in the most famous antitrust suit since 1911. Digital, a 132–64 loser in 1983, bounced back to 111, but many high techs were smashed. Storage Technology lost 84 percent and was the worst of the lot at the NYSE. On the NASDAQ list, nine issues— mainly computer types—lost over 80 percent. Health issues were not immune, either, to more realistic pricing.

Chicago Milwaukee Corporation, a rich shell of the historic railroad, made a most famous run in 1984, from 95 to 196. Its last rail holding, 85 miles of commuter line, would be sold in 1987.

The market's greatest worries came in the spring after a discount rate increase, which put great pressure on the bond market. Treasuries fell by about ten points. A sharp Dow advance in August, aided by a record day of 237 million shares, corrected most of the first-half decline. The index then moved sideways, though with great volatility, for the balance of the year. Sentiment was boosted greatly in the last few weeks by two reductions in the discount rate. President Reagan's re-election had also aided confidence.

1984 DJIA First 1252.74. High 1286.64 Jan 6. Low 1086.57 Jly 24. Close 1211.57, −3.7%.

1985   A host of famous corporate names disappeared or were hyphenated in 1985. Widespread restructuring caused tough times for thousands of workers at firms not involved in the merger game.

Nabisco fell in with R.J. Reynolds and General Foods with Philip Morris. Royal Dutch finally absorbed Shell. American Broadcasting, G. D. Searle, Levi Strauss, Carnation, and Revlon, among others, disappeared from the stock tables. Carl Icahn, at the year end, was zeroing in on TWA, Howard Hughes' former carrier, while another source of the famous recluse's wealth, Hughes Aircraft, signed on with General Motors. One big deal that failed was Ted Turner's attempt on CBS.

Enormous stock buy-backs were also a feature of the 1985 market, which started the second leg of the 1982–1987 advance. Buying back 40 *million* or more of their own shares were: Exxon, Unocal, Arco, Phillips Petroleum, and Allied-Signal.

There was plenty of action outside the mega deals, however. Speciality retailers were hot, along with the pollution control stocks. The Gap moved from 21 to 64; International Technology was up 161 percent. Real estate investments varied. The Rockefellers cut the public in on the most famous address in New York City, but the Rockefeller Center was pricey at $20. California's historic Tejon Ranch, on the other hand, was cheap at 94 in January. It subsequently moved to 304.

Inflation was a non-event. Gold sold at $285 in February, its lowest price since 1979, and oil prices were pressured all year. Drilling companies struggled to avoid Chapter 11 and the energy banks began taking some big hits, Texas Commerce Bankshares dropping from 44 to 26.

In May, when the discount rate was cut to its lowest level since 1978, the Dow quickly moved over the 1300 milestone. It had been a balky bull market, over two years since 1200 was first crested. A splendid rise occupied the last four months of 1985 as the average zipped from a September low at 1298 to 1553. A falling dollar encouraged foreign buying.

Speculative stocks turned easy late in the year, however. Computervision was a big loser, 44 to 9, Mohawk Data, a darling of the 1960s at 111, hit 1¼. It had been 18 in 1983. At the year end, the merger frenzy was increasing, **if** anything, with General Electric committing to buy RCA for over $6 billion.

1985 DJIA First 1198.87. High 1553.10 Dec 16. Low 1184.96 Jan 4. Close 1546.67, +27.7%.

1986 Five years of generally advancing stock prices, as measured by the S&P 500, bowed out to congratulatory headlines at the end of 1986. The last such run by a major average had been by the DJIA, ending in 1928.

The laudatory press, however, couldn't offset the year's tremendous amount of bad type about fraud, insider trading, triple witching, and green mail. And, if insiders Ivan Boesky and Dennis Levine were seen as archetypal villains, they were viewed in the provinces as less dangerous than program trading, equated with the pool operations of an earlier era.

In business, the biggest headlines attached to the astounding collapse of oil prices. West Texas crude, $26 in January, sold at $10 in April. The industry was devastated. Bankruptcies, multimillion dollar reserve writedowns, and Chapter 11 became endemic to the industry. The $50 per barrel crude dream had become a $10 nightmare.

Still, the Dow gained 26 percent during the year, despite three major energy stocks in the average, large profit losses by U.S. Steel and General Motors, and a notable price decline by IBM. Steel and Bethlehem Steel sold at their lowest levels in decades. Merck, however, gave an enormous boost to the Dow, advancing by 81 percent.

Other drug types did even better. Viratek raced from 10 to 99. It would fall back to 10 within a year, there being some doubts and lawsuits regarding claims that the firm's Ribavirin was really a cure for AIDS. Genentech tripled to 99, or about 1,000 times earnings of nine cents.

Many foreign issues sparkled, like Hitachi, Korea Fund, and the gold-miner, Echo Bay. Best of the exotics was Philippine Long Distance Telephone, which gained 580 percent following the Marcos ouster.

During the year, a record of $300 billion in mergers, acquisitions, buy-outs, and divestiture activity were recorded. Again, as in 1985, a large number of famous names were leveraged or merged out—companies like Safeway, Allied Stores, Associated Dry Goods, and Sperry.

Goodyear and Gillette paid raiders green mail to save the corporate perks, but small stockholders were not included. None of the "deals" could match the percentage profits seen in Home Shopping Network, however. An initial public offering by Merrill was sold to the "public" at $18. The stock traded at 44 the next day and 100 several months later.

The insider scandals were triggered in May by Dennis Levine, but the market held together until early July when a record 62-point Dow loss struck unexpectedly, just after the 1900 milestone—fourth of the year—had been passed. In early September, technicians were delighted by a new Dow peak, only to see the average struck down by an 87-point daily loss. The selling wave spread overseas and Tokyo suffered a record drop on the following day.

A high state of nervousness attached itself to the market during the fall. In November, insider Ivan Boesky paid a $100 million fine to the SEC, a staggering levy, even in a year of staggering numbers.

On December 2, the year's high was reached and Dow 2000 seemed a Christmas probability. But the market still had to face triple-witching day, a quarterly phenomenon, when current-period stock options, stock futures indices, and options on the indices expire. The day, December 19, would long be remembered.

A record 245 million shares traded—not all bad. But it seemed quite reckless to critics, who were appalled that about 90 million shares traded in the last minute of the day in a frenzy of program trading and option expiration.

There were also sobering thoughts about the longevity of cheap energy prices. In a rare example of cohesion and avoidance of rancor, the December OPEC meeting broke up with a meaningful agreement. West Texas crude closed the year near $15; it would rally $4 by mid-January.

1986 DJIA First 1537.73. High 1955.57 Dec 2. Low 1502.29 Jan 22. Close 1895.95, +22.6%.

1987   In August 1987, there were a few traders who thought or hoped that the Dow would eventually fall 1,000 points. But no one thought the damage would come by Halloween. Or that on the worst day, which would come on October 19, the Industrials would fall 508 points, nearly 23 percent.

Bona fide bear markets, like that of 1946–1949 have lost little more and the mini bears of 1956–1957 and 1960 considerably less than the great one-day meltdown of 1987.

Fortunes were destroyed in the monstrous October decline and a great deal of faith lost in the Street and financial institutions. Brokers would find annuities and CDs easier sales than stocks and bonds for the next few years.

The amazing thing was that after falling 1,000 points, a year-end rally of rather modest proportions left the sometimes manueverable Dow higher for the 12 months, unlike 1929. But that gay deception could not mask the fact that there were only 810 advances for the year at the Exchange versus 1,444 declines.

Through late August, the Dow Industrials had built an apparently insurmountable cushion again yearly loss, having advanced by 827 points. An insatiable lust for stocks had pushed the New Year into a dazzling start. Dow 2000 was hurdled on January 8 and Dow 2100 on January 19. A record 13 consecutive days of advance helped push the average up 263 points for the month, aided by the first 300 million share day. Even utilities were hot and an astounding $1.2 billion was poured into a new Duff & Phelps closed-end utility fund. The Utility average reached its all-time high the following day.

A bullish frenzy lasted all spring despite advancing crude prices, a falling dollar and further insider scandals. The Dow reached 2400 in April, up over 500 points from the 1986 close. Inflation worries and higher money costs then cooled the enthusiasm, but in June the average was up to a new high and crossed 2500 in July.

On August 10, the index reached 2600 and was at 2700 just a week later. Dow 3600, the widely publicized Elliot Wave goal, suddenly became a dangerous near-consensus. The end was, indeed, near. It came on August 25 at 2722.42, in a week which saw bonds and the dollar smashed.

A few weeks of great volatility were followed by a final rally, which put the Dow back to 2641 in early October, although market breadth remained very poor.

The gathering storm was ominous. Bonds and the dollar continued a terrible collapse. A 92-point record drop on October 6 was followed by a 95-point hit on October 14 and, finally, the long-forecast 100-point decline on Friday, October 16. A few brave souls thought it might be enough, but with little confidence, as there was great fear on the Street. But on Monday, the selling avalanche continued, smashing the market with a 508-point loss on 603 million shares.

It was another of the infamous October massacres. The one-day carnage among quality issues was shocking, the worst since 1929. Digital Equipment fell 43 points. Merck, the No. 1 Dow stock in 1986, was down 33. Dow Chemical, which had closed at 88, was clubbed down to 56 on Monday, but did rally to 71 for a loss of 17. The normally unflappable Procter & Gamble ended at 61, minus 23.

Huge percentage drops hit lesser names and OTC issues. Brunswick fell 40 percent and Holiday Inns, 37 percent. The unique Americus Trust "scores," which offer investors an opportunity for leveraged participation in market appreciation, had a flip side, as it turned out, and were devastated. Amoco scores lost 65 percent and Exxon scores were down 45 percent. Luxury shares were abandoned. Neiman-Marcus, 31 on Thursday, fell to 18. Only 52 stocks at the Board could advance; 1,973 declined.

The October 19 loss was the largest in history and on the largest volume. Its percentage decline, 23 percent, was also a record and almost perfectly duplicated the two-day total loss of October 28–29, 1929.

Monday's bloodbath was followed by a two-day rally of about 290 points, but panic struck again on the following Monday, with the Dow axed for 157 points. The financial storm had spread worldwide and the Hong Kong market, one of the hot Asian markets of the previous year, was forced to suspend.

Reason took over in November and a large, churning market lasted through the year, though in early December several averages edged to new yearly lows. In the meantime a great deal of finger pointing and investigation were going on, concerning the events of October. In the public mind, at least, program trading was seen as most culpable and many houses embargoed the mechanized trading scheme.

Real estate, and not black October, was the cause of some of the year's biggest losses, however. Texas banks had been hurt by oil's slide but that was nothing compared to the real estate collapse. First RepublicBank lost 80 percent of its value, and a pair of other Lone Star banks were in the worst ten at the NYSE.

Lukens, up 228 percent, led Compaq Computer, and Reynolds among the year's big winners, and many software companies were solid gainers, along with the metals and golds. Bethlehem Steel, a Chapter 11 candidate just a year earlier, was up 168 percent. But home shopping, like home cooking, turned out to be overrated and the Home Shopping Network, which had split, fell from 47 to 5.

A few brave souls at the year-end felt that a unique bear market had already come and gone, while the alarmists foresaw October as only the beginning. Both camps, however, visualized a prolonged period of consolidation and sideways movement before a decisive course emerged.

1987 DJIA First 1927.31. High 2722.42 Aug 25. Low 1738.74 Oct 19. Close 1938.83, +2.3%.

1988   The world was a field of financial land mines for overconfident bears in 1988. The looming recession, so clearly forecast by the crash of 1987, was a no-show. The highest-priced market in the world, Tokyo, continued to defy gravity; it rose to a record high in April, and then went higher.

Business, earnings, and dividends bloomed in the United States and by December, the civilian jobless rate was at its lowest point in 14 years.

General Motors totaled up a record $122 billion in sales and IBM a record earnings figure of $5.5 billion, but small investors fled the market, favoring closed-end bond funds, CDs, and annuities. Brokerage house stocks were disappointing performers.

The big winners of 1988 were the merger stocks; seven of ten of the best advances during the year were by takeover issues. Many more historic names disappeared from the Exchange roster, Federated Department Stores, Firestone, and Kraft (National Dairy) among them. The big dollars involved caused many a gasp, but the banks, having nixed foreign loans, boasted plenty of money to throw at the takeover deals. RJR Nabisco was taken privately for a sum of over $25 billion.

Improving trade figures and falling oil prices helped sentiment in the first half, but the Dow marked time during the final six months, beset by the specter of a drought-induced inflation and higher interest rates. In October, the Dow peaked and in the following month the prime rate advanced to 10.5 percent, its highest level in over three years.

Merger candidates like Service Merchandise, up 411 percent, and Best Products, up 260 percent, were among the biggest winners of 1988, while assorted western banks and S&Ls were among the year's worst actors. Texas American Bancshares lost 92 percent of its value. Semiconductors, gold mining, and computer systems were leaders in negative action.

Asset allocation, a subjective division of investment dollars between bonds, stocks, and cash equivalents, continued as a buzz phrase on the Street, but few could agree on the proper recipe for the mixture. The 1988 advance did little for those whose computer set formulated a 10 percent stock position, with 90 percent in bonds and cash.

Big dollar swings in stocks were rather rare—a welcome relief after 1987. The RJR Nabisco takeover pushed the stock from 44 to 94 and Pennwalt sailed up from 43 to 107, but those were exceptional moves. Digital Equipment, a darling of the previous few years, tumbled from 145 to 86 before closing at 98, a 37 percent loss for the year.

Berkshire Hathaway, the highest-priced issue at the NYSE, was a natural exception to limited dollar moves. It advanced from 2755 to 5050 before closing at 4750. It would rise further, to 8875, in 1989.

Merger stocks and the "whisper stocks," those rumored as candidates, got the headlines and action in 1988. The Dow was firm but restrained, though Boeing, up 64 percent, and Woolworth, up 50 percent, performed well. Goodyear, minus nine percent for the year, was the most disappointing Industrial.

While the Dow advance for the year was a modest 12 percent, it was welcome relief after months of financial doomsaying, the near-war with Iran in the Gulf, climbing interest rates, and continued insider revelations along the Street. In December, Drexel Burnham Lambert copped a plea on multiple fraud charges and agreed to pay $650 million in fines and restitution. While the sum seemed large west of the Hudson, it was not much more than Drexel's junk-bond chief, Michael Milken, had been paid in the previous year.

As the year ended, President Reagan could find satisfaction in the fact that his second term had seen four years of advancing Dow prices. The "Reagan Market" had matched a presidential success record last achieved in Calvin Coolidge's market of 1924–1928.

1988 DJIA First 2015.25. High 2183.50 Oct 21. Low 1879.14 Jan 20. Close 2168.57, +11.8%.

1989

Unbeknownst at the time, the most significant market event of 1989 was recorded on the year's last day of trading. The Dow Nikkei reached its record high, 38,915.87. By the spring of 1990, that Tokyo average would be near 28,000. The sun also sets, said the cynics, for the inscrutable levitation of the Japanese market had ended in 1989.

Domestically, the best news for long-term investors was the fact that all three Dow averages overcame their 1987 highs. They were led by the merger-minded Transportation index which, at its high of 1532.01 in September, had more than doubled the 1987 low of 660. A similar advance by the DJIA would have put it over 4000.

For a time, in the early autumn, it seemed that every airline was either a prime merger stock—like UAL—or a whisper candidate. Donald Trump was a daily media event with his plans for American (AMR). Hilton Hotels and others in the travel business were also "in play."

It would not come to pass, however. Banking snags and greed flipped the Transportations upside down and they suffered a true selling panic, tumbling by 24 percent between early September and the end of November. UAL, seen as worth $300 a share, fell quickly from 294 to 146. In a disastrous fallout of the panic, the "junk bond market" lived up to its name. Bids just disappeared.

Exclusive of Exxon's navigational error at Valdez in April, it did seem that most of the year's big news events came in the last quarter. The most stunning involved the overnight democratization of Eastern Europe and the destruction of the Berlin Wall. That encouraged some new global stars and a fierce demand for the deutsche mark. The several national mutual funds—Spain, Asia Pacific, Thai, and German—turned out among the year's top performers at the Big Board.

The Street's fourth-quarter consensus was for a recession in 1990, but the Dow revived after the October massacre and was only 38 points off its October high at the year end. Spain Fund, up 199 percent, was the No. 1 performer at the Big Board but only because the mania for L.A. Gear's sneakers topped out early, leaving it with a gain of but 185 percent on its close at 31. Early in the fall, Gear had reached 47, where it was up by 327 percent.

At the AMEX and in the OTC market really low-priced issues proved their attraction again. Thermo Processors gained 299 percent for the year; its low had been 3. NASDAQ favorite, American Travelers, pushed up by 318 percent; its low had been just over 4.

Despite such speculative successes, it was not much of a year for brokers. Deals declined and brokerage ranks were pruned. Merrill Lynch managed a two-point gain for the year, but Shearson Lehman Hutton was a sinker. It was not much of a year for the S&Ls, either. They dominated the list of poor performers.

Computer stocks were the worst of the industrial groups, with mighty IBM down 23 percent while the telephone companies had one of their truly strong years, aided by falling interest rates. AT&T advanced from a low at 28 to 47 and ended up 58 percent. That could not touch the performance of its rival, MCI, which gained 95 percent.

Several one-time stars came back on stage. Mattel, the toy maker, doubled and the Bank of America was well resurrected. Circle K and American Medical both omitted dividends in the fall and were rudely treated; the convenience store chain dropped from 17 to 3.

Investors were again pummeled by program traders. On October 13, the Dow went into free fall, urged on by the computer strategists, and fell 191 points. The decline ranks as the second worst in history, measured in points, a reminder of October's savage bear reputation.

The decade of the 1980s was the wildest since the 1930s. Gold, crude oil, inflation, and interest rates flew to record peaks in 1980–1981, but stocks and bonds gained investment ascendancy starting in 1982. For the Dow, the 10-year period witnessed an enormous gain of 1893 points, or 226%. The percentage, however, was far below the figures for the 1950s and 1920s.

Retailing issues, not high-techs, dominated the decade's big-winner ranks. Circuit City Stores, 26 cents (adjusted) in 1979, gained 8,265 percent to 21¾. The Limited's gain was near 10,000 percent by 1987, but the stock could never recover from that year's meltdown; its decade advance was plus 6,358 percent. Wal-Mart and Dillard Department Stores were other brilliant retail performers in the period. Oil service shares dominated the list of large losers.

1989 DJIA First 2144.64. High 2791.41 Oct 9. Low 2144.64 Jan 3. Close 2753.20, +27.0.

1990   War—or the threat of war for the United States—finally did in the lengthy 1982–1990 bull market in the summer of 1990. The Dow peak came in July, but it was Iraq's invasion of Kuwait that rolled the market over. American troops landed in Saudi Arabia on August 8. Inflationary pressures appeared immediately and by early October, $40 crude and a looming recession had dropped the Dow Industrials by 20 percent. Congress' inept toil to forge a budget had not only closed Yosemite Park and other federal services, but had encouraged a great emigration of foreign investments to saner shores. The dollar fell to a record low against the deutsche mark.

Dow 2999.75, the record close reached on both July 16 and 17, marked the passage of the long 1982–1990 bull market. If the 3000 mark seemed a glorious figure, it had been accomplished in a rather sullen atmosphere, when measured against the great excitment of typical bull market peaks.

January 1990, had given off ominous warnings with its abrupt collapse, darkened by a serious bond market slump. But a consensus bearishness and rich institutional pockets helped rachet the market higher into mid-summer though the historic bull credentials were just not present. Volume was low, brokerage stocks were sickly, technical indicators were depressing and other indices besides the Industrials seemed to fly warnings.

An alarming divergence between the Transportations and the Dow had begun in October 1989 and continued right into the summer peak of 1990. And even as the DJIA teased the 3,000 level, the Utility index was 12% below its 1989 close.

Perhaps more ominously, the Tokyo Nikkei Index, a source of great comfort to the bulls of the previous decade, had lost bullish steerage. Near 39,000 on the last day of 1989, the leading Japanese stock average traded at the 32,000 level at mid-July.

Early autumn fears were heightened by the astonishing gains for oil prices and when crude pushed over $40 in early October, the sun did set for the Japanese market. The Nikkei fell to 20,222. It was a most serious bear market collapse—a decline of 48% marked within just nine months—and one which ranked with the great declines of the past century for the New York market.

War for the United Nations forces in the Middle East was deemed possible. Iraq's territorial lust seemed akin to that of Germany, Italy, and Japan in the 1930s and hawks felt it better to deal with the problem quickly rather than waiting for Saddam Hussein to overrun the entire Arabian peninsula.

The litany of woes in October seemed endless: high interest rates, the threat of war, increased unemployment, sliding earnings, and the budget clowning in Congressional halls. It seemed to offer a career for crisis management in many fields. Bulls hoped October's reputation as a giant "bear-killer" would survive, but skeptics deemed it unlikely that a bull market lasting almost exactly nine years could be fully corrected in a two-month slide erasing a mere 20% of the Dow's value. Additionally, a reasonable 40% retracement of the total 1982–1990 advance of 2,223 Dow points would call for a drop to near the 2,100 level for the Industrials, according to the pessimists.

If a slight-of-hand had kept the Dow's final 1990 loss at a modest four percent, other indices indicated more pain. The Dow Transports, the AMEX, NASDAQ, and Value Line had all fallen between 18 and 24 percent. Financial confidence had been eroded by the continuing S&L crisis and serious problems at the money center banks and the old-line casualty companies.

Having had five months in which to adjust their portfolios, most investors just hunkered down at the year end, forsaking the perennial optimism of the New Year. The United Nations' countdown to the Iraqi withdrawal deadline was barely two weeks away.

Among the few bright spots was an avid foreign interest in American corporations, spurred by the cheap dollar, and IBM's return to market leadership; it had gained 18 points in a sloppy equity year. Blue chip losers included AT&T, down by a third, and Chase Manhattan, off 70 percent.

1990 DJIA First 2748.72. High 2999.75 Jly 16 Low 2365.10 Oct 11. Close 2633.66, − 4.3%.

3

Bull Markets
since 1890

There have been five great bull markets in the past century and a score of other most pleasing advances. For each of the superadvances, the gain was at least 200 percent.

The first great advance was by the Rails, 1896–1902. The carriers were still the most important segment of corporate America and they enjoyed the fruits of the nation's great expansion at the turn of the century. "McKinley Prosperity," it was called by the GOP. The Rail average is favored in this period as more representative of the market.

The next great advance in the market would commence in 1921, when there was an extreme backwardation in the stock market. The Dow Rails were lower than at the turn of the century. And the Industrials had greatly lagged the blooming of the economy. Stocks would catch up in 1921–1929, riding a "Detroit ripple," the great auto boom, and not the suffering, regulated carriers.

A giant, new bull market seemed remote in the summer of 1932. A quarter of the nation's population was unemployed and banks were failing by the

TABLE 3-1 BULL MARKETS SINCE 1890

The great advances		
Period	Years	Gain (%)
"McKinley Prosperity"	1896–1902	209
The Road to 1929	1921–1929	497
FDR & Hope	1932–1937	372
Born With a Silver Spoon	1949–1956	222
Single-Digit Financials	1982–1990	286

Major bull markets		
Period	Years	Gain (%)
A Golden Age Ends	1903–1906	144
Steel Rigging	1907–1909	90
Quartermaster to Europe	1914–1916	112
Inflation, Oil Frenzy	1917–1919	81
Long Road to Peace	1942–1946	129
Dow's All-Time High	1962–1966	86

Other bull sequences		
Period	Years	Gain (%)
Easy Money	1957–1960	63
A Record Passion	1960–1961	30
The "Sizzle" Market	1966–1968	32
Institutional Dementia	1970–1973	67
Bad Earnings, Good Market	1974–1976	76
"Death of Equities" Exaggerated	1978–1981	38

thousands. But, by Labor Day, stocks had nearly doubled the July low. And by 1937 the stunning advance had pushed the Dow up 372 percent, a figure embossed, to be sure, by the low, low prices of 1932 when a handful of Dow issues were single-digit priced.

In 1949, a skeptical America finally capitulated and decided that the "inevitable" postwar depression was a no-show. Wall Street entered its finest decade, in terms of the Dow Industrial Average. Stocks doubled and redoubled. Computers came of age. The "paperwork explosion" and the space race arrived at about the same time. Something was left behind, however; 1957 was the last year a stock investor could get more return from risky dividends than from AAA bonds. And 1956–1957 were the last back-to-back years in which the politicians could balance the U.S. budget.

The longest peacetime economic expansion in the nation's history drove the bull market of the 1980s. As in 1921, the market, barely higher at mid-1982 than in 1965, had a lot of catching up to do. Lower interest rates and lower inflation were the catalysts. The Dow numbers ballooned up to 2000 and then quickly on to 2500, a tremendous leap from the Dow 1000 ceiling which had sapped the market so often in the years since 1966. Whether measured by the 1982–1987 advance of 250 percent, or the 1982–1990 gain of 286 percent, the sequence remains third in the great bull advances of the past century.

"McKinley Prosperity"
DJRA Aug 8, 1896–Sep 9, 1902: 41.82 to 129.36, +209%.

"McKinley Prosperity" cheered the country in the late 1890s, and the boom lasted well into the twentieth century. In August 1896, the market had made an epic turn, anticipating an end to the inflation threats from the silver cult.

Sound money, high tariffs, and a formal gold standard, along with a frantic gathering of businesses into giant industrial trusts, or consolidations, would be hallmarks of the GOP prosperity.

In 1897, the Dow Industrials and Rails were jointly compiled for the first complete year. It was an auspicious time. In 1898, the country would record its greatest trade balance. An era of great corporate expansion was about to begin. And the public would soon be lured back into a booming stock market.

Rail Average Dominant

The nouveau industrial sector would receive its first great speculative attention in 1898–1899, but the Rails were the dominant average of the period. They were the senior average, long tracked. They carried the higher Dow index level and their members were dominant in size, until the formation of U.S. Steel in 1901.

They were also favored as investments. A sometimes scandalous financial record was, at least, a long record as compared with the Industrials, and the rail functions were seen as longer lived and more essential than those of the new industrial groups. Their 100-year bonds were in demand, as the following box indicates.

The six-year bull market for the Rails would be quite splendid. Bankruptcy and foreclosures, following the "great train wreck" of 1893, had squeezed a great deal of water out of the unfortunate carriers. The Rail Average would gain 209 percent in the 1896–1902 advance, its best until the 1932–1933 sizzler.

After a slow start in 1897, the market regained enthusiasm in July, aided by a favorable court decision on rail rates and the Dingley Tariff Bill. President McKinley, capital, and labor all endorsed the new bill. Consumers were not consulted.

Grain prices advanced to the best level since 1891, but the Cuban annoyance was nagging the country and the market lagged. Cuban guerrillas had been fighting Spanish rule over the island for 25 years and Spanish intransigence and a jingoistic U.S. press fanned the flames.

On February 15, 1898, the battleship *Maine* blew up in Havana harbor and the Industrials slid sharply to a mid-March low at 42.00. On April 24, Spain and the United States squared off. On May 1, the Spanish armada in the

---

100-YEAR BONDS NOW COMING DUE

In the 1890s, farsighted men could see that the demand for capital to pursue the nation's expansion would surely diminish. The Western Frontier had already passed and by 1899 bond yields were at their lowest level in the nation's history.

Rail expansion was slowing and the opportunities for the employment of capital at a good return were expected to shrink.

And so it came to pass that the market demanded and received a series of extremely long-term bonds, many with a maturity of 100 years. Railroad management could see some advantages in postponing debt maturity for a century.

If one closely examines an issue of Moody's Bond Record, there will crop up a number of famous railroad names with century-old bonds coming to maturity in the 1990s.

Included is paper from the Southern Railway, the Chesapeake & Ohio, the Missouri-Kansas-Texas, the New York Central, Norfolk & Western, and Texas & Pacific, among others.

If most of the "century bonds" are about to mature, there will still be some historic paper about. The Northern Pacific general lien, three percent bonds issued in 1897, will not come due until 2047.

Philippines was completely destroyed. Colonel "Teddy" Roosevelt, with others, charged up San Juan Hill on July 1. The Spanish fleet at Santiago, Cuba, was sunk July 3. On July 26, the Queen Regent sued for peace.

By the time the peace accord was signed in August, both averages had far surpassed their 1897 high, under the most prosperous conditions. Pittsburgh boomed as pig iron production set new records. Copper enjoyed its highest pricing since 1883.

A few brave wagon and carriage makers even hitched their wheels to electric engines. Others, like Studebaker, hitched their wagons to gasoline engines and the stars.

Public Reenters Market

Fevered speculation swept over the market in the winter of 1898–1899, with the new industrial shares enjoying their biggest play of the decade. The public's appetite for stocks was whetted by myriad trust amalgamations, and the machinations of New York's ex-Governor Flowers, a leading operator in the Industrials and tractions.

Outside buying was feverish, at a pitch not seen since 1878–1880. In January, 1899, the *Commercial & Financial Chronicle* wrote of the avalanche of business which was taxing the Exchange. "The public is in the market and its capacity for absorbing securities seems at the moment unlimited. . . . placing money indiscriminately during a period of rising prices in enterprises whose current profits and actual assets are practically unknown."[1]

Tennessee Coal & Iron, beneficiary of a semi-corner, advanced from 13 to 126 between 1896 and 1899. Booming electric demands pushed General Electric from 20 to 132, while U.S. Rubber made it from 10, in June 1897, to 57. The newly popular tractions, the "electric railroads," had gained a speculative following. Aided by pools and politicians, they scored some notable gains. The Brooklyn Rapid Transit (BRT) rode up from 18 to 137 and the Metropolitan Street Railway from 79 to 251.

Increasing labor problems, high money costs, and increasing friction between the United Kingdom and the Transvaal worried investors in the early fall of 1899. War in southern Africa came in October, and the London connection, for the third time in the decade, brought chaos to the Exchange. News of British war losses in December caused a plague of selling. James R. Keene, a noted speculator, attacked the "Flower" stocks, and the BRT was driven down to 61.

Within two weeks, the Dow fell by 23 percent and a one-day decline of nearly 9 percent on December 18 would stand as a record for 30 years.

The Twentieth Century

The Dow opened the twentieth century at a level of 68.13. Its two-point advance would be its best day of the year. During the spring, further manipulations in the traction stocks—the Third Avenue Railway was driven down from 126 in January to 45 in March—and price cutting in the steel industry caused considerable tension. Tennessee Coal & Iron, 104 in February, fell to 46.

But the Rails continued firm and the year's index lows came in August, when monthly volume fell to 4 million shares; it had been 13 million one year earlier. For the Industrials, it had been a one-year bear slide.

McKinley's reelection in November as he defeated Bryant again, and by a wider margin, brought a small buying panic to the Street. The Industrials rushed ahead in 11 of 12 sessions in the November period. The Rails easily overcame their 1899 peak and closed the year with a strong surge.

The "Billion-Dollar" Trust

U.S. Steel, a trust, was formed in the spring of 1901. It was the nation's first billion-dollar corporation, if one honors the huge amount of watered paper. The values of the consolidated companies, many of which were themselves puffed-up trusts, were syndicated for nearly $1.4 billion. The intrinsic values were closer to $700 million, or even less. Banking and underwriting groups had, without the use of firearms, looted the endeavor of an amazing $150 million in fees.

---

[1]The Commercial & Financial Chronicle, New York, January 7, 1899, p. 5 col 1.

Danger of a steel trade war was the supposed catalyst for J. P. Morgan's giant undertaking and the nucleus was Andrew Carnegie's great Pittsburgh operation. Carnegie's personal take of $218 million in gold bonds would make him the richest man in America. A part of the sum would make several thousand municipal library boards very happy.

More than 160 other steel trusts and operating companies were brought into J. P. Morgan's steel net within a few weeks. The shares were listed at the Big Board, where they moved up from below 40 to 55 within a short period, aided by the finesse of James R. Keene, the most famous pool operator of the period.

Merger mania gripped the country, as the great steel and rumored rail deals inflamed the public's imagination. Intrinsic values and the market parted company.

The $1,000 Corner

The desperate battle for control of the Northern Pacific remains one of the great Exchange legends. The shares raced from 96 in April 1901 to 1000 on May 9 as Morgan and James Hill of the Great Northern battled the Union Pacific, engineered by E. H. Harriman, and Kuhn, Loeb, for control of the Northern Pacific.

The Northern Pacific and Great Northern had captured joint control of the Chicago, Burlington & Quincy, a vital Chicago gateway line which connected with both the Union Pacific and the Northern Pacific, and the coup threatened Union Pacific traffic. Harriman determined to subvert the move by capturing control of the Northern Pacific, since Morgan and Hill refused to share the Burlington ownership with him. His steady buying pushed the Northern Pacific to 115 on May 1 and a great number of other rails were seized up in a merger frenzy. On April 30, 3,281,000 shares had traded at the Exchange, a volume record.

Control, not a corner, was the goal of the titans. The biggest corner of them all, it turned out, was a "natural." Morgan did not control 50 percent of the shares and Harriman's swift attack found Morgan in France on his annual vacation. His cable to buy 150,000 Northern Pacific shares at the market dealt panic and ruin to the shorts as the stock rocketed from 159 to 1000 within an hour on May 9, creating a firestorm of selling in other securities. "Meanwhile . . . it was suddenly noted with horror by traders that all other stocks were beginning to collapse . . . the men who had been trapped in the NP corner . . . threw all other share possessions overboard."[2]

Morgan's U.S. Steel dropped to 24, down 23 points on Thursday, May 9. Harriman's Union Pacific crashed from 106 to 77. Hill's Great Northern preferred lost more than 40 points. The titans as well as the pygmies were being crushed.

---

[2]Charles Albert Collman, *Our Mysterious Panics 1830–1930, A Story of Events and The Men Involved* (New York, William Morrow & Co., 1931), p. 213.

A quick truce was called. The shorts were allowed "in" at 150. Within a week, trackage and directorship arrangements were worked out. In November, the huge, antagonistic holdings were merged into yet another giant holding company, euphemistically labeled the Northern Securities Company.

The market, of course, had quickly fixed on other worries. A terrible drought stirred up a brief "corn panic." In early September, President Mc-Kinley was shot by an anarchist while in Buffalo and died on the 13th; Vice-President Theodore Roosevelt succeeded. Major steel companies were struck. Copper prices dropped.

Amalgamated Copper, bloated to 130 early in the year, had hoarded a staggering inventory of actuals, holding out for 17 cents a pound. The market proved disagreeable and the copper disgorgement dropped Amalgamated to 61 in December. Meanwhile, the Dow Industrials had completed a mini-peak in June after an advance of but nine months.

Amalgamated's large price drop distorted the narrow, 12-stock Industrial index. If the 20-stock average adopted in 1916 is worked back (through its substitutions) to the 1901–1902 period, one will find that the high point for the industrial sector, based on that broader reading, came in 1902.

General Electric, exiled from the Dow in early 1901, would have helped. It did not peak until 1902, at a price of 334, up from a 1901 low at 184. Its sales had increased from $11 million in 1896, when it sold for 20, to $42 million.

Thanks to the Northern Securities consolidation, the Rails were suddenly perceived as a growth industry. A "new era" would see cut-throat competition contained, it was felt. The Rails' upward divergence from the Dow would continue until September 1902. The Pennsylvania was thus encouraged to buy heavily into B&O, the C&O (where control was jointly held with the New York Central), and the Norfolk & Western. Edward Harriman early in 1901 had broadened the Union Pacific's western community of interest by buying control of the Southern Pacific from the Huntington estate.

It had been a long and prosperous move for those rail speculators willing to buy a ticket in the summer of 1896. Santa Fe reached 94, up from 9. The Rock Island was a 49–230 winner. The St. Paul was up eight times while the the shares of the Norfolk & Western, a noted 1893 failure, steamed up from ⅛ to 81.

On the industrial side, the period had marked the high point of the trustification of America. The peak of consolidations had come in 1899, when such famous names as American Woolen, Bigelow Carpets, Borden, United Fruit, and Union Bag & Paper were born in mostly horizontal amalgamations of companies in the same line of business. In terms of capitalization, the huge steel and tobacco amalgamations made 1901 the top year. International Harvester, put together by Morgan in 1902, was the last great and successful merger of the period.

In the fall of 1902, money tightened and the economy was slowed by a tortuous coal strike which was finally settled only through the intervention of the president. The Northern Securities Company came under attack from Washington and the Minnesota Attorney-General. Prosperity and the trust cycle had peaked. But it had been a splendid advance, one whose dimensions would not be improved until the 1930s. Figure 3-1 shows the long advance, a gain of 209 percent from the Silver Crisis low of 1896.

The Road to 1929
DJIA Aug 24, 1921–Sep 3, 1929: 63.90 to 381.17, +497%.

In the summer of 1921, it was sadly evident that the blossoming of the twentieth century had somehow bypassed the stock market.

The Dow Rail Average was just where it had been in the summer of 1898. Industrial indices were only slightly higher than at the turn of the century. (The Dow's level was distorted by the revisions of 1916.) An Exchange membership sold, in 1921, for something less than its peak value of 1901 and the year's volume would be far below the annual average posted in the first decade of the century.

The dismal state of affairs on Wall Street was paradoxical in view of the industrial boom during the century's first two decades. Automobile production had exploded from 4,100 hand-assembled units to over 2 million in 1920. Nearly 14 million telephones were hooked up versus 1 million in 1900. The gross national product had tripled.

A continuation of amazing economic statistics would enrich the market in the 1920s. Its prosperity would be boosted by a catch-up for its lag of the 1906–1921 period. A legendary advance, the biggest and longest in history, was about to begin. It would push the Industrials up by 497 percent; no other bull market has approached that figure.

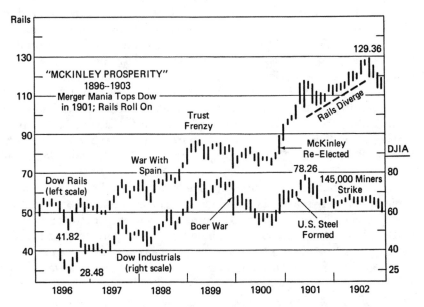

Figure 3.1 Dow Industrials versus Dow Rails, 1896–1902

In the autumn of 1921, good crops, lower interest rates, increasing employment, and an end to deflation and inventory liquidation helped end the depression. By April of the following year, the Dow was back over 100, having gained 56 percent in eight months. Detroit's comeback was even stronger, for America's passionate love affair with the auto was back on track.

The Detroit Ripple

The ripple of Detroit's boom would sweep across every industry, creating a prodigious industrial tidal wave.

> During the roaring twenties, auto production regularly absorbed one-fifth of the yearly production of steel, one-quarter of the machine tools, three-quarters of the sheet glass production and four-fifths of the rubber industry's output.
>
> And, of course, the total output of scores of entirely new auto-created industries— batteries, spark plugs, carburetors, frames, axles, to list only a handful—poured into the car plants.[3]

U.S. Steel, the nation's largest corporation, would become No. 2 in sales in 1926, falling to General Motors.

Consumerism spread beyond the auto showrooms. Vacuum sweepers, motion picture palaces, radios, tractors, and electric ice boxes tempted the public. Electric was a buzz word, adored by the stock market and consumers. General Electric, 28 in 1921, would advance to 403 in 1929, after adjusting for the 1926 split.

Even light bulbs were part of the consumer boom. Moody's calculated that by 1929, 70 percent of the population was living in electric-lighted dwellings. In 1920, 70 percent of the population was still using kerosene lamps.

If 1921–1923 was a heady period for the auto makers, it didn't do much for General Motors. In the latter year, the industry became the largest industrial section of the nation, supplanting the steels, but General Motors, at its best price was only 17½. The dividend had been excised in 1922, when the stock made its all-time low at 8¼. Studebaker, on the other hand, had skipped from 38 to 142 in its 1920–1923 recovery. William C. Durant had formed Durant Motors after being ousted from General Motors and his heavily promoted shares outperformed GM, rushing up from 10 to 84. They would fall to 4 in 1926.

There would be two pauses in the long road to the 1929 heights. The first came in 1923 when a mild depression cost the Dow about 19 percent in a seven-month period. The economy had become overheated from the auto boom, and the FRB had upped the discount rate by a half, to 4.5 percent. The reoccupation of the Ruhr by French and Belgium troops in January had been poorly received.

Despite the economic setback in 1923, Detroit's sales were an extraordi-

---

[3]Stephen W. Sears, *The American Heritage History of the Automobile in America* (New York: American Heritage Publishing Co., Inc.) 1977, p. 190.

nary 3.625 million units, up over 2 million from the 1921 level. The enormous increase had been spurred by price cuts, a lesson since forgotten, an ardent public, the growing acceptance of installment sales, and a large export demand.

Auto sales lagged in 1924, but the market was stable until late in the year when the Republican election victory drove the market sharply higher and above the 1919 peak. The highly successful "Coolidge Market" was under way.

For both the autos and market, 1925 was a splendid year. The Dow neared 160 in October and in the same month NYSE volume broke the venerable record established in 1901, at the time of the great Rail mania. General Motors, with a 1:4 reverse split, brought price creditability back to its shares, which climbed to 150, or 37½ on the old stock.

The first frightening break in the long advance gripped the market in February 1926. The Dow fell 17 percent between February 11 and March 30 and two consecutive days in early March saw volume over 3 million shares, a new experience for floor brokers. The drastic decline was followed by a new high in August, but it would be May 1927 before the Dow was ready for another fast lap.

By December of that year, the Dow was over 200 and the Rails, after a very long haul, had finally been able to overcome their 1906 peak.

The Beginning of the Top

In retrospect, the 1921–1929 market seems easy. There were, however, severe disappointments, like the Durant. Many other independent auto producers peaked in 1924–1925. The building boom crested in 1925, along with some component stocks. Commodity types had a difficult time after 1924 when such issues as American Beet Sugar and American Hide & Leather topped.

More important, the oil group suffered early stagnation. Union Oil of California hit its high in 1926. Richfield, Shell, and Standard of Ohio reached their high marks in 1928. Excess output was the problem. Venezuela and Mexico were pushing output. Iraq had an enormous discovery. West Texas was proving a treasure house with such discoveries as the great Yates pool, source of Marathon's riches. It was still a rich producer when the firm was bought out by U.S. Steel. Titans of the "Seven Sisters," the great international oils, met secretly at Ancharry Castle, Scotland, in 1928 for a bit of hunting and salmon fishing. Such "merriment and diversion," as Adam Smith had warned, often worked to the public's disadvantage.

But the oil spigot could not be shut down. Crude prices in the United States in 1928–1929 were far below the levels of 1924–1926. Coal shares had lost relative strength to the market for years. Retailers also had a difficult time in improving on their 1926 results and Kress, May, Safeway, and Sears peaked in 1928.

Wall Street had no difficulty in finding new darlings, however. In 1927, Charles Lindberg soloed the Atlantic. His craft, the *Spirit of St. Louis,* was powered by a Wright engine. Wright shares flew up 27 points the day after the

---

FEW FOREIGN ENTANGLEMENTS

In 1927, the NYSE began an aggressive program to attract foreign listings. Only four foreign internal securities were on the Board, all in the form of ADRs.

But if New York thought that it could replace London as the great international exchange, it would be disappointed. Thousands of foreign listings had been traded in London for decades and would continue to find a home there, whether they be tea plantations in Ceylon, tin workings in Malaysia, or diamond mines in South Africa.

By 1933, the Exchange had netted only eight European issues and none from Central or South America, Asia, Australasia, or Africa. Only a handful of good neighbor listings from Canada, Cuba, and the sugar islands had been added.

---

flight. Valued at 25 early in 1927, the shares would outfly "Lindy," reaching 289 in the following year.

Big bull speculators like Livermore, Durant, Meehan, Cutten, and the Fisher brothers ramrodded the market. The Fisher brothers had become even richer in 1926 when they sold the balance of their famed body works to General Motors.

Radio Corporation was a symbol of the great times. It was a natural bull leader for a public ecstatic over the future of a device which could bring free entertainment—baseball, comedians, preachers, even politicians—into every room of the home. Sales of radio apparatus and tubes in 1927 was 20 times the dollar amount of 1920. And RCA, with a great deal of undercover muscle, did better. At 41 in the spring of 1927 (already up fourfold after a reverse split), it would rise to 420 in December 1928. Its final high in September 1929 would be 574 before adjusting for the 5:1 split of that year.

A frantic pace in 1928 shoved the Dow up to 296 following the election of Herbert Hoover to the White House. The November volume would be the largest of the entire bull market. A frightening and ominous week in early December sliced the Dow by nearly 12 percent and ushered in six months of vicious volatility. Radio dropped from over 400 to 298 in just three days of the December slaughter.

The Final Convulsions

The bull market of 1929 was just a summer romance. On the 27th of May, the Dow at 293.42 was within one-tenth point of its close on November 30, 1928, despite many violent moves in each direction during the interim. The "great"

1929 bull market lasted barely 90 days, and advanced the Dow 30 percent to the September high.

In the meantime, a frightening glut of new underwriting had been pressed upon the public and almost like thieves in the night a few market leaders had been stealing away from the general celebration.

Chrysler peaked in January and General Motors in late March, along with the leading coppers, Anaconda and Kennecott. Such diverse Dow Industrial members as National Cash Register and International Nickel also recorded their 1929 highs in the first quarter.

The stock market had lagged the twentieth-century blossoming of productivity in America for two decades, but by the late 1920s even modest earnings increases were being over-rewarded in terms of the price-earnings multiple.

General Motors in 1926 had sold for less than 5 times earnings. In the same year, Du Pont, IBM, and National Dairy were all available at less than 7 times earnings. Each sold for over 20 times earnings in 1929. R. H. Macy (Macy's) had earned $4.39 in 1926 and by 1929 had boosted the bottom line over 50 percent to $6.70. The stock rose from 29 to 256, a rather splendid markup for a retailer of modestly-priced lines. Many utilities were valued near 35 times earnings and the biggest and most powerful banks at a multiple of 50X.

And while fundamentals were becoming overpriced on the Street, there were warnings from overseas. Foreign markets had topped in the spring of 1929, or earlier. Berlin's peak had come in 1927.

Obviously the summer rally of 1929 was on thin ice, but that seemed only to add to its excitement. The Dow sped up from 297 at the end of May to 381 on the first trading day of September. This despite the fact that the Cleveland Trust had shown in August that more issues were down than up for the year.

At the peak, the Dow was priced at over 19 times its probable earnings for the year. The new Dow Utility index, first computed in 1929, was at 25 times earnings. The Dow's church steeple top left little time for second guessing, as can be seen in Figure 3-2.

Investment trusts were the final madness. The formation and sale of them became an end in itself. Capital was being raised for the packaging of mutual funds and investment trusts rather than for new plants and equipment.

Many trusts became hot issues, selling at huge premiums to net asset value. Shenandoah was offered at $17.50 in late July and raced to 42 the same day, a mutual fund record. The public was buried with $640 million in new issues in September, including a million shares of Lehman Corp. at 104. It was the final madness. "Professional Management" would take decades to recover its reputation.

If the public was trapped by overpricing and overpromotion, the snare was set by low-margin trading. A few thousand dollars used to purchase stock on 10 percent margin will create a loose-cannon effect in a moderate sea, and a financial typhoon of heroic proportions lay just over the horizon.

There would be little warning of heavy weather save by those who, like

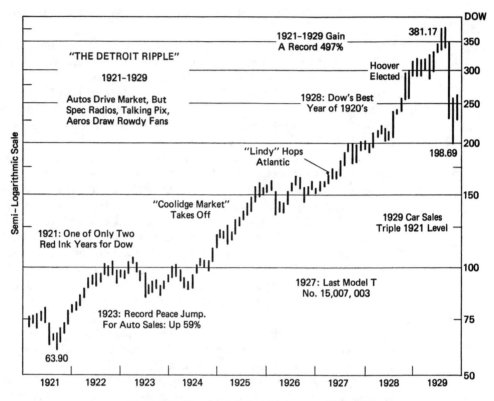

Figure 3.2 Dow Jones Industrial Average, 1921–1929

Roger Babson, had cried "wolf" before. The watch ended on September 3, 1929, with the Dow at 381.17, having lasted for eight years and 11 days through 2,402 trading sessions. The Dow was valued at 19.2 times the ernings it would post for the year. The dividend yield, after the declaration of many fall extras, would turn out to have been 3.3 percent.

FDR & Hope
DJIA Jly 8, 1932–Mar 10, 1937: 41.22 to 194.40, +372%.

Prosperity was not just around the corner when the stock market reached its great bear market low in July 1932. The economic statistics would darken further in 1933, when there would be 4,000 bank suspensions (Iowa had the most) versus 1,453 in 1932. In 1933, only six railroad passenger cars would be manufactured. There had been nearly 2,500 made in 1929.

In June of 1932, it had seemed there was no money and less hope. By mid-July, there was a sudden frenzy of hope and even some money. "Some" was all it took.

For $1,000, a speculator could buy a diversified portfolio made up of corporate names famous then and now. Abbott Labs, Allied Stores, Black &

Decker, Maytag, McGraw-Hill, Phillips Petroleum, and Zenith Radio, among many others, sold between 50 cents and $2.50 a share that summer. Railroads like the Milwaukee, Chicago North Western, Katy, and Nickel Plate were in the same price class. A $1,000 portfolio could have included four or five 100 share holdings.

If nearly one quarter of the American work force was unemployed, three out of four were working. Value sold cheap and speculative hope suddenly surged. From its lowest point in modern history, 41.22 on July 8, 1932, the Industrials exploded to 79.92 on September 3. The Rails streaked to an incredible gain of nearly 200% in the same period. That advance, in percentage terms, was larger than the entire 1921–1929 success of the senior average.

The excitement was greatest in August, when volume in the second week exceeded the monthly total for any of the previous three months. In the long history of the Exchange, no bull/bear reversal has enjoyed such fireworks.

If speculation proved itself alive and well in the late summer of 1932, there were also some tremendous fundamentals arguing for the market. Scores of well-known names sold for less than their net current assets; plants and physical assets came "free." Others were priced below their net cash per share. Dividends, if rare, were rich. AT&T, at 70, yielded nearly 13 percent on its $9 payout. Liggett & Myers (Chesterfield cigarettes) paid $5 and sold at 32.

But hope, not dividends, was the big catalyst for the summer run, and hope waned in the autumn. A huge binge of profit taking on October 5 collapsed prices, with the Rails down 11.1 percent having one of their worst days ever.

FDR was elected in November, an event viewed bearishly for a day or so before a quick recovery. But by February, bank failures, bank holidays, and fear of the unknown had dropped the Dow back to 50 from its September high at 79.93.

Michigan declared a bank holiday on February 14, 1933, and by March 2, state banking holidays were endemic. Illinois, New York, and other states joined the crowd on the night of Friday, March 3, just before the inauguration of FDR. The joys of the summer past were all forgotten.

On March 5, President Roosevelt declared a national bank holiday, embargoed gold and silver exports, and summoned Congress for a special session. Stock and commodity exchanges, barren without banks, closed.

Congress went to work stirring up an alphabet soup, and 1,500 banks were quickly reopened. On March 15, when the exchanges reopened, both the Industrials and Rails enjoyed a record "one-day" advance, up 15 percent for the former and nearly 18 percent for the carriers. Hope had returned, after the new president's first ten days.

A tumultuous 120 days were in store for the market and the nation. From the eve of FDR's term, the Dow doubled its value by mid-summer, 53.84 to 108.67. The Rails moved from 24.76 to 56.65. A huge amount of market hype involved the impending repeal of Prohibition.

The downfall of the 18th Amendment was esteemed to bring happiness to the working man, painless tax revenues, increased employment, and a better society. Mobsters, it was argued, would leave rum-running for honest employment.

These social improvements were not lost on the Exchange floor. Crown Cork & Seal, Owens-Illinois, and National Distillers were enthusiastically toasted. Owens went from 12 in 1932 to 97 in 1933 while Crown advanced from 8 to 65. National Distillers, which owned 50 percent of all the pre-prohibition whiskey, was a "pure play" and leaped from 17 to 125 in the first seven months of 1933. A whiskey pool added to the excitement during the same period, running the shares of American Commercial Alcohol from 13 to 90. Joseph Kennedy, who would become the first SEC Commissioner in the following year, was active in the alcohol and other 1933 manipulations.

The repeal bash got rather out of hand and, inevitably, led to a nasty hangover from July's high point at 108.67, which also marked the year's peak. The "distillers' panic" of July sobered the market quickly, the Dow falling 18 percent in three days. National Distillers dropped from 125 to 66; it would not celebrate 125 again until the end of World War II.

Gold's Price Increased

Bold initiatives and spending programs by Washington helped but did not cure the economy's sickness. Since commodity and farm price inflation was seen as a commendable goal, it was decided to puff up gold's price and see what hap-

---

GOLD "PRICE JIGGLING" AT FDR'S BEDSIDE

One of President Roosevelt's economic objectives was a reflation of commodities to the 1926 price level. Tinkering with the price of gold was one tool.

Citizens had been isolated from their gold and gold-clause contracts by presidential decree and the direction of bullion prices was taken over in October 1933 by the Reconstruction Finance Corporation (RFC).

There was no formula for setting gold's price, outside a strong upward bias, but it was done on a daily basis. The "fix" reached $33.05 in November and $34.01 in early December versus the former value at $20.67.

Jesse Jones, head of the RFC wrote of the "price jiggling" at the White House gold fixing, which occurred each morning.

". . . The President turned to me and said, 'Jess, you and Henry (Morganthau) drop by my bedroom in the morning and we'll fix the price of gold.' "[4] And so they did, finally setting it at $35 on January 31, 1934. Over a period of 11 months the dollar had been devalued to 59.06 cents.

---

[4]Jesse H. Jones with Edward Angly, *Fifty Billion Dollars, My Thirteen Years with the RFC (1932–1945)* (New York: The Macmillan Company, 1951), p. 248.

pened. Formerly at $20.67, it was racheted upward during the autumn of 1933, finally being fixed at $35 in January 1934. The escalating price was fixed by the President and its momentous progress had a delightful informality, as noted by Jesse Jones, head of the RFC.

The large summer-to-summer market advance of 1932–1933 had brought stocks back to decent levels. Deep fear had left and quality issues performed well. Du Pont was a solid winner, 22 to 104. Speculative issues were often remarkable; American Car & Foundry increased tenfold. The Dow reached 111 in February 1934 but then turned flat. Construction and steel output fell sharply. Volume slumped from the heady levels of 1933. In the summer of 1935, the Industrials finally marched on through the 110 barrier, which had posed such a difficult target, and the Rails ended their private bear market, which had begun at the rally peak in July 1933.

They had lost over 50 percent of their value as the Industrials consolidated. The long divergence was caused by continued red ink for the industry. Over 29,000 miles of road entered receivership or bankruptcy in 1935; the 1933 figure had been 21,222. The sizzling rally of 1933 had done too much, too soon for the Rails.

The New Haven, for example, 6 in 1932, reached 35 in 1933 and then fell back to 3 in 1935. Its high in 1929 had been 133.

Great speculation and volume swept into the market in early 1936 and in March, margin requirements were raised to 55 percent, the first change since FRB control. Despite disturbing foreign events, like Hitler's reoccupation of the Rhineland, widespread domestic labor disturbances, sit-down strikes, and John L. Lewis, the market struggled higher. Higher for Homestake was 544, as it reached the end of its great gold rush. An 8:1 split took it out of the stratosphere.

New Highs Over 1929

With the Rails nearly back to their 1933 top, 1936 ended with a strong tone. Many stocks began to peak in this period, most notably the autos. General Motors reached 77, a long ride from its low of 7⅝ in 1932, but rationalized by its new market dominance.

The most exciting stocks, however, had been those capable of flying above their 1929 highs. Douglas Aircraft, Phillips Petroleum, and Philip Morris were among them. The tobacco company posted a great success story in the 1930s. Sales of less than $3 million smoked up to $73 million in 1939. The voice of "Johnny" and his "Call for Philip Morris" radio commercial were heard around the country. By 1937, the $1 dividend basis of 1932, when the stock sold at 8, had increased to nearly $11 and the shares were up 1,250 percent. Coca-Cola (Figure 3-3) had also shown dramatic growth.

Other remarkable gains were achieved, even by those stocks that never approached the 1929 peaks. Wright Aero advanced from 4 to 141 and Youngstown Sheet & Tube from 4 to 102. Square D was a sensation, rising from 50 cents to 90 cents.

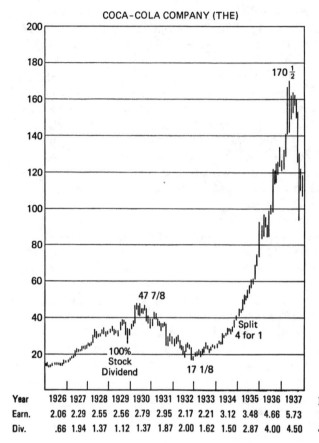

Year   1926 1927 1928 1929 1930 1931 1932 1933 1934 1935 1936 1937
Earn. 2.06 2.29 2.55 2.56 2.79 2.95 2.17 2.21 3.12 3.48 4.66 5.73
Div.   .66 1.94 1.37 1.12 1.37 1.87 2.00 1.62 1.50 2.87 4.00 4.50

Figure 3.3 Coca-Cola: Superstar of the 1930s (*Source: M.C. Horsey & Company, Salisbury, MD*)

Though the distillery and brewery new issues which had been unloaded on the public in the post-Prohibition boom had proven tasteless, the container business had continued its boom. Owens-Illinois, 12 in 1932, rose to 208 in 1937. Earnings had not kept pace with that rapture, however, and after a 2:1 split, the shares would fall back to 40 in 1938.

Fed Brakes

In January 1937, the Federal Reserve Board put the brakes on the overheated economy, tightening Reserve requirements, and the bull market lasted barely six weeks longer, despite some modest new excitement for the Rails. It had been a remarkable success, however, up 372 percent (Figure 3-4) in continuing depression circumstances.

On March 10, almost exactly four years after FDR's inauguration, the stock market peaked at 194.40, with a minimal amount of excitement by standards of past market successes.

As the NYSE bulletin of July 1937 complained, "The volume of transactions on the exchange in relation to the shares listed has experienced practi-

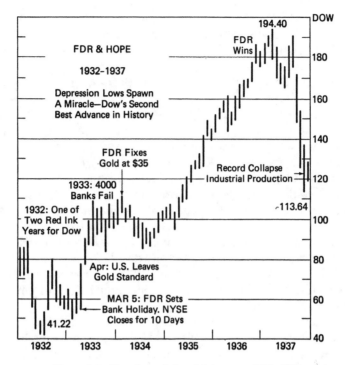

Figure 3.4 Dow Jones Industrial Average, 1932–1937

cally no net recovery from the low points of the depression . . . current turnover is only a fraction of that prevailing in the past."[5]

Born with a Silver Spoon
DJIA Jne 13, 1949–Apr 6, 1956: 161.60–521.05, +222%

The unique 1949–1956 bull market was born with a silver spoon, not spawned in the barrios of glum economic statistics, like most of its sisters. It fell immediate heir to record Dow earnings, higher even than in 1929, and rich dividends.

"Wolf" had been the cry for three years. Masochistic investors, determined to suffer the "inevitable" postwar depression, had chosen to ignore the dramatic improvement in corporate fundamentals which had taken place since the start of World War II.

A classic bear trap was sprung in June 1949. A miniscule new low, which alarmed a legion of Dow theorists, dropped the Industrials to the level of August 1945, just before the first atom bomb. But the market shrugged off the technical threat and within two months was back over 180. It was finally ready to capitalize on good news and ignore bad news—such as the nationwide steel strike.

In late December, the Dow reached 200, then a magic figure, in a month

---

[5]New York Stock Exchange Bulletin, Vol. VIII, No. 7, July, 1937, p. 1, col. 1.

which saw NYSE volume double the June figure. By April 1950, the average had topped its 1946 victory high and was at the highest level in 20 years. Optimism swelled, only to be crushed by the shocking outbreak of the Korean War in late June.

On June 27 a great selling wave, with the largest volume since September 1939, swept over the market. The sharp decline ended in mid-July, a setback of 13.5 percent. It was one of only two severe tests in the entire six-year advance.

The Korean War guaranteed a return of heavy defense spending and the continuance of a busy industrial sector. The stock market, a postwar laggard to the nation's huge increase in productive capacity, would begin to catch up. Earnings would increase sharply for most groups, but the appreciation of those earnings would accelerate even faster.

In October, General Douglas MacArthur's leapfrog invasion of Inchon encouraged new highs and the market closed the year at 235, despite the Chinese hordes pouring south across the Yalu River from Manchuria.

The new bull market had already developed a strong following. Exchange volume in 1950 was the largest since 1933 and nearly double the 1949 figure. Prices would work slowly higher in 1951 and 1952, but both momentum and activity would decline.

In January 1953, concern about recession and lower earnings resurfaced. Rails, drugs, and textiles turned weak, though the strong leaders of the previous years such as aircrafts, oils, and rubbers, among others, only paused.

Bristol-Myers and Parke Davis, in an extraordinary move among quality drugs, both reduced dividends and lost about 50 percent of their peak values. Other dividend slicers included such well-regarded firms as Beatrice Foods, Black & Decker, Crane, Pepperell, J. C. Penney, and Masonite. American Smelting, which had peaked in January 1952, would cut its dividend three years in a row; it fell from 52 to 26 before turning, with the market, in late 1953. Chrysler's payout had peaked in 1950, but its stock price of 62 in the summer of that year would rise to 98 in December 1952, the last strong month of the first segment of the long advance.

The stagnation and correction that then overtook the market lasted until April 1954. Upward momentum then returned and the Dow crested 300—its precise closing level of 1928. By August, volume was pouring into the Exchange. There was only one session in the month when trading fell below 2 million shares. In the entire summer of 1953, there had only been two days with volume over that figure. Laggard groups turned strong after the mild recession of 1953. Pittston Coal, quiet during the early 1950s, would run from 18 to 84 in its 1953–1957 move.

Superior Oil, the highest-priced stock at the NYSE, became pricier. It first crossed 600 in 1953 and would touch 2000 in 1957, when many industrial groups made their bull market highs, having extended the Dow's rise by over a year. Aircrafts were strong leaders during the entire period, also. Douglas had fallen to 49 in 1949, though boasting working capital of $91 per share. It would sell at 571 (unadjusted for three stock splits) in 1956.

Alcoa, Kaiser Aluminum, and Reynolds all took part in a spectacular climb for the specialty metals. Reynolds moved from 4 to 85. Kaiser, which had lagged early on, suffered only minor corrections from 1953 to 1956 as it spurted from 7 to 70. Papers also boomed and St. Regis was a tenfold winner, 6 to 60.

The market was vastly encouraged by a record number of stock splits, given more approbation by the public than they deserved.

Market giants that split their shares at least *twice* and at least 2:1 on each occasion included such diverse names as American Electric Power, Alcoa, American Can, American Cyanamid, General Motors, and Standard Oil of New Jersey. There were scores more.

The storied Santa Fe railroad split 2:1 in 1951 and 5:1 in 1956. The patient buyer of 100 shares in 1949 when the yield was 10 percent ended up with 1,000 shares. Price-adjusted, the shares rose from 8 to 35 in the period.

Acute excitement visited the market in November 1954 when the Dow crossed its 1929 high, 381.17. Trading heated up in both December 1954 and January 1955 as monthly volume approached 100 million shares, the highest level since 1933. The year of 1954 remains the Dow's best since 1933, up 44 percent. Crowded boardrooms and soaring mutual fund sales confirmed the public's new-found fascination with the equity market.

Congress opted to share in the limelight and the Fulbright Committee was convened to study Street activities. In March 1955, Professor John K. Galbraith, a perennially bearish scholar of the 1929 crash, testified before the committee and urged that margins be increased to 100 percent. In another disappointment, interest rates tightened during the summer and in August, the broker loan rate went to 3.5 percent, the highest level since 1931.

Still, the market did not slow until late September, when President Dwight D. Eisenhower suffered a severe heart attack in Denver. It occurred on the weekend, and when the NYSE opened on Monday, it faced the worst crisis day since 1929. Leaders fell from four to eight points with the NYSE list losing about $14 billion in market value, compared to the estimated $16 billion lost on October 29, 1929. Volume of 7,717,000 was the highest since 1929. Both Eisenhower and the market recuperated rapidly and the Dow ended 1955 at the absolute peak of the year, 488.40, up 21 percent for the period.

The early years of the 1950s remain arguably the best since World War II. Employment was high and work stoppages low. Inflation had waned after the Korean War and was actually a negative figure in 1955, a year that auto output set a record. The boom helped Washington to several budget surpluses.

The prime rate had remained between 3 percent and 3.25 percent from December 1951 until late 1955. There were few speculative excesses in the market, considering its duration and substantial gains.

March 1956 saw the Dow surpass the 500 milestone and in April, the index scored its bull market high of 521.05. Many strong groups, however, would not peak until December or even until the summer of 1957. The Dow Industrials worked out a rare triple-top in 1956–57; it is seen in Figure 3-5.

Shares had finally outrun their immediate prospects. A price-earnings multiple of 7X for the Dow in 1949 had more than doubled. The average had gained 222 percent, but earnings were up only 42 percent.

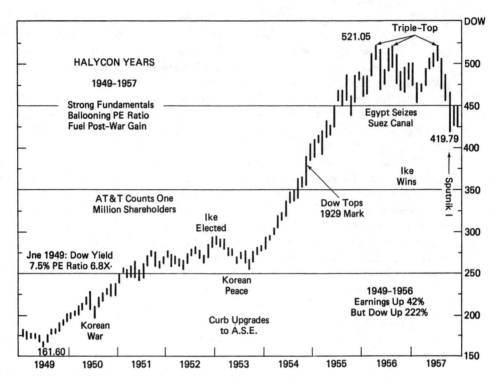

Figure 3.5   Dow Jones Industrial Average, 1949–1957

Du Pont provides an excellent example of the PE puffery. Seen as a classic blue chip at the time, the stock had sold at 43 in 1949 on earnings of $4.53. By 1955, the earnings had doubled to $9.26. The blue chip had been worth 10 times earnings in 1949; at 250 in 1955, it was valued at 27 times earnings.

It was time for a rest. The long advance had been second in duration only to the 1921–1929 marathon.

Single Digit Financials
DJIA Aug 12, 1982–Jly 16, 1990: 776.92 to 2999.75, +286%.

The longest economic advance in history made the bull market of the 1980s into a super star. Only the extravaganzas of the 1920s and 1930's outshone it, but they did so by a wide margin. Dow 4630 would have been required in 1990 to match the great 1921–1929 record.

Single-digit financials ramrodded the Dow's third greatest advance. The Fed's discount rate, 12 percent in 1982, stood at 5.5 percent in 1986. In the same year, the annual CPI rate stood at barely 1 percent; it had been 12.5 percent in 1980. With the inflation haircut removed, improving earnings were given higher esteem and price multiples mushroomed.

Gasoline lines disappeared and crude oil prices slumped into the 'teens, benefitting industry, consumers, and cost-of-living indices.

In its marathon run, the 1980s' market was fueled by falling energy prices, huge mergers, leveraged buyouts (LBOs), corporate raids, and enormous stock buy-back programs. It all managed to keep the populace and the Street's bankers and lawyers in a high state of excitement, along with the SEC.

Along the way, the Dow Industrials, locked between 575 and 1050 since 1965, broke their chains and began a massive move to overtake an economy which had moved far ahead of the index.

In 1982, a recession year, the Dow earned $114 and paid a dividend of $54; its low was 777. The dividend amounted to more than the composite $46 earnings the average had posted in 1964, when the year's high had been nearly 900.

The massive advance of the 1980s started on August 13, 1982 with a starry-eyed hope that Henry Kaufman, Salomon's widely quoted interest rate expert, was correct in predicting a decline in rates. Hope quickly turned to fact.

August's reversal was awarded a heroic start. The NYSE had never recorded a 100-million share day previously. By the end of the month, there had been five century-breakers and the Dow had gained 16 percent in just 13 trading days. Four cuts in the discount rate between July 20 and August 27 had been the convincers.

The first leg of the market lasted until the following July, spurred by the further rate cuts and improving PE ratios.

Hottest issues in 1983 were the small technology stocks and the Street helped feed the addiction by increasing stock offerings tenfold during the year. For many of the high techs, the bull market was already finished. International Rectifier, leading tech gainer at the NYSE—up 243 percent in 1983 and plus 357 percent at one time—had already reached its bull market high.

Strong cyclical stocks, like the motors and steels, helped the 1983 record, but their performance could not equal that of the popular brokerage stocks. Merrill Lynch and many others, curiously, would record their best prices of the decade in 1983. Merrill had gained 438 percent from the 1982 low.

Though many indices tripped in the summer, the Dow moved smartly ahead to a yearly high at 1287 in November, up 66 percent in 15 months. The giddy list of big winners encouraged some advisers to focus on a 1929 repeat. Banking problems had already surfaced and the introduction of options on stock indices added one more dangerous game for speculators.

But 1984 turned out to be neither bull nor bear, only an uneventful correction of about 200 Dow points, a small enough price to pay after an advance of 510 points since 1982. First-half weakness was followed by a stout rally in August and a sideways movement for the balance of the year. A final count showed the Dow with a 47-point loss, though the NYSE and S&P indices both ended higher.

Biggest excitement during the year had come from the frenzied battle for control of some legendary energy companies. Analysts claimed that the country's cheapest oil was on Wall Street and Getty, Gulf, and Superior were all bought out in record-sized deals. But such frenetic merger activity, along with other indicators, caused Joe Granville to write "The Warning," not his first alarum of the period.*

A Perfect "5"

In every year of this century which ends with "5" the stock market has advanced, and 1985 followed the pattern perfectly, with a solid gain of 28 percent. Gold fell back below $300, interest rates continued to decline and merger mania increased. A continued restraint in inflation and energy prices provoked great confidence.

The Fed cut the discount rate to 7.5 percent in May, putting it at its lowest level since 1978 and bonds continued their extraordinary gains, aided by large foreign purchases. Food issues, not oils, were the big merger targets, with R. J. Reynolds taking over Nabisco and Philip Morris grabbing General Foods. As the year ended, the fever was spreading. Carl Icahn was dogging TWA and GE had its sights again set on RCA, which it had once previously controlled after World War I.

Street consensus was that the huge stock buy-backs and merger activity would subside in 1986, and there were doubts that the strong consumer performance of the previous year could be maintained. Specialty retailers in 1985 had been a standout, led by the Gap, up 204 percent, Jewelcor, and Limited. Oil service firms had again run into disaster. Global Marine and McDermott International preferred shares were among the the biggest losers at the Exchange.

Oil Smash Fuels Stocks

The collapse of oil prices in January 1986 helped fuel a buyers' panic. First-half January weakness was reversed and in February the Industrials gained a record 138 points. The high-volume surge continued through March. West Texas intermediate crude, meanwhile, was being smashed down from $26 to near $10, and the enormous weakness in a vital industrial and consumer commodity provided a strong base to the bull arguments. The Dow raced by milestones at 1600, 1700, and 1800 during the first quarter.

With oil near $10, experts were quick to predict a further drop of $5 but a strong rally pushed prices back up, only to see a renewed selling drive in July, when North Sea crude fell to $8.25.

The crumbling oil prices pushed inflation fears to the sidelines and the Fed was able to reduce interest rates; by summer, the discount was at 5.5 percent, its lowest level in nine years. In the meantime, a weak dollar was making U.S. shares attractive to foreign buyers, whose purchases during the year would total about four times the previous record of 1981.

America's air attack on Libya and Russia's Chernobyl tragedy, both in April, had only a short impact on prices, but in May accusations of insider

---

*Joseph Granville, *The Warning, the Coming Great Crash in the Stock Market* (New York, Freundlich Books, 1985).

trading against Dennis Levine would launch the Street's worst regulatory ordeal in 25 years.

It was a year, at least in the second half, for blue chips and not secondary issues. Tobaccos were a lead group, but Merck powered the Dow average. A number of famous old names—Sperry, Associated Dry Goods, Safeway, Allied Stores—were swept up in the merger race. Despite another great year, the market took some hard hits. A record knock on the Dow in July raised eyebrows, but in September following a discount rate cut, the Dow was levered up to a new high.

All seemed right for the bulls until a stunning 87-point drop on September 11 blind-sided New York. Ivan Boesky and Drexel Burnham's junk bond activities and the consequences of a new tax bill would occupy the financial press for the balance of the year.

Giants IBM and General Motors paired again as large cap losers in the Dow, and fabled Bethlehem Steel fell to a historic low, down 60 percent for the year, amidst Chapter 11 rumors.

The footsteps heard at year end at Wall & Broad were those of the Tokyo Stock Exchange. By the end of 1987, it would replace New York as the world's largest.

The Dow close in 1986 had been uncharacteristically sloppy, at the low of the month. But the January bull came on with a most stunning explosion, a buyers' panic which broke record after record.

Days of 200-million shares were common. On January 23, over 302 million shares were traded. For 13 consecutive days, the Industrials closed higher. The milestone at Dow 2000 got only a nod, and 2100 was passed 11 days later. By the end of March, Dow 2200 and 2300 had been topped.

Bears claimed one huge victory, however. On "witching day," January 23, the Industrial average, having been up 64 points, hit a terrible air pocket, falling to a loss for the day of 44 points. It was the first 100-point drop for the average, although it did not make the record book because of its intraday nature.

1929 Clone?

Impressive as the winter surge was, it only encouraged skeptics. Many of them idled away their computer time by constructing 1982–1987 Dow charts in comparison with the 1920s. The similarities were strong enough to attract a wide following of the fearsome. A 1929 clone, they said, was in the making.

But overpowering summer strength led to capitulation by the bears. Dow 3500, a famous forecast target of Robert Prechter, suddenly seemed quite reasonable and latter-day bulls leapfrogged the figure with estimates of Dow 4000.

In July Dow 2500 was easily passed and in August, the average whistled by 2600 and 2700. Notorious post-Labor Day action of previous years was forgotten under the heady influence of worldwide momentum for equities. Tokyo's astronomical price-earnings ratios made American shares seem conservative.

On August 25, the Dow reached a peak at 2722.42, up 25.35. Blue chips coughed up their gains the next day, with IBM, suddenly unpopular, the most active stock at the Board, losing sharply to close at 168.

Even before Labor Day, the Dow was hard hit, down to 2561, and the swift retreat raised the possibility of a 10 percent correction for the market. The Dow had not suffered such a reaction since July 1984, a record time span for such bearish immunity.

But if the corrida was almost over, the bullish forces were not going to be led off docilely. Dow 2500 intraday was struck, then back to 2600. A close under 2500 on September 21 seemed frightening but on the following day, the biggest point advance in history was recorded with the Dow up 75.23. Bullish hopes were regained and the Dow shot back up to 2641 on October 2.

In the meantime, the bond market continued to unravel, as did the dollar. The prime had jumped to 9.25 percent from 7.5 percent in late spring. By October 13, the Dow had slipped to 2508, but was still 15 points above the low of September. In Japan, the Tokyo Stock Exchange was celebrating record highs.

The Panic of 1987, which threatened to meltdown the nation's financial structure, would begin the next day. It would last for but five trading days.

Once again the October-battered market spent the balance of the year in a highly nervous state. Many averages, including the Transports, dropped to a new low in early December, but the Dow resisted and by a sort of artificial miracle, managed to close the year with a slight gain.

A Public Disenchantment

In 1932, at the bottom of the nation's worst depression, stock buyers herded into the market when finally given some hope that better prices lay ahead. In January 1975, after a market experience akin to the 1930s, "cat and dog" buyers rushed for the many really low-priced bargains. They would profit greatly over the next six months.

But the smash of 1987 turned the public away. Small investors either deserted the market or withdrew as gracefully as possible when they could get "almost even." The public was disenchanted with the stock market.

Skepticism and Treasury bills replaced the hope and equities sought at previous market bottoms. Customer funds rolled over into CDs and money funds. Brokerage houses had to turn to special "products" to meet the rent. Closed-end bond funds, real estate partnerships, annuities, and even low- or no-profit CDs were pushed to retain investor assets.

Commission houses tightened belts against the defections. And the high-flying investment bankers also took a hit. They were nailed by an enormous, over-priced underwriting—the U.K. sale of its British Petroleum shares. Syndicate losses were estimated to approach $200 million.

To the discomfiture of the professional bears and doom sayers, corporate earnings and dividends continued to expand in 1988. Tokyo provided world leadership for the bulls, and in April, the Tokyo Nikkei index burst over its 1987 top. The Nikkei magic, however, failed to work any bullish tricks in the American market, where the Dow's advance was but 12 percent for 1988.

LIKE A TORNADO IN THE NIGHT

Like a tornado in the night, the October rout smashed values with an assault of astonishing speed. On October 5, the Dow stood at 2604, only four percent below August's record peak. On Tuesday, October 13, at 2508, the Dow was still above its September low, despite a crumbling dollar and soaring interest rates.

Four days of unparalleled devastation lay ahead, days which would leave the world's financial markets splintered and crushed, as a trailer park might give way to a tornado. A disastrous trade deficit figure drove the market down 95 points on Wednesday. On the following day, the prime was hiked for the second time in five weeks and after early resistance, the Dow lost 53 points in the last half hour.

The market's best support, the merger game, was blind-sided by the increase in interest rates and a possible end to various tax perks. On Thursday, Secretary of Treasury James D. Baker threatened to send the dollar into freefall if German financial intransigence continued; European investors fled for their financial bunkers and the Dow fell 108 points on Friday.

Over the weekend, the news worsened. While New York slept during Monday's early morning hours, world markets were hammered, starting on the Pacific Rim. At the NYSE, the Dow's opening level was 200 points below Friday's close. Margin liquidation, a United States air attack on one of Iran's military platforms, unfettered program selling and fear that the SEC might shutter the Exchange led to the worst one-day panic in history.

With the tape over two hours late, the crippled Dow fell 220 points in the last hour, ending the day with a loss of 22.6 percent. Enormous damage had been dealt even the strongest blue chips. Coca-Cola was down 25 percent and Procter & Gamble a bit more. Exxon owners were stunned by a 31 percent drop.

But Monday's record 508 point collapse on 604 million shares had finally accomodated all the sellers. The panic was over. It had vaporized an estimated $500 billion in market values. "Meltdown," they would call it.

In the spring of 1989, the NWA (Northwest Airlines) LBO helped punch the Transports above their 1987 high. Feverish buying followed, as merger rumors flew around all the airlines. UAL, the parent company of United Airlines, was put in play, along with AMR (American Airlines) and the carrier average overflew the 1300, 1400, and 1500 milestones in August.

In the meantime the Dow managed to rise above its 1987 peak on August 24, a near-perfect second anniversay. September slippages was followed by a Dow peak on October 9 at 2791, but the Transports failed to confirm.

Its action lagged the Transports, however. UAL, the parent company of United Airlines, had been put in play, along with AMR, American Airlines, and the carrier average overflew the 1300, 1400, and 1500 milestones in August. Slippage in early September was followed by a new Dow peak on October 9 at 2791, but the Transports failed to confirm that strength.

A Frightful Anniversary

Fretful types were already worrying about the October malaise and the 1987 meltdown anniversary and their fears came into focus on Friday, October 13. The financing for the $300 share buy-out of United Airlines suddenly came unglued; the late-session announcement cost the Dow 134 points in the last hour. Trading was halted in both United Airlines and American, the latter a proposed takeover target by Donald Trump. Mergers and whispered mergers were suddenly seen as suspect credit risks, given the quicksands of the junkbond market.

Speculators and arbitrageurs dumped the lot, and a score of merger candidates were hacked up in the carnage. Hilton, which had volunteered that it might be had for a rich bid, dropped 20 percent to 85. Other diverse takeover stocks losing about 10 percent included U.S. Steel, Delta Airlines, Chevron, and Campbell Soup.

It all added up to history's second worst day for the Dow, down 191 points, to 2561, though the percentage decline of 6.9 percent was bearable. Alarmists predicted a rerun of 1987. But for most shares the Monday morning panic selling was quickly over. By the end of the day, the Dow was plus 88 points on volume of 416 million shares, and by the weekend, the average was near 2700, despite a plunging carrier index.

There was no quarter for the airlines. On October 16, UAL was down 50 points from Friday's frozen level at 280. Speculators forced out of the stock were lucky. By the weekend the shares had fallen to 165, as British Airways denied any further interest in the deal. Donald Trump disappointed his groupies by opting out of the proposed $120 tender offer for AMR, and its shares ended at 71. The Transportation index had lost 17 percent in five sessions and UAL had lost abut 42 percent of its value.

A great amount of finger pointing followed the bad scene of October 13, for it was evident that "circuit breakers" did not insulate the market from nasty shocks. For the Street, the sad thing was that the crash had come just as small investors had started to slip back into the market.

And the Street was primed, with four-color brochures, to try and lure part of October's mammoth CD maturities into stocks. Or bonds, bond funds, mutual funds, or any other of the "financial products" on the shelves.

Sadly, a large part of the CDs just rolled over into new certificates. Program trading had taken its toll again.

Fortunately, a consensus outlook for lower interest rates helped the market during the balance of the year and on December 29, the three Dow averages were at their highest yearly closing levels in history, even though the Transportations had suffered greatly in the previous 120 days. The Dow, at 2753, was only 38 points below its record October peak.

For AT&T, up 58 percent for the year, it was a return to leadership, while IBM's glory faded badly. Its shares had lost 23 percent, falling beneath the 1987 panic low. Foreign entanglements were the surprising group leaders in 1989. The Asia-Pacific, Thai, and Germany funds were all among the Big Board's top ten performers.

1990: An Ominous Beginning

An ominous turn marked the beginning of the 1990s. On January 2, the Dow vaulted up 57 points to close at a record 2810.15. Outside the Utilities, no other major index could match the lonely high. Volume was a disappointing 162 million shares.

Prices quickly faded during the balance of the week. Was it to be another frightening sea change, seen so often in the first few days of January? Mother Russia's children were in "civil war." Tokyo's bond market started to slip and the Nikkei was not far behind.

Other false January starts were recalled. The Dow's brilliant peaks in 1906, 1960, and 1973 had been followed by a lower monthly closing and a fresh bear market.

A commanding consensus for lower interest rates, seen at the year end, splintered. Long-term government bonds quickly broke a surprising seven points from their 1989 highs, as seen in the Christmas week.

The January effect, which called for higher prices as December's tax victims revived, was forgotten. Record cold and soaring energy prices fostered new inflation fears.

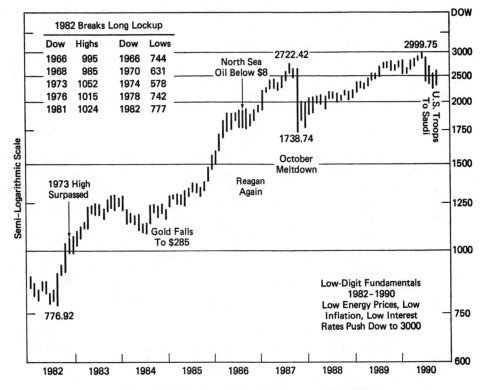

Figure 3.6 Dow Jones Industrial Average, 1982–1990

By late January the Dow had fallen nearly 400 points by hourly measurements, with strong bearish company in both London and Tokyo.

The January glass was falling.

But once again, as had happened so often in the previous six years, the bears could not capitalize on weakening indicators. Despite a stricken Tokyo market and poor action among the broader indices as well as the Transportations, the Dow would soar to the 3000 level by mid-July. (See Figure 3-6.) Unbeknownst to the market, the winds of war lay just over the horizon. With little fanfare, the great 1982–1990 bull market had passed in the third week of July.

MAJOR BULL MARKETS

The Rails: A Golden Age Ends
DJIA Nov 9, 1903–Jan 19, 1906: 42.15 to 103.00, +144%.

The early years of the twentieth century were, arguably, the golden years of the Rail Age. Between Boston and New York, the New Haven Railroad ran 19 trains each way each day. The *Twentieth Century* and the *Broadway Limited*, respective flagships of the New York Central and Pennsylvania, raced between New York and Chicago in 18 hours and on time. Bigger engines, heavier rails, and huge, new steel boxcars promoted operating efficiency in freight handling.

Rail shares had enjoyed a golden age. Index values had tripled in the previous ten years, aided by strong performances by the western roads and coal carriers, particularly those "dewatered" in the courthouse a decade earlier. Norfolk & Western, ⅛ in 1896, reached 98. The Union Pacific, less than 4, made it to 196 in 1906. Railway operating income at the Santa Fe was up 356 percent in ten years.

The Dow Rail average peaked in January 1906 at 136.36. It would not pass that milepost again until 1927. Its secular advance had been large but its 1903–1906 gain, of less than 40 percent that of the Industrials, was a bad omen. If 1906 was not the end of the railroad domination of the American business scene, it was surely the beginning of the end.

There was no clue that the Rails' secular trip was over. Earnings were robust and dividends increased to the point where the ICC ordered an investigation into the Union Pacific's largesse, at 10 percent of par. Business generally was enjoying a boom not seen since the early 1880s. Earnings for U.S. Steel in 1906 would be a third better than the record year of 1902, and 14 times the depleted 1904 level.

After the bear market low of late 1903, the bull advance had dragged in the first half of 1904. In February, Japan staged a full-scale Pearl Harbor raid on Vladivostock and subsequently wiped out the Russian fleet. A bit later, the Turks and Greeks loaded up for one of their eternal conflicts.

More important domestically, great uneasiness was caused in March when the Supreme Court upheld an order dissolving the Northern Securities

Company—the holding company for the Northern Pacific and Great Northern. The holding company was ruled to be in restraint of interstate commerce.

During the first half of 1904, the Street was still working off the paper it was stuck with from the 1902–1903 glut. In May, U.S. Steel reached its all-time low at 8⅜, with Morgan's consortium finally checking Harriman's bear operations in the stock. Two dividend cuts by the world's largest corporation had assisted the raiders. Steel's order file suddenly bloomed and Morgan's favorite raced up to 34 as large volume swept into the market. NYSE activity in October–November was six times that of May–June. Railroad construction, in its last great frenzy, boomed the iron trade. Each year from 1904 through 1907 would see over 5,000 miles of new track laid. A decade later, the figures would be generally under 1,000 miles, and often less than 500 miles in the 1920s.

In November, President Roosevelt was easily voted back into the White House with at least nominal support from the Street, for his election seemed assured. Following the election, the market quickly pushed higher.

Prosperity was spotty in 1905. A number of Rails increased their payouts, despite worries about increasing state regulation, but 3,300 miles of road went under receivership. Earnings for the Dow approached the 1902 level and, after a late spring slump, stocks reversed sharply higher in the late summer. Both indices overcame their previous record peaks of 1901 and 1902; the Industrials led the way.

The success came despite another painful financial investigation. The life insurance industry and its close ties with the "money kings" of the city, as Thomas W. Lawson termed them in his exposé in *Everybody's Magazine*, were subjected to 57 public hearings, not ending until December 30. In the following year, New York legislation would bar life insurance firms from underwriting securities and prohibit them from investing in common stocks. This was not all bad. Some insurance companies were still carrying their underwriting commitments from Morgan's International Mercantile Marine. The 1902 shipping trust had never left the ways.

The existing trusts of the period did not fade away after the Northern Securities ruling. U.S. Rubber, whose tire business still revolved around bicycles, bounced from 7 in 1903 to 60 in 1906. U.S. Cast Iron Pipe was a 6–53 winner and National Lead went 11–96.

And as had been learned in 1903, the trust format did not guarantee profits or stock pricing. American Can, Union Bag, and Swift all struggled after their 1904 rallies. The "meat trust" lost its reputation to the muckrakers. Swift's peak price in 1906 was 55 points below its 1902 top.

A great copper frenzy seized the market in late 1905. The burgeoning electric utilities and traction lines, it seems, were about to effect a shortage of the metal. The commodity frenzy topped the market. Volume in January 1906 was 39 million shares, second only to April 1901. It marked one of the two times in this century for a bull market and volume peak to coincide.

January was an extraordinary high for the market. It was a watershed year for the Rails, marking an elevation which would not be crested for 21 years. And the Dow, peaking just over 100, had reached for the first time a tough psychological level which would bedevil it for years.

Steel Rigging
DJIA Nov 15, 1907–Nov 19, 1909: 53.00 to 100.53, +90%.

The 1907 financial panic ended in November. A depression came in 1908, along with lower Dow earnings and higher Dow prices. It was the same scenario that would be repeated in 1974–1975—panic and depression followed by lower earnings and higher stock prices.

In 1908, the Industrials' earnings fell by 21 percent, yet the Dow gained 47 percent for the year. U.S. Steel's earnings plummeted from $15.61 to $4.05, but the stock's 1908 high at 59 was almost eight points above the 1906 and 1907 peaks and marked the first time that the pricey buyers of 1901 could have earned a small profit.

The Rails had been the best investments early in the decade and the coppers at mid-term. Now it was time for the steels, boosted, some cynics said, by the Gary dinners.

The Gary Dinners

Depressed by prospects for business and the steel industry in November 1907, Judge Elbert Gary, president of U.S. Steel, invited the country's steel executives to a dinner in New York. The meeting was so convivial that it seemed to encourage a great harmony of pricing and production. The dinners—and fellowship—were continued for a few years and became known as the Gary dinners.

Adam Smith had written in 1776 that "People of the same trade seldom meet together, even for merriment and diversion, but the conversation ends in a conspiracy against the public, or in some contrivance to raise prices."[6]

Cynics contend that such fellowship explains the great rise in the steel stocks during the 1907–1909 advance. U.S. Steel, 22 in 1907, soared to 94 in 1909. Republic Iron and Steel gained fourfold, 12 to 50, and Colorado Fuel & Iron made it from 14 to 50. Steel's earnings advanced to $10.59 and its annual volume in 1909 was a record 34 million shares. Small by modern standards, but a huge turnover rate, as there were but 5.1 million shares outstanding.

Morgan's pool, which had bought about 500,000 shares of stock in the fall panic of 1907, gave the shares a blue-chip sponsorship. Rails, meanwhile, lacked the steam of the early 1900s. They were badgered by state rail commissions and legislatures and their 65 percent gain in the two-year period was far below that of the Industrials, though the Denver & Rio Grande and the Cotton Belt both tripled.

Market scholars often compute this period as the time when the Industrials took over as the leading market average, though total rail capitalization at the Exchange would exceed that of the Industrials for several more years.

After a slow business year in 1908, commercial activity blossomed in

---

[6]Adam Smith, *An Inquiry Into The Nature and Causes of The Wealth of Nations, Second Edition* London: Methuen & Co. Ltd., 1920), Vol. I, p. 130.

1909. Pig iron production, advancing by 60 percent, set a record. Grain crops were good. Six of the 20 Rail stocks paid a higher dividend than in 1906; only three had cut their payout. But only the class western roads materially outdid their 1906 highs.

AT&T, on an $8 dividend basis since late 1906, enjoyed a solid gain. Having fallen to 88 in 1907, it made it to 145 in 1909. One of the biggest point gainers in the period was Wells Fargo, which climbed from 223 to 670, a large part of the markup coming in 1909, after the death of the legendary E. H. Harriman. He was on the board of 27 railroads at the time of his death, but that was only part of his influence as he and Kuhn, Loeb controlled the historic express company, among other important concerns. After his death, Fargo's huge surplus—a melon—was cut and distributed. It amounted to a $115 cash and 20 percent stock dividend.

Though there were no listed automobile shares in the period, Ford put out over 10,000 cars in 1908. General Motors was organized in the same year.

At the autumn peaks in 1909, both the Rails and Industrials were a trifle shy of their 1906 peaks. It was, as the chartists can now recognize, a true double top. The activity for the second year of the advance, at 212 million shares, was far below the 1901 and 1906 figures.

If activity was contained, there was plenty of optimism on the floor. A NYSE seat changed hands for a record $94,000, a price which would not be exceeded until the bull market of 1919. The record came despite the fact that the Dow had been unable to climb above its high of 1906, as seen in Figure 3-7.

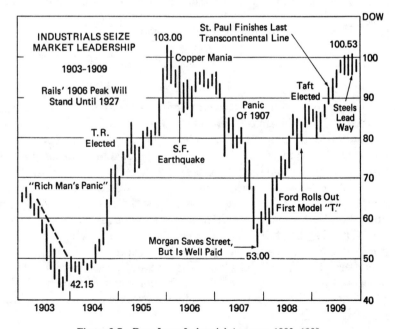

Figure 3.7 Dow Jones Industrial Average, 1903–1909

United States: Quartermaster to Europe
DJIA Jly 30, 1914–Nov 21, 1916: 51.88 to 110.15, +112%. (New Dow average.)

Depression turned to feverish war boom within months in 1914–1915 as America, almost overnight, became quartermaster to the armies of Europe.

The domestic economy and even grain shipments were seen in August 1914 as imperiled by the outbreak of World War I. Scores of firms, including U.S. Steel, cut their dividends in the autumn. Railroad trunkline profits were at a 15-year low. By December, unemployment was widespread.

THE WAR'S FIRST CASUALTY

When World War I broke out in the last week of July 1914, the NYSE was the first American casualty. It closed and other United States stock exchanges followed suit.

European bourses had closed earlier in the week and a wave of world selling orders forced the Exchange to shutter on Friday morning, July 31. It would not reopen until December 12.

Trading was allowed through the clearing-house, but only at minimum prices, which generally reflected the closing level of July 30. Activity was very slow, save in the sugar stocks, which commanded premium prices.

An active outlaw or "gutter" market swiftly developed. Trading there was most active, with the lowest prices coming in the last week of October. There was no pretense of minimum pricing in this outdoor market.

Further details on this historic emergency closing, the first at the NYSE since 1873, can be found in the retrospect of 1914.

But the economy was about to enjoy a record acceleration from the November low. The Exchange, more or less padlocked since July, would reopen in December, with continued apprehension about the potential for heavy European selling. London and the continent owned a half-billion dollars in both U.S. Steel and the Pennsylvania stocks, among other large holdings.

When the stock market reopened, prices advanced sharply. Jules S. Bache, quoted in the *Wall Street Journal,* capsuled the atmosphere, "We know the worst, and when that stage is reached, the country is ready for improvement."[7]

That is what followed, in sensational fashion. The year 1915 would be the greatest ever in the history of the Dow Industrial Average, which advanced 81.7 percent. "War babies" led the advance, as orders for munitions, steel, processed commodities, shells, and powder poured into America's factories.

The year was a nervous opener, however. Germany's submarine threats

---

[7]The *Wall Street Journal,* New York, Dec 14, 1914, sec. 1, p. 2, col. 2.

were frightening and U.S. Steel eliminated its dividend. Since the NYSE still enforced minimum pricing, the price at which U.S. Steel could trade had to be cut and cut again, finally to 38. Minimum-price restrictions at the NYSE were finally removed in April.

On May 7, a German sub torpedoed the *Lusitania,* dropping the Dow by more than 7 percent within a week. It was the only serious decline of the year.

Bethlehem Steel would be the great war leader. On July 30, 1914, the stock sold at 29 and in early January 1915 at 46. It was then swept up in a mercurial advance which took it to 155 in March, 275 in July, and 600 in October. Armor plate, shells, and shipbuilding were big-ticket items. The export of billets, ingots, and bloom increased tenfold in the first ten months of 1915 over 1914's annual figure.

A huge harvest helped the farm sector to a rare prosperity when both prices and exports rose dramatically. Nearly every commodity was in heavy demand, and the 1915–1916 commodity mania enriched both producers and fabricators. Copper-miner Calumet & Hecla advanced from 350 to 640. South Porto Rico Sugar was a 28–240 winner. Cuban-American Sugar did nearly as well, 38–270.

New York had become the financial center of the world within months. Both the Germans and Allies sought and received large credits. J.P. Morgan became the purchasing agent for England and France. It was a year of enduring speculation and market advance. Late in the year, there were frequently 25 to 50 points between Bethlehem trades; there were only 148,620 shares outstanding. The Dow, typically, reached its high between Christmas and the New Year.

The greatest market year in history was not without its skeptics, of course. In January 1916, the *Commercial & Financial Chronicle* reported, "So far as the rise . . . was based on supposed larger profits from war orders, it was mainly the result of speculative manipulation. It will take many years of exceptional profits to justify the extreme figures to which many war stocks have been boosted."[8] Such war stocks, often separately tabulated by the *Wall Street Journal,* included such issues as: American Brass, Atlas Powder, Colt Arms, Du Pont Powder and Winchester Arms (1200 bid, 1400 offered in one listing).

Although 1915 had been sensational, the first half of 1916 was correctional. It would be September before the market could overcome the 1915 top. General Motors was the hardest driver in the final lap of the raging autumn market. The stock had closed in 1915 at 500, up from 82 at the first of the year. William Crapo Durant had pegged the price and then put a move on it, recovering the control he had forfeited to the bankers in 1911. In 1916, the shares raced on to 850, covering the last 150 points in a few leaps and bounds.

General Motors had peer company. There were no restrictions on auto production and a newly affluent society was eager to trade in their carriages. Ford's output rose from 300,000 units in 1914 to 700,000 in 1916 and 1 million the following year. Maxwell's stock raced from 15 to 99 during the period. Studebaker reached 167 after a 1914 low at 20. War-boosted earnings were

---

[8]The *Commercial & Financial Chronicle,* New York, January 8, 1916, p. 103, col. 2.

widely discounted, however. U.S. Steel would earn $109.75 in the 1916–1918 years, but its peak price was 137.

Retailers also enjoyed the largesse of wartime prosperity. May Department Stores doubled. Shipping space was at a premium as the weapons of war poured across the Atlantic, and J. P. Morgan would have been pleased to see his greatest underwriting failure salvaged. The International Merchant Marine shares had foundered off the ways in 1902 and the preferred fetched but 3 in 1914. The heated demand for bottoms pushed it up to 126 in 1916. The common stock did better, percentagewise.

Unfortunately, the Rails enjoyed only a nominal advance during the war years and on November, 15, 1916, the "new" 20-stock Industrial index crossed above the carriers' average for the first time in history, though that historical ascendance had been made by the old Industrial average in the summer of 1915.

The Industrials peaked in November 1916. Bethlehem Steel had reached 700 on wild rumors of an enormous "melon" cutting and was up 2,300 percent from the July 1914 low. General Motors, the other giant of the early war years, had gained 1,445 percent, 55 to 850.

Inflation, Oil Fever
DJIA Dec 19, 1917–Nov 3, 1919: 65.95 to 119.62 +81%.

The winds of peace advanced the stock market during 1918. Fundamentals lagged. Earnings were curtailed by increased taxes, shortages, and government supply allocations. Urged on by the Post Office Department, the government took over operations of American Telephone & Telegraph.

Volume in August was the lowest of the war years, despite encouraging prospects for peace. And when the armistice came, November 11, it would be discovered that it was already discounted; the year's high had come in mid-October. The market was worrying about a mini-recession and the abrupt cancellation of large war orders.

But both Europe and America needed the goods of peace and an intense economic boom burst on the nation in early 1919. Inflationary pressures, restrained during the war, mushroomed and the market viewed such price action as friendly. A swift ascent was accompanied by huge speculations, corners, and near corners.

NYSE volume was at the highest level since the blow-off of January 1906. The Wholesale Price Index nearly doubled the 1915 level. The Dow's rise was inflation driven, for earnings would decline for the third consecutive year.

Commodity shares could relate to the inflation. American Linseed rose to 89 from a 1917 low at 16. American Woolen saw a 37–170 stretch. Purveyors of cotton oil, hides, and sugar did nearly as well.

Oil Boom

Economists had perceived a lessened demand for crude in 1919, but demand increased sharply, rising to a figure far above U.S. production. A drilling boom took place and oil shares enjoyed a huge speculative demand. Not until 1980 would the industry again command such market popularity.

Standard of Jersey, 475 in 1917, would reach 880 in 1920, though its dividend remained at $20. Houston Oil was a big speculative winner, 14 to 172. Mexican Petroleum, a pool favorite and owner of extremely rich Mexican concessions, was pushed up from 67 to 264.

The advance of 1919 was both steep and broad. May Department Stores ran to 132 off a bear low at 43 and Associated Dry Goods increased six times. American Tobacco benefitted from a change of smoking habits and rose from 123 in 1917 to 315 in 1919. Cigarette production had tripled since 1914.

A federal bureaucracy continued to control the rails and higher wages and ceiling freight rates just didn't jibe with inflation. But if the railroads did poorly, the equipment shares did well as the carriers repaired and replaced their war-worn equipment. Baldwin Locomotive steamed up from 42 to 156, and American Car & Foundry was not far behind.

The stunning promise of the auto industry was also exploited, even though 1918 had notched the industry's first sales decline in history, due to steel restrictions. General Motors, 75 in 1917 (it had split since 1916) was propelled up to 407. General Motors lusted for Fisher Bodies, a major supplier, and the latter's stock gained nearly 150 points from the 1917 low at 25. The "auto play" spread to other industries. Kelly-Springfield bounced from 37 to 164. General Asphalt, seen as having great highway promise, gained from 15 to 161.

But war and inflation had sown the seeds of a volatile increase in interest rates and by November 1919, monthly call loan renewals at the NYSE averaged 10.9 percent, a vast increase from the 2 percent rate seen in the boom winter period of 1915–1916. In the same month, coal miners went out on strike, joining the steel unions off the job since September. Labor and interest rate pressures suddenly seemed intolerable.

The bull movement had advanced swiftly since March, up 42 percent, and would end quickly, peeling off 12 percent of the Dow's value from November 3 to the post-Thanksgiving session. It would take five years to recover the peak level of 120. A firestorm of deflation was about to sweep the market.

The Long Road Back
DJIA Apr 28, 1942–May 29, 1946: 92.92 to 212.50, +129%.

The scent of victory in World War II was far afield in April 1942 when the Dow recorded its low for the war years. Corregidor would fall in May and General Rommel's Tiger tanks still roved the North African desert, almost at will. Spring had brought the war's darkest hours.

General Jimmy Doolittle's April B-25 raid on Tokyo, launched from the carrier *Hornet*, had strengthened American hopes, but not the stock market. Following the raid, the Dow continued its decline, persistent since Pearl Harbor; the index lost another 4.4 percent within a few days.

On April 28, the Dow reached 92.92, the lowest level of the war and a level not seen since the autumn of 1934. The market's labored turn from that point was an unusual trend reversal. There was no high-volume day, no final panic, no frenzied bargain hunting. And no hard news to account for the reversal.

Grudgingly, the Dow climbed back over 100 in May. That seemed to say only that the war would at least become more two-sided. But the month's volume was the lowest since 1918. There were no big bettors around.

On May 31, a thousand RAF bombers struck Cologne. Essen suffered a similar raid June 2. And U.S. naval forces won a vital victory at the Battle of Midway in the first week of June. The war news improved.

In July, the Nazis invaded Russia and the U.S. Marines were bloodily opposed after their August invasion of Guadalcanal. But perceptions were changing. Winston Churchill put it best in late November. "It is the end of the beginning," he said in a London speech. So it was at the Exchange, where the Dow had finally crept up to its pre-Pearl Harbor level.

Still, the young bull market moved only timidly. War news rather than economic news was the driving force. Business activity was feverish, pushed to the limit to satisfy Allied war needs and the domestic economy, though the expansion of earnings, hobbled by war taxes, would be minimal. In 1945, the Dow 30 would earn $10.56 versus $9.22 in 1942.

But the three Dow averages would mount splendid gains. The Utilities started from a record low of 10.52 and then registered their best bull advance in history, gaining 313 percent. The Rails would also outperform the Industrials during the war years, and the gain was even superior to their move in the 1920s.

At the end of 1942, the Dow was barely above its Pearl Harbor level and volume for the year, the lowest since 1900, illustrated the crisis of confidence.

In early 1943, the war news brightened. The Russians broke the Stalingrad siege. The British captured Tripoli. The scent of victory was savored.

For the first time in several years, aggressive buying entered the market. In March, each session saw volume of over 1 million shares. There were only two such days in all of 1942.

In May 1943, the Axis forces surrendered in North Africa and the Dow finally pushed above its rally peak of late 1940. Sicily and mainland Italy were invaded, but as the news grew more encouraging, a pause gripped the market.

A Fear for Peace

Investors grew more cautious, concerned about what peace might mean to the economy. Volume dried up. At the end of May 1944, the Dow was no higher than the previous year. There had been several months when no trading session reached 1 million shares. But D-Day, June 6, 1944, shattered the consolidation and stocks moved higher through the balance of the year.

It was a long road back, however. Not until mid-February 1945 would the Dow rise above its high of September 1939. And at V.E.-Day, in May, the average was barely a dozen points above the prewar level and was still 30 points under the peak of 1937. It was not until January 1946 that the Industrials could top 200, when they were helped by the largest NYSE volume recorded during the the four-year bull market. The final peak came May 29, at 212.50 (Figure 3-8).

Blue chip stocks had been solid performers during the war years. "Lucky Strike Green" went to war, but American Tobacco survived, advancing from 34 to 101. General Motors pushed to 80 from a war low at 29. Auto demand was correctly perceived as being enormous whenever the war ended. Quality oils did well. Jersey Standard and the Texas Co. moved from 30 to about 70.

Stunning Speculative Gains

Springing from an extremely low-value base after years of depression, speculative stocks ran up the really stunning gains. The airlines were a lead group. Before 1940, only thousands had flown. By the end of the war, millions. TWA soared from 8 to 78 during the wartime advance; Northwest Air from 8 to 64.

Full employment and full pockets pushed consumer issues sharply higher. Gimbel's ran from 4 to 110; Allied Stores from 5 to 63; Schenley from 13 to 99. Some really speculative shares made staggering gains. The obvious "War Babies" of 1939 were not the big winners.

Electric Bond & Share, the utility holding company, moved up from 1 to 26. Tri-Continental's perpetual warrants gained over 17,000 percent in a move from pennies to 5⅝. Bankrupt and semi-bankrupt Rails saw earnings highball to undreamed levels. Texas & Pacific Railway lost money in 1939, earned a meager $1 in 1940 but $20.17 in 1942, when the shares sold under 8.

Gotham Hosiery enjoyed a run from 2 to 43 and Twentieth Century Fox paced the Hollywood producers, advancing from 7 to 64.

The scent of victory, not the victory march, had been the sweetest gift to the market. By the time General Douglas MacArthur accepted the Japanese

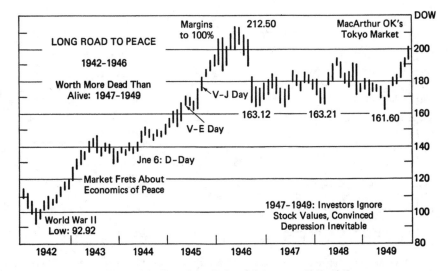

Figure 3.8 Dow Jones Industrial Average, 1942–1949

surrender documents in Tokyo Bay, 68 percent of the 1942–1946 Dow gains had been realized. For the Rails, the figure was 71 percent.

Dow's All-Time "High"
DJIA Jne 26, 1962–Feb 9, 1966: 535.76 to 995.15, +86%.

Almost unnoticed, 1966 stands as one of the great tops in stock market history. If the Dow Industrial Average is adjusted for inflation, 1966 is the all-time high. The subsequent secular decline lasted for 17 years, to 1982. Figure 3-9 shows the inflation adjusted decline in that period.

The great bull market of the 1980s left the weighted Dow well below the 1966 peak. The 1987 peak (real Dow 2722) remains the best level since 1966. Despite a climb to 3000 in July, 1990 by the actual average the inflation compensated index failed to crest the 1987 level.

The watershed year, 1966, also marked the end of the 1962–1966 advance and of the long upward march stretching back to the war-time low of 1942. A number of stocks marked up gains of 100:1 in the longer period, including quality names like Boeing, Fairchild Camera, Gilette, IBM, Motorola, Superior Oil, and Zenith. Boeing and Gilette made their final peak in 1967.

A Symbolic End to Smokestack America

Smokestack America also came to a symbolic end. General Motors, a legendary market leader since World War I, recorded its all-time high in late 1965, at 113¾ (56⅞ adjusted for the 2:1 split of 1989).

The period marked an end to the "olden" days when the steels and motors

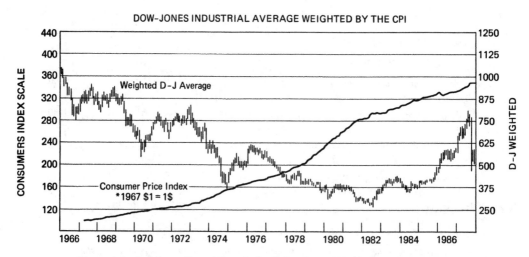

Figure 3.9 Inflation adjusted Dow Industrials, 1966–1987 (*Source: M.C. Horsey & Company, Salisbury, MD*)

were the great market movers, U.S. Steel and Bethlehem Steel having already reached their historic peaks in 1959.

If the Pittsburgh/Detroit axis was to come under eclipse, the motors, at least, put on a grand finale helped by a sizzling run from Chrysler, 10 to 68 between 1962 and 1964. General Motors's advance to above par had started from the 45 level.

The frightening Cuban missile crisis of October 1962 had staggered the market only four months after the finish of the Kennedy Panic and the bear market low of June. After that, booming auto sales, superior earnings progress, an exciting space program, low inflation, and stable interest rates combined to push the market steadily higher.

Along the way, the market overcame the shocking assassination of President Kennedy, a huge commodity scandal ("salad oil"), and increasing involvement in Vietnam. The president's assassination had forced an emergency early closing of the NYSE, its first since 1933. More than 2 million shares traded in the last seven minutes.

Autos were among the classical leaders of the advance, but the big action was airborne. TWA got a big speculative play with a marvelous flight from 8 to 101. Braniff, whose troubles still lay far ahead, did even better with a move from 4 to 98. Aircraft and defense issues responded well, along with the electronic issues. Motorola moved from 32 to 234 in the 1962–1966 period.

Xerox duplicated its great action of the 1950s with a run from 18 to 238 and the drugs were sensationally strong, urged on by Medicare legislation. Syntex continued a volatile pattern, accentuated by its controversial birth control pill. It rose from 4 to 95 between 1962 and 1964 before collapsing to 24 in the same year. It quickly revived and reached 125 in 1966.

There were disappointments, of course. Cigarette smokers got a warning ticket from the government and American Tobacco could only recover about half its 1961–1962 loss. Fairchild Camera's private bear market lasted from 1960 to 1964 with a loss of more than 75 percent of its value, but it reversed at 21 and overzealous bears suffered a forced conversion as the stock rocketed to 217 in 1966.

Huge volume at the NYSE had developed in 1963, as activity finally topped the 1929 mark, though margin requirements had been raised to 70 percent. Volume would continue to increase for the next five years and, in 1964, would help the long laggard Rail and Utility indices push through their highs of 1929.

A "Multiple" Disappointment

In the spring of 1965, the market became clearly overheated and a sharp break, starting in May, cost the Dow 100 points. The decline, a modest 10.5 percent, was the worst setback for the Industrials during the entire rise.

Though it had been a remarkably carefree advance, the percentage gain at the end in February 1966 was but 86 percent. This left the move far down on the list of major sequences, despite its longevity and splendid individual performances.

The reason: No bull market has ever started from such a high earnings appreciation base as that of 1962, when the Dow was valued at nearly 15X earnings at the bear market low. So, while earnings expanded dramatically from 1962 to 1966, there was little leverage for a PE explosion because of the rich starting endowment.

The Utilities had peaked early, in April 1965, being coveted for growth and not their traditionally rich dividend returns, which had fallen below 3 percent for some popular issues. The index had enjoyed a great secular multiple expansion. Having been valued at barely 5.5X earnings in 1942, it topped out at over 19X earnings.

Nevada Power, though not in the average, was one of the growth-anointed. The Las Vegas "play" moved it from 16 to 55 between 1962 and 1965, where it was seen as worth 33X earnings. In the end, fears of higher interest rates, a growing concern with inflation, and a tougher regulatory atmosphere combined to dim the electrics.

———————————— **OTHER BULL SEQUENCES** ————————————

Easy Money
DJIA Oct 22, 1957–Jan 5, 1960: 419.79 to 685.47, + 63%.

A most extraordinary buying panic erupted in the summer of 1958. Over the next 12 months, bulls would roll up marvelous profits in dozens of stocks benefitting from a new age in computers, missiles, and electronics. One had only to believe.

Sandwiched between the great bull market of the early 1950s and the 1960s, the intense advance of 1957–1960 never has received its proper due. Starting in March 1958, both the Dow Industrials and Rails would close higher for 12 straight months. In December 1957, the low for the Rail average had been 95.67, or about the closing level in 1900. In 1958, the average recorded its greatest annual advance, up 63 percent. The Milwaukee and North Western both tripled.

Among the Industrials, old favorites were shunted aside in favor of missile stocks and new product adventures. Or even, "improved" products. Haloid-Xerox had been making copy machines for several years, but improvements caught the Street's attention, and the shares rose from 36 to 120.

Such companies as Texas Instruments, Polaroid, Fairchild Camera, and Aerojet-General were the new breed of market giants. Texas Instruments, 16 in 1957, reached 194. Fairchild did a bit better, 16 to 204.

Amontok's pride, IBM, couldn't even double, but gathered a lot of attention with a giant step from 300 to 552.

Disney's wonderful new park struck the fancy of vacationing Americans, and the stock moved easily from 13 to a high of 60 in early 1959. Dow dowagers looked on with amazement. General Motors's gain was 34 to 52 during the period, though U.S. Steel did better in one of its patented, steam-roller advances.

In October 1958, volume poured into the Exchange with the month registering its highest activity since 1933, despite a pair of margin increases in the early fall. The second pushed the rate to 90 percent, a level second only to the 100 percent requirement of 1946.

Aircraft manufacturers, meanwhile, lost allure to the missile stocks. Even Boeing, whose 707s were introduced commercially in 1958, was a disappointment after a brilliant start in that year. While Aerojet-General, 16 in early 1957, blew up to 98 in 1959, United Aircraft, Douglas, and Boeing would all drop below their worst levels of 1957. Thiokol, into propellants, was 6 in early 1957 and 72 in early 1959.

In February 1959, the Dow 600 milestone was easily passed but in March, finally, the Dow was trimmed for a miniscule monthly loss of about two points. Despite the continuing rash of prime-rate increases, still further gains lay ahead, though Superior Oil, no longer a merger target of Texaco, had already made its famous high at 2165 as shown in Figure 3-10.

Gold bugs, alarmed at the loss of Treasury bullion, bought the mining

Year	1952	1953	1954	1955	1956	1957	1958	1959	1960
Earn	28.13	28.38	24.54	8.04	11.94	44.71	39.20		
Div.	2.00	1.00	2.00	3.00	–	–	3.00		

Figure 3.10 Legendary oil finder topped at 2165 (*Source: M.C. Horsey & Company, Salisbury, MD*)

shares, but their gains were modest compared with the consumer stocks. Maytag jumped up nearly fourfold, 12 to 46, while Polaroid's new camera magic developed its stock into a huge winner, 25 to 150.

The pace was so furious that there was not even a minor correction until mid-1959, by which time many issues were finishing off their steep advances with spike tops. Both the NYSE index and the S&P 500 peaked in the late summer. A rash of splits among the Dow 30 helped that average hold on through the year end. Eight Dow stocks, headlined by AT&T, voted share distributions. Telephone made its patient shareholders happy with a 3:1 division.

The new darlings of the market had enjoyed enormous and almost unchallenged success, but the reward for the Dow was a modest 63 percent, the most restrained major move since 1911–1912. The year 1959 had wound up a fabulous era for the Dow. The decade's 239 percent gain remains the best ever. Dreams of the "Soaring Sixties" would prove premature, however.

A Record Passion
DJIA Oct 25, 1960–Dec 13, 1961: 566.05 to 734.91, +30%.

Frustrated bulls of early 1960 regrouped from the January ground loop and marched back to the flight line in October. They had just suffered the first intrayear bear market since 1890. Fortunately, it had been shallow.

Enthusiasm and volume expanded enormously as the Dow advanced for eight consecutive months. In March 1961, the NYSE registered a volume record. In April, the index high of 1960 was exceeded and margin debt rose to a 20-year peak.

The 1961 passion for stocks would exceed the 1929 record. Eager buyers pushed the Dow's price-earnings level to 23X in December, much higher than the 19.2X reading at the 1929 peak. The extreme burst of enthusiasm seen in 1961 for the Dow 30 has not been matched since.

It is perhaps surprising that such frenzy developed in a year which had increasing international tensions. The United States broke off diplomatic relations with Cuba in January and followed that with the aborted Bay of Pigs invasion. Frequent airline kidnappings to Cuba would exacerbate the differences. In August, the Berlin Wall mushroomed overnight and in September, the Soviets exploded a nuclear bomb in the atmosphere. Direct military support was sent to Vietnam in December and in the same month the Office of Emergency Planning proposed a $700 million program to build community fallout shelters.

Leaders of the speculative pack in early 1961 were the bowling stocks. Brunswick, a $8 number in 1959, rolled up to 75. AMF did nearly as well before the industry caught a split in the early spring. By June, despite a higher market, both bowlers had suffered sharp losses. Brunswick's terrible decline would take it to 13 in 1962, a drop of 83 percent.

The market found new favorites, however. Avnet Electronics ran up from 17 to 68 within about seven months; it was seen as worth about 100X earnings at that advanced price. Denny's menu was valued at over 80X earnings and

Polaroid advanced to a multiple of 72. Computers were assayed nearly as richly. Even such mundane issues as Western Union and Twentieth Century-Fox were priced at over 40X earnings. Drugs were also overpriced; Miles Lab soared to 116X its 1961 earnings, even higher than IBM's 81X multiple.

No Dow stocks were accorded such accolades, and such former leaders as Alcoa, Anaconda, Chrysler, Dow, General Electric, Westinghouse, and the steels failed to exceed their best levels of 1959–1960.

At the AMEX, however, there was plenty of excitement. Turnover rate was at a record and the Exchange enjoyed its first 5-million share day in May. Such frenetic speculative activity has often spelled regulatory trouble and in the same month the SEC announced its first exchange investigation since 1940 and went on to do battle with the "Curb."

Such was the public's esteem for stocks that underwriters could promote a record number of new issues. It was not a basic industries play. Many of the offerings were "hot," by reason of hope or manipulation. Remarkable names were fabricated, like Rocket Jet Engineering and Hydro-Space Technology. Vending machine operations were granted a cachet their hardware hardly deserved.

Small business investment companies were seen to offer rewarding social and financial benefits (they invested in a portfolio of small companies), and partly because of special tax advantages the SBICs were also "hot." An imaginative label like Electro-Science Investors helped propel that SBIC from a new issue price of 11 to 54. After splitting 3:1, the venture capital firm headed for 80 cents. Speculation, not a sophisticated nose for small electronics firms, shot Electronics Capital up to 69 from a 1960 low at 15. A niggardly NAV and earnings of but two cents were ignored in the madness of the SBIC crowd. Capital's shares would slump to 5 in the humming bull market year of 1964.

The frothy market was clearly brewing its own undoing. At the NYSE, the advance-decline ratio, a measure of breadth in the market, peaked in May and several groups, like the semiconductors, lost public esteem as rapidly as the bowlers. Texas Instruments suffered a stunning loss, 207 to 95, but would fall further in the 1962 crash to 40.

During the autumn, the market lost momentum and technical strength, with the Rails topping in October. The Industrials' final high on December 13 was barely one percent above its early September peak. Despite great speculative gains and its own inflated fundamentals, the Dow's move had been disappointing, both short and thin. The gain, only 30 percent, remains the second poorest in bull market history.

The "Sizzle" Market
DJIA Oct 7, 1966–Dec 3, 1968: 744.32 to 985.21, +32%.

"Sizzle" drove the 1966–1968 market. Blue-chip stocks, which had anchored the 1962–1966 advance, struggled as the public embraced secondary issues with a lust not felt for a generation.

The Dow did gain 32 percent in the period, but Table 3-2 shows the

TABLE 3-2 "SIZZLE MARKET" LEFT DOW QUALITY AT THE POST

Stock	1965–1966 High	1966 Low	1968 High
AT&T	71	50	58
Du Pont	266	143	178
General Electric	120	80	100
General Motors	114	66	90
Standard of California	86	65	77
U.S. Steel	56	35	46

astonishing decline of a half dozen previous all-time favorites. It was a market for junk stocks and the Dow, for the first time since the 1930s, failed to surpass the previous bull market top.

Franchisors, mobile home builders, software vendors, and conglomerates were leading "go-go" issues. Scores of minor issues at the NYSE and AMEX gained ten times. Many speculative issues were up by 20 times.

University Computing was a huge gainer, 3 to 186. Mohawk Data exploded from 4 to 111, though current earnings were but 39 cents. Equity Funding, an insurance/mutual fund scam, was pumped up from 3 to 82 while International Industries (House of Pancakes) was moved from 3 to 58.

Those four issues, like so many other sensational performers of the period, would live longer in speculative lore than corporate manuals. By 1974, they had all collapsed to a price of less than 2. Equity, which was suspended, had no market value.

Name changes, reverse splits, and bankruptcy would haunt dozens of the 1966–1968 favorites.

AMEX Super Year

The AMEX lived up to its speculative reputation in 1968. Volume exploded to a figure nearly four times that of 1964. More significantly, the activity amounted to 49 percent of that at the NYSE, a figure not equaled before or since. The turnover ratio 65.5 percent, was the highest at either Exchange since 1929.

A number of superstars at the AMEX gained over 1,500 percent in the two-year bull market, even if they lacked first-rate credentials. Leasco, Levin-Townsend, and Computing & Software were among the group. Redman Industries, a mobile home play, hiked up from 3 in late 1966 to 113 in December 1968.

In this third bull market of the 1960s the best year of the sequence (1967) mounted an advance of but 15 percent versus a gain of 17 percent in 1963 which was the best year of the 1962–1966 advance, and the 19 percent gain of 1961. The two best gains of the 1950s had been 44 and 34 percent.

Stocks and concepts were puffed up to ridiculous evaluations, despite a great deal of social unrest. Black riots, college sit-ins, hippie love-ins, and antiwar marches grabbed the headlines but didn't seriously impede the market, which was more impressed by the temporary reversal of interest rates. In January 1967, the first prime rate reduction in six years had been announced.

International tensions continued. War in the Middle East broke out, and a confrontation with China over the Vietnam War seemed possible. Gold and silver fled the United States and in November, the British pound was devalued. Still, the market held together, though there were some important departures. The airlines, including American, the aircrafts, including Lockheed, and even a few high flyers like Texas Instruments and LTV had already peaked.

The spring of 1968 brought the crucial test for the market. The North Koreans seized the *Pueblo;* the Vietcong shelled Saigon and Red China shot down an American plane. Disturbing also was the surrender of the London gold pool, pledged to maintain an orderly gold price at or near $35. It surrendered to world buying panic and the London gold market was forced to close March 15. By late March, amidst wild rumors, the Dow was 825, its lowest point since January 1967.

President Johnson's speech to the nation on Sunday, March 31, staggered the bears when he revealed that he did not "choose to run" again; he also announced a curtailment of bombing over Vietnam. The Dow responded with a huge upside gap the next day, closing with a 21-point gain and triggering the final leg of the 1966–1968 advance.

The London gold market reopened on Monday, but Johnson's speech and the two-week cooling-off period restrained the action. There were no $50 or even $40 gold bids. The final London fix was at $37.70. A world currency upheaval would be postponed. Free market forces later in the year put the price over $40 and Benguet, the Philippine mining company, advanced to 20 from a 1967 low of 2.

Johnson's announcement proved to be the catalyst for a renewal of sizzle in the market. And dreams of overnight wealth. Four Seasons Nursing Centers was a tenfold winner in 1968. TelePrompTer went 24 to 83.

Sizzling along with the stock market was inflation, driven by the war, and the temperatures at the Federal Reserve Board. Between November 1967 and December 1968, the Board raised the discount rate four times, with but a single cut, and that for one-quarter point. In June 1968, margins were raised to 80 percent from the 70 percent level in effect for nearly five years. A large number of high-volume, speculative stocks carried "special" 100 percent margin requirements at the Exchange.

It all had little impact on the Street, where business was so great that brokers had to go on a four-day week, starting in June. Back offices couldn't handle the volume, which was up fourfold in ten years. Even a 10 percent income tax surcharge in August couldn't halt the advance.

Richard Nixon's election to the White House spurred the market to its final 40-point advance, but by December, synergism and computer leasing had exhausted all charms. Mushrooming interest rates began to refocus attention on stock yields. And dividends had not been so easy to cook as the high-flying earnings reports. The composite Dow dividend in 1968 of $31.34 was less than the payout of 1966.

Institutional Dementia
DJIA May 26, 1970–Jan 11, 1973: 631.16 to 1051.70, +66.6%.

Institutional dementia—a lust for growth stocks at any price—would climax the 1970–1973 bull market. It would be a real case study, where anointed issues were valued by money professionals at 50, 60, even 80 times earnings.

But, in the summer of 1970, sheer survival of stock values and even the NYSE itself were the only concerns. The most savage attack on speculative stocks since the great depression had ended in the last week of May 1970. But not the bad news.

In June, the Penn Central, which controlled 10 percent of the Class I railroad mileage in the country, declared bankruptcy. Orvis Brothers, a member of the Exchange for 98 years, was forced to shutter. Rumors of insolvency for many other long-time members swept the Street. Dempsey-Tegler, the big St. Louis house, closed in July.

But, in late June, a few rays of light could be seen. President Nixon announced that all U.S. troops had left Cambodia. A threatened general rail strike was averted by a White House order for a 90-day moritorium—and just in time. The carrier index had continued to fall after the Dow low and had lost 58 percent of its value in just 17 months, despite a late game substitution of nine airlines and truckers into the average at the beginning of January.

A Middle Eastern cease-fire in August and a reduction in bank reserve requirements in the same month boosted confidence and the market swept higher in the early autumn, disregarding a strike at all General Motors plants.

The recession ended officially November 1. Three prime rate cuts between then and Christmas, and five more by mid-March, sparked a buying panic which carried the Dow from 750 in mid-November to 951 in April 1971.

An April hike in the prime cooled an overheated market in which the Transports had already doubled. But new worries surfaced. Mutual fund redemptions, for the first time in history, exceeded sales. U.S. Steel cut its dividend and fell to its lowest level since 1954. IBM had a slow quarter and slid 83 points off the spring high. Additional prime rate hikes hurt confidence.

On Sunday, August 15, President Nixon, in a surprise move, announced a freeze on wages, prices, and rents until November 13. The market opened on a huge, upside gap and the day's volume was the largest in history. But the rally turned sour and by November, the Dow was back below 800, having fallen 123 points from the August bulge. Attractive pricing and a trio of prime cuts enticed buyers back and the Dow raced back to kiss the 900 level again on December 29.

Market attention, during 1970–1971, had focused on fresh faces and stories. Winnebago, the recreational vehicle pride of Forest City, Iowa, advanced more than 20 times from the 1970 low to the 1971 high, as shown in Figure 3-11. Recreational shares were broadly favored, including swimming pool fabricators, amusement parks, snowmobiles, and even motel stocks.

Bausch & Lomb received FDA approval for its soft contact lens in March

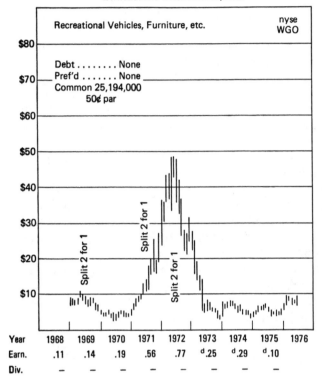

WINNEBAGO INDUSTRIES, INC.

Recreational Vehicles, Furniture, etc.

nyse
WGO

Debt . . . . None
Pref'd . . . . None
Common 25,194,000
50¢ par

Split 2 for 1

Split 2 for 1

Split 2 for 1

Year	1968	1969	1970	1971	1972	1973	1974	1975	1976
Earn.	.11	.14	.19	.56	.77	d.25	d.29	d.10	
Div.	–	–	–	–	–	–	–	–	

Figure 3.11 OPEC reversed Winnebago's success (*Source: M.C. Horsey & Company, Salisbury, MD*)

1971 and by the end of the year had traded as high as 191, up from 28 in the summer of 1970.

Hysterical Pursuit

April 1972 brought a new Dow high over that of 1971, but the market had entered a complex period. Investment advisors were bitterly divided. While many indicators and indices topped out, the institutions hysterically pursued growth and the illusions of growth. In the 12 months ending September 1972, Vickers' Favorite Fifty outpaced the Dow 4 to 1, while time-tested market leaders lagged. Farm equipments were an exception and Deere & Co. nearly doubled its previous 1967 high, gaining from 14 to 65.

"One decision stocks" were seen as rational choices by the institutions. One had only to select the proper issue. Price and timing were immaterial, since projected growth would overcome any bad detailing. Generally, there was little fault with the quality of choices. The spurious growth stocks of the 1966–1968 era were ignored. Genuine growth, or the perception thereof, was demanded and handsomely rewarded. Tropicana, TelePrompTer, Rite Aid, Avon, Johnson & Johnson, and International Flavors were all elevated to at least 60X earnings.

Disney, McDonald's, and Wang were seen to possess supergrowth, worth 80X earnings. Polaroid, despite a choppy record, was valued at 115X earnings at the 1972 peak.

There was even some hope that with all the quality shares locked up in institutional vaults there might be a shortage of high-grade growth stocks. In July 1972, the *Commercial & Financial Chronicle* headlined an article on institutional investing, "Growth Stock Scarcity." Institutions wanted to believe. Since the classics had been given scandalously high PE ratios, a genuine shortage of shares was needed to encourage further improvement. Table 3-3 shows the mushrooming appreciation for growth issues.

In November 1972, the Dow finally conquered the 1000 level and a great number of skeptics were convinced that the historic passage meant much higher prices in the year ahead.

Although 1973 opened brightly, eight glorious days finished the bull market. Where growth had been miscalculated—for Scotty's, TelePrompTer, and Wang—there would be no tomorrow. Even where the growth mystique had been truly visioned, there would be an exceptionally long wait for the promised land. In the case of McDonald's Corp. it would be ten years before the 1972 high was matched. Disney fans would wait for 13 years.

Despite the dementia for growth at any price, portfolio managers were proven not certifiable. It was not, after all, their money.

Bad Earnings, Good Market
DJIA Dec 6, 1974–Sep 21, 1976: 577.60 to 1014.79, +76%.

Earnings for the Dow Industrials in the first half of 1975 were the worst since 1971. But by mid-July, the Dow was up 34 percent from its bear market low of December. The bad news had been in the market for months.

Sellers in the autumn panic had discounted the end of the world. Values had become cheap and prices more so. Forty percent of stocks at the NYSE traded for 10 or less. Chrysler, Westinghouse, and Woolworth all sold near 8 and a half dozen other Dow veterans were priced in the teens. Woolworth would gain 238 percent over the next two years.

The great market strength in first half of 1975 was sparked by falling interest rates and a sudden passion by money managers to convert cash into

TABLE 3-3 PRICE-EARNINGS RATIOS FOR SOME LEADING GROWTH STOCKS

Company	Business	Dec 1970	Dec 1971	Peak 1972–1973
Automatic Data Processing	data processing	66X	85X	118X
Disney	recreation	41	70	82
McDonald's	fast-food	31	57	82
Rite Aid	discount drugs	26	46	71
Schlumberger	oil service	21	33	55

equities. The discount rate, 8 percent in early December at the market's low, would be cut four times before June, ending at 6 percent.

There would be no further reductions in 1975 and the first leg of a two-year advance came to a sudden halt in July. For the balance of the year, a choppy market frustrated both bulls and bears. New York City's fiscal collapse, inflation fears, large unemployment, and a record peacetime budget kept the reins on stock prices. Short-term, tax-free notes of New York City had sold at a 60 percent annual-yield basis in May when the state senate rejected Big Apple aid.

A running battle between President Gerald Ford and the Democratic Congress was another source of concern. From mid-July to the year end, the Dow lost 30 points.

In January 1976, the discount rate was cut again and feverish buying reentered the market. On February 20, daily volume ran over 40 million shares for the first time and in March, the Dow climbed to 1009 before falling victim to profit taking. Steels had been among the popular leaders, with both U.S. Steel and Bethlehem Steel climbing to 15-year highs. General Motors was a strong ally; it advanced to 79, up 50 points from the 1974 low.

OPEC's growing greed would push many energy shares to even larger gains. The coals had strongly resisted the 1973–1974 slump. Westmoreland Coal's low in 1973 was 8, but it did not sell below 12 in the following year. By 1976, it would be 65. Smith International, a leading oil industry supplier, jumped from 10 to 43.

The brokerage shares, battered victims of the crash, had one of their best moves ever. Merrill Lynch was a 6–33 winner while Paine Webber had an even larger percentage move, 2 to 13.

Spring's massive enthusiasm for stocks pushed some groups, including the chemicals, to an early bull market top. Union Carbide, 32 in 1974 reached up to 77, but by the year end would fall back to 56. Du Pont and Dow Chemical mirrored that performance.

Other special situations kept rolling. Teledyne, which had tendered at $40 for its own shares in February, astounded its defectors by continuing on to 81. In 1974, it had been 7. Volatile National Semiconductor advanced from 6 to 55.

Not every stock participated. Americans' lust for gold, finally legalized at the end of 1974, had been overestimated—at least at $200 per ounce. Bullion fell steadily to the $100 level, reached in August 1976. Homestake was a 70–25 victim. Eli Lilly's growth slowed and the shares, which had rallied to 80 in 1975 from a bear low at 56, fell back to 43, its lowest level since 1970.

In September, the Dow notched up six points over its March peak, but enthusiasm was restrained. The big earnings gains had already been achieved. Other indices would move higher into 1977, including the Rails, but the Dow had crested.

And so had IBM. The powerful market leader had failed, for the first time since World War II, to even approach its previous bull market high. Its 1976 peak was 289 compared with 365 in 1973.

"Death of Equities" Exaggerated
DJIA Feb 28, 1978–Apr 27, 1981: 742.12 to 1024.05, +38%.

Business Week's stunning cover headline of August 13, 1979 announced the "Death of Equities." Fortunately, the dramatic headline proved premature.

The six-year period from 1976 to August 1982 was one of great frustration for bulls and bears alike. Net changes were modest but there was great price turbulence and, in 1979, a great gloom.

George Lindsay, the veteran timing seer, saw it all perfectly in his "Annual Forecast 1978" when he wrote in the *Advisor,* "We are going through a series of moderate bull and bear markets, which began two years ago. Neither a great boom nor a devastating collapse is in sight."[9]

Such words rang of heresy in an industry geared to dramatic changes, but the Dow was involved in a baffling and tremendously broad consolidation move.

Performance of the Dow in 1978 was consistent with Lindsay's forecast. The bear market low came at 742 on the last day of February. By early fall, the average was over 900, only to drop back below 800 by November.

The year ended with a small loss for all three Dow averages, but the result was negated by the large number of solid gainers at the NYSE where 118 issues gained 50 percent or more while only five lost that amount.

Consensus Bears

Inflation, scrambled charts, and divergence between the Dow and broader indices had convinced most investment advisors by the spring of 1979 to capitulate to the bearish arguments and gloom became the consensus. Depression, "killer waves," and Dow 400 were popular forecasts from even those veteran writers not given to reckless statements. Possibly, it was the aggravation of long gas lines.

The news budget was appalling. Inflation's sting hurt more each month. Interest rates soared and bond values, regardless of quality, slumped. Small investors, drawn to high bond yields, found that AAA quality was no guarantee of price if interest rates rose. They took a "quantum leap in financial sophistication," according to Salomon's Henry Kaufman.

Paper money was widely forecast to become worthless, but a hundred programs were conceived to separate the public from such. "Hard assets," such as collectibles, silver ingots, survival foods, and case lots of light bulbs were hawked by book, tract, and TV.

Even as OPEC pumped up oil prices and the twin deficit towers—trade and budget—grew taller, the Dow struggled back over 900 intraday in early October 1979. Paul Volcker and the Fed then shocked the Street with a weekend credit-tightening move—dubbed the "Saturday Night Special"—and inter-

---

[9]George Lindsay, Annual Forecast 1978, *Advisor,* Houston, Vol. III, No. 24, December 28, 1977, p. 4.

est rates rushed sharply higher. The Dow plunged from the year's high to the year's low within a few weeks.

In November, "students" seized the American Embassy in Teheran and in December, Russia invaded Afghanistan. Quality shares like IBM, AT&T, Sears, Kodak, GE, MMM, and Du Pont were all losers for the year. Smokestack stocks were sacked.

What was going up were the natural resource stocks. Commodity prices were in the fast lane and inflation plays were enormously popular. Blue chip anxieties didn't faze speculators at the AMEX, where a large listing of small energy companies and Canadian resource firms helped to push the AMEX index up 64 percent during the year.

Amazingly, the Dow on December 31, 1979 showed a nominal gain for the decade, up 38 points. Amazing, because the market had been battered in those ten years by two depressions, three bear markets, a record corporate bankruptcy, the worst inflation in 60 years, a fourfold increase in oil prices, Watergate, the Nixon resignation, and Gotham's flirtation with Chapter 11.

A Rush for Gold

A speculative explosion in the precious metals in January 1980 ushered in the most turbulent year since the 1930s. A towering madness for gold, below $400 in December, rocketed its price to $850 at the London fix on January 21. A $1,000 price was seen as inevitable. Silver, with strong-arm support by the Dallas billionaire and friends, rushed up to $50.

But, easy up was easy down. The precious boom caught the vapors and a "correction" turned to panic. A billion dollars in margin calls brought unrestrained selling into the market. Silver, on March 27, fell 32 percent in one day, touching $10.25. The SEC shut down trading in the stock of Bache & Co., principal broker for the participants in the alleged silver corner. Stocks were sacrificed at any price by the mangled longs.

It was all typical of a most volatile year. The prime rate, 15 percent at the end of 1979, reached 20 percent in April. By July, the rate had almost been halved, to 10.75 percent. An astounding 19 consecutive increases then pushed the bank charge to 21.5 percent by mid-December.

If the financials were on a yo-yo course, the price direction of oil was, at least, reliably one way, advancing quickly to $32 for Saudi light versus the 1979 close at $24. Inflation cloned oil price advances.

The Dow, after an April low at 759, ignored the nation's problems and achieved a significant success by Thanksgiving. There were, of course, defectors in the market, most notably energy-impacted firms. Yellow Freight, 34 in 1978, fell to 12. United Airlines dropped from 46 to 14 in the same period, even as the rail segment of the Transportation index prospered. Union Pacific, which had been 21 in 1978, powered up to 96, its best move in decades.

Fueling the market's big autumn advance were the oils and oil service stocks. Sohio, which had doubled in 1979, doubled again. Superior's gain from the 1978 low was 430 percent. Schlumberger was a 19–87 winner and Hughes

Tool's bull move was from 10 to 48. Dozens of lesser issues did even better in percentage terms.

Gold mining shares overcame the spring shock to metal prices and made their peaks in late autumn, spurred by the Iran-Iraq war, which started in September. Western Deep, 10 in 1979, rose to 85. Homestake moved from 19 to 88, and the high-cost Canadian, Lake Shore, drove from 5 to 40.

Raging bull excitement also worked quick wonders for the brokers, badly wounded in the March rumor-mill. Shearson Loeb Rhodes spun up from 10 to 38.

Though not heavily publicized, a number of specialty stocks continued highly successful careers. Metromedia, 4 in 1974, reached 176 in 1981. Waste Management and Warner Communications were sevenfold winners from 1978 to 1981. Mary Kay and United Cable did even better.

A heavily discounted Ronald Reagan victory and the return of a 20 percent prime rate finally did the celebration in, with the Dow turned back once again at the 1000 level. In December, the oils were heavily smashed, for reasons not entirely clear at the time, since $50 crude was an unarguable certainty in the Oil Patch. Nevertheless, many energy-related stocks had already recorded their peak prices for the 1980s.

On January 7, 1981, Joe Granville's famous "abandon all hope" alarm staggered the market, exciting the largest volume in history. But by mid-February the Dow, at least, had recovered and recorded a series of closes over 1000 in April, finally peaking at 1024, strangled once again by an escalation of the prime.

The great inflation play had ended. There had been heavy casualties on the bond lists, but few reported equity obituaries; they would appear later in an aftershock of deflation.

BUYING PANICS

Stock market panics are not confined to the sell side. And while a buying panic lasting several months seems a misnomer, such periods of high-volume, uncorrected upside activity have been cast into the Street glossary as panics. In recent decades, they had been institutionally driven.

They last about two to four months and can come in any phase of a bull market, or as part of a serious bear market rally. True buying panics, those lasting but a day or so, have been startling in their successes. On October 6, 1931, the Dow rammed up 15 percent as an enormous short-covering move got under way. That huge gain was matched in the "daily" advance of March 15, 1933, when the Exchange reopened following the bank holiday. The important one-day rallies are tabulated following the multimonth sequences.

Those longer episodes are mostly restricted to sequences where gains exceeded 25 percent in a period of not over four months. Many improved vastly on those credentials, with advances equal to that of some minor bulls markets.

The following is a list of the major Dow buying panics since 1890.

1893 —Jly 26–Oct 28 Erie bankruptcy exhausts bear forces. Rails rise 33%.

1896 —Aug 8–Nov 12 Silver threat, Bryan campaign fade. Explosive 58% rise.

1897 —Jne 1–Sep 20 Big upside volume develops based on favorable rail decision and Dingley Tariff. Industrial advance: 44%.

1898 —May 2–Aug 26 War victories at Manilla, Santiago, San Juan boost Dow 25%.

1899 —Jan 2–Apr 25 First big speculative play for Industrials, helped by many pools and manipulations. Gain: 28%.

1900 —Sep 24–Nov 20 "McKinley Prosperity" wins second term and 30% jump for Dow.

1904 —Sep 6–Dec 5 Post-Labor Day action leads to explosive volume; October sees more million-share days than all of 1903. Dow up 32%.

1905 —Nov 13–Jan 19, 1906 Copper capers and other manipulations push Dow up 27% to highest level of 1897–1914 period.

1915 —Mar 20–Apr 30 Wartime economic fears fade. Dow up 25% as U.S. Steel reverses sharply.
Jly 9–Oct 22 Superior gain of 42% marred by 6 percent setback in August.

1916 —Aug 8–Nov 21 Bethlehem Steel and General Motors lead intense advance of 25%.

1919 —Apr 7–Nov 3 Inflation blow-off, oil frenzy stir volume to 13-year peak. Dow gains 33% in longish episode.

1928 —Aug 14–Nov 28 Easy money. No correction of more than 2% in Jly–November period. Pools help force Industrials up 38%.

1929 —May 27–Sep 3 This is the 1929 bull market, as Dow was still minus for year at end of May. Summer rally a strong 30%.

1930 —Jan 7–Apr 17 Short on advance statistic, up only 19%, but April's volume second greatest in upside history, lagging only November 1928.

1931 —Oct 5–Nov 9 Shorts panic and run Dow up by 35% in a month.

1932 —Jly 8–Sep 7 Dow up 94% in two months. Rails, Utilities do even better.

1933 —Apr 1–Jly 18 Up 95% as bulls toast FDR leadership and upcoming repeal of Prohibition. March–July gain of 117% omitted because of 12% slide late March.

1938 —May 31–Aug 6 Recession ends. Retail sales boom. Dow rises 35%.

1962 —Oct 23–Feb 18, 1963 Reflex from Cuban missile crisis boosts Dow by 23% and Rails 32%.

1974 —Dec 6–Mar 17, 1975 Reflex from worst market since 1930's. Dow gain: 36%.

1975 —Dec 5–Mar 24, 1976 Gain only 23%, but January's advance remains the best for any month since World War II.

1980 —Apr 21–Aug 15 Longish buying stampede takes market up by 27% in rebound from silver crisis. Sliding interest rates big booster.

1982 —Aug 12–Nov 3 One of history's great buying panics is ignited by sudden collapse of interest rates. Explosive volume pushes Dow up 37%.

1986 —Jan 23–Mar 27 Institutional demand heats up. Dow plus 21%.

1987 —Jan 2–Mar 27 Market whizzes by Dow milestones at 2000, 2100, 2200, and 2300. Average advances 475 points, or 25%. Classic buying panic.

IMPORTANT ONE-DAY BUYING PANICS

REFLEX FROM PANIC CONDITIONS

		Pct. Gain	
1893	—Jly 27	6.6	(20-Stocks). Erie bankruptcy ended Rail panic July 26.
1901	—May 10	6.5	Rebound from Northern Pacific panic.
1903	—Oct 16	5.1	Bargain hunting. Rockefeller a heavy buyer of U.S. Steel preferred.
1907	—Mar 15	6.7	Rush to buy following mysterious March 14 collapse.
1926	—Mar 3	4.4	Multiple bear records broken March 2. Panic low still four weeks away.
1929	—Oct 30	12.3	Aggressive bargain hunting after 23% drop of October 28–29.
1937	—Oct 20	6.1	Reflex follows big reversal day. Dow had lost 34% since mid-August.
1962	—May 29	4.7	Biggest point advance since 1929. Ended "Kennedy Panic," though prices dragged lower.
1963	—Nov 26	4.5	JFK assassinated Friday. NYSE closed Monday. Record point gain.
1970	—May 27	5.1	Bear market of 1968–1970 ended previous day. Another record Dow up.
1974	—Oct 9	4.7	Interest rates fall. Hope returns.
1980	—Apr 22	4.0	Technical end to silver crisis. Lower rates. Granville buys.

1987 —Oct 21   10.1   Meltdown cools. Record up-day in points and volume.

NEWS ORIENTED

1920 —Nov 22   4.3   Finger in the dike. Du Pont interests take over stricken General Motors.

1930 —Jne 19   4.6   FRB discount cut to 2.5%, lowest ever. Bargain hunting.

1931 —Oct 6   14.9   Hoover seeks solons' cooperation for economic recovery. Sterling crisis over.

1932 —Sep 21   11.4   C&O, other rails report strong August loadings and earnings. Heavy short covering.

1933 —Mar 15   15.3   FDR action during bank holiday encourages record up-day.

1934 —Jan 15   4.6   President asks for devaluation of dollar in attempt to reflate commodity prices and boost exports.

1938 —Apr 9   5.2   New Deal defeat in Congress. More pump priming slated.

1940 —Nov 7   4.4   Inflation: Treasury seeks debt boost, halt to tax exempts.

1957 —Oct 23   4.1   Space race begins. Sputnik panic ends. Biggest daily point gain since 1929.

1978 —Nov 1   4.5   U.S. will risk recession, fight for $. Discount rate up, gold down.

1982 —Aug 17   4.9   Interest rates in collapse. Institutional buying frenzy.

WAR-INFLUENCED RALLIES

1895 —Dec 21   5.3   (20 Stocks). "War" with England suddenly seems laughable.

1898 —May 2   5.7   Dewey torpedoes Spanish fleet at Manilla. Short war foreseen.

1899 —Dec 19   4.7   British war reverses slow in Transvaal. War panic ends.

1915 —May 11   4.2   Wilson intimates no war. Lusitania had been sunk May 7.

1916 —Dec 22   5.5   Bargain hunting follows bizarre sequence peace-war scares.

1939 —Sep 5   7.3   Buying frenzy follows Nazi invasion of Poland.

Armistice in 1918 and V.E.-Day and V.J.-Day at end of World War II were market nonevents, victory having been well discounted.

4

Bear Markets since 1890

The period of 1929–1932 remains the nonpareil among the bear markets of the past century. No other decline has even approached its loss of 89 percent. Its human and financial tragedies have been remorselessly explored.

Often forgotten is the fact that the century's second worst market crash also occurred in the 1930s, in 1937–1938. It was a devastating affair, lasting but 12 months, and cutting the Dow Industrials by 49 percent. In this study, it is seen as part of a longer bearish episode, "The Winds of War, 1937–1942," with a loss of 52 percent, but it is identified separately in the statistical section under "Major Price Movements Dow Jones Industrials."

Five other bitter periods have found the Dow falling between 45 percent and 49 percent. The 1916–1917 slide dropped the Dow 40 percent in just a year, a minimum qualification for the list of great declines.

In each of these bear markets, the final bottom has come only when all excesses had been wrung out and when the news was so black that it could get

TABLE 4-1　BEAR MARKETS SINCE 1890

The great declines		
Periods	Years	Loss (%)
The Great Train Wreck	1890–1896	47%
"Rich Man's Panic"	1901–1903	46
The Great Copper Capers	1906–1907	49
Peace Scare, War Scare	1916–1917	40
War's Hangover	1919–1921	47
The Bankrupt Years	1929–1932	89
Winds of War	1937–1942	52
"Blood and Tiers"	1973–1974	45
Major bear markets		
Periods	Years	Loss (%)
Big Business Battered	1909–1914	29
The "Kennedy Panic"	1961–1962	27
Worst Year Since 1937	1966–1966	25
A Broadening Experience	1968–1970	36
Market Up, Dow Down	1976–1978	27
Other bear sequences		
Periods	Years	Loss (%)
Worth More Dead Than Alive	1946–1949	24
Bears Fumble Opportunity	1956–1957	19
The "Soaring Sixties"?	1960–1960	17
Inflation's Ugly Flip Side	1981–1982	24

no worse. By that time, stressed longs had exhausted their purses and been forced to liquidate their margin accounts.

The Great Train Wreck
20-Stocks Jne 4, 1890–Aug 8, 1896: 78.38 to 41.82, −47%.

The panic of 1893 placed 74 railroads with nearly 30,000 miles of track in receivership or bankruptcy. It was the greatest train wreck of all time. Many historic names like the Reading, Erie, Union Pacific, Southern Pacific, and Santa Fe would head for the courthouse during the year.

The primary decline seen in February 1892 to July 1893 dropped the 20-Stock Average by 43 percent and ended in panic. It was the centerpiece of three separate bear sequences during the early 1890s which resulted in a six-year market slide.

During these six years, the economy was blighted by low farm prices, severe unemployment, bitter strikes, and social unrest. The year of 1894 was a period of hard depression with commercial failure liabilities amounting to three times the figure in 1892.

For the railroads, the most important section of the business economy, the roots of the period's problems went back to the 1880s when a glorious expansion of railroad mileage had made a thousand hamlets happy. Some 40,000 miles of new track had been added between 1886 and 1890. Much of the new track, however, was in low-traffic spur and connecting lines in competitive areas. And much of it was heavily capitalized, often built under crooked contracts.

Junk bonds were not an innovation of the 1980s. They were a railroad specialty over 100 years ago.

If hamlets were happy, railroad traffic agents were not. Net revenues had eroded to the point where J. Pierpont Morgan repeatedly convened the rail chiefs in an effort to stabilize rates. Unfortunately, each truce was quickly followed by another outbreak of guerrilla rate wars.

The decade of the 1890s had started out brightly enough. The 20-Stock Average (18 Rails, 2 Industrials) rose to 78.38 in June 1890, having gained 35 percent from the major low of April 1888. From that point, the market would suffer through a series of lower highs and lower lows until 1896. Table 4-2 shows the secular erosion of some popular stocks during the 1890–1896 period.

A minor bear market had occupied the balance of 1890, climaxing in December. "Gaucho finance" had done in London's great merchant banking firm, the House of Baring, and when Argentine credits became sticky in October, London selling pressured prices at the NYSE. Further damage was done when a speculative pool in Northern Pacific was crushed in November. The Baring crisis ended swiftly in December, thanks to aid from the Bank of England.

Up: December 1890 to March 1892

Over the next 14 months, the market struggled higher, helped immensely in 1891 by a record grain crop and export demand. A high-volume, manipulated blow-off came in February 1892. It was spurred by a powerful pool in the Philadelphia & Reading, whose president conspired to monopolize the production and transportation of anthracite coal. The Rail high came shortly later, on March 4, though prices would move only grudgingly lower. The bitter Homestead steel strike and the receivership of the Richmond Terminal system with its far-flung, 8,000-mile system were frustrating for bulls during the summer.

TABLE 4-2   TYPICAL DOWNTRENDS, 1890–1896

	1890 High	1890 Low	1892 High	1893 Low	1895 High	1896 Low
Chicago, Rock Island	99	62	94	51	84	49
Illinois Central	120	85	110	86	106	84
Missouri Pacific	79	53	66	17	43	15
New York, New Haven	270	250	255	188	218	160
20-Stock Average	78.38	58.10	75.68	43.47	63.77	41.82

More damaging was the 1892 collapse of three major railroad traffic associations. They had enjoyed considerable success in patching together rate agreements and their dissolutions led to immediate and savage pricing competition, hastening the great rail tragedies of 1893.

For the balance of 1892, however, the market had moved sideways until November, when the strong vote for Grover Cleveland and Democratic friends turned stock prices decisively lower.

These early years of the 1890s witnessed a huge expansion of industrial trusts, generally large combinations of firms within one line of business. Greedy and unscrupulous men, among others, were impressed by the success of the trusts formed in the late 1880s in such diverse lines as sugar, whiskey, and cotton oil. They moved rapidly to forge new combinations of trade which were grandly watered, capitalized far in excess of their tangible assets. Pine and twine, glue, matches, even soda fountains were seen as products where profits might be enhanced by consolidation and, hopefully, monopoly. General Electric and U.S. Rubber were formed in 1892.

Hard times would come in 1893–1894, when it was quickly discovered that it was one thing to water stock and quite another to pay dividends on it. Many cartels would fail quickly, though none had been more surely doomed than the United States Buggy Whip trust.

The Silver Problem

In 1890, a political trade-off resulted in the passage of the Silver Purchase Act, pleasing to western miners and southern inflationists, and the McKinley Tariff Act, which was heartily endorsed by the eastern manufacturers and the GOP.

The Treasury was required to purchase 4.5 million ounces of silver monthly, issuing silver certificates in payment. The certificates, which were recirculated, could be exchanged for either gold or silver.

Europe's passion for silver was something less than that of the western Senators. Distrustful of the dollar and the threat of a silver currency basis, Europe chose to realize her credits in gold, creating a growing currency crisis.

In 1893, the railroad problems, the watered stock problems, and a silver crisis matured simultaneously, sparking both a financial and Exchange panic.

The first severe blow to the market came February 20, 1893, when the Reading, a victim of its own greedy plots, was foreclosed. Shares, 53 in January and 65 one year earlier, would drop to 12.

In May, the manipulated National Cordage Trust collapsed. It had been a speculative spring feature, with help from the master pool operator, James R. Keene, and had delighted shareholders with a split and handsome dividend in April. On May 1, peculiarly, the company ran out of cash. The preferred shares were knocked down from 104 to 45 within the week. The common suffered even more.

Panic swept the Exchange. Industrial trusts, even monopolies, it was suddenly learned, offered no portfolio insurance. The "whiskey trust," 66 in January, fell to 13. Gold was hoarded. The New York Clearing House Association was forced to issue loan certificates to facilitate bank clearings. There would be 15,000 commercial failures during the year.

At the same time, the silver problem reached a stage of crisis. In late June, Parliament closed the mints of India to free silver coinage. Bullion's bloated price of $1.27/oz. in 1890 and 81.5 cents before the announcement, plunged to 62 cents. Treasury gold reserves fell dangerously.

With a full-blown commercial and currency crisis at hand, the smash of stock prices did not end until July 26, when the Erie suffered a financial derailment. Distress margin liquidation wreaked its usual havoc. The Evansville & Terre Haute, 127 bid on July 25, fell to 75, while the 20-Stock Average ended at 43.00 on the day, having lost about 43 percent of its value in 17 months. The news, but not the market, would worsen. Pig iron production would fall to an eight-year low in the second half.

Up: July 1893 to September 1895

President Cleveland called Congress into a special August session, asking for repeal of the Silver Act. After interminable Senate debate, fostered by the inflationists and silverites, the repeal bill was passed in the late fall. The move had already been market-discounted; Rails had rallied by 33 percent from the summer low.

Depression in 1894 followed the panic of 1893, but the market moved sideways despite the bad news. Railroad earnings per mile were at their worst level in history. Extensive strikes plagued the country, headlined by the Pullman troubles. Dividends were cut. Commodity prices slumped and gold continued to emigrate. Stocks bought at the panic levels of the previous summer showed surprising gains, however. National Lead ran from 11 in July 1893 to 45 and Chicago Gas doubled, 39 to 80.

When the Democrats had returned to power in March 1893, they were resolved to lower tariffs. Exorbitant duties and the greedy trusts were blamed for high city prices. The Wilson-Gorman Tariff Act, passed in August 1894, did lower some duties, though gouging consumers with a sugar increase, and also introduced an income tax in a populist victory over the East and Wall Street. The income tax cast a pall over the market until it was ruled unconstitutional in the late spring of 1895.

By February 1895, Treasury gold reserves had fallen to $41 million, but J. P. Morgan and friends replenished the stock, trading $65 million in bullion for 30-year government bonds at 4 percent. Patriotism was not its own reward. The bonds, taken in at 104, were immediately sold for 112. Silverites equated the principles and principals with Benedict Arnold. But the temporary relief from the gold run and a labored prosperity boosted the market until September. The 1893–1895 gain had been 47 percent.

Down: September 1895 to August 1896

A summer rally peaked in September and prices drifted lower until December, when President Cleveland seemed to threaten war with Great Britain. The issue involved arbitration of a boundary dispute between that country and Venezuela.

Waving the Monroe Doctrine in front of America's largest creditor was taken poorly by the market, which dropped 15 percent within a week. General Electric, 41 in September, fell to 20. But the selling bash ended as quickly as it had started and at year end the 20-Stock Average was only a point away from the nested closes of 1893 and 1894. The year's range was less than seven points.

More bonds for gold were traded in January, but there was a huge oversubscription and the dollar's reputation seemed temporarily assured. The market steadied, though the Baltimore & Ohio (which had paid its first dividend in 1831) joined the receivers' bench in March.

In the summer, "16-to-1" mania seized the agrarian and southern states once again. William Jennings Bryan mesmerized the inflationists at the Democratic convention in Chicago with his "Cross of Gold" oratory. A brief, but severe "Bryan Panic" fell upon the market. The Rock Island, 73 in mid-June, fell to 49; Chicago Gas slumped from 70 to 45. General Electric, which had come off the mat at 20 in December for a rally back to 40 in the spring, collapsed to 20 once again.

But the silver issue had driven "gold Democrats" away from the party and Bryan's threat by late August was seen as diminishing; the market lows of that month would not be threatened for decades. The third and last bear sequence of the 1890s had cost the Rail Average 34 percent in a decline lasting 11 months.

The six-year decline (Figure 4-1) had amounted to a loss of 47 percent, a figure typical of the most serious bear markets of the past century.

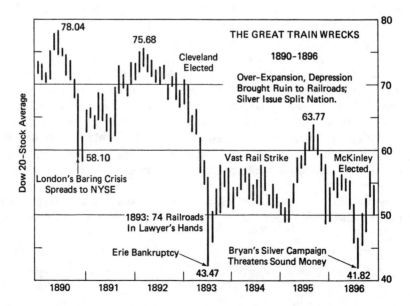

Figure 4.1 Dow Jones 20-Stock Average, 1890–1896

The "Rich Man's Panic"
DJIA Jne 17, 1901–Nov 9, 1903: 78.26 to 42.15, −46%.

The great age of trustification, 1899–1903, came to an abrupt end. Every industry that could be consolidated had been "trustified," including many, like the witch hazel amalgamation, that would have been better left unexploited.

The Rails' popularity continued into early autumn 1902, but trouble for the Industrials had been under way since June 1901. Amalgamated Copper, the Rockefeller copper trust, had assayed a dream of monopolistic pricing for its huge hoard. The price slipped a few pennies on 130 million pounds of metal and Amalgamated collapsed from a summer high of 130 to 61 in December.

U.S. Steel had started trading in February 1901, though the shares had been so watered that they had no intrinsic evaluation. But James R. Keene's adroit manipulation took the stock up to 55 in April, allowing many insiders to slip away. U.S. Steel would not see its April price again until 1908.

The public was bagged in all of the trusts, not the least of which was the grossly overcapitalized American Can. It had disappointed by failing to qualify for the steel amalgamation, after quickly throwing together over 120 plants into the "tin can trust" in the spring of 1901.

In September 1901, the assassination of President McKinley put Theodore Roosevelt in the White House. His exuberance did not carry over to the Industrials, which slid lower for the balance of the year, despite firmness in the Rails which were encouraged by the holding company concept displayed in the Northern Securities blending of Northern Pacific and the Great Northern. Investors anticipated a lessening of rate competition.

Both Industrial and Rail shares steadied in 1902, with the firmness lasting into late summer, despite a Justice Department suit against the Northern Securities Company and a bitter coal strike. But harvest time brought tight money and both averages slumped, deterred late in the year by a large bankers' pool thrown together to slow the decline.

U.S. Steel was to be the sad news in 1903. The world's largest corporation, 40 in January, would fall to 10 in November. In October, its dividend was cut and at the January 1904 board meeting, it would be eliminated. Even in 1901 the $4 dividend basis had been sharply criticized as too much, too soon.

Adding to Morgan's woes was his underwriting failure for a North Atlantic Shipping trust, the International Mercantile Marine. It would be a long-lived disaster. The account, according to one Morgan historian, was ". . . finally closed in July, 1906, with the underwriters still holding 75% to 80%" of the offering.*

Banks and insurance firms were also buried under large blocks of trust paper, since they were active security underwriters and distributors at the

---

*Vincent P. Carosso, with the assistance of Rose C. Carosso, *The Morgans, Private International Bankers, 1854–1913* (Cambridge, MA and London, England: Harvard University Press, 1988), p. 486.

STOCK TICKER SYMBOLS

In 1903 upon the opening of its new building, the NYSE published its first guide to ticker symbols. Single-letter symbols, originally developed among telegraph operators seeking to conserve time and wire space, were already a sign of some corporate status, but were only fitted to high-volume stocks.

Thus, the Atchison was "A." The Brooklyn Rapid Transit was "B" and the Canadian Pacific "C." Despite many bankruptcies, the Erie Railroad had remained an active trader and held on to its historic "E" symbol. Only three Industrials merited a one-letter call, including Western Union (W).

Over the next 50 years, the Rails' dominance eroded. Auto shares were the big market leaders and Chrysler, Hupp, and Packard (K) were in the single-letter peerage. Other transportation modes had also moved on the Rails. Douglas Aircraft had become "D" and Greyhound, "G."

Rather sadly, few of the famous designations remain. Sears, to be sure, has been "S" for decades and AT&T, despite the split-up, remains "T." Woolworth is still "Z." But few other classics remain, as merger and attrition have removed old names. When public relations and advertising types transformed Standard of New Jersey into something called Exxon (XON), its famous "J" symbol was not retired to some stock exchange hall of fame. Rather, it became the designation for Jackpot Enterprises, a Nevada slot machine operator.

---

time. Undigested securities or, as some said, indigestible securities had become the Street's worst problem.

By the summer of 1903, it was obvious that the magic of the trust was no armor against a bearish tide, even for Standard of Jersey. Its dividend was cut to $40 from $48 and would reduce further to $36 in 1904. The shares dropped nearly $300 during the period from a high at 830.

Others did worse on a percentage basis. The American Bicycle trust's preferred fell from $52 to 50 cents. Union Bag & Paper lost two thirds of its value. Colorado Fuel was a big loser, 83 to 24. Steel production slid by 60 percent between August and December 1903. Steel preferred made its low that year at 50, a shattering decline for the $7 dividend shares, whose payout would be maintained. The stock had sold at 102 in 1901. Steel common would suffer more in early 1904, dropping to 8⅜.

The Rails lost but 31 percent in their September to September decline of 1902–1903. Santa Fe was cut down from 94 to 54 and Illinois Central from 178 to 125. Passion for the transit fancies cooled dramatically, however. Brooklyn Rapid Transit, a member of the Dow Rail Average, fell from 72 in April 1902 to 21. Quality rails held decently, but the speculative carriers suffered; the Cotton Belt dropped from 30 to 12 within a few months.

When the decline was over, it was obvious that the principal victims had been the glorified trusts—and their syndicators. The nation had not suffered severely, despite some tight money. There had been no panic, no extreme depression, and no midnight lights at the New York Clearing House.

The 1903 slump became known as the "Rich Man's Panic," since that constituency was most heavily concentrated in the trusts.

The Rails fell to 88.80; it was a nominal loss in relation to their 1896–1902 gains. Figure 4-2 shows the striking divergences between the two averages in the 1896–1902 period.

The Great Copper Capers
DJIA Jan 19, 1906–Nov 15, 1907: 103.00 to 53.00, −49%.

The last great financial panic of a type so common in the nineteenth century struck in the autumn of 1907. New York banks were easily identified by the long lines of desperate depositors demanding a refund.

The road to those troubled days had been marked by an intense period of speculation in both the copper shares and the metal, rather than the traditional rail and steel favorites. News of marvelous ore discoveries in the great Anaconda mine had spurred the Dow's January 1906 top.

The *Wall Street Journal* uncovered an early-day version of insider trading in the coppers, based on rich new ore finds. Their correspondent reported on January 19 that "Miners rushed to friends to pledge their names and proper-

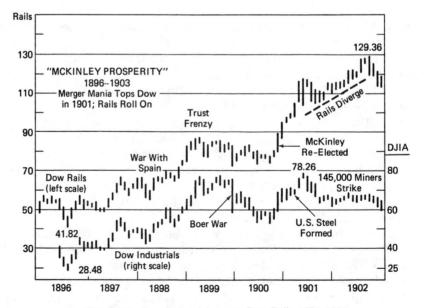

Figure 4.2 Dow Industrials versus Dow Rails, 1896–1902

THE ELECTRIC CITY

A primary reason for the fascination with copper shares, copper corners, and copper manipulations in the early 1900s was the immense growth in electric demands.

An all-electric city seemed on its way. The employment of electric current for transportation, illumination, distribution of power, and the transmission of speech and words was wondrous—and all over copper wires.

Even the statistical drones at the Census Bureau were impressed. "The rapidity of growth in these (electric) fields is probably unsurpassed in any other branch of human activity" was the fulsome praise of a Bureau bulletin.

Unfortunately for the copper manipulators, growing world production and technological improvements took the metal off the endangered species list. Its last big play as a market leader was in the 1905–1907 period.

ties. They mortgaged their homes and telegraphed Wall Street for the purchase of Anaconda shares."[1]

The news was out and easier pricing followed. Anaconda had already tripled its low price of 1905 and was up 400 percent from the bear market low of 1903.

If Anaconda was a rich producer, it was also rich in claim litigation. But the new bonanza made it worthwhile to buy out F. Augustus Heinze, a Montana smelter operator, whose assets it was once claimed were 100 lawsuits. His quit-claim price was in the exorbitant millions, but Amalgamated, which controlled Anaconda and was associated with the Standard Oil interests, would have its revenge in 1907.

A spring slump was climaxed by the havoc of the San Francisco earthquake and it was not until August that a sustained rally could take place. Then E. H. Harriman and the Union Pacific, enriched by the return of monies from the dissolution of the Northern Securities Company, launched an enormous buying program, centered on the N.Y. Central, the Baltimore & Ohio, and the Sante Fe, spending about $56 million in the heated rail sessions of August.

Harriman was so busy that his Union Pacific neglected to report a large increase in the line's dividend for two days and this lamentable if legal lapse caused talk, and a bit later in the year, an investigation by the ICC. There was little follow-through to the August excitement, however, and both averages continued to work on a stretched-out top, which lasted until January 1907.

In the winter, the market seemed to tire of its lengthy consolidation. Inflation and tightening interest rates were unsettling and on March 14, for

---

[1]The *Wall Street Journal*, New York, January 22, 1906, sec. 1, p.2, col. 3.

reasons still poorly explained, the Dow was suddenly slashed by 7 percent. The seeds of panic had been sown, though a large pool operation patched the market back together by the month end.

At about this time, the United Metals Corporation, a Perth Amboy metals refiner and sales agent, also allied with Standard of Jersey interests, developed a sudden lust for copper actuals, instituting a hoarding program. Their inventory of pods, pigs, electrolytic, and Mexican metal bloomed at a prodigious rate, from 30 million pounds in February to 141 million pounds in early autumn.

When the corner failed, the asking price of 25 cents per pound was not quite "on" the market, and the billets went out the door at about 13 cents. Five years later, Congress's Pujo committee developed an innovative thesis that the metal had been withdrawn from the market to allow stockholders of certain copper mining companies to work off their equity positions under the false umbrella of "25 cent copper."

In August, Judge Kenesaw Landis gaveled Indiana Standard with a $29 million fine for rate rebatements and the Rails came under heavy selling from London where American bills of exchange had become unpopular.

It would take one more copper caper, however, to capsize the market. F. Augustus Heinze had taken his millions from Butte to New York, where he fell in with various monied players, including the president of the Knickerbocker Trust Company. The group pushed a corner in the shares of United Copper, a dangerous game late in the bear sequence, and when the plot unraveled, United Copper shares fell from 84 to 10 within a day.

The Knickerbocker and its allied banks circled the wagons, but there was no help from the establishment or the Clearing House. The copper manipulators were broken, but the resulting banking panic nearly brought the Street down. Amalgamated, however, had gained its revenge on Heinze.

The Panic of 1907

The panic was short and brutal, with a loss of 32 percent between early August and mid-November. In Pittsburgh, Westinghouse failed.

Cash was nonexistent and clearing house script acted as currency between banks. In California, trendy even then, the state constructed a revolving bank holiday which would extend until December 23.

The Knickerbocker had been abandoned by the establishment for several reasons, one being its status as a trust which allowed it certain liberal practices denied regular banks. But the abandonment boomeranged in the resulting bank runs. Bethlehem Steel laid off 7,000 workers. New York City was at the wall. The city's financial leaders turned once again to J. P. Morgan.

Aid also came from the Treasury and the Bank of England. Morgan put together a consortium which, with the aid of $25 million and confidence in Morgan, brought succor. But only after call money had gone to 125 percent.

Morgan saved the banks. He also captured the enormously rich Tennessee Coal & Iron with a squeeze play on the White House, which was seen to grant antitrust immunity in return for assistance in halting the panic. Morgan and friends had blotted up various bank and brokerage house accounts which were facing ruin because of thinly margined Tennessee Coal & Iron. The ploy afforded Pierpont a double joy. It enriched U.S. Steel at a bargain takeover price and removed from the active New York scene the noisome John W. Gates, whose large margin position in Tennessee was sacrificed. "Bet a Million" Gates had been a director and large shareholder of the Tennessee and had earned Morgan's enmity by stealing the L&N from his clutches in 1902. And then selling the road back to Morgan at a highwayman's profit.

The panic ended on November 15. Coppers, cornered or otherwise, were not the only severe losers, though few groups could match their huge totals. Amalgamated was smashed from 122 to 42; Calumet & Hecla was axed from 1000 to 535.

Westinghouse Electric dropped from 154 to 32. In the money panic, even the highest-quality paper yielded huge returns. Jersey Standard sold at 390 for a 10 percent yield. AT&T saw its $6 preferred at 60. The preferred of American Can yielded nearly 14 percent, as did the common stock of American Tobacco. An important bear market low for bonds was also made in the autumn months.

The great panic had nearly brought the Street down but need not have been so severe. The Knickerbocker could have been saved, but it had no friends in the establishment. In the spring of 1908, having had time to realize its assets, the trust company repaid its depositors 100 percent.

Peace Scare, War Scare
DJIA Nov 21, 1916–Dec 19, 1917: 110.15 to 65.95, −40%.

The bear market of 1916–1917 was triggered by a peace scare, fueled by a war scare and, finally, war itself for America.

The United States, armorer to the Allies, was geared up to produce the rations of war. Since 1914, a wave of expansion and new plants had occupied the country. Employment, inventories, and backlogs had soared in the arming process. The stock market, a toll-man for the march to prosperity, had more than reflected that expansion and was not prepared for peace, which seemed to threaten in early December 1916.

President Woodrow Wilson had been secretly working for a peace conference since September, following receipt of a peace note from Kaiser Wilhelm. After his reelection, the president pushed additional peace feelers.

Suddenly, the war babies were denied. Insiders, some would say later, were liquidating and selling short long before Wilson's public peace messages to the war leaders on December 18. Bernard Baruch and Jesse Livermore were later found to have been huge short operators in the fall.

Heavy selling hit the list in the second week of December and liquidation accelerated as peace rumors leaked. If the market was unprepared for peace, it was also unprepared for American intervention and was shocked on December 21, when Secretary of State Robert Lansing stated that the United States was being drawn into the war. The Dow suffered its worst drop since July 1914.

Volume was the heaviest since the "Nipper" panic of 1901 and would not be matched again until 1925.

War in Europe had been bullish. Peace in Europe had been seen as bearish. But, the United States at war in Europe was even more bearish.

On January 31, 1917, Germany announced a program of unrestricted submarine warfare and the Dow fell sharply to 87 on February 2, having lost 26 percent of its bull market peak value in about ten weeks. President Wilson broke off relations with Germany on February 3, and on April 2 asked for a declaration of war.

Being a gunsmith was one thing. Being a gunner was something else, as the market had anticipated. In March, an excess profits tax was passed. Inflation exploded. In May, the Chicago Board of Trade closed, wheat having raced from $2 bushel to $3 within weeks. Cotton traded to its highest level since the Civil War. In October, price controls were slapped on steel and in December, the government took over control of the railroads.

In the meantime, the coveted war stocks of 1915–1916 were taking a beating. Bethlehem Steel slumped to 265 (basis the old $700 shares). The previously disappointing Rails turned into a disaster. The St. Paul dropped from 103 to 35; Chicago North Western fell to its lowest price since 1896. Sears lost 114 points from its January 1917 high of 238. Maxwell Motors dropped from 99 to 19.

In September, the Rail Average fell below its prewar level and the plunge continued into December. The sharp 13-month bear market, now almost forgotten in the other events of the war, erased 40 percent of value, as earnings for the Dow fell by 18 percent. About 78 percent of the 1914–1916 gain was lost in the slide.

War's Hangover
DJIA Nov 3, 1919–Aug 24, 1921: 119.62 to 63.90, −47%.

The wild economic and stock market binge of 1919 was followed by a hangover of classic proportions. Though the market had already peaked, America would suffer continued acute inflation in the first half of 1920. In the second half of the year, a forest fire of deflation raced across the country, spreading from commodity to commodity, industry to industry.

Bituminous coal, $9.51 a ton in the spot market in September, would fall to $2.40 nine months later. Composite steel prices, which averaged $85.50 in July, would fall to $42.20 in 1921.

Wall Street was not spared and on one frightening afternoon, September 16, it even came under bomb attack. Thirty innocents were killed outside the Morgan offices, but it was never determined whether anarchists or disgruntled stockholders were the culprits.

In the spring of 1920, the Street's attention had been riveted on a pair of stunning automotive corners. Allen A. Ryan, president of Stutz Motor Car, maker of the sporty Bobcat, launched a lightning attack against the Stutz bears and within weeks pushed the price up from near par to 391 at the end of

March. It was the most sensational corner since the Northern Pacific "natural" of 1901.

Late on March 31, the Exchange announced that it was suspending the shares of the Indianapolis car maker. A few lambs paid over $700 to buy in their shorts in the OTC market, but great push and shove finally allowed the bears an escape price of $550.

Ryan, like many manipulators before and after, then found the corpse impossible to bury, for he had no place to lay off his great holdings. Lawyers and his final bankruptcy would claim a moral victory for the bears. The stock fell to 5 in 1923. Ryan's father, the ultra-rich Thomas Fortune Ryan, a true lion in the Street, had no part in his son's misadventure.

The name William Crapo Durant has pleased every chronicler of his life. A founder of General Motors, he had been ousted as its president in 1911, only to recapture the job. By 1920, he was headed for the door a second time.

His stock manipulations would receive enormous attention in 1920 and during the rest of the decade. He was possessed by the market and maintained his General Motors office in New York, not Detroit. In the early winter of 1920, he and a pool entered the market in an attempt to corner the shares of General Motors. Corral them they did, driving the price as high as 410 in late March against a value of 228 at the end of February. Their corner was in the "old" $100 par shares for which a 10:1 split had been effected, but the new shares were not good delivery against the old.

The shorts were put against the wall but a reprieve arrived just before the firing squad, when the NYSE ruled that the split shares would be good delivery. Twenty million new shares busted the corner and Durant and friends were lucky to recover their chits.

If the Street's attention had been focused on the great auto manipulations, management attention was fixed on the astonishing melt in sales and showroom traffic. Waiting lists for new cars had disappeared. The sizzling inflation had aroused a great public clamor and a loosely organized but devastating buyers' strike swept the country. The Justice Department launched a war on "profiteering."

The Fed hiked the discount rate to 7 percent in June and suddenly business inventories, already expensive, seemed bloated. Commercial activity just faded away. Detroit was in crisis. A General Motors underwriting was cold-turkeyed and the stock fell below 13 (130 on the presplit shares). A postwar depression had arrived worldwide and foreign exchange markets were in disarray.

Ford cut prices and then closed the nation's largest auto plant, laying off thousands. General Motors was in deep trouble, along with the stock, even though Durant had wasted millions during the summer in price-support operations. He would be ousted in November as the Du Pont interests strengthened their control.

The rubber stocks suffered immensely, having earlier hoarded a raw inventory at record prices. Even the cork market was compressed. Armstrong Cork wryly noted in a January 1921 tombstone advertisement for its ten-year, 7 percent gold notes that 1920 profits were a record, except that millions had to be written off "to adjust present inventories to current market conditions."

Depression and unemployment took over. Jobless figures were the worst since 1898. Another farm crisis dropped American Agricultural Chemical from 114 to 27. John Deere's well-regarded preferred was ploughed under, from 103 to 59.

Atlantic Refining, the highest-priced issue at the Exchange, fell over 800 points, from 1650 to 820. Sears had to mark down inventory and dropped from 174 to 54.

With inflation wrung out of the economy, the Fed relented and a series of discount rate cuts helped turn the economy. But it was too late for the bottom line. In 1921, for the first time in its history, the Dow Industrials showed a composite loss. The red ink would never be repeated, save in 1932. In the great deflation, the Industrials had lost 84 percent of their entire war and postwar advance. Figure 4-3 shows the war and postwar action.

The Bankrupt Years
DJIA Sep 3, 1929–Jly 8, 1932: 381.17 to 41.22, −89%.

On December 29, 1929, the famous Stutz Motor Car Company, manufacturer of the Stutz Bearcat Roadster, was thrown into bankruptcy. It was the symbolic end of the age of flappers, coonskin coats, and bathtub gin.

Already bankrupt were the margin accounts of thousands of investors

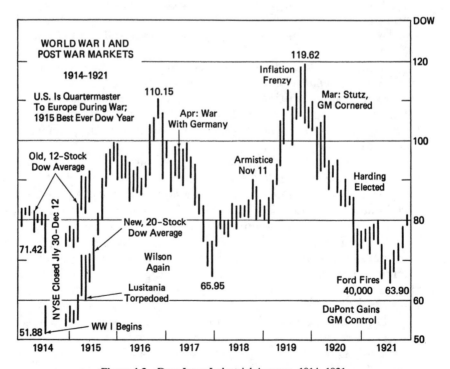

Figure 4.3   Dow Jones Industrial Average, 1914–1921

and the age of "new era" market thinking. Over 9,000 banks would go to the wall in the next three years, joining the sad list of 659 institutions already sacked in a year of "high prosperity."

Bloated securities products and prices, exacberated by 10 percent margins, wrote the sell tickets for the greatest financial panic of the century, in the last quarter of 1929. On its lowest day of that terrible autumn, November 13, the Dow Industrial Average had fallen 57 percent from the peak of September 3. No other stock market panic in history, no bear market in history (save 1929–1932) has approached such destruction. The worst damage was concentrated in the five weeks from October 10 to November 13. The Dow loss: 352.86 to 198.60, or 44 percent in that brief period.

On Monday and Tuesday, October 28–29, the Dow fell by over 23 percent. Tuesday's reported volume of 16,410,000 at the NYSE, a figure much lower than the true volume, was a record which stood for decades.

The lengthy 1921–1929 bull market had ended on Tuesday, September 3. Superstitious traders would suspiciously eye September morns forevermore. The balance of the month was hectic, although there was no clear sign that the end had come. Underwritings were promoted in record volume in September.

There were, to be sure, a few pessimists about. But most, like Roger Babson, who had irked the bulls in early September by predicting a crash of 60–80 points, were only repeating earlier warnings.

On September 20, a bloke named Clarence Hatry did the London Exchange in, what with counterfeit stock certificates and the like, and the trans-Atlantic fallout left the Dow at 343.45 at the month end.

On October 11, the Massachusetts Department of Public Utilities nixed a 4:1 stock split by Boston Edison. The shares were overpriced, the commission reasoned. Splitting it might seduce innocent widows, lured by a new "cheap" price. The Dow stood at 353.

Suddenly, and without the consent of any regulatory agency, it appeared that many stocks had already split. Auburn fell from 540 to 120. General Motors lost almost two thirds of its peak value, though its high had come in the spring. Hershey Chocolate, between October 15 and November 13, fell from 144 to 45, and Case Threshing Machine lost big dollars, 467 to 130.

Gravity was the dominant force, aided by enormous margin debt. On 10 percent margin, customer equity could barely stand a bump, let alone a bruising tumble. An estimated 600,000 clients were in margin, as opposed to cash accounts, and most of them, as it would turn out, would have a high mortality. Margin debt had reached a record high of $8.5 billion on October 1.

That huge loan figure then "contracted with unparalleled swiftness and violence," as the NYSE pointed out, falling to $6.1 billion November 1 and $4.0 billion on December 1. Over 50 percent of all margin debt was wiped out in two months. The enforced liquidation was mostly over by mid-November, the Dow having struck its panic low at 195.59 intraday on November 13. Bargain hunters took over.

The rally of late 1929 continued into 1930, regaining 50 percent of the panic loss by April. J. I. Case threshed a few bears in the spring, climbing back to 363 from its low at 130. Alcoa, victimized in the previous fall with an enormous smash from 540 to 180, was pushed back up to 356. Motion picture issues surpassed their 1929 peaks. Politicians, economists, and brokerage firms scored a new high for "encouraging words."

But summer brought the Hawley-Smoot tariff bill, a severe blow to the market, and a weakening economy. In August, auto production abruptly fell to less than half the figure seen in the same month of the two previous years. October, the crash anniversary month, saw the Dow drop below the worst figure of 1929. By December, the immediacy of the depression was in sharp focus.

Not all the tricks in New York City were downtown. The Bank of the United States, having learned a very little about third mortgages and a lot about massaging the books, was closed by state banking authorities in December. The bank had 60 branches and 400,000 depositors. It was the largest bank padlock in U.S. history.

The market did not take kindly to the closing, smashing down to a new low. The new year had barely started when Sears revealed that its 1930 sales were down by over 11 percent—no great surprise—but important December sales were 22 percent below the Christmas period of the previous year.

Unemployment was estimated at 4–5 billion at the year end. A world-class, worldwide depression had arrived.

Things Get Worse

In 1931, things got worse. Though "1929" remains the digital readout for all that went bad in the market, it pales by comparison with 1931. The Dow suffered its worst loss in that year, down 52.7 percent. September rolled out to the worst monthly loss in history and the Dow's percentage drop in the week ending October 3 was also a record.

Bank failures became epidemic worldwide. There were 2,294 closings in the United States, doubling the 1930 figure. In May, Austria's Creditanstalt had closed and the impact rolled across Europe, never slowing for customs.

A sharp rally at the end of June was sparked by President Hoover's war-debt moratorium proposal, but the world's spreading financial crisis quickly pushed prices lower.

In September, Great Britain abandoned the gold standard. The resulting "sterling crisis" was the world's worst since the onset of World War I. The British pound, a $4.85 stalwart for decades, was crushed to $3.25. The Bank of England was forced to rush its discount rate up from 2.5 percent to 6 percent within a few months, and the Reichsbank's rate jumped from 7 percent to 15 percent in September.

Japan invaded Manchuria, an omen of further Tokyo military adventures in the decade, and the Dow fell below 100 for the first time since 1921.

Huge short-covering followed the September crisis; it would last for just five weeks. It was a move typical of the 1930–1932 period. General Motors' short position fell from 365,700 to 170,000 shares. But by late November, the market was again in serious trouble, losing nearly 37 percent between November 9 and December 28.

There were still many bullish manipulations, however. Auburn Automobile supplied a speedy lap for the adventuresome. Even then, the Indiana manufacturer was known for its classic car lines and the firm enjoyed a record output of 28,103 autos in 1931. Such progress and a rumored corner propelled the stock from a 1930 low of 61 to a 1931 peak of 296.

Such was not the luck of AT&T. The firm lost over 291,000 phones during the year—the first time it had ever lost net customers on an annual basis.

By the end of 1931, there were believed to be nearly 8 million unemployed. But, again, things would get worse.

The steel industry, which had operated at only 25 percent of capacity in 1931, saw the figure fall to 18 percent in 1932. Though the carnage in stock values had gone nearly unchecked for over two years, the market's worst period lay ahead as the year of 1932 began.

Between mid-January and the first week of July, the Industrials were stripped of 52 percent of their value. Even those firms that continued to pay regular dividends were brutalized, for fear of future cuts. AT&T sold at 310 in 1929 and 70 in 1932, though it paid the same $9 dividend in each year. In the trench warfare of 1932, IBM became briefly a yield stock. At the low point of the year, its dividend return was 11 percent, a figure never matched by Big Blue, before or since.

Single-Digit Blue Chips

Dozens of name stocks sold in the single digits for the first time in history. General Electric, General Motors, and Bethlehem Steel fell to 8½ or less. John Deere hit 3½; its adjusted high (1930) had been 163. Anaconda, Borg-Warner, Goodrich, Marshall Field, and Continental Oil all sold for less than 4. U.S. Rubber dropped to 1½; it would be 25 the next year, while "penny stock" survivors like Lockheed, Richfield Oil, Louisiana Land & Exploration, and Warner Brothers would do rather better than that over a longer period.

Quality, defensive stocks did hold values, however; $800 wouldn't buy 100 shares of every stock. Singer sewing machines were in obvious demand for economical home sewing. The stock's low was 75. The A&P grocery chain shares never sold below 100. Kellogg's cereal filled out a lot of skimpy meals besides breakfast, and its low was 75. Coca-Cola increased its dividend to $8 in 1932 and the stock held at 69.

If officials at Telephone thought the loss of phones in 1931 was disturbing, 1932 would be a real shocker. Over 1.6 million net phones were unhooked, a loss of more than 10 percent of all in service.

In April, Paine Webber wrote in its semi-monthly review, ". . . the brunt of selling has fallen on favorite stocks of the 1928–29 boom. Measured by the Dow Jones Industrial average, this is the seventh wave of liquidation."[2] This is shown in Figure 4-4.

---

[2]Paine, Webber & Co. Semi-Monthly Review, April 25, 1932, p. 1, col.1.

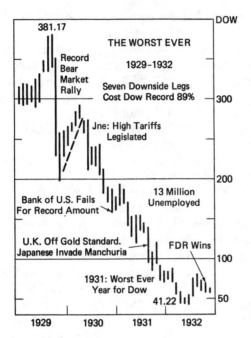

Figure 4.4 Dow Jones Industrial Average, 1929–1932

The fierce contraction was still less than that dealt to many individual issues. Stock owners who exited the market in the crash of 1929 were lucky, compared with investors who held on. Among well-known rails losing at least 95 percent of their peak 1929 value were Southern Pacific, the Pennsylvania, the Illinois Central, and the Atlantic Coast Line. A few among many.

Alcoa, Bethlehem, Goodyear, and Otis Elevators were among scores of high-quality Industrials suffering a similar haircut. Rather surprisingly, individual stock ownership increased materially during the hard times. Odd-lot traders were net buyers of stock in every month from September 1929 to August 1932, often in record amounts.

On July 3, 1932, Franklin D. Roosevelt, in his Chicago acceptance speech for the Democratic presidential nomination, said, "I pledge you, I pledge myself to a new deal for the American people—a call to arms."

The stock market believed. Or perhaps, it was the May–June reversal seen in the European markets, where buyers were encouraged by plummeting interest rates. On Friday, July 8, for reasons still not known, the long bloodbath quietly ended. Only 720,000 shares were traded and there were 114 advances against 218 declines for the day, which saw the Dow end at 41.22. The Dow Rails, having lost 93 percent of their 1929 value, bottomed the same day as did the Utilities.

In the Saturday session which followed, there were few bullish converts. The market barely moved, up 0.41 on 235,000 shares. But the most incredible, bear-busting rally in stock market history was about to begin. It had a lot of ground to make up, as the chart of the fallen 1929 favorite, RCA, shows in Figure 4-5.

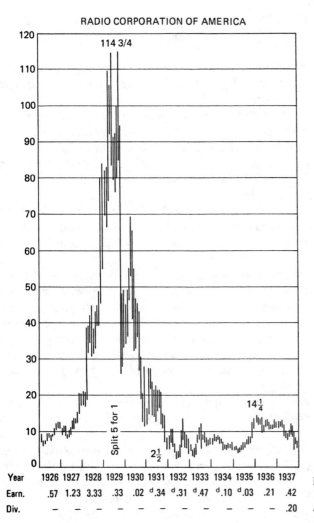

RADIO CORPORATION OF AMERICA

Year	1926	1927	1928	1929	1930	1931	1932	1933	1934	1935	1936	1937
Earn.	.57	1.23	3.33	.33	.02	d.34	d.31	d.47	d.10	d.03	.21	.42
Div.	–	–	–	–	–	–	–	–	–	–	–	.20

Figure 4.5 Historic RCA smash, 1929–1932 (*Source: M.C. Horsey & Company, Salisbury, MD*)

The Winds of War
DJIA Mar 10, 1937–Apr 28, 1942: 194.90 to 92.92, −52%.

In 1937, the winds of war had already engulfed Spain. War or the threat of war would overtake Japan and China, Austria, Czechoslovakia, Germany, Poland, Italy, England, France, and Russia. The United States and the rest of the free world would join by 1942. German and Japanese threats were taken seriously, even in 1937, but the American economy—finally believed to be free of the great depression—was still the major market catalyst. Sadly, soup lines were about to reappear.

The industrial collapse of 1937 was devastatingly swift. The demand for steel, autos, tools, and a huge variety of factory products evaporated overnight in the autumn of the year. A fierce panic, the worst since 1929, swept the market, plunging prices on the Dow from 190 in August to 114 in November. That 40 percent drop alone equals the damage done in some very serious bear markets.

The collapse also ushered in another severe, agonizing depression and, unbelievably, tilted the market down for another five years, though it would be a bitter see-saw battle between bear and bull.

Never in the history of the country has business turned so bad-so fast as in the late months of 1937. Steel production fell from over 5 million tons in May to 1.8 million tons in December, when the industry operated at less than 20 percent of capacity versus 82 percent in August. By early 1938, auto production had fallen to less than half the level of early 1937. Movie attendance in 1938 would be 40 percent below that of the previous year.

The stock market was poorly situated to withstand such news. The Dow had vastly outgained the recovery of earnings and at the March peak of 194.40 was valued at a lofty 19.3 times its trailing earnings. Margin debt had also increased sharply.

Thus, the market was sensitive to any real or imagined threat. In the spring, the president launched a full-court press on the Supreme tribunal, seeking to increase its membership, a move which caused great political turmoil. In April, the president took offense at industrial inflation, as opposed to farm inflation, and attacked business, particularly the copper industry.

Later in the month, the FRB put the hammer on, raising reserve requirements for the second time in two months. The Dow fell quickly to a low of 166 in late May.

Sellers got a second chance in August, when the Dow struggled back to 190, only five points below the March peak. It was an important double top, as it turned out.

In early October, London stock prices crashed and panic struck New York a bit later, with the Rails falling by 18 percent within six trading days. On October 17, Aluminum Corporation fell 14½ points on the Curb. Chrysler and Coca-Cola, both on the Big Board, lost 11 and 13½ points, respectively.

Such hysterics were puzzling to fundamentalists, who noted that General Electric—typical of many other blue chips—had just posted a huge, 38 percent increase in earnings for the first nine months.

But puzzlement, war, and the threat of war continued to dog the market. In December, the Japanese sunk the American gunboat, *Panay,* in Chinese waters, chilling an incipient rally. In March 1938, the market caved in to renewed war fears as Germany marched to control of Austria, in the infamous Anschluss.

Confidence was not improved when Richard Whitney, president of the NYSE, was expelled on March 17 for conduct unbecoming. He subsequently was sent up the river.

The shocking crash ended on March 31, with the Dow at 98.95. Individual issues had been maimed. General Motors was clubbed down from 70 to 26 in the 12-month rout. Akron and Goodrich suffered with Detroit, the tire maker falling from 51 to 10. Crown Cork, a Prohibition-repeal favorite, dropped from 101 to 22. Gimbels was discounted from 30 to 5.

The steel industry rushed from its best profit in eight years, in 1937, to widespread red ink. The large wage increases of 1937 had come at just the wrong time. Jones & Laughlin dropped over 100 points, 126 to 21.

For some pretty good Rails, it was a 1932 repeat. Southern Pacific had taken five years to fight its way from 6½ to 65. The journey was swiftly de-railed, and the shares dropped all the way back to 9 in 1938. Santa Fe's chart looked about the same, 18 in 1932 to 95 in 1937 and back to 22 the next year.

The "FDR Depression," as political opponents dubbed it, was lethal but short. The one-year collapse, part of a bearish trend lasting to 1942, cut 49 percent off the value of the Dow, a figure fractionally more than the bear moves of 1906–1907 and 1919–1921.

A Fierce Bear Market Rally

Having plunged below 100 at the end of March for the first time in three years, the Dow dumbfounded the bearish consensus by opening with a sharply higher gap on April 1. The index closed well above 100, up 4 percent for the day.

The next 17 months would see the Dow twist through a series of confusing manuevers—mini-bull and bear markets—but all a part of the longer down-ward slope.

By June 1938, hope and business had revived and the Industrials were at their best level since the previous November. Anticipation of better times was the basis for the sharp advance which lasted until November, for 1938's eco-nomic number were appallingly bad, primarily because of the disastrous first half figures.

Unemployment was at an annual average of 19 percent for the year and earnings were attacked. The Dow's dividend payout was cut to $4.98 from $8.78, about equal to the 1932–1933 reduction.

But the fierce bear market rally shot the Dow up by 60 percent in the April–November effort. Figure 4-6 shows this sharp advance in a longer-term context, but some scholars count the period as a minor bull market, despite its short life span.

Many stocks quickly undid the spring's damage. Aluminum Ltd., the Canadian producer, at 149 in 1937, sold down to 67 in early 1938 and then reached back to 136 in the same year. Douglas Aircraft, which had fallen from 77 to 31, rammed up to 81 in the same time frame.

Unfortunately, the problems with and within Nazi Germany would not go away. Turmoil there caused the Berlin bourse to suffer its worst decline of the Hitler regime in July. A few weeks later the London Stock Exchange gave consideration to closing if the war scare worsened.

Peace did, however, have a final fling. Prime Minister Neville Chamber-lain envisioned "peace in our time" following the Munich appeasement of late September and stocks rallied strongly through the mid-term election.

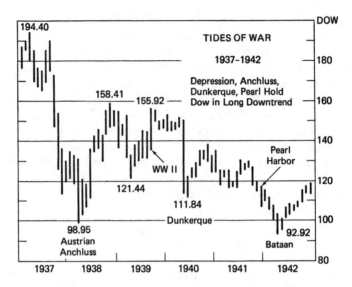

Figure 4.6 Dow Jones Industrial Average, 1937–1942

At that time, with unprecedented brutality, the Nazis launched new attacks on their Jewish citizens, stunning the civilized world. The American envoy to Berlin was recalled and Chamberlain and FDR discussed plans to assist the Nazi victims.

The Dow peaked at 158 on November 12 and, at the year end, was within four points of that level. It had been a marvelous rally, but the advance had fallen far short of the 1937 high and the year's volume was the lowest since 1924.

War Tensions of 1939

Year-end 1938 found business leaders highly optimistic, despite many war caveats. Net employment had gained 1 million in the last half and auto analysts foresaw a possible gain of 35 percent in car production for 1939. Du Pont envisioned a great future for its newest miracle product, nylon.

But war tensions overwhelmed the sharp improvement in the domestic economy. In March, Germany invaded Czechoslovakia. Sabers rattled over all of eastern Europe and the Dow fell about 20 percent in four weeks, ending the slide at 121 in April. Steels were heavy losers during the period, with both Alleghany-Ludlum and Armco dropping about 50 percent during the mini-bear market. Pan American Airways fell from 19 to 11.

Those market students who see the 1938–1939 dip as a stand-alone bear market count it the shortest in history, lasting for but 120 trading sessions into April. It would be followed by a bullish interlude of equally short duration. Table 4-3 shows the bearish cast of some leading stocks during the confusing 1937–1942 market period while Figure 4-6 (above) displays the Dow action.

Prime Minister Chamberlain's 1938 autumn appeasement would bring

TABLE 4-3 TYPICAL DOWNTRENDS 1937–1942

Stock	1937 High	1938 Low	1938–1939 High	1940 Low	1941 High	1942 Low
Addressograph	36	17	30	13	16	10
Eastman Kodak	198	121	186	117	145	108
General Electric	65	27	45	26	35	22
Goodyear	47	15	39	13	21	10
NY Central	55	10	23	9	15	7
Reynolds Tobacco	58	34	45	31	34	20
Union Oil	28	17	20	12	16	10
Dow Industrial	194	99	143	112	138[a]	93

[a]Rally high for DJIA was in November 1940.

war, not peace, in our time. But for one more summer at least, the world enjoyed a facade of peace.

In April of 1939, the Industrials suddenly reversed themselves in dramatic fashion, leaving behind a three-day, high-volume island reversal—a formation much admired by chart classicists.

For a few months, further military outrages were missing and the market could fret over such domestic problems as the big muscle of John L. Lewis and his CIO, along with the coal mining shutdown.

The New York World's Fair drew millions and the air age took a great jump forward when Pan-Am began regular air service to Europe. Rail traffic was booming, along with exports, but stock prices were closely contained.

World War II

The war exploded at 0445 hours on Friday, September 1, when Germany invaded Poland. A buying panic erupted in New York. It ran the Dow, which had been 131 in late August, to 156 on September 12. Paradoxically, all European markets were also steady to firm. In Tokyo, trading was so bullishly violent on September 4 (when the NYSE was closed for Labor Day) that the afternoon session had to be cancelled so that brokers could check and balance their trades.

On Tuesday, when the NYSE reopened, the Dow spiked up by over ten points. The Rails ran up over 10 percent, one of their best days in history.

Old-timers recalled the extraordinary advance of Bethlehem Steel and the other flyers of World War I. "Bessie" jumped 14½ points on September 5.

Brokerage houses abetted the hysteria by rushing to the printers summaries of the great individual and industry moves of the earlier war.

Bethlehem, near 50 in August, touched 100 in late September. Alcoa pushed to 141 from 90. New York Central doubled. Wright Aero flew straight up for 24 points in one day. Anaconda was a big percentage gainer.

Many "war brides" enjoyed their happiest days in September 1939. Bethlehem would not see 100 again during the war years. United Aircraft and Sperry fans, bagged in the September frenzy by aviation's obvious promise, would not get even until the 1950s. The great stock advances of World War II were to come from issues unheralded in the frantic mobilization of early September.

Within days of the German invasion, the world was at war. On September 17, Russia invaded Poland and by the month end had partitioned the remnants of that battered nation with the Nazis.

Dunkerque to Pearl Harbor

The craze for defense issues was cooled by their excessive price markup in September, but the general market held stubbornly to its gains.

The Industrials moved in a long, horizontal formation without serious damage and on April 8, 1940, stood just over 151, five points below the autumn peak. The fighting in Europe seemed stalemated, but in May, the sitzkreig turned to blitzkreig. The Germans swept into the Low Countries, drove the British off the beaches at Dunkerque and, in June, forced France to surrender. The American stock markets were swamped with global sell orders and stocks dropped under classic high-volume conditions. The Dow fell almost in a straight line from May 9 to June 10, when an important low was registered at 112. That defense would hold until Pearl Harbor, despite stupendous Nazi successes.

The Battle of Britain moved to the skies over England in August, but the RAF held, and the Dow ended the month 16 percent above the June low. Yugoslavia surrendered and the Germans rolled into Athens and across Africa, all without seriously threatening the market. In July 1941, the Germans invaded Russia, but that shocking news could not change the market much either.

Meanwhile, the favorites of 1939 had been unmercifully pruned. Chrysler fell to 54 from a peak at 94. Bethlehem Steel dropped to 63. U.S. Rubber, 53 in 1939, was hard hit within the next year, falling to 15.

Even the railroads, swamped with more business than they could efficiently handle, made many new lows, despite an astounding improvement in the trend of earnings. Illinois Central earned 13 cents in 1940, $6.95 in 1941 (when it traded for 4¼) and $17.52 in 1942. Many roads sold for less in 1940–1941 than they had in 1932–1933.

Business was good and getting better during the early 1940s, but the market ignored it. War news was dreary. Japan invaded French Indo-China. U.S. troops, by invitation, were stationed in Iceland. Japanese assets in the United States were frozen. Two American destroyers were torpedoed by U-boats. Price ceilings, excess profits taxes, and supply shortages made profit forecasting more dicey than ususal.

For the market, the 1940–1942 period was one of siege, movements being hostage to war news which was mostly bad. In 1942, the Rails had their smallest range in history, less than six points. Exchange volume was less than that of 1900 and a NYSE seat sold for $17,000, a level last recorded in 1897.

Pearl Harbor

On Saturday, December 6, 1941 the Industrials closed at 116.60 and the Rails at 27.16, a slight plus for both averages. A Japanese air attack staggered Pearl Harbor and the nation early Sunday morning.

The Dow fell by about 7.5 percent in the next few sessions while the Rails lost nearly 10 percent. Stocks scored a modest rally in January, but the litany of bad war news including the loss of Wake, Singapore, Bataan, and two of England's mightiest battleships was too much.

In early April, the Industrial average fell below 100 and the 1938 low. Even Jimmy Doolittle's daring air raid over Tokyo could not stop the slide. On April 28, the Dow closed at 92.92. There was great gloom but no panic, although the five-year downtrend had erased two thirds of the 1932–1937 gain.

At the same time, the Utility average recorded its lowest level in history, 10.58, an appalling loss for a "conservative" group of stocks which had been gauged at 144.61 in 1929.

The Rails, somewhat confused by their new-found prosperity, delayed their war low until June 2, at 23.31. At that level, the average was selling for 2.6X the previous year's earnings, and only 1.7X the 1942 bottom line. Never has any American market average been appraised so cheaply.

From that low point, the carriers would enjoy a period of great relative strength as compared to the Industrials. That trend, the most powerful in decades, would continue until victory in Europe.

"Blood and Tiers"
DJIA Jan 11, 1973–Dec 6, 1974: 1051.70 to 577.60, −45%.

The trendy, two-tier market philosophy of the early 1970s was smashed by bearish forces which took no prisoners and gave no quarter. Growth stocks suffered an unmerciful deflation of tier and plain blue chips were badly bloodied. It was the worst crash since the 1930s and, as usual, the most severe damage was dealt to the most popular darlings of the previous advance.

In 1972 and early 1973, portfolio managers had pursued a few score growth issues with religious fervor. No price was too dear for issues grouped in the "Nifty Fifty." While the titles in the peerage occasionally changed, the listing usually started with Avon and ended with Xerox.

When the bloodbath came, professional anointment proved no armor against the bear. IBM, everyone's first choice, had been valued at about 40X earnings in early 1973. The stock would fall to 12X earnings in 1974. The drop was from 365 to 151 and wiped out over $20 billion of market value.

McDonald's perfect record of growth in the fast-food business had been greatly admired, and the shares were boosted to over 80X earnings in 1972. Perfection would continue, but the PE multiple melted to 13X in 1974 as the stock dropped from 77 in 1973 to 21.

Bad economic and political news proliferated all through 1973, keeping the market under the most severe pressure. The dollar was a pariah. Foreign currency markets had to be closed for a time. Gold bugs were clamoring, bullion having doubled in the first seven months of the year. Domestic interest rates were on an up escalator.

In July 1973, the existence of White House taping procedures was disclosed, and Watergate disclosures and political scandals dominated the news. Vice-President Spiro Agnew, convicted of tax evasion, was forced to resign in October. Gerald Ford would take his place in December.

By August, the Dow had fallen to 852, when an extraordinary rally emerged. It was so strong that it overrode the Yom Kippur war, OPEC price increases, the Arab oil embargo, and Agnew's ouster. On October 26, the Dow, having rallied 135 points, was at 987, only 6 percent below its January top. Startling as the rally was, the retreat from the high was more amazing, as the Dow fell 200 points by early December, led by the suddenly stricken glamors.

Aided by a margin cut, from 65 percent to 50 percent, the Dow managed another rally back to the 900 level in the spring, but that was all. Gold and silver were hot items; the latter had crossed the $6 mark. But bulging oil prices and a prime at 11.5 percent kept the lid on stocks. The slump for stock prices began in June, with the Dow cascading from 860 to 657 at the end of August. It was not a year to test the summer rally theorem.

In late July, the Supreme Court had ordered the White House to deliver up the "tapes," and on August 8 President Nixon announced his resignation, effective the next day. It could not slow the market's slide. The Utilities struck their low in early September, but the Dow took another 100-point hit, with the panic ending on October 4 for most averages.

Bargain Prices

Fear of what 1975 might bring drove stock prices to evaluations not seen since 1949—a Dow PE ratio at 5.8X on record earnings of $99.04. The end of Western Civilization, some said, must be near, considering the level of stock values.

Scores of good names sold at 3X earnings or less. Veteran survivors like Allied Stores, American Standard, Boeing, Mead Corporation, Goodrich, and Grumann were included. Oils were ostracized. Texaco sold at 20 and paid $2.10 in dividends.

Woolworth, with a dividend record reaching back to 1912, sold down to 8, where its yield was 15 percent. Its earnings were $2.14 and would be $3.24 in 1975. Other, lesser names sold at 1X and 1.5X earnings. Moore-McCormack Resources sold at 12 in October. Its expected and realized earnings of over $10 would help the stock flash back to 30 by the year end.

The fallen-away growth stocks were granted no mercy. Rite Aid, the discount drug chain, had sold at 43, over 62X trailing earnings of 68 cents in 1973. Sadly, the earnings would slip in 1973 and 1974, to 50 cents. The stock price dropped below 2, or less than 4X earnings. From that low price and appreciation level, of course, significant profits would be made.

The 1973–1974 crash was the worst since the 1930s, and it wasn't just the fancy names that got killed. A hot new "product," real estate investment trusts (REITs), had been off-loaded on the public in the early 1970s, but the magic wore off quickly. Nineteen of 20 of 1974's biggest losers at the Exchange were REITs. The best of the sorry lot was down by 87 percent. Chase Manhattan Mortgage & Realty was a disappointment, as Figure 4-7 shows.

If bargains abounded in October 1974, buyers had one more test. A pair of miscreants dragged the Dow to a new low on December 6, but every other important average refused to confirm. A modest rally into the year end still left the Dow with its largest percentage loss since 1937 and at the lowest level since 1962.

For the Industrials, the three bear markets in an eight-year period, shown in Figure 4-8, had been most sobering, but the destruction of values at the AMEX and among the stocks in the Value Line Index had been much worse.

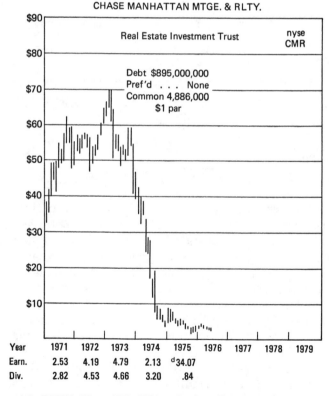

Figure 4.7 REITS: Worst 1973–1974 performers (*Source: M.C. Horsey & Company, Salisbury, MD*)

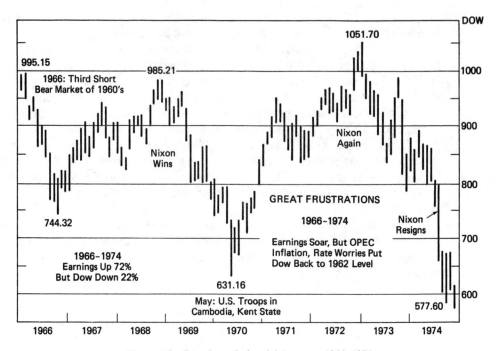

Figure 4.8   Dow Jones Industrial Average, 1966–1974

MAJOR BEAR MARKETS

Battered Big Business
DJIA Nov 19, 1909–Jly 30, 1914: 100.53 to 71.42, −29%.

Feverish attacks on big business and the trusts by both state and federal authorities battered business from 1909 to 1914. Many feared that government interference and harassment of the railroads would spread to all the great manufacturing concerns. Serious suggestions were heard that AT&T and the U.S. Post Office should merge under the latter's management.

Market psyche was damaged by the antitrust rhetoric and court actions, which had accelerated after November 1909, when a circuit court declared Standard Oil to be in restraint of trade. It was all very distasteful to foreign investors and selling from London would pressure both the industrial and rail sectors for the next few years.

Despite a modest 12-month advance during 1911–1912, the general trend for the market was down from 1909 to 1914. For both averages, the 1912 peak would fail that of 1909. The lows in 1914, at the outbreak of World War I, would fall below the worst figures seen in the first two years of the decade. Many individual issues were treated in similar fashion, as noted in Table 4-4.

TABLE 4-4 TYPICAL DOWNTRENDS 1909–1914

Stock	1909 High	1910–1911 Low	1912 High	1914 Low
Anaconda	54	29	48	24
Colorado Fuel & Iron	53	23	44	21
Brooklyn Gas	165	125	149	118
Corn Products	27	10	22	7
Pullman	200	154	175	150
New York Central	148	100	121	77
Southern Pacific	138	105	116	81
Dow Industrials	101	73	94	71

Down: November 1909 to September 1911

The many manipulations of the period also hurt confidence. In a 1909–1910 classic the legendary pool operator, James R. Keene, levitated the shares of the Columbus Hocking Coal & Iron Company from 21 to 92 and then "pegged" trading at the 90 level.

By January 22, 1910, the bull operations had ended, and the stock went free fall, plunging from 89 to 24 in a single day. Several firms were forced to suspend, including the specialist, who turned out to be a poor sport, claiming that various brokers had welched on their buy orders.

The NYSE investigated and ruled the specialist guilty of "abusive language." Faith, it seems, had simply outrun judgment, giving invitation to disaster.

Pools were legal but other brokerage scams like bucket shops were not. The Secret Service and other gumshoe agencies spent a great deal of time in 1910 tracing down Western Union wire drops to the many covert operations.

In the first half of 1910, business was strong and the market weak, a situation reversed in the last six months. In 1911, both Europe and the Justice Department were in a warlike stance. Germany and France carried on threatening "war games," as they quarreled over the latter's protectorate in Morocco.

Oil and Tobacco Balkanized

In May 1911, the Supreme Court ordered both the Standard Oil and American Tobacco trusts dissolved, concluding years of litigation. Other campaigns were plotted by the Justice Department against the "kindling wood," "bathtub," and "poultry" trusts.

Europe's concern over the antitrust problems had been well grounded, but months of untidy market behavior had discounted the court's results. The Dow advanced after the oil and tobacco decisions.

The Balkanization and distribution of holdings from the two enormous combinations proved rewarding to those investors who had purchased in the uneasy period before the 1911 decisions. Jersey holders would prosper greatly from the split-up, gathering up small holdings of the "little" Standard companies, like Standard of Cal, Indiana, Kansas, New York and Ohio, and so on—plus South Penn Oil, Buckeye Pipe, and Vacuum Oil. Distributions were made pro rata in the shares of 33 firms.

In London, confidence was worsened by a constitutional crisis and a general railroad strike in August, and in New York there were rumors of an antitrust suit against the nation's largest corporation, U.S. Steel. President Taft, on a nationwide rail tour, seemed to threaten capital and in September the Dow slipped a shade below its important low of July 1910 and established a bear market trough. The average was still composed of but 12 issues and it took only a pair of weaklings to cause the mischief.

It had been a mild, 22-month bear move in which the Dow lost 27 percent of its value, though a few blue chips had been treated more roughly. Sears, 190 in November 1910, fell to 126 the following September. American Smelting, under government attack, dropped from 104 to 57. Texas Company, newly listed and still headquartered in Houston, lost nearly 50 percent, 144 to 74. Its yield was still meager, as the dividend was cut from $1.50 to $1.25.

Recovery: September 1911 to September 1912

On October 26, 1911, an antitrust suit was filed against U.S. Steel, accusing about every action since the trust was conceived, including the Tennessee Coal & Iron acquisition of 1907. Thirty-seven corporations and 18 individuals, including the likes of J. P. Morgan, John D. Rockefeller, and Andrew Carnegie, were named in the suit.

It was summer rumor turned to fact, and both Dow averages flipped higher after a one-day setback. A trusting but modest recovery set in. Business conditions improved, despite many labor disturbances. Unemployment dropped sharply. Bell system telephones increased to over 5 million, having doubled since 1907. Stock underwritings in 1912 doubled the 1911 total. U.S. Steel's sales climbed to $745 million, only $40 million below the peak of 1907, though earnings did not compare with the previous period.

The Rails continued a modest climb, but the minor bull movement from 1910 to 1912 was their smallest gain in history. Holders were disheartened during the era by harassment of the rails. Quoting the *Commercial & Financial Chronicle,* "ICC 'suspends rate advances' is . . . so familiar of late as almost to warrant keeping it in type."[3] The Rock Island, Texas & Pacific, and many other closely watched lines recorded lower highs in each year from 1909 to 1914.

Most rails failed to move significantly. Pennsylvania, always a great public favorite, had a most narrow range in 1912, 59^{15}/$_{16}$ to 63¼.

While bitter Justice Department campaigns against such giants as AT&T and the Union Pacific would be initiated or continued during the year, the effect of such actions seemed diminished. Demands for a federal incorporation law died.

---

[3]The *Commercial & Financial Chronicle,* New York, January 4, 1914, p. 8, col. 1.

General Motors made an historic if unimpressive debut at the Exchange in August 1912, trading at 52; by the next spring, the stock would be 30. But American Can finally turned in a good performance. The trust shares found some wonderful new friends and moved up from 11 to 48 in 1912. Shares had been 3 in 1907. Standard of Indiana, insiders suspected, would split a huge stock melon and while the issue was a bit pricey for the Curb market, it became pricier, making a $2,700 move, from 1400 to 4100 before the news was leaked.

Enthusiasm at the Exchange was contained by European selling, high interest rates there, American gold losses, and the early winds of war. In the spring, St. Petersburg and Paris fell on rumors of a Russo-Turk conflict over Persia. In September, the French fleet massed in the Mediterranean, fearing an Anglo-German war.

In the same month, the minor bull advance, which had lasted barely a year, ended. The Dow's gain was but 29 percent and it failed the peaks of both 1906 and 1909.

End of Many Eras

For the Republicans, an era ended in 1912 when Democrat Woodrow Wilson won a landslide victory in the presidential race. The GOP had assured his victory by splitting the ticket between Roosevelt's "Bull Moose" group and the backers of the equally hefty, 300-pound incumbent, President Howard Taft.

Other eras would end in the period before the outbreak of World War I. In 1913, the horse and buggy era trotted off into the twilight. Auto production at 485,000 units exceeded that of wagons and buggies for the first time. The lender of last resort would no longer be J. P. Morgan, and not just because he died in the spring of 1913. The Federal Reserve was about to come into being.

The endless Balkan conflicts would be replaced by something much more serious—World War I. Tariff reductions and a relevant income tax bill, to make up for lost custom duties, would be approved.

And, in the eyes of some, a new radical era was beginning in Washington. Populism had not perished. In December 1913, the Postmaster General recommended that the government take over the country's telephone and telegraph lines and modestly allowed that they might be most effectively operated by the postal service.

In Congress, a bill was pushed to halve Telephone's dividend payout, pending a valuation of the company's properties. AT&T, 140 at the beginning of the year, fell to 110 in December.

The *Commercial & Financial Chronicle,* which viewed with alarm Wilson's passage from Princeton to Washington, noted in January 1914 that the advent to control of an "administration . . . determined to emphasize and flaunt its adherence to radical doctrines . . . furnished occasion for the deepest anxiety."[4]

Such anxieties encouraged both domestic and foreign selling, and the market was further demoralized during most of 1913 by the Balkan Wars,

---

[4]The *Commercial & Financial Chronicle,* New York, January 11, 1914, p. 93, col. 2.

which destabilized the bourses of Europe and pushed central bank rates there to the highest figure since 1875. Volume at the NYSE fell to its lowest point of the century and at the year end, the backlog of U.S. Steel was 45 percent below that registered 12 months earlier.

Despite threatening war clouds, values held up during the first five months of 1914, though Europe continued a heavy seller. Then, in June, came a shocking commercial failure. H. B. Claflin, the great wholesale dry goods company formed in 1843, unexpectedly went into receivership. Claflin controlled many other mercantile and retail establishments and, indirectly, Lord & Taylor.

At almost the same time, the Balkan powder keg exploded. Archduke Ferdinand, Crown Prince of Austria, was assassinated in Sarajevo. War between Serbia and Austro-Hungary swiftly followed and within weeks all of Europe was drawn into the conflict.

Stock markets around the world collapsed. In the last week of July, General Motors lost 39 points under panic conditions. Rails, weak all year, were pounded. Canadian Pacific, 221 in early 1914, fell to 156; it had always been a London favorite. Southern Railway's price was cut in half.

Many carriers dropped below their depression low of 1903, including such former investment favorites as the Baltimore & Ohio, the New York Central, the scandal-ridden New Haven, and the Illinois Central. The few Industrial

---

A CHURCHILLIAN COUP

In 1913, England's First Lord of the Admiralty determined that a modern British navy could no longer operate efficiently with coal for fuel. Reluctant to depend upon either the Dutch Shell or American Standard Oil for the navy's bunker oil requirements, he recommended that the government acquire an interest in the Anglo-Persian Oil Company.

The result would be one of the world's most fabulous stock investments.

It was proposed that the British government subscribe £2 million for a half interest in Anglo-Persian. The necessary bill, introduced into the House of Commons in May, 1914, was argued in person by the First Lord. He had to overcome the objections of crusty admirals, the coal interests, oil magnates, and those conservatives who feared commercialization by the State.

But the First Lord overcame all arguments and the bill passed, receiving the Royal Assent only a week before the start of World War I. Anglo-Persian became, in 1935, Anglo-Iranian, and in 1954 the British Petroleum Company. In 1987, the British government sold its holdings for £7.2 billion.

The vast sum realized would have been pleasing to the memory of that long-ago First Lord of the Admiralty, who had pushed the Royal Navy from coal to oil and acquired, for the British government, the rich stake in the world's third largest oil company. His name: Winston S. Churchill.

stalwarts that held above their 1913 lows included most motors and both Bethlehem Steel and U.S. Steel.

The panic ended the bear market on Thursday, July 30, 1914, if only because London and New York exchanges would shut down; other world bourses had closed earlier in the week. The padlock, shortly before Friday's scheduled opening, came just in time. The Dow had lost 7 percent on Thursday and overnight cables and telegrams were loaded on the sell side.

Thursday's close, 71.42, would stand as the wartime low. The NYSE would not reopen until December 12, when the Industrials would post a 4 percent gain.

For the Industrials, the five-year downtrend had been mild—a 29 percent loss, as seen in Figure 4-9. The loss for the Rails had been somewhat larger and their relative weakness would continue throughout the decade.

The "Kennedy Panic"
DJIA Dec 13, 1961–June 26, 1962: 734.91 to 535.76, −27%.

The 1961–1962 bear market was the shortest in modern history. It lasted barely six months. The decline of 27 percent for the Dow was modest.

But for a devastating few weeks in May, the "Kennedy Panic" gripped the market, forcing the most dramatic sell-off since Dunkerque. The collapse on May 28, a loss of 34.95 points, was the worst since 1929 and the new high-speed ticker fell two-and-one-half hours behind floor transactions. But the crash forced stock values to a much sounder basis and the Dow's PE ratio reached its most attractive level since 1957.

The days of panic were triggered by a bitter quarrel between President John F. Kennedy and the steel industry's price chiefs. But the bear market,

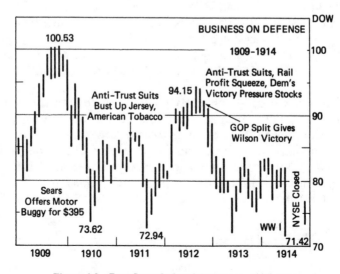

Figure 4.9 Dow Jones Industrial Average, 1909–1914

which had been slow to develop, was rooted in the bloated price-earnings ratios which had developed in the 1961 market sizzle. IBM had sold at over 80 times earnings and Polaroid went for 100 times earnings.

Other more disturbing problems had intruded. The SEC was on a justified tear. Insider trading, unregistered stock sales, falsified prospectuses, manipulations, and margin violations were all under investigation at the end of 1961. The chief of the scandal-ridden American Stock Exchange had been forced to resign in December. The increasing U.S. military presence in Vietnam was receiving more publicity and concern as the American position escalated from advisor to participant.

Yet, the market seemed resigned to living with those problems throughout the winter of 1962. It was the April face-off between JFK and the steel industry that triggered the sudden collapse for stocks.

The president had been intimately involved in the steel-union wage negotiations since January and had seen the March 31 contract signing as a fair trade-off, with no general wage increase and no price hike. On April 6, however, in a shocking move, U.S. Steel raised its prices an average of $6 per ton, hoping to reverse an irregular five-year downtrend for earnings.

President Kennedy exploded. Under fierce duress, including pressure from Robert Kennedy's Justice Department, the industry rescinded the price hike. But the unparalleled White House pressure against U.S. Steel and the other companies raised the immediate perception that the president was antibusiness.

On April 24, the Kennedy Panic locked on, with the Dow still only about 40 points below its December peak. A drop continued through May 29, peeling off a quick 22 percent of the Dow's value and putting some former market leaders into free fall.

American Tobacco's bear market loss was 56 to 24. Addressograph fell from 110 to 39. American Home Products was cut from 90 to 44, to list a few "A's." Bell & Howell became a battered victim of the 1961–1962 crash, 70 to 16. Certain-Teed was sliced from 60 to 11 within the 1962 year.

U.S. Steel, a natural selling target, dropped to 38 from 91. Bethlehem Steel performed a bit better, though 1962 earnings would be the worst since 1948.

Sheer panic ended abruptly on May 28, though the bear market would sullenly grind lower through June. Along the way, it wiped out the previous bear market low of 1960, causing great technical fears. But, for a change, the market's slide failed as an economic forecaster. There was panic but no recession. In July, auto sales would set a record. The year of 1962 would see peak Dow earnings, despite the dismal first-half performance when the swift drop recorded by the index had cancelled 57 percent of the total 1957–1961 advance.

1966: Worst Year since 1937
DJIA Feb 9, 1966–Oct 7, 1966: 995.15 to 744.32, −25%.

Unique to the 1960s were three ultra-short bear markets, all of which are shown in Figure 4-10. The intrayear decline of 1966 was the third. Though

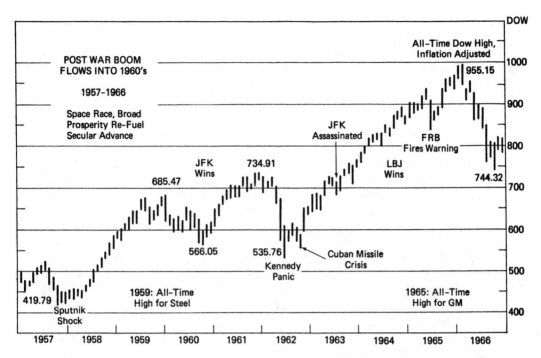

Figure 4.10 Dow Jones Industrial Average, 1957–1966

largely forgotten, it was nasty. The decline was only 25 percent, but some heavy hits helped turn 1966 into the worst year for the Industrials since 1937.

Dow 1000 had proven an unyielding barrier early in the winter, but it was Vietnam, inflation, and a credit crunch that undid the market. At the end of January, LBJ decided to renew Vietnam bombing after a 30-day moratorium and within a few days the 1962–1966 bull market had ended.

Credit strains were already at work. The prime, at 4.5 percent since 1960, had been hiked in December and it would be raised three more times by late spring. Inflation's threat, bred by a guns-and-butter policy, was growing and FRB Chairman Martin in early May suggested new tax hikes to rein it in, an unpopular nostrum which encouraged fierce selling at the Exchange. In the summer, Hanoi was bombed for the first time and a credit crunch developed with bonds under great pressure. Dow theory storm signals were hoisted.

Though the bear market was short and relatively mild, as gauged in the record book, extraordinary losses were mounted within just a few months. Interest-related stocks were natural selling targets but the list of issues losing at least 50 percent was long and diversified. It included such popular names as Boeing, Boise Cascade, and Burlington Industries. And also Chrysler, Joy Manufacturing, Occidental Pete, Parke Davis, and Texas Gulf Sulphur. The volatile Fairchild Camera suffered a big dollar loss, 144 to 65.

Howard Hughes, a bit earlier in the year, had unloaded 75 percent of his TWA holdings on the public and they had only a short time to enjoy their flight before the stock was taken down from 101 to 52.

By autumn, the credit crisis had passed, the Dow having struck a three-year low. October was the bear killer, followed by a stiff rally from 744 to 820 in mid-November. Tax selling took over in December, and the Dow ended the year at 786, a loss of nearly 184 points. This left the annual tally in poor shape, with 916 issues down and but 288 on the plus side.

A Broadening Experience
DJIA Dec 3, 1968–May 26, 1970: 985.21 to 631.16, −36%.

In 1969, there were few investors or brokers who had been blooded by a serious bear assault. Both groups had come into the market since World War II. Their market experience would be considerably broadened in the next 17 months.

To be sure, there were a few battered victims left from the giddy new-issue market of 1961, but in the previous 20 years, no bear market had lasted longer than eight months. Since 1942, the average decline in such bear sequences had been but 22.5 percent and the worst damage, during 1961–1962, was 27 percent. The enormous losses for individual stocks in the 1930s—80 percent and 90 percent—were regarded as historical oddities. Such market innocence was about to be destroyed.

The speculative fireworks of the 1960s had come to an end in December 1968. In its place came a nasty downdraft of 18 months and a bear trend which, adjusted for inflation, would continue until 1982. Enormous losses, up to 90 percent in well-known companies, would be visited upon the market.

Ratcheting interest rates, virulent inflation, and the frustrations of Vietnam fragged the market. Between mid-November and January 7, 1969, the prime rate was kicked up four times, a velocity of change never approached before.

Inflation was soaring. The war had driven the 1968 CPI to its largest increase since 1951, and prices were still rising. Massive antiwar protests were common.

In the spring of 1969, the market seemed off balance, but not in serious trouble. Strikes, Suez troubles, a discount rate hike, and the gunning down of an American plane by the North Koreans failed to seriously wound prices.

A sharp bear market rally in May had poor technicals but pushed the Dow back to 968, where it was only 16 points off the 1968 peak. But when summer began, a prime rate increase of 1 percent jumped the bank charge to 8.5 percent, a blow compounded by the breakdown of Vietnam peace negotiations in Paris. Bull scenarios swiftly unraveled.

University Computing, 187 in late 1968, traded down to 53, and still had 40 points to fall before the end of the bear attack. Anaconda dropped to 27 from a January top at 66.

July's moon landing brought no Street cheer, but near the end of the month the cascade of selling dwindled, the Industrials having fallen intraday below 800.

There being no additional broadsides from the banks, the market welded together a modest advance lasting until November. Heavy tax selling then conspired to turn December into a disaster. Dow 770 was reached before hope arose that the FRB might recast its tight-money policy.

After a new market low in January 1970, encouragement returned in March when the prime was cut. The push ended abruptly when President Nixon announced that American and Vietnamese troops had invaded Cambodia in pursuit of the North Vietnamese. The tragedy of Kent State, May 4, sacked the market.

No Air Support

In the meantime, the Rail average had been doing rather worse than the Industrials, despite the fact that it had been upgraded to the "Dow Transportation" index on January 1. Nine airline and truck carriers were substituted into the average of 20 stocks, ousting such wonderful names as the Chesapeake & Ohio, Illinois Central, and Missouri Pacific.

Unfortunately, the embattled Rails got no air support from their new allies. Four of the six airlines added to the list lost 50 percent of their value in the first half of 1970. TWA fell from 24 to 10; its 1966 high had been 100.

In the meantime, the long-delayed dream merger of two historic lines, the Pennsylvania and the New York Central, in 1968, had proven the worst financial nightmare in railroad history. The Penn Central shares slid from 87 to 6. Bankruptcy and accusations of insider selling followed in June 1970.

Overhyped stocks were more spectacular victims of the 18-month slide. LTV was smashed from 170 to 7. Levin-Townsend lost 94 percent of its value, 68 to 3. Data Processing Financial & General took a 92–7 hit.

No one in early 1970 wanted to take the market darlings of 1968— franchisors, nursing homes, computer leasors—home to mother. Synergism, it was discovered, had no loan value and conglomerate was shortened to a four-letter word. Susquehanna Corp., which had parlayed bricks, uranium, and missiles into a $80 stock, dropped to 5. Unexcelled, Inc. found that meat packing and discount stores didn't meld and lost 60 points off a top at 63.

A large number of good names were badly hurt, though they survived. Admiral Corp., Boeing, Collins Radio, Litton, and Lockheed all lost 90 percent of their value. Natomas fell from 130 to 13. Atlantic Richfield's North Slope riches couldn't halt a slide from 136 to 45. IBM, at an all-time high in January 1970 at 387, was struck down to 219 within about four months.

And J. Ross Perot, who owned an enormous block of his firm, Electronic Data Systems, suffered the sad distinction of becoming the largest "paper" loser in history. His favorite stock, 164 in April, fell to 29.

The bear market climaxed in panic. Mutual funds were hit by big redemptions. Commercial paper was suspect. Brokerage house insolvencies were rumored. On May 24, there were but 130 advances versus 1,370 declines at the NYSE, a 1:10 ratio typical of many previous market lows.

The bitter ordeal, worst since the early war days, ended suddenly on May 26 at Dow 631. Within four trading days, the average was back to 710, though the Penn Central derailment would keep the carriers under pressure until

July. Their multiyear loss was a massive 58 percent, the worst in history, save for the 1930s. The 1968–1970 experience had been a very broadening if not enrichening experience for market newcomers of the previous 25 years.

Market Up, Dow Down
DJIA Sep 21, 1976–Feb 28, 1978: 1014.79 to 742.12, −27%.

In a bear market full of paradoxes, secondary and small stock issues generally prospered in 1976–1978 even as the Dow and institutional favorites were eroded by persistent, if not heavy, selling.

Lesser issues had been unexploited in terms of price–earnings ratios during the 1974–1976 advance and were not subject to the affection alienation which hit the institutional growth darlings. Disney, priced at 82X earnings in 1972, had been battered down to a PE ratio of 10X in 1974.

But by 1976, Mickey Mouse and friends were back on stage, applauded at 27X earnings. A second PE meltdown took the multiple back to 10 in 1978, even though earnings had increased nearly 100 percent since 1974. Disney lost half its 1976 top value. Other popular growth issues suffered a similar dismal treatment.

Industrial giants were decimated along the Pittsburgh-Detroit axis during 1977. Cheap steel imports were one reason for the Dow's troubles. U.S. Steel, Bethlehem Steel and the steel-related Inco made up 10 percent of the Dow's membership. The last two lost 50 percent of their value in the mini bear market, with "Bessie" falling to its lowest level since 1954.

General Motors posted consecutive record earnings in 1976, 1977, and 1978 but fell from 79 to 54 while Chrysler, losing market share, was cut down from 22 to 8.

It had all begun with a strange ending to the 1974–1976 advance. Perfection seemed to mark the high for the Dow. On September 21, the Industrials pushed up 20 points to close at 1014.79. General Motors was the volume leader, up 3. Following General Motors on the active lists were such "good" names as Polaroid, Chrysler, Westinghouse, AT&T, Texaco, Gulf, Fannie Mae, and Exxon. But the Dow immediately reversed, despite autumn strength in other averages and the divergence would continue for several years.

By May 1977, the Industrials had fallen below 900, though the AMEX and OTC averages each reached an all-time high in that month. The Dow continued its sullen withdrawal, even as the NYSE advance-decline line charted a new high in July, a most unusual divergence coming ten months after the DJIA peak.

By October, urged down by an escalation of interest rates, the Dow set a record. It had fallen for nine months without a single rally of 5 percent—the most stubborn decline in history, and one egged on by new tax considerations.

Bulls did not really capitulate, however, until 1978. The year started badly and immediately got worse. On January 3, the dollar suffered a record drop compared to the Swiss franc. On January 4, a grand jury went after the option market makers at the AMEX. On January 6, the Fed raised the discount rate. IBM, which had held against the grain in 1977, tumbled from 275 in December to 235. Texas Instruments tested its 1974 low.

The bear low came on the last day of February, the Dow having lost about 10 percent since the year end. But, despite the 17-month bear market, other broader averages had actually gained. The AMEX index, 104.15 on September 21, 1976, closed at 122.85 on February 28, 1978. The OTC composite was up 10 percent in the same period. The tiered social structure for stocks had undergone a great leveling.

Many stocks had 1978 lows above their 1976 highs, including such well-known names as American Broadcasting, Boeing, and Columbia Pictures. Other unheralded issues were plugged into solid, if unexciting earnings gains. American Standard's earnings had increased in each year from 1971 through 1978, rising from 24 cents to $7.23. The shares were valued at 4X earnings at the low point of 1978, not untypical of secondary issues. Earnings for the firm, a 1929 consolidation of two turn-of-the-century trusts—American Radiator and Standard Sanitary—would continue to rise until 1980.

Many sturdy, small companies did not identify with the sharp slump of early 1978, just as they had ignored the discouraging action of 1977. Retailers, electronic warfare issues, and restaurants, like Church's Fried Chicken and Denny's, maintained excellent chart patterns. Oil service firms, like Rowan, and the gambling shares, led by Resorts International, were other strong groups.

Major oils were hard hit in the final decline, despite a nagging coal strike and the worst winter weather in a century. OPEC's promise to maintain a price freeze through 1978 put Standard of Ohio at 58, down from a high of 91 in 1977. Major integrated oils sold at about 6X earnings.

In a most unusual switch, investors in small stocks had actually prospered as blue chips spiraled down in the 1976–1978 period. The divergence would continue to the upside in 1978 and 1979 as broader indices outperformed the Dow.

——————— OTHER BEAR SEQUENCES ———————

Worth More Dead Than Alive
DJIA May 29, 1946–Jne 13, 1949: 212.50 to 161.60, −24%.

The bear market of 1946–1949 made stocks worth more dead than alive. If such a boothill philosophy bred few gunslingers, it was only because the leveraged-buyout specialists were born a generation too late.

Stocks were value-cheap. Scores came to be priced for less than their net quick assets. Many sold for less than the cash in the till. Share prices continued to erode even as earnings and dividends surged. The sum of the parts, if a company could be broken up, far exceeded market value.

Some of the great fundamental stock bargains in history could be uncovered with no tool other than the *Wall Street Journal*. Other bear markets have afforded superior speculative opportunities, but only at much greater risk. The bear market low of 1949 was accompanied by record earnings and dividends for many firms.

Stocks were cheaply priced because the market was obsessed with the probability of a terrible postwar depression. In the 1930s, the nation had suffered a series of seemingly endless depressions; the pain was not forgotten. And the archives proved that great depressions followed great wars.

Stock followers were not the only ones to foresee economic chaos. Economists unanimously endorsed the script. So did Avery L. Sewell, chief of Montgomery Ward. He halted expansion just as Sears began an aggressive campaign to open new stores. Montgomery Ward was forever doomed to be No. 2.

The bear market began in the tough transition year of 1946. Strikes and work stoppages hit a record level, as in 1919. War contracts of $35 billion were cancelled. Railroad net income was a third of the 1942 figure.

The Dow had struck a 16-year high on May 29, 1946 at 212.50 and, after a July dip, climbed back near 205 in August. It was an ominous double top, for September opened with a fearsome drop in the post-Labor Day session. By October 9, the Dow had fallen to 163.12. Over the next several years, that level would be repeatedly attacked and even slightly fractured, but 97 percent of the 1946–1949 loss had already been recorded in October 1946, though a mild recession would finally make an appearance in November 1948.

Until mid-1949, in a development frustrating to both bulls and bears, the average churned in a sideways formation. During the consolidation, stock fundamentals improved dramatically. By 1949, many market giants were selling at 2 to 4 times earnings. The Dow's own impressive statistics, shown in Table 4-5 received few plaudits.

The drastic discounting of equity fundamentals was so bizarre that *Life* magazine featured some of the rare stock bargains. "The stock market," the magazine wrote in mid-March 1949, "surpasses all understanding . . . stocks are worth more dead than alive."[5]

While the bears awaited the "inevitable" postwar depression, industry after industry moved through its transition cycle. The rolling readjustment saved the market from serious trouble. Aircrafts, office equipment, and textiles, among others, reached their postwar lows in 1947. The Dow Utility Average made its low in 1948.

The automobile industry had even reversed gears in 1946, after an ultrashort decline. Detroit was the prime beneficiary of the explosive demand for goods. There had been no civilian auto production during the war and the United States could not get enough new wheels. Passenger car production boomed from 2,148,700 units in 1946 to 5,119,500 in 1949 with that total finally surpassing the 1929 figure.

Chrysler, typically, had lower earnings in 1946. But the bottom line of

---

[5]William Miller, The Strange State of the Market, *Life*, March 21, 1949, p. 115.

TABLE 4-5   DOW EARNINGS AND DIVIDENDS IN POSTWAR PERIOD

	1946	1947	1948	1949
Earnings	$13.63	$18.80	$23.07	$23.54
Dividend	7.50	9.21	11.50	12.79
Year's Low	163.12	163.21	165.39	161.60
PE Ratio[a]	12.0X	8.7X	7.2X	6.9X

[a]At low.

$3.09 per share more than doubled in 1947 and reached $10.25 in 1948. In 1949, the company earned $15.19, though the stock sold as low as 44, where the shares were priced at less than 3X earnings.

Some unique industry leaders just bulled their way to record earnings in every postwar year, as can be seen in Table 4-6. When 1949's recession finally eased the trend, Gulf and Sante Fe stock prices held at the 1948 lows.

While good news was ignored in the postwar period, the Russians' intransigence—the Iron Curtain, Czechoslovakia, and the Berlin Blockade— failed to excite serious selling.

War-bred enthusiasms led to some serious casualties, however. Trans World Airlines was one, as shown in Figure 4-11. It had soared from 9 to 79 during the war but was smashed back to 9 in 1946 and in 1949 sold as low as 10, though revenues had in 1948 tripled the 1945 figure. A costly expansion had hurt it. It was an industry problem; Northwest Airlines fell from 63 to 7.

Hughes Aircraft helped out TWA's financial situation by converting $10 million in debt to about 1 million common shares, giving them 74 percent control. The debt swap turned into another gold mine for the reclusive billion- aire, Howard Hughes.

Other industries, stripped of wartime demands, suffered equally with the airlines. The Milwaukee railroad had shot up from 6 to 39 during the war years, but by 1949 was down to 5. Pepsi Cola was a 41–8 postwar loser.

In November 1948, President Harry S. Truman's stunning reelection tripped the market, just when it seemed poised for better things. This made stocks exceedingly cheap once again, as earnings and dividends continued to climb. The state of market depression became so acute that *Barron's* financial

TABLE 4-6   FOR SOME, EARNINGS NEVER SLOWED AFTER WORLD WAR II

	1945	1946	1947	1948	PE Ratio[a]
Gulf Oil	$4.98	$6.42	$10.52	$13.54	4.27X
Jones & Laughlin	2.92	3.80	8.46	12.00	2.44
Santa Fe Railroad	9.60	13.50	17.10	23.30	3.61

[a]Lowest price-earnings ratio in 1948.

TRANS WORLD AIR LINES, INC.

Year	1942	1943	1944	1945	1946	1947	1948	1949
Earn.	.33	.31	.43	.29	d1.35	d.71	d.78	
Div.	–	–	–	–	–	–	–	

* 10% stock div.

Figure 4.11 Post-war airline crash victim (*Source: M.C. Horsey & Company, Salisbury, MD*)

weekly took investors to the couch, accusing them of discounting the end of the world. The publication editorialized in early January 1949:

> The Possibilities: Expectation of a mild, orderly recession does not seem wholly logical. Since everybody has been predicting it, everybody likewise has taken measure to protect his business against it . . . Where, then are the over-extended positions that need to be corrected?[6]

Despite the admonition from Dow Jones, the Industrials drifted lower throughout the spring, as did the Rails.

AT&T Victimizes Dow

The final low for the postwar period for the Dow 30 came at 161.60 on June 13, 1949. It was more illusion than fact, a statistical freak engineered by American Telephone & Telegraph, whose shares had been consistently weak throughout the entire period.

The 1946 low for "T" had been 160, while the 1949 bottom was 138. That 22-point loss differential was the primary reason for the index's new low. To the

---

[6]*Barron's*, January 3, 1949, p. 1, cols. 2,3.

consternation of the Dow theorists and dedicated bears, that low turned into a nonevent.

Technicians, perhaps, were not as surprised. The advance-decline line had recorded its low point in 1946. Margin debt had been more than halved since its 1945 peak. The Dow Utilities, often an indicator, had bottomed in 1948, as had Standard & Poor's composite.

Fundamentalists were rewarded with rare bargains. The Industrials in June 1949 sold at 6.86 times their trailing earnings and the dividend yield, based on the year's payout, was 7.9 percent. And, in a historical rarity, the average was priced below book.

The "inevitable" had proven evitable. The depression-siege mentality lifted. Stocks would prove to be worth a great deal more alive than dead by the time the coming bull sequence ended in 1956.

Bears Fumble Opportunity
DJIA Apr 6, 1956–Oct 22, 1957: 521.05 to 419.79, −19%.

In 1956–1957, the bears missed their best opportunity in two decades to smash the market. They had the ball, first and goal, with everything in their favor.

The line-up included: rising interest rates, increasing inflation, falling profits, the Suez war, Russian tanks in Budapest, and a recession. And Ike back in the hospital.

If all that wasn't enough, consumerism suffered a sudden fatigue. Record U.S. auto production of 7.9 million passenger units in 1955 would slump to 4.3 million in 1958, a 46 percent drop. Farm machinery sales declined. Retailers were hurt, with Sears dropping from 41 to 25. Appliance makers were also hit hard, and Admiral was a 30–7 victim. Bellwether General Motors would endure three consecutive years of falling earnings.

Despite a discouraging news budget, the bull died hard. The Dow reached its high April 6, 1956, at 521.05. Both the Industrials and the Rails fell sharply later that month. But by August, the Dow had recovered to 520.95. Other important averages, like the S&P 500 and the NYSE Index made new highs. There was great confidence.

But the year's second increase in the prime lending rate, to 4 percent, was announced August 21, cooling the summer heat. It all seemed to promise a severe market shakeout. But when the down thrust was finally over one year later in October 1957, the Industrials' loss was but 19 percent.

Defensive rotation confused the bears. Excluding gold, *Barron's* at that time tracked 31 industrial groups on a weekly basis. Eleven groups, including the autos, made their market highs in 1955, far ahead of the Dow. Eleven groups topped in 1956. But nine more were still bulling it in 1957.

Lukens Steel, the leading plate maker, typified the rotation. Its gain in 1956–1957 was over 100 points, from 14 to 123. National Lead, a 9–138 winner in the previous six-year advance, added 50 points after the Dow peaked. IBM put on over 100 points in the same time frame.

Still, as in the rolling readjustment of 1946–1949, a few segments of the market were blind-sided. Ford went public in 1956 at 64½ in the biggest "hot" deal ever, and the shares climbed on to 70. But the buyers were Edseled in 1957 when the new marque was released and the stock fell to 36.

Aircraft makers, high flyers in the previous advance, were brought back to earth. Boeing tumbled from 65 to 29. Air transports, coppers, and textiles also proved vulnerable.

TWA dropped from 36 to 10. Heavily touted Magna Copper suffered a bad cave-in, from 139 to 32, while Pacific Mills experienced a lesser run, falling from 56 to 20. Speculative rails suffered large percentage losses. The Katy dropped from 22 to 4. Rail operating revenues for the nation's carriers would not exceed the 1956 level for ten years.

Despite such individual hits, the Dow in July 1957 made its third assault on the 521.05 peak. It failed by less than one-half point. A recession began in August and when the prime got a big hike late in the month, the Dow quickly faded.

Sputnik Shock

On October 4, the Russians launched Sputnik I, shocking the West. Iron Curtain paranoia was expected from the Kremlin, but not scientific wizardry. The Dow dropped heavily on the news and continued the free fall before closing, with huge volume, at 419.76 on October 22.

That was the end. The next day, the Dow opened higher and ended with its biggest daily gain since 1929. The Rails climbed for a few days, but then demurred and lost 15 percent more by December. For the market and most industrial groups, the bear episode was over.

The damage had been minimal by any standard—only 19 percent in 18 months. The bears had fumbled a supurb opportunity.

By Christmas, a few groups and specialty stocks like Polaroid and Merck were recording all-time highs, though the Dow was off about 64 points for the year.

An oft-forgotten casualty of the period was Alcoa Corporation. The Dow member had been an early favorite of the growth cult and the shares had pushed up from below 20 in 1952 to 134 in 1956, where they were valued at over 31X earnings, an extraordinary rapture for the period. It would be three decades before Alcoa would recover its 1956 level.

The "Soaring Sixties"?
DJIA Jan 5, 1960–Oct 25, 1960: 685.47 to 566.05, −17%

The "Soaring Sixties" lost altitude on the decade's third day of trading. The Dow rolled over from its bull market high and fell on 13 of the next 17 trading days.

In early January, expectations had been too high, considering the hype and enormous markups of the special issues so favored in the previous two years. And the Dow's ascent to a record high on January 5 had been a lonely one sparked by multiple stock splits. Broader indices, as well as the Rails, had peaked in the previous summer.

Actually, the entire decade of the 1960s would be disappointing, despite three separate bull sequences. The largest and most solid advance of the period from 1962 to 1966 failed to double the Industrials. And the ten-year gain through 1969 would be but 18 percent, the poorest showing since the 1880s, save for the extreme of the 1930s.

The year 1960 is best remembered in the marketplace for the fact that its intrayear, mini-bear decline of only 17 percent remains the smallest on record. Some market chroniclers give it no official recognition. For a few industrial groups, however, 1960 was the serious end of a rather nasty three-year bear market.

Aircraft and oil shares had been in a bear trend since 1957. In most cases they bottomed in 1960. United Aircraft, 81 in 1957, fell further from 55 to 22 during 1960. Amerada, valued at 148 in 1957, did not end its slide until July, when it hit 55. The great oil explorer would run to 120 in 1961.

Auto shares suffered during the mini-bear. General Motors, 59 in 1959, hit 40 in December. Ford put up its second best public earnings in history but slumped from 93 to 61. The heavy-handed treatment for cyclic issues pulled Goodrich down from 90 to 45 and Bucyrus-Erie, 36 in 1959, did not stop until it had touched 13.

By early autumn, the market had discounted a Kennedy victory, falling to a low in late October, even as gold and the mining shares came under sharp demand from those who saw renewed inflation in Democratic rule. When the Dow reached its low, the contrary Utility average was nicely above its close of 1959, an indicator of the exceptional strength it would show in the next few years.

Inflation's Ugly Flip Side
DJIA APR 27, 1981–Aug 12, 1982: 1024.05 to 776.92, −24%.

Inflation's flip side—deflation—turned ugly in the 1981 daylight. Down on the farm, the inflation of 1980 was recalled with nostalgia.

Soybean futures prices fell by $3 per bushel. Wheat and corn lost $1.50. Cattle and hog prices plunged during the last six months. Deflation and a recession which began in July gave the market plenty of pain. And the FRB's tight money policy made it almost unbearable. The discount rate stood at 14 percent during the summer of 1981 with a 4 percent surcharge for active borrowers. Banks hopped the prime up from 17 percent to 20.5 percent and by early October, long-term Treasury bonds were yielding 15 percent.

Such avarice in the counting house had helped top the Dow in April at 1024 and that unimpressive peak was followed by extreme weakness during the summer. By July, the Dow was flashing bear market in plain language. Easing rates in the late fall ended the first down leg, but there was little room on the upside, given a weakening economy. Unemployment in December was already worse than in 1974.

Higher interest rates returned in January and the market's second leg down took the Dow below 800 only to recover quickly to a May high at 869. A third down leg then commenced; it would end in August.

Oils were the major victims of the 1981–1982 slump in terms of market capitalization. The losses in individual stocks ran into the billions. Exxon's fall from 44 to 25 was not impressive in points, but it added up to over $16 billion in evaporated wealth, based on Exxon's 865 million outstanding shares. Standard of Ohio lost paper value of about the same amount in a drop from 92 to 27. Service companies were more severely hurt percentagewise. Western Co. of North America's price was cut from 32 to 7.

Mining shares broke the hearts of the bullion bugs, but their losses were minor compared to the energy group in terms of total dollar meltdown. Homestake was an 88–17 loser but had only 17 million shares on the books. Sunshine, the veteran Idaho miner, lost 80 percent of its value, 26 to 5, as silver valued at $50 per ounce in early 1980 plummeted to $6.

Financial scandals made the summer of 1982 difficult. Oklahoma City's Penn Square Bank folded; it had bad loans farmed out all over the country, Continental Illinois being a principal loser. Drysdale Government Securities had been padlocked in May.

Nevertheless, a few groups and niche stocks ignored the travails. Publishers such as Prentice-Hall, Commerce Clearing House, and Dow Jones moved against the grain. Limited Stores and Service Corporation, the funeral/cemetery company, found it easy to chalk record highs.

Perhaps the saddest Dow news of the harsh 1981–1982 years was the meltdown into single-digit figures of such legendary market names as Chrysler, International Harvester, Inco, and Manville. Chrysler was ousted from the average. Its shares at 3, seemed doomed to join the likes of Stutz, Pierce Arrow, Hudson, and Studebaker. Manville dropped to 4 and Inco to 8.

International Harvester, one of J. P. Morgan's great trust successes, sank to 2¾. A new name and face-lift would do little for the shares. Retitled Navistar International and stripped of its famed farm equipment business, the shares—still in the DJIA—would have a high in 1990 below 5.

In July 1982, the Fed finally showed mercy and made two swift cuts in the discount rate, dropping it to 11 percent, the lowest level since 1980.

The last act in the confusing Dow drama of 1965–1982 was about to end. The average had etched out an enormous diamond pattern in that 17-year period and the massive formation would survive its final downside test, on August 12, at Dow 777.

At least, the low held above the bear market figure of 1977 and the silver panic mark of 1980, as seen in Figure 4-12. But it was little better than the 1966 bear low at 736, made 16 years previously, and when adjusted for inflation is in reality much lower. That chart can be seen on page 152.

The recession would last until November, but the Street was already convinced that a great sea change had occurred for both inflation and interest rates, a troublesome pair since the LBJ years. An outrageous advance began in

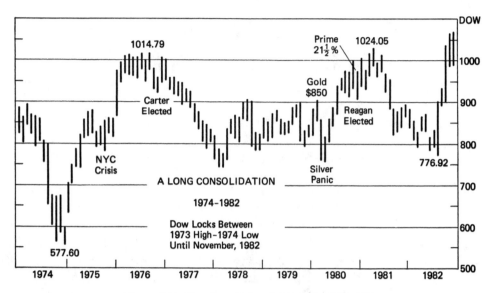

Figure 4.12 Dow Jones Industrial Average, 1974–1982

late August. On November 3, it would crest the multiple and difficult heights between 1000 and 1050 which had turned back every ascent since 1966.

PANIC EPISODES

SELLING PANICS

Bear markets seem unending but they are actually made up of multiple periods of intense selling pressure, relieved by sharp rallies and longish periods of dullness. In the 1929–1932 disaster, which lasted nearly three years, there were seven distinct down legs to the market, separated by some record-breaking rallies.

Serious slides in the past century have typically run for about two months and cut the leading average 20 percent or more. Most of these painful episodes have come at the end of a torturous bear market. But in 1916, a high-volume smash developed directly off a bull market top; it was caused by a "peace scare."

In 1980, the silver panic afforded courageous buyers a bag full of bargains, though the 1978–1981 advance was already two-thirds over. The startling collapse, seen in figure 4.12, was not quite sharp enough to make the following list. Notable bear slides with losses of around 20 percent in a short period follow.

1893 —Apr 29–Jly 26 Trust shares collapse. Widespread rail bankruptcies, with 20-Stock Average (18 rails) down 31%.

1895 —Oct 15–Dec 21 President Cleveland's shocking war threat against England torpedoes market, Rails losing 22%.

1896 —Jne 17–Aug 8 Sound money threatened by Bryan and Silverites. 24% loss.

1899 —Nov 18–Dec 18 London selling account Transvaal war losses. Dow −23%.

1907 —Feb 13–Mar 25 Pools and manipulations begin to unravel. Minus 19%.
—Sept 6–Nov 15 Copper corners and squeezes unwind. Commercial panic ended by Morgan's banking pool. Loss: 28%.

1910 —May 21–Jly 26 ICC rail-rate decision disappoints. Dow falls 18%.

1916 —Nov 21–Dec 21 "Peace scare" ends bull market, costs market 18%.

1920 —Jan 3–Feb 25 Deflation, Prohibition sorrows cut Dow 18%, but historic bull corners in Stutz, GM already underway.
—Sep 17–Dec 21 Auto, steel business collapse, along with all commodity prices. Ford lays off 40,000. Dow drops 26%.

1929 —Oct 10–Nov 13 Nothing equals pain of this historic, one-month 44% collapse.

1930 —Aug 15–Oct 5 A 28% slide convinces players spring rally had been a bull trap.

1931 —Aug 15–Oct 5 Bourses in crisis as England leaves gold standard. 41% loss.
—Oct 24–Dec 17 Frantic short-covering rally had left market naked of support. Banking crisis worsens. Loss: 33%.

1932 —Mar 8–May 31 Last convulsion of the bear market kills all hope. Dow loses 50%. Prices drift lower until July 8.
—Sep 7–Oct 10 Depression not over despite summer's boom. Short, sharp correction erases 27% of Dow value. Carriers derailed, down 40%.

1933 —Jly 18–Jly 22 "Whiskey Panic" cuts Dow 19% in four trading days.
—Sep 19–Oct 21 Second thoughts on the New Deal. Loss: 21%.

1937 —Aug 31–Oct 18 Industrial collapse takes Dow down 34%.

1938 —Feb 23–Mar 31 Nazis annex Austria. NYSE President Richard Whitney cuffed. This final month of a year-long bear move pulls Industrials down 25%.

1939 —Mar 10–Apr 8 Germany marches on Czechoslovakia. Dow loss: 20%.

1940 —May 9–Jne 10 Dunkerque. Nazis to Paris. Italy volunteers as German war partner. Dow cut by 25%.

1946 —Aug 13–Oct 15 Postwar adjustments, shortages push Dow down 20%.

1962 —Apr 5–Jne 26 JFK-U.S. Steel confrontation melts Industrials down 24%.

1970 —Apr 9–May 26 Cambodia, Kent State, margin liquidation spark final crash phase of 1968–1970 decline. Six-week loss: 20%.

1973 —Oct 26–Dec 6 Oil embargo, Nixon tapes, Mid-East war take murderous 200-point toll within less than six weeks, equal to 20%.

1974 —Aug 7–Oct 4 Watergate waterfall drowns market. Nixon resignation no help. Brutal slump of 28% ends worst bear sequence since 1930s.

1987 —Oct 5–Oct 19 Brutal, two-week purge costs Dow 34%.

———— BEARISH DIVERGENCES, INDUSTRIALS ———— AND TRANSPORTS

BEARISH DIVERGENCES BETWEEN AVERAGES ————————————

Divergences between the leading Dow averages, the Industrials and Transportations, are never bullish and are always unsettling to market technicians.

"Failure to confirm" is the buzz phrase, and it can be marked in many ways, to the upside or downside, and in either major or minor phases of the market.

A minor misfire occurred in October 1989. The Industrials were moving easily in new high ground, but the Transportation index, despite a merger mania which had ballooned airline shares to giddy heights, refused to confirm. It was unable to rise above its peak of early September. Within days, the dreadful air pocket of Friday, October 13, sucked both averages into a nasty crash.

Longer-term divergences are more important and clearly ominous. In 1980, the Transportation index soared far above its peak level of 1972, while the Industrials continued to despair below their 1973 high of 1052. The next major move in the market was the 1981–1982 bear market.

In 1972–1973, the sequence was reversed. The Transportations peaked in April 1972. Their failure to make further progress, despite the Dow's upward move through the 1000 level, kept technicians and Dow theorists nervous for months. Though the Industrials did not top until January 1973, the great crash which followed proved the validity of the warning.

The longest running divergence occurred from 1899 to 1902. The Rails were the most important of the two averages, and had mounted a really long bull campaign, lasting from August 1896 until the autumn of 1902. Part of the reason was that many of the Rail components had been "dewatered" or recapi-talized in the great epidemic of railroad reorganizations after 1893.

Industrials, on the other hand, included many new trusts, all of which were grossly overcapitalized. Their speculative frenzy of early 1899 rolled over in September into a year-long downtrend. That was followed by a short, mini-bull market which ended in the summer of 1901. The great trust flotations of 1901 had sucked up all the Industrial money.

The Rails steamed on, oblivious to the problems in steel and copper until September 1902, and the differences were settled in the bear market that followed. The long time frame was really exceptional, which testifies to the relative strength of the carriers in the turn-of-the-century economy.

Rails Often Relatively Weak

Since that period, however, the most serious divergences have struck down the Rails. In 1919, a heated inflation drove the industrial sector hard all year. Government control of the railroads continued despite the war's end and left investors indifferent to the carriers, whose possible returns were seen as akin to bonds. The average was unable to rise above its peak of Armistice week, 1918, while the Dow pushed higher for another year. The great deflation of 1920–1921 resolved the impasse.

Long extended advances by the Industrials in the 1920s and 1950s found the Rails set back by mini-bear attacks in 1922–1923 and 1953–1954, but the divergence was mild, similar to two positive moves by the Rails in the 1940s when the Dow was suffering.

One exceptionally long and dangerous divergence was finally resolved in a favorable mode. In July 1933, the Rails had advanced by 376 percent within 12 months—a record. It was too much, too fast considering the tough economic days still ahead. The carriers entered a two-year slump. In the meantime, the Dow struggled in a sideways consolidation.

Bullish hopes and firming traffic finally revived the Rails in March 1935, and both averages rolled up huge gains in an advance which lasted until March 1937.

But in 1990, a pointed divergence gave off a very bearish signal. Even as the Dow struck the magic 3000 level, the Transports were trading 22 percent below their high of 1989, an ominous indicator by historical standards.

5

The Dow Jones Stock Averages

The Dow Jones & Co. did not invent the NYSE or, as it sometimes seems, Wall Street. But one of the *Wall Street Journal*'s founders did originate the first Dow average and his name will, apparently, grace the evening news forevermore.

"How's the market?" means: What is the Dow Jones Industrial Average doing? And has for decades. The Industrials are the best-known market index in the world.

The Industrial and Rail stock averages, more or less as we now know them, were first jointly computed in 1896, although Dow Jones & Co. had published on an irregular basis an index of NYSE active stocks since 1884. The daily antecedent of the present 20-stock Transportation index can be traced back to late 1889; it contained two "industrials"—Pacific Mail and Western Union—and 18 rails. It was loosely referred to as the Rail average.

While trade in rail stocks and bonds dominated the Exchange until early in the twentieth century, the proliferation of new industrial ventures, particularly the giant trusts, had made a separate industrial average desirable and on May 26, 1896, a 12-stock industrial average was first published in the *Wall Street Journal*. It ended the day at 40.94.

Later in the year, the 20-Stock Average, which had been the best market index for the previous years of the 1890s, became a pure rail index. Substitutions were made for the two industrial members, but they melded well.

Scores of other substitutions have been made in both lists over the years. Only General Electric survives from the 1896 cast. The Atchison (Sante Fe Pacific) and a few other renamed rails live in the Transports.

Dow Jones & Company remains the sole arbiter of membership in the averages and many popular stocks such as Coca-Cola, General Motors, IBM, and the Chicago, Rock Island, among others, have been drummed in and out of the lists. The original 12-stock industrial group now numbers 30.

A 20-stock Utility average was created in 1929; later, the membership was cut back to 15. Interestingly, AT&T was an original member of the index, but in 1939 was promoted to the Industrials, bumping IBM. Dow 1000 would have come years earlier without that infamous substitution. The Utilities join the 30 Industrials and 20 Transportations to make up the 65-stock Composite index.

In 1970, a major change was wrought in the Rails. Reflecting new transportation patterns, the name was changed to the Transportation Average and nine rails were replaced by a cross section of other transportation issues.

The Dow averages, of course, have their critics. A principal fault, it is often maintained, is the restricted membership. But the Dow Jones & Co. has heeded those critics. On September 24, 1889, the *Wall Street Journal,* writing about the old 12-Stock Average, noted that "It has occasionally been attacked as not including stocks enough to fairly represent the market."[1] Whereupon, the *Journal* introduced the new 20-Stock Average. And the Industrial list was, after all, expanded from 12 stocks to 20 in 1916 and increased again to 30 in 1928.

The pace of expansion may be glacial, but the averages have remained, for nearly a century, the most popular and often the only market statistical guide used by many investors. No other averages boast their longevity and rich statistical history.

It will be the Dow theory of market average movements, and not a Value Line/NYSE Index theory that technicians will bicker about in the twenty-first century.

---

[1]The Wall Street Journal, New York, September 24, 1889, p. 2, col. 2.

TABLE 5-1　STOCKS LISTED IN DOW AVERAGES

30 Industrials

Allied-Signal	Exxon	Primerica
Alcoa	General Electric	Procter & Gamble
American Express	General Motors	Sears, Roebuck
American Telephone &	Goodyear	Texaco
Telegraph	IBM	USX
Bethlehem Steel	International Paper	Union Carbide
Boeing	McDonald's Corp.	United Technologies
Chevron	Merck	Westinghouse
Coca-Cola	Minnesota Mining/Mfg.	Woolworth
Du Pont	Navistar	
Eastman Kodak	Philip Morris	

20 Transportations

AMR Corp.	Consolidated Freight	Santa Fe Pacific
Airborne Freight	Consolidated Rail	Southwest Airlines
Alaska Air Group	Delta Air Lines	UAL Corp.
American President	Federal Express	Union Pacific
Burlington Northern	Norfolk & Southern	USAir Group
CSX	Pan Am	XTRA Corp.
Carolina Freight	Ryder System	

15 Utilities

American Electric Power	Consolidated Natural	Panhandle Eastern
Centerior Energy	Gas	Peoples Energy
Columbia Gas	Detroit Edison	Philadelphia Electric
Commonwealth Edison	Houston Industries	Public Service Enterprise
Consolidated Edison	Niagara Mohawk	SCEcorp.
	Pacific Gas & Electric	

The 12 Original Industrials[a]

American Cotton Oil	Distilling & Cattle Feed.	North American
American Sugar	General Electric	Tennessee Coal & Iron
American Tobacco	Laclede Gas	U.S. Leather preferred
Chicago Gas	National Lead	U.S. Rubber

The 20 Original Rails[b]

Atchison	Louisville & Nashville	Rock Island
Burlington	Manhattan Elevated	St. Paul
CCC & St. Louis	MKT preferred	Southern Railroad pre-
Chesapeake & Ohio	Missouri Pacific	ferred
Chicago & North Western	NY Central	Susquehanna preferred
Erie	Northern Pacific pre-	Wabash preferred
Jersey Central	ferred	
Lake Shore	Philadelphia & Reading	

[a]May 26, 1896. By year's end, U.S. Rubber was out, Pacific Mail in and Standard Rope had already replaced Cordage preferred which had ousted North American.

[b]October 26, 1986 was first posting of all-rail index, two industrials having been previously included.

TABLE 5-2   MAJOR PRICE MOVEMENTS FOR DOW JONES INDUSTRIALS

Dates		Total move		Point change	%
Aug 8, 1896	Sep 5, 1899	28.43 to	77.61	+ 49.18	173
Sep 5, 1899	Sep 24, 1900	77.61 to	52.96	− 24.65	32
Sep 24, 1900	Jne 17, 1901	52.96 to	78.26	+ 25.30	48
Jne 17, 1901	Nov 9, 1903	78.26 to	42.15	− 36.11	46
Nov 9, 1903	Jan 19, 1906	42.15 to	103.00	+ 60.85	144
Jan 19, 1906	Nov 15, 1907	103.00 to	53.00	− 50.00	49
Nov 15, 1907	Nov 19, 1909	53.00 to	100.53	+ 47.53	90
Nov 19, 1909	Sep 25, 1911	100.53 to	72.94	− 27.59	27
Sep 25, 1911	Sep 30, 1912	72.94 to	94.15	+ 21.21	29
Sep 30, 1912	Jly 30, 1914	94.15 to	71.42	− 22.73	24
Jly 30, 1914	Nov 21, 1916[a]	51.88 to	110.15	+ 58.27	112
Nov 21, 1916	Dec 19, 1917	110.15 to	65.95	− 44.20	40
Dec 19, 1917	Nov 3, 1919	65.95 to	119.62	+ 53.67	81
Nov 3, 1919	Aug 24, 1921	119.62 to	63.90	− 55.72	47
Aug 24, 1921	Sep 3, 1929	63.90 to	381.17	+ 317.27	497
Sep 3, 1929	Jly 8, 1932	381.17 to	41.22	− 339.95	89
Jly 8, 1932	Mar 10, 1937	41.22 to	194.40	+ 153.18	372
Mar 10, 1937	Mar 31, 1938	194.40 to	98.95	− 95.45	49
Mar 31, 1938	Nov 12, 1938	98.95 to	158.41	+ 59.46	60
Nov 12, 1938	Apr 8, 1939	158.41 to	121.44	− 36.97	23
Apr 8, 1939	Sep 12, 1939	121.44 to	155.92	+ 34.48	28
Sep 12, 1939	Apr 28, 1942	155.92 to	92.92	− 63.00	40
Apr 28, 1942	May 29, 1946	92.92 to	212.50	+ 119.58	129
May 29, 1946	Jne 13, 1949	212.50 to	161.60	− 50.90	24
Jne 13, 1949	Apr 6, 1956	161.60 to	521.05	+ 359.45	222
Apr 6, 1956	Oct 22, 1957	521.05 to	419.79	− 101.26	19
Oct 22,1957	Jan 5, 1960	419.79 to	685.47	+ 265.68	63
Jan 5, 1960	Oct 25, 1960	685.47 to	566.05	− 119.42	16
Oct 25, 1960	Dec 13, 1961	566.05 to	734.91	+ 168.86	30
Dec 13, 1961	Jne 26, 1962	734.91 to	535.76	− 199.15	27
Jne 26, 1962	Feb 9, 1966	535.76 to	995.15	+ 459.39	86
Feb 9, 1966	Oct 7, 1966	995.15 to	744.32	− 250.83	25
Oct 7, 1966	Dec 3, 1968	744.32 to	985.21	+ 240.89	32
Dec 3, 1968	May 26, 1970	985.21 to	631.16	− 354.05	36
May 26, 1970	Jan 11, 1973	631.16 to	1051.70	+ 420.54	67
Jan 11, 1973	Dec 6, 1974	1051.70 to	577.60	− 474.10	45
Dec 6, 1974	Sep 21, 1976	577.60 to	1014.79	+ 437.19	76
Sep 21, 1976	Feb 28, 1978	1014.79 to	742.12	− 272.67	27
Feb 28, 1978	Apr 27, 1981	742.12 to	1024.05	+ 281.93	38
Apr 27, 1981	Aug 12, 1982	1024.05 to	776.92	− 247.13	24
Aug 12, 1982	Aug 25, 1987	776.92 to	2722.42	+1945.50	250
Aug 25, 1987	Oct 19, 1987	2722.42 to	1738.74	− 983.68	36
Oct 19, 1987		1738.74 to			

[a]New 20-Stock Industrial Average, effective in 1916, but computed back to beginning of World War I.

TABLE 5-3   MAJOR PRICE MOVEMENTS FOR DOW JONES RAIL-TRANSPORTS[a]

Dates		Total move		Point change	%
Apr 2, 1888	Jne 4, 1890	58.11 to	78.38	+ 20.27	35
Jne 4, 1890	Dec 8, 1890	78.38 to	58.10	− 20.28	26
Dec 8, 1890	Mar 4, 1892	58.10 to	75.68	+ 17.58	30
Mar 4,1892	Jly 26,1893	75.68 to	43.47	− 32.31	43
Jly 26, 1893	Sep 4, 1895	43.47 to	63.77	+ 20.30	47
Sep 4, 1895	Aug 8, 1896	63.77 to	41.82	− 21.95	34
Aug 8, 1896	Sep 9, 1902	41.82 to	129.36	+ 87.54	209
Sep 9, 1902	Sep 28, 1903	129.36 to	88.80	− 40.56	31
Sep 28, 1903	Jan 22, 1906	88.80 to	138.36	+ 49.56	56
Jan 22, 1906	Nov 21, 1907	138.36 to	81.41	− 56.95	42
Nov 21, 1907	Aug 14, 1909	81.41 to	134.46	+ 53.05	65
Aug 14, 1909	Jly 26, 1910	134.46 to	105.59	− 28.87	21
Jly 26, 1910	Oct 5, 1912	105.59 to	124.35	+ 18.76	18
Oct 5, 1912	Dec 24, 1914	124.35 to	87.40	− 36.95	30
Dec 24, 1914	Oct 4, 1916	87.40 to	112.28	+ 24.88	28
Oct 4, 1916	Dec 19, 1917	112.28 to	70.75	− 41.53	37
Dec 19, 1917	Nov 9, 1918	70.75 to	92.91	+ 22.16	31
Nov 9, 1918	Jne 20, 1921	92.91 to	65.52	− 27.39	29
Jne 20, 1921	Sep 11, 1922	65.52 to	93.99	+ 28.47	43
Sep 11, 1922	Aug 4, 1923	93.99 to	76.78	− 17.21	18
Aug 4, 1923	Sep 3, 1929	76.78 to	189.11	+112.33	146
Sep 3, 1929	Jly 8, 1932	189.11 to	13.23	−175.88	93
Jly 8, 1932	Jly 7, 1933	13.23 to	56.53	+ 43.30	376
Jly 7, 1933	Mar 12, 1935	56.53 to	27.31	− 29.22	52
Mar 12, 1935	Mar 17, 1937	27.31 to	64.46	+ 37.15	136
Mar 17, 1937	Mar 31, 1938	64.46 to	19.00	− 45.46	71
Mar 31, 1938	Sep 27, 1939	19.00 to	35.90	+ 16.90	89
Sep 27, 1939	May 21, 1940	35.90 to	22.14	− 13.76	38
May 21, 1940	Aug 1, 1941	22.14 to	30.88	+ 8.74	39
Aug 1, 1941	Jne 2, 1942	30.88 to	23.31	− 7.57	25
Jne 2, 1942	Jne 13, 1946	23.31 to	68.31	+ 45.00	193
Jne 13, 1946	May 19, 1947	68.31 to	41.16	− 27.14	40
May 19, 1947	Jly 14, 1948	41.16 to	64.95	+ 23.79	58
Jly 14, 1948	Jne 13, 1949	64.95 to	41.03	− 23.92	37
Jne 13, 1949	Dec 22, 1952	41.03 to	112.53	+ 71.50	174
Dec 22, 1952	Sep 14, 1953	112.53 to	90.56	− 21.97	20
Sep 14, 1953	May 9, 1956	90.56 to	181.23	+ 90.67	100
May 9, 1956	Dec 24, 1957	181.23 to	95.67	− 85.56	47
Dec 24, 1957	Jly 8, 1959	95.67 to	173.56	+ 77.89	81
Jly 8, 1959	Sep 29, 1960	173.56 to	123.37	− 50.19	29
Sep 29, 1960	Oct 11, 1961	123.37 to	152.92	+ 29.55	24
Oct 11, 1961	Oct 1, 1962	152.92 to	114.86	− 38.06	25
Oct 1, 1962	Feb 15, 1966	114.86 to	271.72	+156.86	137
Feb 15, 1966	Oct 7, 1966	271.72 to	184.34	− 87.38	32
Oct 7, 1966	Feb 7, 1969	184.34 to	279.88	+ 95.54	51
Feb 7, 1969	Jly 7, 1970	279.88 to	116.69	−163.19	58
Jly 7, 1970	Apr 7, 1972	116.69 to	275.71	+159.02	136
Apr 7, 1972	Oct 3, 1974	275.71 to	125.93	−149.78	54
Oct 3, 1974	May 18, 1977	125.93 to	246.64	+120.71	96
May 18, 1977	Mch 9,1978	246.64 to	199.31	− 47.33	19
Mch 9, 1978	Apr 16, 1981	199.31 to	447.38	+248.07	124
Apr 16, 1981	Aug 12, 1982	447.38 to	292.12	−155.26	35
Aug 12, 1982	Aug 14, 1987	292.12 to	1101.16	+809.04	277
Aug 14, 1987	Dec 4, 1987	1101.16 to	661.00	−440.16	40
Dec 4, 1987	Sep 5, 1989	661.00 to	1532.01	+871.01	132
Sep 5, 1989	—	1532.01 to	202.8	− 64.95	26

[a]20-Stock Dow Average (18 rails) until October 1896. Dow Rails until 1970. Dow Transportations since January 1, 1970.

HISTORICAL RECORDS

TABLE 5-4   ANNUAL RANGES AND CHANGES

Year	Dow Jones Industrial Average					Dow Jones Rail-Transports Average				
	Closing high	Closing low	Close	Point change	% change	Closing high	Closing low	Close	Point change	% change
1890**						78.38	58.10	61.96	− 10.21	− 14.1
1891**						73.25	61.50	72.88	+ 10.92	+ 17.6
1892**						75.68	66.86	68.10	− 4.78	− 6.6
1893**						70.87	43.47	51.35	− 16.75	− 24.6
1894**						57.60	50.73	51.06	− 0.29	− 0.6
1895**						63.77	48.56	52.23	+ 1.17	+ 2.3
1896**	na^c	28.48	40.45	na	na	56.79	41.82	51.33	− 0.90	− 1.7
1897	55.82	38.49	49.41	+ 8.96	+ 22.2	67.23	48.12	62.29	+ 10.96	+ 21.4
1898	60.97	42.00	60.52	+ 11.11	+ 22.5	74.99	55.89	74.99	+ 12.70	+ 20.4
1899	77.61	58.27	66.08	+ 5.56	+ 9.2	87.04	72.48	77.73	+ 2.74	+ 3.7
1900	71.04	52.96	70.71	+ 4.63	+ 7.0	94.99	72.99	94.99	+ 17.26	+ 22.2
1901	78.26	61.52	64.56	− 6.15	− 8.7	117.86	92.66	114.85	+ 19.86	+ 20.9
1902	68.44	59.57	64.29	− 0.27	− 0.4	129.36	111.73	118.98	+ 4.13	+ 3.6
1903	67.70	42.15	49.11	− 15.18	− 23.6	121.28	88.80	98.33	− 20.65	− 17.4
1904	73.23	46.41	69.61	+ 20.50	+ 41.7	119.46	91.31	117.43	+ 19.10	+ 19.4
1905	96.56	68.76	96.20	+ 26.59	+ 38.2	133.54	114.52	133.26	+ 15.83	+ 13.5
1906	103.00	85.18	94.35	− 1.85	− 1.9	138.36	120.30	129.80	− 3.46	− 2.6
1907	96.37	53.00	58.75	− 35.60	− 37.7	131.95	81.41	88.77	− 41.03	− 31.6
1908	88.38	58.62	86.15	+ 27.40	+ 46.6	120.05	86.04	120.05	+ 31.28	+ 35.2
1909	100.53	79.91	99.05	+ 12.90	+ 15.0	134.46	113.90	130.41	+ 10.36	+ 8.6

Year										
1910	98.34	73.62	81.36	− 17.69	− 17.9	129.90	105.59	114.06	− 16.35	− 12.5
1911	87.06	72.94	81.68	+ 0.32	+ 0.4	123.86	109.80	116.83	+ 2.77	+ 2.4
1912	94.15	80.15	87.87	+ 6.19	+ 7.6	124.35	114.92	116.84	+ 0.01	+ na
1913	88.57	72.11	78.78	− 9.09	− 10.3	118.10	100.50	103.72	− 13.12	− 11.2
1914	83.43	71.42	74.73	− 4.05	− 5.1	109.43	87.40	88.53	− 15.19	− 14.6
1915[a]	99.21	54.22	99.15	+ 44.57	+ 81.7	108.28	87.85	108.05	+ 19.52	+ 22.0
1916	110.15	84.96	95.00	− 4.15	− 4.2	112.28	99.11	105.15	− 2.90	− 2.7
1917	99.18	65.95	74.38	− 20.62	− 21.7	105.76	70.75	79.73	− 25.42	− 24.2
1918	89.07	73.38	82.20	+ 7.82	+ 10.5	92.91	77.21	84.32	+ 4.59	+ 5.8
1919	119.62	79.15	107.23	+ 25.03	+ 30.5	91.13	73.63	75.30	− 9.02	− 10.7
1920	109.88	66.75	71.95	− 35.38	− 32.9	85.37	67.83	75.96	+ .66	+ 0.8
1921	81.50	63.90	81.10	+ 9.15	+ 12.7	77.56	65.52	74.27	+ 1.69	+ 2.1
1922	103.43	78.59	98.73	+ 17.63	+ 21.7	93.99	73.43	86.11	+ 11.84	+ 15.9
1923	105.38	85.76	95.52	− 3.21	− 3.3	90.63	76.78	80.86	− 5.25	− 6.1
1924	120.51	88.33	120.51	+ 24.99	+ 26.2	99.50	80.23	98.33	+ 17.47	+ 21.7
1925	159.39	115.00	156.66	+ 36.15	+ 30.0	112.93	92.98	112.93	+ 14.60	+ 14.8
1926	166.64	135.20	157.20	+ .54	+ 0.3	123.33	102.41	120.86	+ 7.93	+ 7.0
1927	202.40	152.73	202.40	+ 45.20	+ 28.8	144.82	119.29	140.30	+ 19.44	+ 16.1
1928	300.00	191.33	300.00	+ 97.60	+ 48.2	152.70	132.60	151.14	+ 10.84	+ 7.7
1929	381.17	198.69	248.48	− 51.52	− 17.2	189.11	128.07	144.72	− 6.42	− 4.2
1930	294.07	157.51	164.58	− 83.90	− 33.8	157.94	91.65	96.58	− 48.14	− 33.3
1931	194.36	73.79	77.90	− 86.68	− 52.7	111.58	31.42	33.63	− 62.95	− 65.2
1932	88.78	41.22	59.93	− 17.97	− 23.1	41.30	13.23	25.90	− 7.73	− 23.0
1933	108.67	50.16	99.90	+ 39.97	+ 66.7	56.53	23.43	40.80	+ 14.90	+ 57.5
1934	110.74	85.51	104.04	+ 4.14	+ 4.1	52.97	33.19	36.44	− 4.36	− 10.7
1935	148.44	96.71	144.13	+ 40.09	+ 38.5	41.84	27.31	40.48	+ 4.04	+ 11.1
1936	184.90	143.11	179.90	+ 35.77	+ 24.8	59.89	40.66	53.63	+ 13.15	+ 32.5
1937	194.40	113.64	120.85	− 59.05	− 32.8	64.46	28.91	29.46	− 24.17	− 45.1
1938	158.41	98.95	154.76	+ 33.91	+ 28.1	33.98	19.00	33.98	+ 4.52	+ 15.3
1939	155.92	121.44	150.24	− 4.52	− 2.9	35.90	24.14	31.83	− 2.15	− 6.3

TABLE 5-4 Continued

Year	Dow Jones Industrial Average					Dow Jones Rail-Transports Average				
	Closing high	Closing low	Close	Point change	% change	Closing high	Closing low	Close	Point change	% change
1940	152.80	111.84	131.13	− 19.11	− 12.7	32.67	22.14	28.13	− 3.70	− 11.6
1941	133.59	106.34	110.96	− 20.17	− 15.4	30.88	24.25	25.42	− 2.71	− 9.6
1942	119.71	92.92	119.40	+ 8.44	+ 7.6	29.28	23.31	27.39	+ 1.97	+ 7.7
1943	145.82	119.26	135.89	+ 16.49	+ 13.8	38.30	27.59	33.56	+ 6.17	+ 22.5
1944	152.53	134.22	152.32	+ 16.43	+ 12.1	48.40	33.45	48.40	+ 14.84	+ 44.2
1945	195.82	151.35	192.91	+ 40.59	+ 26.6	64.89	47.03	62.80	+ 14.40	+ 29.8
1946	212.50	163.12	177.20	− 15.71	− 8.1	68.31	44.69	51.13	− 11.67	− 18.6
1947	186.85	163.21	181.16	+ 3.96	+ 2.2	53.42	41.16	52.48	+ 1.35	+ 2.6
1948	193.16	165.39	177.30	− 3.86	− 2.1	64.95	48.13	52.86	+ 0.38	+ 0.7
1949	200.52	161.60	200.13	+ 22.83	+ 12.9	54.29	41.03	52.76	− 0.10	− 0.2
1950	235.47	196.81	235.41	+ 35.28	+ 17.6	77.89	51.24	77.64	+ 24.88	+ 47.2
1951	276.37	238.99	269.23	+ 33.82	+ 14.4	90.08	72.39	81.70	+ 4.06	+ 5.2
1952	292.00	256.35	291.90	+ 22.67	+ 8.4	112.53	82.03	111.27	+ 29.57	+ 36.2
1953	293.79	255.49	280.90	− 11.00	− 3.8	112.21	90.56	94.03	− 17.24	− 15.5
1954	404.39	279.87	404.39	+123.49	+ 44.0	146.23	94.84	145.86	+ 51.83	+ 55.1
1955	488.40	388.20	488.40	+ 84.01	+ 20.8	167.83	137.84	163.29	+ 17.43	+ 11.9
1956	521.05	462.35	499.47	+ 11.07	+ 2.3	181.23	150.44	153.23	− 10.06	− 6.2
1957	520.77	419.79	435.69	− 63.78	− 12.8	157.67	95.67	96.96	− 56.27	− 36.7
1958	583.65	436.89	583.65	+147.96	+ 34.0	157.91	99.89	157.65	+ 60.69	+ 62.6
1959	679.36	574.46	679.36	+ 95.71	+ 16.4	173.56	146.65	154.05	− 3.60	− 2.3
1960	685.47	566.05	615.89	− 63.47	− 9.3	160.43	123.37	130.85	− 23.20	− 15.1
1961	734.91	610.25	731.14	+115.25	+ 18.7	152.92	131.06	143.84	+ 12.99	+ 9.9
1962	726.01	535.76	652.10	− 79.04	− 10.8	149.83	114.86	141.04	− 2.80	− 1.9
1963	767.21	646.79	762.95	+110.85	+ 17.0	179.46	142.03	178.54	+ 37.50	+ 26.6
1964	891.71	766.08	874.13	+111.18	+ 14.6	224.91	178.81	205.34	+ 26.80	+ 15.0
1965	969.26	840.59	969.26	+ 95.13	+ 10.9	249.55	187.29	247.48	+ 42.14	+ 20.5
1966	995.15	744.32	785.69	−183.57	− 18.9	271.72	184.34	202.97	− 44.51	− 18.0
1967	943.08	786.41	905.11	+119.42	+ 15.2	274.49	205.16	233.24	+ 30.27	+ 14.9
1968	985.21	825.13	943.75	+ 38.64	+ 4.3	279.48	214.58	271.60	+ 38.36	+ 16.4
1969	968.85	769.93	800.36	−143.39	− 15.2	279.88	169.03	176.34	− 95.26	− 35.1

Year									
1970	842.00	631.16	838.92	+ 38.56	+ 4.8	183.31	116.69	171.52	− 4.82	− 2.7
1971	950.82	797.97	890.20	+ 51.28	+ 6.1	248.33	169.70	243.72	+ 72.20	+ 42.1
1972	1036.27	889.15	1020.02	+129.82	+ 14.6	275.71	212.24	227.17	− 16.55	− 6.8
1973	1051.70	788.31	850.86	−169.16	− 16.6	228.10	151.97	196.19	− 30.98	− 13.6
1974	891.66	577.60	616.24	−234.62	− 27.6	202.45	125.93	143.44	− 52.75	− 26.9
1975	881.81	632.04	852.41	+236.17	+ 38.3	174.57	146.47	172.65	+ 29.21	+ 20.4
1976	1014.79	858.71	1004.65	+152.24	+ 17.9	237.03	175.69	237.03	+ 64.38	+ 37.3
1977	999.75	800.85	831.17	−173.48	− 17.3	246.64	199.60	217.18	− 19.85	− 8.4
1978	907.74	742.12	805.01	− 26.16	− 3.1	261.49	199.31	206.56	− 10.62	− 4.9
1979	897.61	796.67	838.74	+ 33.73	+ 4.2	271.77	205.78	252.39	+ 45.83	+ 22.2
1980	1000.17	759.13	963.99	+125.25	+ 14.9	425.68	233.69	398.10	+145.71	+ 57.7
1981	1024.05	824.01	875.00	− 88.99	− 9.2	447.38	335.48	380.30	− 17.80	− 4.5
1982	1070.55	776.92	1046.54	+171.54	+ 19.6	464.55	292.12	448.38	+ 68.08	+ 17.9
1983	1287.20	1027.04	1258.64	+212.10	+ 20.3	612.57	434.24	598.59	+150.21	+ 33.5
1984	1286.64	1086.57	1211.57	− 47.07	− 3.7	612.63	444.03	558.13	− 40.46	− 6.8
1985	1553.10	1184.96	1546.67	+335.10	+ 27.7	723.31	553.03	708.21	+150.08	+ 26.9
1986	1955.57	1502.29	1895.95	+349.28	+ 22.6	866.74	686.97	807.17	+ 98.96	+ 14.0
1987	2722.42	1738.74	1938.83	+ 42.88	+ 2.3	1101.16	661.00	748.86	− 58.31	− 7.2
1988	2183.50	1879.14	2168.57	+229.74	+ 11.8	973.61	737.57	969.84	+220.98	+ 29.5
1989	2791.41	2144.64	2753.20	+584.63	+ 27.0	1532.01	959.95	1177.81	+207.97	+ 21.4
1990	2999.75	2365.10	2633.66	−119.54	− 4.3	1212.77	821.93	910.23	−267.58	− 22.7

aNew 20-stock average adopted in 1916, but computed back to 1914. Year 1914 is last for old 12-stock average in this tabulation.

bThe Transporation Average figures from 1890–1896 represent the 20-Stock Average, composed of 18 rails and two industrial issues.

cna = Dow Industrials were first computed in May 1896, so there are no "change" statistics available. Individual stock figures show that the August 8 low was the low for the year.

Series best and worst years:
Industrials: Plus 81.7%, 1915; Minus 52.7%, 1931.
Rail/transports: Plus 62.6%, 1958; Minus 65.2%, 1931.

TABLE 5.5 ANNUAL RANGES AND CHANGES

Utility average

Year	Closing high	Closing low	Close	Point change	% change
1929a	144.61	64.72	88.27	+ 2.63	+ 3.1
1930	108.62	55.14	60.80	− 27.47	− 31.1
1931	73.40	30.55	31.41	− 29.39	− 48.3
1932	36.11	16.53	27.50	− 3.91	− 12.4
1933	37.73	19.33	23.29	− 4.21	− 15.3
1934	31.03	16.83	17.80	− 5.59	− 23.6
1935	29.78	14.46	29.55	+ 11.75	+ 66.0
1936	36.08	28.63	34.83	+ 5.28	+ 17.9
1937	37.54	19.65	20.35	− 14.48	− 41.6
1938	25.19	15.14	23.02	+ 2.67	+ 13.1
1939	27.10	20.71	25.58	+ 2.56	+ 11.1
1940	26.45	18.03	19.85	− 5.73	− 22.4
1941	20.65	13.51	14.02	− 5.83	− 29.4
1942	14.94	10.58	14.54	+ 0.52	+ 3.7
1943	22.30	14.69	21.87	+ 7.33	+ 50.4
1944	26.37	21.74	26.37	+ 4.50	+ 20.6
1945	39.15	26.15	38.13	+ 11.76	+ 44.6
1946	43.74	33.20	37.27	− 0.86	− 2.3
1947	37.55	32.28	33.40	− 3.87	− 10.4
1948	36.04	31.65	33.55	+ 0.15	+ 0.4
1949	41.31	33.36	41.29	+ 7.74	+ 23.1
1950	44.26	37.40	40.98	− 0.31	− 0.8
1951	47.22	41.47	47.22	+ 6.24	+ 15.2
1952	52.64	47.53	52.60	+ 5.38	+ 11.4
1953	53.88	47.87	52.04	− 0.56	− 1.1
1954	62.47	52.22	62.47	+ 10.43	+ 20.0
1955	66.68	61.39	64.16	+ 1.69	+ 2.7
1956	71.17	63.03	68.54	+ 4.38	+ 6.8
1957	74.61	62.10	68.58	+ 0.04	+ 0.1
1958	91.00	68.94	91.00	+ 22.42	+ 32.7
1959	94.70	85.05	87.83	− 3.17	− 3.5
1960	100.07	85.02	100.02	+ 12.19	+ 13.9
1961	135.90	99.75	129.16	+ 29.14	+ 29.1
1962	130.85	103.11	129.23	+ 0.07	+ 0.1
1963	144.37	129.19	138.99	+ 9.76	+ 7.6
1964	155.71	137.30	155.17	+ 16.18	+ 11.6
1965	163.32	149.84	152.63	− 2.54	− 1.6
1966	152.39	118.96	136.18	− 16.45	− 10.8
1967	140.43	120.97	127.91	− 8.27	− 6.1
1968	141.30	119.79	137.17	+ 9.26	+ 7.2
1969	139.95	106.31	110.08	− 27.09	− 19.7
1970	121.84	95.86	121.84	+ 11.76	+ 10.7
1971	128.39	108.83	117.75	− 4.09	− 3.4
1972	124.14	105.06	119.50	+ 1.75	+ 1.5
1973	120.72	84.42	89.37	− 30.13	− 25.2
1974	95.09	57.93	68.76	− 20.61	− 23.1
1975	87.07	72.02	83.65	+ 14.89	+ 21.7
1976	108.38	84.52	108.38	+ 25.73	+ 30.8
1977	118.67	104.97	111.28	+ 2.90	+ 2.7
1978	110.98	96.35	98.24	− 13.04	− 11.7
1979	109.74	98.24	106.60	+ 8.36	+ 8.5
1980	117.34	96.04	114.42	+ 7.82	+ 7.3
1981	117.81	101.28	109.02	− 5.40	− 4.7
1982	122.83	103.22	119.46	+ 10.44	+ 9.6
1983	140.70	119.51	131.84	+ 12.38	+ 10.4
1984	149.93	122.25	149.52	+ 17.68	+ 13.4
1985	174.96	146.54	174.81	+ 25.29	+ 16.9
1986	219.15	169.47	206.01	+ 31.20	+ 17.8
1987	227.83	160.98	175.08	− 30.93	− 15.0
1988	190.02	167.08	186.28	+ 11.20	+ 6.4
1989	235.98	181.84	235.04	+ 48.76	+ 26.2
1990	236.23	190.96	209.70	− 25.34	− 10.8

a Dow Utility Average first computed in 1929

Years: Series best and worst; Plus 66.0%, 1935; Minus 48.3%, 1931.

TABLE 5-6 DOW AVERAGES—ANNUAL CLOSING HIGHS AND LOWS WITH DATES

Year	Closing Highs			Closing Lows			Year
	Industrials	Rail-Transports	Utilities	Industrials	Rail-Transports	Utilities	
1890		78.38 Jne 4			58.10 Dec 8		1890
1891		73.25 Dec 28			61.50 Jly 30		1891
1892		75.68 Mar 4			66.86 Dec 23		1892
1893		70.87 Jan 21			43.47 Jly 26		1893
1894		57.60 Aug 27			50.73 Jan 2		1894
1895		63.77 Sep 4			48.56 Dec 21		1895
1896	Not available	56.79 Feb 24		28.48 Aug 8	41.82 Aug 8		1896
1897	55.82 Sep 10	67.23 Sep 17		38.49 Apr 19	48.12 Apr 19		1897
1898	60.97 Aug 26	74.99 Dec 30		42.00 Mar 25	55.89 Apr 21		1898
1899	77.61 Sep 5	87.04 Apr 3		58.27 Dec 18	72.48 Dec 22		1899
1900	71.04 Dec 27	94.99 Dec 31		52.96 Sep 24	72.99 Jne 23		1900
1901	78.26 Jne 17	117.86 May 1		61.52 Dec 24	92.66 Jan 3		1901
1902	68.44 Apr 24	129.36 Sep 9		59.57 Dec 15	111.73 Jan 14		1902
1903	67.70 Feb 16	121.28 Jan 9		42.15 Nov 9	88.80 Sep 28		1903
1904	73.23 Dec 5	119.46 Dec 3		46.41 Mar 12	91.31 Mar 14		1904
1905	96.56 Dec 29	133.54 Dec 29		68.76 Jan 25	114.52 May 22		1905
1906	103.00 Jan 19	138.36 Jan 22		85.18 Jly 13	120.30 May 3		1906
1907	96.37 Jan 7	131.95 Jan 5		53.00 Nov 15	81.41 Nov 21		1907
1908	88.38 Nov 13	120.05 Dec 31		58.62 Feb 13	86.04 Feb 17		1908
1909	100.53 Nov 19	134.46 Aug 14		79.91 Feb 23	113.90 Feb 23		1909
1910	98.34 Jan 3	129.90 Jan 4		73.62 Jly 26	105.59 Jly 26		1910
1911	87.06 Jne 19	123.86 Jly 21		72.94 Sep 25	109.80 Sep 27		1911
1912	94.15 Sep 30	124.35 Oct 5		80.15 Feb 10	114.92 Feb 5		1912
1913	88.57 Jan 9	118.10 Jan 9		72.11 Jne 11	100.50 Jne 11		1913
1914	83.43 Mar 20	109.43 Jan 31		71.42 Jly 30	87.40 Dec 24		1914
1915	99.21 Dec 27	108.28 Nov 4		54.22 Feb 24	87.85 Feb 24		1915
1916	110.15 Nov 21	112.28 Oct 4		84.96 Apr 22	99.11 Apr 22		1916
1917	99.18 Jan 3	105.76 Jan 3		65.95 Dec 19	70.75 Dec 19		1917
1918	89.07 Oct 18	92.91 Nov 9		73.38 Jan 15	77.21 Jan 15		1918
1919	119.62 Nov 3	91.13 May 26		79.15 Feb 8	73.63 Dec 12		1919
1920	109.88 Jan 3	85.37 Nov 3		66.75 Dec 21	67.83 Feb 11		1920
1921	81.50 Dec 15	77.56 Jan 15		63.90 Aug 24	65.52 Jne 20		1921
1922	103.43 Oct 14	93.99 Sep 11		78.59 Jan 10	73.43 Jan 9		1922

231

TABLE 5-6 Continued

Year	Closing Highs			Closing Lows			Year
	Industrials	Rail-Transports	Utilities	Industrials	Rail-Transports	Utilities	
1923	105.38 Mar 20	90.63 Mar 3		85.76 Oct 27	76.78 Aug 4		1923
1924	120.51 Dec 31	99.50 Dec 18		88.33 May 20	80.23 Feb 18		1924
1925	159.39 Nov 6	112.93 Dec 31		115.00 Mar 30	92.98 Mar 30		1925
1926	166.64 Aug 14	123.33 Sep 3		135.20 Mar 30	102.41 Mar 30		1926
1027	202.40 Dec 31	144.82 Oct 3		152.73 Jan 25	119.29 Jan 28		1927
1928	300.00 Dec 31	152.70 Nov 27		191.33 Feb 20	132.60 Feb 20		1928
1929	381.17 Sep 3	189.11 Sep 3	144.61 Sep 21	198.69 Nov 13	128.07 Nov 13	64.72 Nov 13	1929
1930	294.07 Apr 17	157.94 Mar 29	108.62 Apr 12	157.51 Dec 16	91.65 Dec 16	55.14 Dec 16	1930
1931	194.36 Feb 24	111.58 Feb 24	73.40 Mar 19	73.79 Dec 17	31.42 Dec 17	30.55 Dec 28	1931
1932	88.78 Mar 8	41.30 Jan 15	36.11 Sep 7	41.22 Jly 8	13.23 Jly 8	16.53 Jly 8	1932
1933	108.67 Jly 18	56.53 Jly 7	37.73 Jly 13	50.16 Feb 27	23.43 Feb 25	19.33 Mar 31	1933
1934	110.74 Feb 5	52.97 Feb 5	31.03 Feb 6	85.51 Jly 26	33.19 Sep 17	16.83 Dec 26	1934
1935	148.44 Nov 19	41.84 Dec 9	29.78 Dec 7	96.71 Mar 14	27.31 Mar 12	14.46 Mar 14	1935
1936	184.90 Nov 17	59.89 Oct 14	36.08 Oct 31	143.11 Jan 6	40.66 Jan 2	28.63 Apr 29	1936
1937	194.40 Mar 10	64.46 Mar 17	37.54 Jan 13	113.64 Nov 24	28.91 Dec 28	19.65 Oct 19	1937
1938	158.41 Nov 12	33.98 Dec 31	25.19 Oct 27	98.95 Mar 31	19.00 Mar 31	15.14 Mar 31	1938
1939	155.92 Sep 12	35.90 Sep 27	27.10 Aug 2	121.44 Apr 8	24.14 Apr 8	20.71 Apr 8	1939
1940	152.80 Jan 3	32.67 Jan 4	26.45 Jan 3	111.84 Jne 10	22.14 May 21	18.03 Jne 10	1940
1941	133.59 Jan 10	30.88 Aug 1	20.65 Jan 13	106.34 Dec 23	24.25 Dec 10	13.51 Dec 19	1941
1942	119.71 Dec 26	29.28 Nov 2	14.94 Jan 6	92.92 Apr 28	23.31 Jne 2	10.58 Apr 28	1942
1943	145.82 Jly 14	38.30 Jly 24	22.30 Jly 14	119.26 Jan 8	27.59 Jan 2	14.69 Jan 2	1943
1944	152.53 Dec 16	48.40 Dec 30	26.37 Dec 30	134.22 Feb 7	33.45 Jan 3	21.74 Jan 3	1944
1945	195.82 Dec 11	64.89 Dec 8	39.15 Dec 10	151.35 Jan 24	47.03 Jan 31	26.15 Jan 23	1945
1046	212.50 May 29	68.31 Jne 13	43.74 May 29	163.12 Oct 9	44.69 Oct 9	33.20 Oct 9	1946
1947	186.85 Jly 24	53.42 Feb 8	37.55 Feb 8	163.21 May 17	41.16 May 19	32.28 May 20	1947
1948	193.16 Jne 15	64.95 Jly 14	36.04 Jne 14	165.39 Mar 16	48.13 Feb 10	31.65 Feb 10	1948
1949	200.52 Dec 30	54.29 Jan 7	41.31 Dec 30	161.60 Jne 13	41.03 Jne 13	33.36 Jan 3	1949
1950	235.47 Nov 24	77.89 Dec 28	44.26 May 20	196.81 Jan 13	51.24 Jne 29	37.40 Jly 26	1950
1951	276.37 Sep 13	90.08 Feb 5	47.22 Dec 31	238.99 Jan 3	72.39 Jne 29	41.47 Jan 2	1951
1952	292.00 Dec 30	112.53 Dec 22	52.64 Dec 30	256.35 May 1	82.03 Jan 9	47.53 Jan 2	1952
1953	293.79 Jan 5	112.21 Jan 30	53.88 Mar 13	255.49 Sep 14	90.56 Sep 14	47.87 Jne 22	1953
1954	404.39 Dec 31	146.23 Dec 29	62.47 Dec 31	279.87 Jan 11	94.84 Jan 11	52.22 Jan 4	1954
1955	488.40 Dec 30	167.83 Nov 25	66.68 Jly 26	388.20 Jan 17	137.84 Jan 17	61.39 Oct 11	1955
1956	521.05 Apr 6	181.23 May 9	71.17 Aug 7	462.35 Jan 23	150.44 Nov 29	63.03 Jan 23	1956

Year							Year
1957	62.10 Oct 22	95.67 Dec 24	419.79 Oct 22	74.61 May 21	157.67 Jan 10	520.77 Jly 12	1957
1958	68.94 Jan 2	99.89 Jan 2	436.89 Feb 25	91.00 Dec 31	157.91 Nov 19	583.65 Dec 31	1958
1959	85.05 Sep 21	146.65 Nov 17	574.46 Feb 9	94.70 Mar 18	173.56 Jly 8	679.36 Dec 31	1959
1960	85.02 Feb 16	123.37 Sep 29	566.05 Oct 25	100.07 Dec 29	160.43 Jan 5	685.47 Jan 5	1960
1961	99.75 Jan 3	131.06 Jan 3	610.25 Jan 3	135.90 Nov 20	152.92 Oct 11	734.91 Dec 13	1961
1962	103.11 Jne 25	114.86 Oct 1	535.76 Jne 26	130.85 Mar 19	149.83 Feb 2	726.01 Jan 3	1962
1963	129.19 Jan 2	142.03 Jan 2	646.79 Jan 2	144.37 Aug 23	179.46 Dec 18	767.21 Dec 18	1963
1964	137.30 Mar 31	178.81 Jan 3	766.08 Jan 2	155.71 Nov 20	224.91 Oct 26	891.71 Nov 18	1964
1965	149.84 Dec 20	187.29 Jne 28	840.59 Jne 28	163.32 Apr 20	249.55 Dec 17	969.26 Dec 31	1965
1966	118.96 Aug 29	184.34 Oct 7	744.32 Oct 7	152.39 Jan 12	271.72 Feb 15	995.15 Feb 9	1966
1967	120.97 Nov 8	205.16 Jan 3	786.41 Jan 3	140.43 Apr 20	274.49 Aug 4	943.08 Sep 25	1967
1968	119.79 Mar 25	214.58 Mar 5	825.13 Mar 21	141.30 Nov 19	279.48 Dec 2	985.21 Dec 3	1968
1969	106.31 Dec 9	169.03 Dec 17	769.93 Dec 17	139.95 Jan 31	279.88 Feb 7	968.85 May 14	1969
1970	95.86 Jne 30	116.69 Jly 7	631.16 May 26	121.84 Dec 31	183.31 Jan 5	842.00 Dec 29	1970
1971	108.03 Nov 24	169.70 Jan 4	797.97 Nov 23	128.39 Jan 19	248.33 Sep 7	950.82 Apr 28	1971
1972	105.06 Jne 19	212.24 Oct 20	889.15 Jan 26	124.14 Nov 24	275.71 Apr 7	1036.27 Dec 11	1972
1973	84.42 Dec 5	151.97 Aug 22	788.31 Dec 5	120.72 Mar 2	228.10 Jan 2	1051.70 Jan 11	1973
1974	57.93 Sep 13	125.93 Oct 3	577.60 Dec 6	95.09 Jan 7	202.45 Jan 3	891.66 Mar 13	1974
1975	72.02 Jan 2	146.47 Jan 2	632.04 Jan 2	87.07 Jne 24	174.57 Nov 17	881.81 Jly 15	1975
1976	84.52 May 25	175.69 Jan 2	858.71 Jan 2	108.38 Dec 31	237.03 Dec 31	1014.79 Sep 21	1976
1977	104.97 Feb 25	199.60 Oct 25	800.85 Nov 2	118.67 Jly 22	246.44 May 18	999.75 Jan 3	1977
1978	96.35 Nov 14	199.31 Mar 9	742.12 Feb 28	110.98 Jan 3	261.49 Sep 8	907.74 Sep 8	1978
1979	98.24 Oct 24	205.78 Feb 27	796.67 Nov 7	109.74 Dec 17	271.77 Aug 15	897.61 Oct 5	1979
1980	96.04 Mar 27	233.69 Mar 27	759.13 Apr 21	117.34 Nov 18	425.68 Nov 28	1000.17 Nov 20	1980
1981	101.28 Sep 28	335.48 Sep 25	824.01 Sep 25	117.81 Jan 5	447.38 Apr 16	1024.05 Apr 27	1981
1982	103.22 Jly 30	292.12 Aug 12	776.92 Aug 12	122.83 Oct 11	464.55 Dec 7	1070.55 Dec 27	1982
1983	119.51 Jan 3	434.24 Jan 3	1027.04 Jan 3	140.70 Oct 31	612.57 Nov 22	1287.20 Nov 29	1983
1984	122.25 Jne 15	444.03 Jly 25	1086.57 Jly 24	149.93 Dec 18	612.63 Jan 9	1286.64 Jan 6	1984
1985	146.54 Jan 4	533.03 Jan 4	1184.96 Jan 4	174.96 Dec 20	723.31 Dec 16	1553.10 Dec 16	1985
1986	169.47 Jan 22	686.97 Jan 10	1502.29 Jan 22	219.15 Aug 20	866.74 Dec 2	1955.57 Dec 2	1986
1987	160.98 Oct 19	661.00 Dec 4	1738.74 Oct 19	227.83 Jan 22	1101.16 Aug 14	2722.42 Aug 25	1987
1988	167.08 May 18	737.57 Jan 21	1879.14 Jan 20	190.02 Jan 29	973.61 Dec 29	2183.50 Oct 21	1988
1989	181.84 Feb 24	959.95 Jan 3	2144.64 Jan 3	235.98 Dec 15	1532.01 Sep 5	2791.41 Oct 9	1989
1990	190.96 Aug 24	821.93 Oct 17	2365.10 Oct 11	236.23 Jan 2	1212.77 Jne 6	2999.75 Jly 16	1990

[a] na =

Series high and low records:
Industrials: 2999.75 (1990)–28.48 (1896)
Rail-Transports: 1532.01 (1989)–13.23 (1932)
Utilities: 236.23 (1990)–10.58 (1942)

TABLE 5-7   LONG TERM RECORDS FOR DOW AVERAGES

Industrials (since 1897)	Rail-Transports (since 1890)	Utilities (since 1929)
Plus years: 59	Plus years: 56	Plus years: 38
Minus years: 35	Minus years: 45	Minus years: 24

Record From 1950		
Plus Years: 34	Plus years: 29	Plus years: 33
Minus years: 17	Minus years: 22	Minus years: 18

THE DIRTY THIRTIES

The 1929 crash shoved the nation and the market into its most frightening economic decline in history.

The year 1930 was a smashing opener. Both major Dow averages lost one third of their value. In 1931, things would get worse.

The market improved during the mid-years, but then the panic of 1937 struck. Industrial production would fall faster than it had in 1930. The market's recovery from that depression would be handicapped by war uncertainties.

Three of five of the century's worst years, for both leading averages, were suffered in the 1930–1939 decade. And 1932—down 23 percent for both—almost made the list, saved by a giant rally. In early July, the Dow was minus 47 percent from the 1931 close and the Rails were down a shocking 61 percent.

TABLE 5-8   CONSECUTIVE YEAR SERIES RECORDS

Industrials	
Advancing:	1924–1928, 1985–1989 (5 years). Best series 1924–1928: plus 214%.
Declining:	1929–1932 (4). Loss: 80%.

Rail-Transports	
Advancing:	1897–1902 (6). But best series was 1942–1945 (4), plus 172%.
Declining:	1929–32 (4). Loss: 83%.

Utilities	
Advancing:	1954–1958, 1960–1964, 1982–1986 (5). But best series was 1942–1945 (4), plus 172%.
Declining:	1929–1933 (5). Loss: 80%.

TABLE 5-8 Continued SERIES BEST AND WORST YEARS
Ranked By Percent

Best Yearly Gains					
Dow Industrials		Dow Rail-Transports		Dow Utilities	
Year	Gain (%)	Year	Gain (%)	Year	Gain (%)
1915	81.7	1958	62.6	1935	66.0
1933	66.7	1980	57.7	1943	50.4
1928	48.2	1933	57.5	1945	44.6
1908	46.6	1954	55.1	1958	32.7
1954	44.0	1950	47.2	1976	30.8
1904	41.7	1944	44.2	1961	29.1
1935	38.5	1971	42.1	1989	26.2

Worst Losses					
Dow Industrials		Dow Rail-Transports		Dow Utilities	
Year	Loss (%)	Year	Loss (%)	Year	Loss (%)
1931	52.7	1931	65.2	1931	48.3
1907	37.7	1937	45.1	1937	41.6
1930	33.8	1957	36.7	1930	31.1
1920	32.9	1969	35.1	1941	29.4
1937	32.8	1930	33.3	1973	25.2
1974	27.6	1907	31.6	1934	23.6
1903	23.6	1974	26.9	1974	23.1

TABLE 5-9 BEST AND WORST MONTHS OF EACH YEAR
Ranked by Percent

| | Industrials | | | | | | Rail-Transports | | | | | |
| | Advances | | | Declines | | | Advances | | | Declines | | |
Year	Month	% +	Points +	Month	% −	Points −	Month	% +	Points +	Month	% −	Points −
1890[a]							Apr	5.5	3.93	Nov	6.2	4.18
1891							Aug	13.0	8.04	May	4.6	3.19
1892							Feb	3.3	2.42	Nov	5.2	3.68
1893							Aug	10.4	4.72	Jly	18.4	10.22
1894							Aug	8.8	4.53	Sep	4.7	2.63
1895							Mar	7.6	3.69	Dec	9.0	5.15
1896							Sep	9.0	4.15	Jly	9.2	4.76
1897	Aug	14.5	6.93	Sep	7.0	3.83	Aug	10.1	5.76	Mar	6.4	3.41
1898	May	14.7	6.74	Sep	11.4	6.91	May	13.3	7.77	Feb	6.4	4.24
1899	Mar	11.3	7.55	May	12.0	9.20	Jan	8.9	6.64	May	8.9	7.55
1900	Nov	12.8	7.55	Apr	7.1	4.69	Nov	11.7	9.33	Jne	5.9	4.66
1901	Apr	8.0	5.88	Sep	9.3	6.81	Apr	10.8	11.32	Jly	8.4	9.82
1902	Mar	3.8	2.38	Nov	6.1	4.01	Jly	4.5	5.47	Nov	3.5	4.20
1903	Dec	10.8	4.78	Jly	14.1	8.32	Dec	4.8	4.53	Sep	8.5	8.30
1904	Nov	14.3	8.99	Dec	3.3	2.41	Nov	4.9	5.57	Feb	5.6	5.62
1905	Dec	7.0	6.31	Apr	4.9	3.94	Jly	5.0	3.84	Apr	5.7	7.08
1906	Jly	6.2	5.40	Jne	7.2	6.74	Aug	4.7	6.09	Apr	6.5	8.67
1907	Apr	5.2	4.15	Oct	14.8	10.02	Jne	4.1	4.14	Oct	14.6	14.33
1908	Mar	11.5	6.97	Sep	5.6	4.73	Nov	6.9	7.53	Feb	6.2	5.67
1909	Mar	5.2	4.27	Nov	3.1	3.05	Mar	4.5	5.28	Nov	2.7	3.56
1910	Oct	6.3	5.05	Jan	7.2	7.14	Aug	2.7	2.91	Jne	6.7	7.99
1911	Nov	6.8	5.18	Aug	7.9	6.77	Jan	4.2	4.76	Aug	8.2	10.09
1912	Mar	8.4	6.87	Dec	3.9	3.53	Mar	3.1	3.53	Dec	3.2	3.91
1913	Jly	4.8	3.59	Jan	4.7	4.15	Jly	2.1	2.16	Feb	3.9	4.55
1914	Jan	5.2	4.07	Jly	11.5	9.24	Jan	5.5	5.71	Jly	12.7	13.00
1915	Apr	18.0	10.95	May	9.9	7.11	Jan	9.3	9.11	May	5.4	5.29
1916	Sep	11.5	10.65	Dec	10.4	10.95	Oct	9.3	5.00	Jan	6.8	7.30
1917	May	4.5	4.15	Oct	11.1	9.31	Sep	4.8	3.93	Oct	8.0	6.94
1918	Jan	7.3	5.42	Nov	5.1	4.38	Dec	4.9	4.20	Dec	3.2	2.76
1919	May	13.6	12.62	Nov	13.0	15.32	May	5.3	6.05	Aug	6.1	5.29
1920	Mar	12.6	11.50	Feb	12.0	12.51	May	7.2	4.47	Nov	6.1	5.07
1921	Jan	5.8	4.18	May	6.8	5.40	Aug	6.1	3.77	Feb	3.7	2.85
							Nov	5.2				

Year												
1922	Feb	5.1	4.16	Sep	4.4	4.48	Jly	5.4	4.53	Nov	5.3	4.69
1923	Aug	7.5	6.55	Jne	9.9	9.68	Feb	3.8	3.30	Jne	7.5	6.19
1924	Dec	8.2	9.13	Mar	4.3	4.21	Nov	7.9	7.07	Feb	1.3	1.09
1925	Oct	9.1	13.06	Mar	4.9	5.96	Dec	5.0	5.41	Mar	5.9	5.94
1926	Jne	6.7	9.61	Mar	9.1	13.99	Aug	4.3	5.04	Feb	3.1	3.40
1927	Nov	9.1	16.48	Oct	8.0	15.86	Feb	5.7	6.93	Oct	5.5	7.78
1928	Nov	16.3	41.22	Jne	4.2	9.26	Nov	7.1	10.12	Jne	4.1	5.89
1929	Jne	12.2	36.38	Oct	20.4	69.94	Aug	8.8	15.33	Oct	8.0	13.96
1930	Jan	7.5	18.66	Jne	17.7	48.73	Mar	3.2	4.94	Jne	11.0	15.86
1931	Jne	16.9	21.72	Sep	30.7	42.80	Jne	16.9	12.30	Sep	21.4	15.59
1932	Aug	34.8	18.90	Apr	23.4	17.17	Aug	68.0	14.79	May	33.3	7.14
1933	Apr	40.2	22.26	Feb	15.6	9.51	May	31.0	10.05	Sep	21.9	11.51
1934	Nov	10.3	9.58	Jly	8.0	7.67	Jan	21.9	8.97	Jly	21.1	9.30
1935	Apr	8.6	8.64	Jan	2.5	2.65	Nov	13.3	4.59	Feb	10.0	3.38
1936	Oct	5.6	9.37	Apr	6.8	10.67	Jan	14.1	5.72	Apr	7.8	3.65
1937	Jly	9.6	16.29	Sep	12.9	22.84	Mar	6.4	3.72	Sept	16.8	8.35
1938	Jne	24.3	26.14	Mar	23.7	30.69	Jne	28.1	5.71	Mar	36.5	10.90
1939	Sept	13.5	18.13	Mar	10.5	15.46	Sep	36.4	9.51	Mar	18.8	6.10
1940	Jne	4.9	5.65	May	21.7	32.21	Jne	13.5	3.03	May	24.6	7.54
1941	Jne	6.4	7.38	Oct	7.1	9.00	Jly	7.7	2.20	Dec	5.7	1.54
1942	May	5.8	5.53	Mar	6.8	7.26	Jan	11.1	2.82	Mar	9.6	2.65
1943	May	4.9	6.58	Nov	6.3	8.70	Feb	9.8	2.85	Nov	10.6	3.74
1944	May	4.4	6.01	Apr	1.9	2.61	Dec	12.9	5.52	Apr	1.8	0.73
1945	May	7.1	11.03	Mar	3.7	5.99	Apr	12.6	6.37	Jly	5.8	3.50
1946	Jan	6.1	11.76	Sep	8.9	16.77	Jan	7.7	4.82	Sep	16.7	9.57
1947	Jne	4.8	8.05	Apr	3.7	6.56	Dec	11.4	5.36	Apr	7.0	3.42
1948	Mar	5.9	9.90	Jly	4.3	8.13	Mar	9.1	4.46	Nov	15.4	9.43
1949	Jly	5.1	8.50	Feb	3.4	6.06	Dec	9.7	4.65	Feb	9.2	4.86
1950	Sep	4.4	9.49	Jne	6.4	14.31	Dec	13.3	9.11	Jne	7.2	4.04
1951	Jly	6.3	15.22	May	3.7	9.48	Jan	11.5	8.94	Jne	9.1	7.25
1952	Nov	5.4	14.43	Apr	4.4	11.83	Mar	11.2	9.49	Sep	2.9	2.96
1953	Oct	4.5	11.77	Aug	5.1	14.16	Oct	3.6	3.36	Aug	9.7	10.23
1954	Nov	9.8	34.63	Aug	3.5	12.12	Dec	10.9	14.39	Aug	5.9	7.11
1955	Nov	6.2	28.39	Oct	2.5	11.75	Nov	11.4	17.12	Oct	3.6	5.52
1956	Mar	5.8	28.14	May	7.4	38.07	Mar	7.6	12.20	May	6.5	11.53
1957	Apr	4.1	19.55	Sep	5.8	28.05	Jly	2.3	3.33	Oct	10.3	12.76
1958	Dec	4.7	26.19	Feb	2.2	10.10	Jan	12.5	12.08	Feb	5.6	6.09
1959	Jly	4.9	31.28	Sep	4.9	32.73	Apr	5.1	8.17	Sep	3.7	6.05
1960	May	4.0	23.80	Jan	8.4	56.74	Nov	3.4	4.27	Sep	8.3	11.30
1961	Jan	5.3	32.31	Sep	2.6	18.73	Jan	8.3	10.86	Jne	3.8	5.44
1962	Nov	10.1	59.53	Jne	8.5	52.08	Nov	15.1	18.26	Jne	8.2	10.56
1963	Apr	5.2	35.18	Jne	2.8	20.08	Apr	7.1	10.86	Jly	3.9	6.70

TABLE 5-9. Continued

	Industrials						Rail-Transports						
	Advances			Declines			Advances			Declines			
Year	Month	% +	Points +	Month	% -	Points -	Month	% +	Points +	Month	% -	Points -	
1964	Sep	4.4	36.89	Aug	0.3	2.62	Sep	5.8	11.92	Aug	5.3	11.55	
1965	Sept	4.2	37.48	Jne	5.4	50.01	Jly	7.2	14.04	Jne	5.5	11.35	
1966	Oct	4.2	32.85	Aug	7.0	58.97	Jan	5.7	14.21	May	10.4	26.40	
1967	Jan	8.2	64.20	Oct	5.1	46.92	Jan	12.3	25.04	Oct	9.3	24.83	
1968	Apr	8.5	71.55	Jan	5.5	49.64	Apr	8.2	18.01	Feb	4.5	10.33	
1969	Oct	5.3	42.90	Jne	6.9	64.37	Aug	2.7	5.30	Jne	9.2	21.41	
1970	Jly	7.4	50.59	Jan	7.0	56.30	Dec	11.8	18.16	Jne	16.5	23.89	
1971	Dec	7.1	58.86	Oct	5.4	48.19	Aug	16.0	33.12	Jly	4.3	9.21	
1972	Nov	6.6	62.69	Jne	3.3	31.69	Nov	7.6	16.83	Jne	9.5	24.41	
1973	Sep	6.7	59.53	Nov	14.0	134.33	Dec	12.0	21.01	May	11.4	21.08	
1974	Oct	9.5	57.65	Sep	10.4	70.71	Oct	19.1	24.53	Aug	10.8	17.02	
1975	Jan	14.2	87.45	Jly	5.4	47.48	Jan	11.3	16.18	Jly	5.4	9.30	
1976	Jan	14.4	122.87	Oct	2.6	25.26	Jan	15.5	26.70	Oct	3.2	6.97	
1977	Jne	2.2	19.64	Jan	5.0	50.28	Apr	5.2	11.54	Aug	6.1	14.07	
1978	Apr	10.6	79.76	Oct	8.5	73.37	Jly	9.7	21.28	Oct	14.5	35.40	
1979	Mar	6.6	53.36	Oct	7.2	62.97	Mar	9.4	19.34	Oct	11.0	28.54	
1980	Jly	7.8	67.40	Mar	9.0	77.39	Nov	17.8	64.37	Mar	14.9	43.14	
1981	Nov	4.3	36.43	Aug	7.4	70.87	Mar	11.5	45.28	Aug	8.7	35.20	
1982	Aug	11.5	92.71	Feb	5.4	46.71	Aug	20.1	61.93	May	6.7	22.99	
1983	Apr	8.5	96.17	May	2.1	26.22	Jne	8.7	46.87	Jly	6.0	35.15	
1984	Aug	9.8	109.10	May	5.6	65.90	Aug	9.9	46.93	Feb	7.9	43.58	
1985	Nov	7.1	97.82	Mar	1.3	17.23	May	12.4	71.42	Sep	7.3	50.09	
1986	Feb	8.8	138.07	Sep	6.9	130.76	Aug	7.8	55.87	Jly	8.5	66.62	
1987	Jan	13.8	262.09	Oct	23.2	602.75	Jan	8.4	67.71	Oct	27.7	290.44	
1988	Feb	5.8	113.40	Aug	4.6	97.08	Jne	9.9	81.84	Aug	4.5	39.58	
1989	Jly	9.0	220.60	Feb	3.6	83.93	Aug	18.1	231.68	Oct	16.9	245.03	
1990	May	8.3	219.90	Aug	10.0	290.84	Feb	8.0	83.22	Aug	17.6	241.26	

aDow Industrial Average not computed until May, 1896.

Series Best & Worst Months:

Industrials: +40.2%, April 1933; Minus 30.7%, September 1931.

Rail-Transports: +68.0% August 1932; Minus 33.3%, May 1932.

TABLE 5-10 SERIES BEST & WORST MONTHS
Ranked By Percent

Best Months					
Industrials		**Rail-Transports**		**Utilities**	
Date	Gain (%)	Date	Gain (%)	Date	Gain (%)
Apr 1933	40.2	Aug 1932	68.0	Aug 1932	45.2
Aug 1932	34.8	Sep 1939	36.4	Apr 1933	29.8
Jne 1938	24.3	May 1933	31.0	Oct 1938	25.3
Apr 1915	18.0	Jne 1938	28.1	Jne 1929	22.2
Jne 1931	16.9	Jan 1934	21.9	Jne 1940	20.0
Nov 1928	16.3	Aug 1982	20.1	Jan 1975	16.7
May 1898	14.7	Oct 1974	19.1	Jan 1934	16.1

Worst Months*					
Industrials		**Rail-Transports**		**Utilities**	
Month	Loss (%)	Month	Loss (%)	Month	Loss (%)
Sep 1931	30.7	Mar 1938	36.5	Sep 1931	33.9
Mar 1938	23.7	May 1932	33.3	Oct 1929	31.7
Apr 1932	23.4	Oct 1987	27.7	May 1932	26.8
Oct 1987	23.2	May 1940	24.6	May 1940	24.7
May 1940	21.7	Sep 1933	21.9	Mar 1938	23.6
Oct 1929	20.4	Nov 1931	21.7	Jne 1930	19.6
Jne 1930	17.7	Jly 1934	21.1	Feb 1933	18.8

*Table 5-10 would be changed, if allowed multiple entries from a single year. May 1932 (−20.3%) would qualify among the worst Industrial months. April 1932 (−27.5%) and September 1931 (−21.4%) would be inserted in the list of Rail losses.

TABLE 5-10A   CONSECUTIVE MONTH SERIES RECORDS

Industrials	
Advancing Months	Declining Months
Apr 1935–Mar 1936 (12) plus 55.1%	Aug 1941–Apr 1942 (9) minus 35.1%
Mar 1958–Feb 1959 (12) plus 37.2%	Apr 1920–Sep 1920 (6) minus 19.3%
May 1942–Mar 1943 (11) plus 46.9%	Jan 1953–Jne 1953 (6) minus 8.8%
Jly 1949–May 1950 (11) plus 33.4%	Apr 1981–Sep 1981 (6) minus 15.3%

Rail-Transports	
Mar 1958–Feb 1959 (12) plus 57.6%	Apr 1917–Nov 1917 (8) minus 24.4%
Oct 1962–Jne 1963 (9) plus 50.1%	Jne 1919–Jan 1920 (8) minus 18.0%
Nov 1963–Jly 1964 (9) plus 28.5%	Aug 1967–Feb 1968 (7) minus 19.6%
Oct 1975–Jne 1976 (9) plus 44.1%	Dec 1983–May 1984 (6) minus 22.9%

Utilities	
Jan 1954–Sep 1954 (9) plus 17.2%	Nov 1965–Jne 1966 (8) minus 16.7%
Nov 1957–Jly 1958 (9) plus 21.0%	Jan 1972–Jly 1972 (7) minus 9.7%
Jly 1949–Feb 1950 (8) plus 24.4%	Sep 1934–Feb 1935 (6) minus 22.4%
Jne 1976–Jan 1977 (8) plus 28.2%	Aug 1937–Jan 1938 (6) minus 36.2%

Series Best & Worst:
  Advance: Rails, 1958–1959, plus 57.6% (12)
  Decline: Utilities, 1937–1938, minus 36.2% (6)

FEW RECENT BLUE-CHIP MONTHS

High index prices have restrained upside percentage gains in recent years. Only one period in the bull market of the 1980s made the blue-chip list of monthly gains; that was August 1982, when a dramatic downturn in interest rates helped the Transports gain over 20 percent.

January 1976 is the most recent Industrial entry and was the best percentage performer for that average since June of 1938. The enormous percentage gains of August 1932 came during the administration of President Herbert Hoover, but were too late to help the GOP.

TABLE 5-11 BEST & WORST DAYS OF EACH YEAR
Ranked By Percent

| | Industrials | | | | | | Rail-Transports | | | | | |
| | Advances | | | Declines | | | Advances | | | Declines | | |
	Date	%	Points	Date	%	Points	Date	%	Points	Date	%	Points
1890a							Nov 12	3.7	2.23	Nov 10	4.2	2.67
1891							Nov 10	2.3	1.58	Sep 24	2.5	1.80
1892							Jan 20	2.0	1.42	Jly 5	2.1	1.49
1893							Jly 27	6.6	2.88	Jly 26	7.4	3.47
1894							Jan 15	2.7	1.41	Jan 8	2.0	1.06
1895							Dec 23	5.3	2.55	Dec 20	8.5	4.70
1896							Aug 10	5.9	2.45	Dec 18	5.3	2.77
1897	Aug 31	3.0	1.58	Oct 12	3.9	2.00	Apr 20	2.1	1.03	Sep 21	3.0	1.95
1898	May 2	5.7	2.60	Feb 24	3.2	1.49	Mar 28	5.4	3.09	Apr 1	3.0	1.77
1899	Dec 19	4.7	2.75	Dec 18	8.7	5.57	Jan 25	3.0	2.36	Dec 18	4.3	3.30
1900	Jan 2	3.1	2.05	Apr 16	4.4	2.85	Nov 7	2.1	1.67	May 8	1.9	1.50
1901	May 10	6.4	4.29	May 9	6.1	4.34	May 10	6.5	6.69	May 9	7.4	8.25
1902	Sep 30	3.2	2.08	Sep 29	3.3	2.21	Sep 30	3.6	4.37	Sep 29	3.7	4.57
1903	Oct 16	5.1	2.16	Aug 19	4.1	2.18	Jne 11	2.8	2.78	Apr 13	2.8	3.16
1904	Dec 16	3.2	2.11	Dec 12	6.1	4.24	Mar 15	2.0	1.79	Dec 12	3.2	3.78
1905	Nov 27	2.9	2.49	Apr 27	3.4	2.73	Aug 11	2.1	2.64	Apr 27	2.5	3.16
1906	May 4	3.0	2.63	Apr 27	2.7	2.52	May 4	2.5	2.99	May 1	2.7	3.36
1907	Mar 15	6.7	5.10	Mar 14	8.3	6.89	Mar 15	6.3	6.24	Mar 14	7.3	7.81
1908	Nov 4	2.4	1.97	Dec 17	2.2	1.89	Jne 1	2.9	2.91	May 23	2.2	2.24
1909	Jan 7	2.1	1.81	Feb 23	3.5	2.91	Sep 1	2.2	2.82	Feb 23	2.8	3.25
1910	Jne 7	3.0	2.45	Feb 7	3.4	3.04	Jne 7	2.4	2.79	Jly 26	2.4	2.65
1911	Nov 9	2.9	2.28	Oct 27	3.0	2.32	May 16	1.5	1.73	Feb 24	2.6	2.16
1912	Nov 6	1.8	1.65	Jly 5	2.2	2.01	Nov 6	1.7	2.03	May 3	1.5	1.82
1913	Jne 12	3.0	2.17	Jan 20	4.9	4.20	Jne 12	2.7	2.68	Jne 2	1.7	1.86
1914**	Dec 12	4.4	3.14	Jly 30	6.9	5.30	Dec 14	2.3	2.08	Jly 30	5.0	4.71

TABLE 5-11 Continued

| | Industrials | | | | | | Rail-Transports | | | | | |
| | Advances | | | Declines | | | Advances | | | Declines | | |
Date	Date	%	Points	Date	%	Points	Date	%	Points	Date	%	Points
1915	May 11	4.2	2.58	May 7	4.5	3.10	Jly 27	2.8	2.50	May 7	1.9	1.80
1916	Dec 22	5.5	4.93	Dec 21	5.4	5.10	Dec 22	2.3	2.38	Oct 5	3.0	3.40
1917	Feb 3	3.4	2.96	Feb 1	7.2	6.91	Dec 27	9.0	6.41	Feb 1	3.3	3.40
1918	Jan 31	3.7	2.82	May 27	3.1	2.51	Nov 7	2.4	2.16	Nov 25	2.8	2.41
1919	Jne 17	3.7	3.72	Aug 4	4.8	5.17	Nov 14	2.9	2.33	Aug 4	3.9	3.41
1920	Nov 22	4.3	3.12	May 19	4.2	3.85	Feb 17	4.5	3.15	Nov 12	4.0	3.24
1921	Jly 6	3.2	2.15	Jne 20	3.5	2.35	Apr 15	3.6	2.42	Jne 20	3.4	2.33
1922	Nov 2	2.4	2.27	Jne 12	2.6	2.47	Jly 6	3.4	2.92	Oct 30	2.0	1.87
1923	Oct 31	3.0	2.62	Jly 27	3.0	2.69	May 24	2.2	1.79	May 7	4.3	3.64
1924	Dec 31	2.1	2.49	Feb 15	3.4	3.42	Nov 7	2.4	2.17	Jan 15	2.2	1.77
1925	Sep 3	2.0	2.69	Nov 10	3.7	5.83	Nov 13	2.2	2.35	Mar 23	1.7	1.69
1926	Mar 4	4.4	6.32	Oct 15	2.7	4.15	Mar 31	3.0	3.12	Mar 30	2.6	2.74
1927	Sep 6	3.0	5.65	Oct 8	3.7	7.21	Dec 2	2.0	2.85	Oct 28	2.0	2.68
1928	Nov 22	3.5	9.81	Dec 8	5.1	13.72	Jne 13	2.1	2.85	Dec 6	2.2	3.29
1929	Oct 30	12.3	28.40	Oct 28	12.8	38.33	Nov 14	6.0	7.68	Oct 28	6.6	10.91
1930	Jne 19	4.6	10.13	Jne 16	5.8	14.20	Dec 19	4.0	3.88	Nov 7	3.6	3.96
1931	Oct 6	14.9	12.86	Sep 24	7.1	8.20	Dec 18	14.3	4.49	Sep 24	10.2	6.28
1932	Sep 21	11.4	7.67	Aug 12	8.4	5.79	Feb 13	11.6	4.13	Oct 5	11.8	3.94
1933**	Mar 15	15.3	8.26	Jly 21	7.8	7.55	Mar 15	17.9	4.43	Jly 21	9.6	4.74
1934	Jan 15	4.6	4.53	Jly 26	6.6	6.06	Jan 15	6.3	2.64	Jly 26	8.8	3.30
1935	Dec 3	2.0	2.86	Oct 2	2.6	3.45	Feb 18	5.8	1.88	Oct 2	4.5	1.55
1936	Nov 4	2.3	3.99	Apr 27	3.2	4.88	Jly 14	3.3	1.66	Apr 27	4.3	1.92
1937	Oct 20	6.1	7.71	Oct 18	7.8	10.57	Oct 20	8.5	2.56	Oct 18	8.3	2.78
1938	Apr 9	5.2	5.75	Mar 25	5.3	6.07	Jne 23	9.5	2.14	Mar 25	9.3	2.04
1939	Sep 5	7.3	10.03	Jan 23	3.7	5.44	Sep 5	10.6	2.78	Mar 31	7.8	2.23

Year	Date			Date			Date			Date		
1940	Nov 7	4.4	5.77	May 14	6.8	9.36	Jne 12	6.2	1.47	May 21	7.7	1.84
1941	Dec 30	3.5	3.76	Dec 8	3.5	4.08	Jly 21	3.5	1.03	Dec 8	5.6	1.51
1942	Jly 8	2.1	2.18	Mar 3	2.3	2.45	Jan 2	4.9	1.24	Apr 14	2.9	0.72
1943	Mar 25	2.0	2.60	Apr 9	3.2	4.30	Apr 5	3.1	1.07	Nov 8	5.2	1.75
1944	Dec 28	1.2	1.76	Sep 6	1.5	2.14	Dec 14	2.6	1.20	Sep 6	3.4	1.36
1945	Aug 23	1.9	3.10	Jly 17	2.0	3.39	Nov 15	2.7	1.70	Jne 28	3.7	2.31
1946	Oct 15	3.6	6.08	Sep 3	5.6	10.51	Oct 31	5.2	2.42	Sep 3	8.2	4.68
1947	Jne 11	2.1	3.58	Apr 14	3.0	5.07	Jne 11	3.0	1.29	Apr 14	3.7	1.69
1948	May 14	2.0	3.78	Nov 3	3.8	7.30	May 14	3.9	2.33	Nov 3	5.6	3.45
1949	Jan 6	1.8	3.14	Sep 20	1.9	3.38	Sep 13	3.0	1.36	May 31	4.0	1.83
1950	Jly 18	2.2	4.25	Jne 26	4.7	10.44	Oct 2	3.6	2.44	Jne 26	6.2	3.46
1951	Jan 2	2.0	4.51	Oct 22	1.9	5.13	Jly 5	2.9	2.13	Jne 25	3.5	2.72
1952	Mar 4	1.5	3.87	Feb 19	1.5	3.98	Mar 27	3.1	2.75	Oct 15	2.3	2.27
1953	Oct 15	1.4	3.71	Apr 6	2.1	5.93	May 20	2.8	2.98	Jne 9	3.4	3.48
1954	Nov 3	2.1	7.54	Jne 8	2.1	6.96	Jne 15	2.4	2.65	Jne 8	3.2	3.56
1955	Sep 27	2.3	10.37	Sep 26	6.5	31.89	Nov 25	2.7	4.41	Sep 26	6.8	11.15
1956	May 29	1.9	8.87	Apr 10	1.6	8.48	Dec 6	2.6	4.04	May 28	2.4	3.96
1957	Oct 23	4.1	17.34	Oct 21	2.5	10.77	Oct 23	5.5	5.91	Oct 21	5.5	6.28
1958	Nov 26	1.6	8.63	Nov 24	2.6	14.68	Sep 19	2.8	3.81	Nov 24	3.0	4.58
1959	Dec 8	1.5	9.72	Aug 10	2.2	14.78	Aug 20	3.0	4.73	Aug 10	1.9	3.10
1960	Jly 29	1.8	11.06	Mar 3	1.5	9.32	Jan 5	2.1	3.25	Mar 3	2.7	3.92
1961	Jan 4	1.8	11.24	Apr 24	1.8	12.60	Oct 4	3.7	5.40	Mar 23	1.5	2.22
1962	May 29	4.7	27.03	May 28	5.7	34.95	May 31	3.7	4.66	May 28	5.3	6.88
1963	Nov 26	4.5	32.03	Nov 22	2.9	21.16	Nov 26	2.6	4.39	Nov 22	1.9	3.28
1964	Sep 11	0.9	7.63	Dec 1	1.3	11.00	May 20	2.2	4.42	Nov 9	1.6	3.40
1965	Jne 30	2.0	16.63	Jne 28	1.6	13.77	Jne 30	2.6	4.95	Jly 20	1.8	3.53
1966	Oct 12	2.6	19.54	Jly 25	1.9	16.32	Oct 12	2.9	5.35	Aug 29	2.3	4.55
1967	Jne 6	1.8	14.94	Jne 5	1.8	15.54	Jne 1	2.2	5.36	Aug 8	3.2	8.79
1968	Apr 1	2.4	20.58	Jly 22	1.5	13.60	Jne 7	2.1	5.53	Jly 22	1.4	3.59
1969	Apr 30	1.7	16.08	Dec 18	1.8	13.86	Dec 24	2.4	4.16	Nov 24	2.3	4.50
1970	May 27	5.1	32.04	May 25	3.1	20.81	May 27	6.2	8.22	May 25	3.9	5.38
1971	Aug 16	3.8	32.93	Jne 18	1.9	17.09	Aug 16	5.1	10.99	Nov 1	2.6	5.89
1972	Jly 24	1.6	14.91	Dec 18	1.4	13.99	Apr 4	2.3	6.08	Apr 25	2.2	5.79
1973	May 24	3.3	29.42	Nov 26	3.4	29.05	Dec 26	4.7	8.40	May 17	4.1	7.32

TABLE 5-11 Continued

	Industrials						Rail-Transports					
	Advances			Declines			Advances			Declines		
	Date	%	Points	Date	%	Points	Date	%	Points	Date	%	Points
1974	Oct 9	4.7	28.39	Nov 18	3.5	22.69	Oct 9	5.1	6.85	Sep 12	3.4	4.61
1975	Jan 27	3.9	26.05	Mar 24	2.6	19.63	Oct 8	3.1	5.04	Jly 23	2.7	4.43
1976	Jan 5	2.2	19.12	May 24	1.9	19.22	Nov 4	2.8	5.83	Oct 11	2.0	4.24
1977	Nov 10	1.7	14.12	Jly 27	2.2	19.75	Nov 11	2.4	5.01	Dec 6	2.1	4.52
1978	Nov 1	4.5	35.34	Oct 16	2.4	21.92	Nov 1	4.9	10.32	Oct 27	2.4	5.26
1979	Nov 26	2.1	16.98	Oct 9	3.0	26.45	Nov 26	2.1	5.21	Oct 9	3.9	10.37
1980	Apr 22	4.0	30.72	Mar 17	2.8	23.04	Mar 28	3.6	8.52	Mar 17	3.2	8.47
1981	Mar 12	2.3	22.15	Jan 7	2.4	23.80	Mar 12	3.3	13.15	Aug 24	3.2	12.89
1982	Aug 17	4.9	38.81	Oct 25	3.5	36.33	Aug 17	5.1	15.21	Oct 25	4.0	17.53
1983	Jly 20	2.6	30.74	Jan 24	2.2	22.81	May 5	2.9	15.09	Sep 27	2.9	16.95
1984	Aug 2	3.1	36.00	Feb 8	2.0	24.19	Aug 2	5.4	25.99	Feb 8	3.2	17.06
1985	Jan 21	2.8	34.01	Aug 6	1.6	21.73	Dec 4	2.7	18.84	Sep 17	2.1	13.70
1986	Mar 11	2.5	43.10	Sep 11	4.6	86.61	Sep 4	2.7	20.63	Sep 11	4.3	33.63
1987	Oct 21	10.1	186.84	Oct 19	22.6	508.00	Oct 21	6.3	46.76	Oct 19	17.5	164.78
1988	Jan 4	3.9	76.42	Jan 8	6.9	140.58	May 31	2.7	21.65	Jan 8	5.6	44.53
1989	Oct 16	3.4	88.12	Oct 13	6.9	190.58	Aug 7	7.5	94.06	Oct 16	7.3	102.06
1990	Aug 27	3.3	78.71	Aug 23	3.3	93.31	Aug 27	4.4	38.82	Aug 6	5.7	58.76

[a]Dow Industrial Average not computed until May, 1896.

**The "daily" changes of March 15, 1933 were recorded on the first day of trading following the banking holidays of early March. The Exchange had closed on March 5. The "daily" change of December 12, 1914 for the DJIA came after a four-month shutdown due to WW I.

Series Best & Worst Days:

Industrials Up: Mar 15, 1933 plus 15.3% Rail-Trans. Up Mar 15, 1933 plus 17.9%
Industrials Down: Oct 19, 1987 minus 22.6%. Rails-Trans Down: Oct 19, 1987 minus 17.5%

TABLE 5-12   SERIES BEST AND WORST DAYS
Ranked by Percent

Best Days

Industrials			Rail-Transports			Utilities		
Date	+%	+Points	Date	+%	+Points	Date	+%	+Points
Mar 15, 1933	15.3	8.26	Mar 15, 1933	17.9	4.43	Oct 30, 1929	18.1	13.44
Oct 6, 1931	14.9	12.86	Dec 18, 1931	14.3	4.49	Apr 20, 1933	15.9	3.38
Oct 30, 1929	12.3	28.40	Feb 13, 1932	11.6	4.13	Oct 6, 1931	13.2	4.60
Sep 21, 1932	11.4	7.67	Sep 5, 1939	10.6	2.78	Sep 21, 1932	12.2	3.59
Oct 21, 1987	10.1	186.84	Jne 23, 1938	9.5	2.14	Oct 20, 1937	10.2	2.00
Sep 5, 1939	7.3	10.03	Dec 17, 1917	9.0	6.41	Oct 21, 1987	8.3	14.17
Mar 15, 1907	6.7	5.10	Oct 20, 1937	8.5	2.56	Jan 15, 1934	7.4	1.81
May 10, 1901	6.4	4.29	Aug 7, 1989	7.5	94.06	May 6, 1938	7.2	1.33
Oct 20, 1937	6.1	7.71	Jly 27, 1893	6.6	2.88	Jne 19, 1939	5.4	4.30
May 2, 1898	5.7	2.60	May 10, 1901	6.5	6.69	May 29, 1962	5.2	5.38

Worst Days

Industrials			Rail-Transports			Utilities		
Date	-%	-Points	Date	-%	-Points	Date	-%	-Points
Oct 19, 1987	22.6	508.00	Oct 19, 1987	17.5	164.78	Oct 28, 1929	17.0	17.79
Oct 28, 1929	12.8	38.33	Oct 5, 1932	11.8	3.94	Oct 19, 1987	15.3	29.16
Dec 18,1899	8.7	5.57	Sep 24, 1931	10.2	6.28	Jly 20, 1933	9.1	3.28
Aug 12, 1932	8.4	5.79	Jly 21, 1933	9.6	4.74	Nov 6, 1940	7.6	1.77
Mar 14, 1907	8.3	6.89	Mar 25, 1938	9.3	2.04	Sep 24, 1931	7.4	3.36
Jly 21, 1933	7.8	7.55	Jly 26, 1934	8.8	3.30	May 28, 1962	7.3	8.22
Oct 18, 1937	7.8	10.57	Dec 20, 1895	8.5	4.70	Oct 5, 1932	7.3	2.33
Feb 1, 1917	7.2	6.91	Oct 18, 1937	8.3	2.78	Sep 3, 1946	6.9	2.71
Sep 24, 1931	7.1	8.20	Mar 31, 1939	7.8	2.23	Jne 16, 1930	6.4	5.70
Jly 30, 1914	6.9	5.30	May 9, 1901	7.4	8.25	Mar 31, 1939	6.0	1.38

CONSECUTIVE ADVANCE-DECLINE DAYS

Extended consecutive day moves fascinate market followers, though such surges have only rarely signaled the start of a major trend reversal.

In January 1987, 13 whirlwind advances by the Dow Industrials—good for 209 points—caused many investors to think that the blow-off signaled the end for a bull market already four-and-one-half years of age. The Dow advanced another 600 points by August. Fourteen days of straight declines for the Rail average in 1941 reflected the dismal war situation but the low of World War II would not come for another eight months.

Duration of the consecutive day moves has had small correlation with the extent of the gain or loss. In August 1932, a five-day advance rushed the Dow up over 27 percent. Eleven straight gains in 1944 helped the index by less than 3 percent. Table 5-13 shows the record Dow and Transport consecutive day movements. It is shown on page 247.

TABLE 5-13   BIGGEST DAILY DOW GAINERS & LOSERS*
Ranked By Percent

Gainers					
Dow Industrials		Rail-Transports		Utilities	
	%		%		%
Mar 15, 1933	+15.3	Mar 15, 1933	+17.9	Oct 30, 1929	+18.1
Oct 6, 1931	14.9	Dec 18, 1931	14.3	Apr 20, 1933	15.9
Oct 30, 1929	12.3	Sep 23, 1931	14.0	Nov 14, 1929	13.7
Sep 21, 1932	11.4	Oct 6, 1931	13.1	Oct 6, 1931	13.2
Oct 21, 1987	10.1	Feb 13, 1932	11.6	Sep 21, 1932	12.2
Feb 11, 1932	9.5	Sep 21, 1932	11.5	Oct 20, 1937	10.2
Nov 14, 1929	9.4	Jne 4, 1932	11.2	Aug 3, 1932	10.1
Dec 18, 1931	9.4	Aug 15, 1932	10.8	Jly 24, 1933	9.9
Feb 13, 1932	9.2	Sep 5, 1939	10.6	Feb 13, 1932	9.6
May 6, 1932	9.1	Oct 14, 1932	10.5	Oct 31, 1929	8.6
Apr 19, 1933	9.0	Aug 22, 1932	10.2	Oct 21, 1987	8.3

Losers					
Industrials		Rail-Transports		Utilities	
	%		%		%
Oct 19, 1987	−22.6	Oct 19, 1987	−17.5	Oct 28, 1929	−17.0
Oct 28, 1929	12.8	Oct 5, 1932	11.8	Oct 19, 1987	15.3
Oct 29, 1929	11.7	Sep 24, 1931	10.2	Oct 29, 1929	14.5
Nov 6, 1929	9.9	Oct 26, 1987	10.0	Nov 6, 1929	12.2
Dec 18, 1899	8.7	Sep 12, 1932	9.8	Jly 20, 1933	9.1
Aug 12, 1932	8.4	Jly 21, 1933	9.6	Nov 6, 1940	7.6
Mar 14, 1907	8.3	Mar 25, 1938	9.3	Sep 24, 1931	7.4
Jly 21, 1933	7.8	Jly 26, 1934	8.8	May 28, 1962	7.3
Oct 18, 1937	7.8	Sep 21, 1933	8.6	Oct 5, 1932	7.3
Feb 1, 1917	7.2	Dec 20, 1895	8.5	May 14, 1940	7.2
Oct 5, 1932	7.2	Oct 18, 1937	8.3	Sep 3, 1946	6.9

The Series Best and Worst Days (Table 5-12) allows only one entry per year. Table 5-13 gives overall rankings, dominated by multiple yearly entries of the 1929–1932 period.

Utility Outage

The Dow Utility Average in 1967 set a record never approached by the other Dow indices. It declined for 21 consecutive days from September 27 to October 26, rallied for one day, and then fell for another seven sessions. Twenty-eight losses in 29 days. Total loss was 7.5 percent. In October–November of the same year, the Rails dropped for 12 days, rallied for one day and then declined for another 12 days. Total loss was 13 percent.

THE LONGEST MILES

The Dow 100 milestone was first passed in 1906, only to see the panic of 1907 plunge the average down to 53. The milestone was reached again in 1909, 1916 (revised average), and 1919. Each time the Dow faded away from that psycho-

TABLE 5-14 CONSECUTIVE DAY SERIES RECORDS
Ranked By Percent

Consecutive Days of Gain				Consecutive Days of Loss			
				Industrials			
Year	Period	Days	Pct. (+)	Year	Period	Days	Pct. (−)
1916	Sep	11	7.9	1941	Jly–Aug	14	3.4
1921	Oct	11	6.4	1960	Jly	11	7.0
1929	Jne–Jly	11	7.9	1968	Jan	12	5.1
1944	Apr–May	11	2.9	1971	Oct	11	6.4
1955	Jan–Feb	11	5.5	1974	Sep–Oct	11	13.3
1970	Nov–Dec	12	6.5				
1987	Jan	13	11.0				

Gain				Loss			
				Rail-Transports			
Year	Period	Days	Pct. (+)	Year	Period	Days	Pct. (−)
1897	Jly–Aug	11	7.5	1930	Dec	12	14.5
1938	Sep–Oct	11	34.2	1953	Dec	11	8.0
1957	Jne–Jly	11	6.3	1966	Aug	12	9.8
1964	Jne–Jly*	11	5.9	1967	Oct**	12	5.7
1971	Mar–Apr	14	10.8	1967	Oct–Nov**	12	8.3
1973	Sep–Oct	11	12.2	1968	Oct–Nov	11	3.0
	Dec–Jan	13	12.8	1969	Feb–Mar	12	9.7
1980	Oct	11	9.5	1972	Apr–May	11	8.0

*Rails did not suffer a loss in 19 sessions. One day was unchanged.

**Rails fell for 12 days, rallied for one and then declined for 12 more days.

logical barrier. It was not until 1924 that the level seemed permanently crested.

The 1929 advance to Dow 381 made the 100 level seem an anachronism, but by 1932 the average had fallen to 41.22 and 100 again became a coveted goal. In 1937, the Industrial average climbed to 194, but a second depression and war in Europe made 100 an easier target than 200.

The final pit stop at Dow 100 came in the bleakest days of World War II when the Industrials, in the late spring of 1942, fell once again below 100. It had been 36 years since that level had first been tested on the upside. May 26, 1942 was the last time the index would close below the century mark.

Dow 1000 also proved a tough milestone. The Industrials nicked the figure intraday many times in early 1966, but could never close above that level. In late 1968, another failure occurred and it was November 1972 before the Dow could pass the psychological milestone. Table 5-15 details milestones for the three averages.

TABLE 5-15   MILESTONES FOR DOW AVERAGES

Record Closing Prices—First Time		
Industrials	Rail-Transports	Utilities
Over 100 Jan 12, 1906	Over 100 Mar 13, 1901	Over 100 Jne 6, 1929
Over 150 Oct 20, 1925	Over 150 Nov 20, 1928	Over 125 Jly 20, 1929
Over 200 Dec 19, 1927	Over 200 May 12, 1964	Over 150 Aug 3, 1964
Over 300 Jan 2, 1929	Over 300 Jly 17, 1980	Over 175 Jan 3, 1986
Over 400 Dec 29, 1954	Over 400 Nov 18, 1980	Over 200 Jne 30, 1986
Over 500 Mar 12, 1956	Over 500 Mar 1, 1983	Over 225 Jan 22, 1987
Over 600 Feb 20, 1959	Over 600 Nov 14, 1983	
Over 700 May 17, 1961	Over 700 Jly 16, 1985	
Over 800 Feb 28, 1964	Over 800 Mar 11, 1986	
Over 900 Jan 28, 1965	Over 900 Feb 4, 1987	
Over 1000 Nov 14, 1972[a]	Over 1000 Jne 8, 1987	
Over 1100 Feb 24, 1983	Over 1100 Aug 11, 1987	
Over 1200 Apr 26, 1983	Over 1200 Jly 10, 1989	
Over 1300 May 20, 1985	Over 1300 Aug 7, 1989	
Over 1400 Nov 6, 1985	Over 1400 Aug 9, 1989	
Over 1500 Dec 11, 1985	Over 1500 Aug 29, 1989	
Over 2000 Jan 8, 1987		
Over 2500 Jly 17, 1987		
Over 3000**		

[a]Intraday, Dow first over 1000 Jan 18, 1966.

**Intraday, Dow over 3000 Jly 16, 1990, but could not close there.

OTHER LEADING STOCK AVERAGES

THE AMEX INDEX

The American Stock Exchange has progressed through several indices to its current version, the ASE Market Value Index (AMVI). It is market-value weighted and measures more than 800 issues at the ASE, including ADRs and warrants. Changes are measured against a July 5, 1983 base value of 50.00. Uniquely, it assumes that cash dividends paid by component stocks are reinvested and thus a total return is gauged.

The present series can be traced back to 1968. Like the Value Line, the index displayed miserable relative strength in the early 1970s, despite a powerful Dow and S&P. High for the AMEX count had been 84.49 in 1969; at the 1972 bull peak, the average could only reach 69.18. By 1974, the index had taken a terrible beating, having lost 65 percent of its 1969 value.

That weak pattern would reverse and by 1979 when there was a heated demand for the natural resource stocks, the average was in an almost unheralded bull market, having far outpaced its 1969 high. Meanwhile, the major averages seriously lagged their 1973 tops and would not overcome them until 1982.

Series high for the AMEX index was 397.03 in 1989. Series low was 29.13 in 1974.

NASDAQ COMPOSITE INDEX

This index of over-the-counter stocks is a market-value weighted measurement of all stocks traded on the National Market System of the National Association of Security Dealers (NASDAQ). It was first computed in February 1971 and began to get serious attention later in the decade when it outperformed the Dow and S&P averages.

Over 4,000 securities are included in this very broad index. Many are small speculative issues, but it also hosts a great number of the newer technology stocks. MCI, Intel, Apple, Lotus, and Sun Microsystems have been among the most active and popular issues in recent years.

When speculative fever focuses on lower-priced stocks and such occasionally high-flying groups as the computers, softwares, and biotechs, the index outperforms the blue-chip averages.

The series high was reached in 1989 at 485.73. Its low in 1974 was 54.87.

NYSE COMPOSITE INDEX

In 1925, the NYSE initiated a monthly market index, seeking a representative and all-inclusive measurement for stock prices at the Big Board. The effort was abandoned when the monthly *Exchange Bulletin* was folded in 1939. Thirty-three major stock groups had also been tallied and charted.

The present NYSE Composite Index was developed in 1966. It consists of all common shares listed at the Board. Total daily market value is measured with the market value of each stock obtained by multiplying its price by the number of shares listed.

Aggregate market value is then expressed relative to the base market period of 50.00, that figure being close to the actual price average of all common shares listed at the Exchange at the end of 1965. Four sub-indices are also compiled: Industrials, Transportation, Utility, and Finance.

Historically, the composite can be traced on a weekly basis to early January 1939. The series low was 4.64 in 1942, and the high at 201.13 in July 1990. That figure was only a point better than the 1989 peak. Stock index futures and options are traded on the composite at the New York Futures Exchange.

STANDARD & POOR'S MAJOR INDICES

The antecedent of the S&P 500 was first computed by Standard Statistics in 1923, 18 years before the firm merged with Poor's Publishing. Prices were figured weekly at the time and computed back to 1918, with 198 stocks covered. By 1937, 419 issues were tabulated.

In 1957, the "500" was created adding 25 rails and 50 utilities to 425 industrial stocks. A later change consolidated 40 utilities, 20 transports, and 40 financials with 400 industrials. Both the 400 and the 500 are market-value weighted and the 500 represents about 80 percent of the market value of all issues traded at the Exchange. The index base is 1941–1943: 10.

Until 1976, the indices were limited to NYSE listings, but since then some AMEX and OTC stocks had been added. A number of "index" funds attempt to mirror the S&P performance and money managers strive desperately to keep their results level or ahead of this broad, historic market gauge. A daily chart of the index appears in the *New York Times*. Futures based on the 500 attract enormous institutional volume at the Chicago Mercantile Exchange and the futures options are huge traders at the Chicago Board.

Series low for the S&P 500 was 4.40 on June 1, 1932, so its depression trough preceded the Dow Industrials by some five weeks. Series high in 1990 at 368.95 was barely 1.5 points over the October peak of 1989.

VALUE LINE COMPOSITE INDEX

The Value Line Investment Service has its own composite index, made up of approximately 1,700 stocks that are tracked in the voluminous Value Line Investment Survey book. The weighted geometric average has a 1961 base figure of 100.

A goodly number of small-growth issues are followed, making the index rather broad in scope. It was a leader on the downside in the 1968–1974 period, unable in 1973 to even approach its peak of the previous decade.

Like the AMEX and NASDAQ indices, the Value Line showed great relative strength in the late 1970s, compared with the Dow. When the Industrials struck their bear market low in February 1978, the three indices were all above their level of September 1976, when the Dow had recorded its last bull market peak.

Series low was 47.03 in 1974. The high in 1989 was 278.98. Value Line futures are traded at the Kansas City Board of Trade and index options at the Philadelphia Stock Exchange.

WILSHIRE 5000 INDEX

It's called the "5000" but over 6,000 capitalization-weighted security prices are used in the Wilshire Index which measures the dollar performance of all U.S. common equity securities with readily available price data. Capitalization is about 86 percent NYSE, 11 percent OTC and 3 percent AMEX, and the index is an excellent approximator of dollar changes in the American equity market.

The index was created in 1974 by Wilshire Associates as a performance measure and month-end history was computed back to December 1970. Since

December 1979, the index has been calculated on a daily basis and its closing level appears in the leading metropolitan and financial papers.

The series' low (monthly) was in October 1974 at $550.035 billion. Its base is December 31, 1980 at $1,404.596 billion and the record high was $3,523.57 billion in 1989. A double top at $3,518.32 billion was recorded in July 1990.

MEDIA AVERAGES

For decades, the *New York Times*'s 50-stock average was one of the most popular indices with investors. It had a long record, having originated in 1911, and its graphics were displayed each day in the *New York Times*. The average, composed of 25 industrials and 25 rails, was folded in the 1970s.

The *New York Herald Tribune*'s industrial and rail averages were begun in 1923 and a Curb average was added in 1929. Other media types developing their own averages include the Associated Press and *Barron's*. *Investor's Daily* charts its very broad, 6,000-stock average each day.

WORLD MARKET INDICES

In foreign markets, the Nikkei 225 is the famous big number index of the Tokyo market. It threatened the 40,000 level in late 1989. In London, the Financial Times-Stock Exchange 100-share index is the best known average, though there is also a FT-SE 30-share indicator.

Toronto's 300 is closely followed by world investors in the Canadian market. The FAZ 100-share index in Frankfort drew considerable attention and a splendid gain in 1989 as the communist walls in Eastern Europe crumbled. The knowledge or even curiosity level about world indices drops rather sharply after Germany. In France, its the CAC-40 and in Italy the BCI index. Spanish investors watch the Madrid General average, and in Australia the All-Ordinary index keeps tabs at the southern end of the Pacific Rim. Hong Kong's riotous Hang Seng index, with a 1989 range of 2094–3440 marks the colony's stock fortunes, though its life expectancy will be suspect when Beijing assumes control of the island.

6

Market Activity
Records

The New York Stock Exchange did not officially tabulate volume figures until 1930 and there are discrepancies from the several sources around the turn of the century.

Compounding the problem is the fact that unlisted trading was permitted at the Exchange between 1885 and March 1910. That volume is included in the following tables, although the Exchange excludes it in the annual computations of its Fact Book. The same source, however, includes unlisted trades in its daily reported stock volume.

The *New York Times,* the *Wall Street Journal,* and the *Commercial & Financial Chronicle* often have slightly different volume numbers in this earlier period. For example, the *Wall Street Journal* has always listed April 30, 1901 as the peak volume day of that year. Other authorities name May 9, the day of the Northern Pacific panic, as the volume leader. Generally, differences are not so material. Tables 6-1 through 6-7 capsule vital volume statistics.

Annual turnover (shares traded divided by average shares listed) in the 1900–1910 period excludes unlisted shares and tends to mildly exaggerate the era's activity rate. Volume figures in the following tables are so-called "reported" volume, "the most commonly used measure of stock market activity," according to the NYSE. These are the numbers reported on the tape and in the media.

TABLE 6-1 ANNUAL SHARE VOLUME (in millions)

Year	NYSE volume[a]	% turnover	AMEX volume	As % of NYSE
1890	71.3			
1891	69.0			
1892	85.9			
1893	81.0			
1894	49.1			
1895	66.6			
1896	54.7			
1897	77.3			
1898	112.7			
1899	176.4			
1900	138.3	172		
1901	265.6	319		
1902	188.3	207		
1903	160.7	168		
1904	186.5	191		
1905	263.0	244		
1906	284.0	240		
1907	195.4	160		
1908	196.8	161		
1909	214.4	179		
1910	163.8	127		
1911	125.8	90		
1912	131.5	88		
1913	82.8	54		
1914	47.4	31		
1915	172.5	111		
1916	232.6	145		
1917	184.6	103		
1918	143.3	74		
1919	318.3	153		
1920	227.6	91		
1921	172.8	59	15.5	09
1922	260.9	77	21.7	08
1923	236.5	60	51.0	22
1924	284.0	67	72.2	25
1925	459.7	99	88.4	19
1926	451.9	84	115.5	26
1927	581.7	94	125.1	22
1928	930.9	132	242.3	26
1929	1,124.8	119	476.1	42
1930	810.6	67	222.3	27
1931	576.8	44	110.3	14
1932	425.2	32	57.1	13
1933	654.8	50	100.9	15
1934	323.8	25	60.1	19
1935	381.6	29	75.7	20
1936	496.0	37	134.8	27
1937	409.5	30	104.2	25
1938	297.5	21	49.6	17
1939	262.0	18	45.7	17
1940	207.6	14	42.9	21
1941	170.6	12	34.7	20
1942	125.7	9	22.3	18
1943	278.7	19	71.4	26
1944	263.1	18	71.1	27
1945	377.6	24	143.4	38
1946	363.7	22	137.3	38
1947	253.6	14	72.4	27
1948	302.2	15	75.0	25
1949	272.2	13	66.2	24
1950	524.8	23	107.8	21
1951	443.5	18	111.6	25
1952	337.8	13	106.2	31
1953	354.9	12	102.4	29
1954	573.4	19	162.9	28
1955	649.6	19	229.0	35
1956	556.3	13	228.2	41
1957	559.9	12	214.0	38
1958	747.1	15	240.4	32
1959	820.3	15	374.1	46
1960	766.7	12	286.0	37
1961	1,021.3	15	488.8	48

TABLE 6-1 Continued

Year	NYSE volume[a]	% turnover	AMEX volume	As % of NYSE	Year	NYSE volume	% turnover	AMEX volume	As % of NYSE
1962	962.2	13	308.6	32	1976	5,360.1	23	648.3	12
1963	1,146.3	15	316.7	28	1977	5,273.8	21	651.9	12
1964	1,236.6	14	374.2	30	1978	7,205.1	27	992.2	14
1965	1,556.3	16	534.2	34	1979	8,155.9	28	1,161.3	14
1966	1,899.5	18	690.8	36	1980	11,352.3	36	1,525.8	13
1967	2,530.0	22	1,145.1	45	1981	11,853.7	33	1,343.5	11
1968	2,931.6	24	1,435.8	49	1982	16,458.0	42	1,337.8	08
1969	2,850.8	20	1,240.7	44	1983	21,589.6	51	2,081.3	10
1970	2,937.4	19	843.1	29	1984	23,071.0	49	1,545.0	07
1971	3,891.3	23	1,070.9	28	1985	27,510.7	54	2,100.9	08
1972	4,138.2	23	1,118.0	27	1986	35,680.0	64	2,978.5	08
1973	4,053.2	20	759.8	19	1987	47,801.3	73	3,506.0	07
1974	3,517.7	16	482.2	14	1988	40,849.5	55	2,515.2	06
1975	4,693.4	21	540.9	11	1989	41,698.5	52	3,125.0	07
					1990	39,664.5	46	3,328.9	08

[a]Annual volume figure is for reported volume and includes unlisted securities in the 1890–1910 compilations.

Sources: *The New York Times, New York Stock Exchange Year Book, AMEX Datebook, and Commercial & Financial Chronicle.*

TABLE 6-2 NASDAQ ANNUAL SHARE VOLUME (in millions)

Year	Volume	Listed companies	Year	Volume	Companies	Year	Volume	Companies
1972	2,221	3,288	1978	2,762	2,475	1984	15,159	4,097
1973	1,681	2,761	1979	3,561	2,543	1985	20,699	4,136
1974	1,180	2,436	1980	6,692	3,894	1986	28,737	4,417
1975	1,390	2,467	1981	7,823	3,353	1987*	37,890	4,706
1976	1,684	2,495	1982	8,432	3,264	1988	31,070	4,451
1977	1,932	2,456	1983	15,909	3,901	1989	33,530	4,293*
						1990	33,363	4,132

*Record daily total volume: 288,059,700 October 21, 1987.

TABLE 6-3   NYSE MONTHLY VOLUME RECORDS (Millions of Shares)

Year	High		Low	
	Month	Volume	Month	Volume
1890	May	11.1	Jly	3.0
1891	Sep	11.2	Jly	3.2
1892	Feb	11.4	Jly	3.5
1893	Feb	10.8	Sep	4.7
1894	May	5.1	Jly	2.8
1895	May	8.9	Feb	3.0
1896	Nov	5.9	May	2.8
1897	Sep	12.9	Feb	2.8
1898	Dec	15.3	Apr	6.0
1899	Jan	24.3	Jly	8.4
1900	Dec	23.4	Aug	4.0
1901	Apr	41.7	Aug	10.8
1902	Apr	26.5	Jne	7.8
1903	Jne	15.5	Feb	10.2
1904	Oct	32.6	Jne	5.0
1905	Dec	31.5	Jne	12.3
1906	Jan	38.7	Jly	16.3
1907	Mar	32.3	Jne	10.2
1908	Nov	24.9	Jne	9.4
1909	Aug	24.6	Feb	12.4
1910	Jan	24.2	Sep	7.7
1911	Sep	17.6	Apr	5.0
1912	Apr	16.1	Jne	7.1
1913	Jne	9.6	Nov	3.8
1914	Jan	10.1	Jne	4.0
1915	Oct	26.6	Feb	4.4
1916	Nov	34.5	Jly	9.2
1917	May	19.6	Aug	11.7
1918	May	21.1	Aug	6.9
1919	Oct	37.4	Jan	11.9
1920	Mar	29.1	Jne	9.3
1921	Jne	18.4	Jly	9.3
1922	Apr	30.7	Jan	16.6
1923	Mar	25.9	Jly	13.5
1924	Dec	43.9	May	13.8
1925	Oct	54.7	Apr	25.1
1926	Mar	52.3	May	23.5
1927	Dec	62.3	Jan	34.6
1928	Nov	114.8	Jly	38.8
1929	Oct	141.7	Jne	69.5
1930	Apr	111.0	Aug	39.9
1931	Mar	65.7	Aug	24.8
1932	Aug	82.6	Jne	23.0
1933	Jne	125.6	Jan	18.7
1934	Feb	56.8	Sep	12.6
1935	Nov	57.5	Feb	14.4
1936	Jan	67.2	May	20.6
1937	Jan	58.7	Jne	16.4
1938	Oct	41.6	May	14.0
1939	Sep	57.1	Jne	12.0

TABLE 6-3 Continued

	High			Low	
Year	Month	Volume	Month	Volume	
1940	May	39.0	Jly	7.3	
1941	Dec	36.4	Feb	9.0	
1942	Dec	19.3	May	7.2	
1943	Mar	37.0	Oct	13.9	
1944	Jne	37.7	Apr	13.8	
1945	Jne	41.3	Jly	20.0	
1946	Jan	51.5	Jly	20.6	
1947	Oct	28.6	Aug	14.2	
1948	May	42.8	Aug	15.0	
1949	Dec	39.3	Feb	17.2	
1950	Dec	59.8	Feb	33.4	
1951	Jan	70.2	Nov	25.7	
1952	Dec	40.5	Aug	20.9	
1953	Mar	42.5	Jly	22.2	
1954	Dec	76.5	Feb	33.3	
1955	Jan	74.7	Aug	41.8	
1956	Mar	60.4	Jne	37.2	
1957	Oct	64.0	Mar	35.7	
1958	Oct	95.1	Feb	40.2	
1959	Jan	83.3	Aug	51.1	
1960	Dec	77.4	Jly	53.9	
1961	Mar	118.0	Jly	60.9	
1962	May	111.0	Sep	62.9	
1963	Oct	122.3	Mar	74.8	
1964	Apr	123.5	Aug	82.3	
1965	Dec	191.2	Jly	85.2	
1966	Mar	191.5	Jly	119.9	
1967	Dec	229.5	Feb	183.1	
1968	Apr	295.6	Feb	174.5	
1969	Oct	310.2	Mar	199.2	
1970	Dec	335.3	Mar	213.0	
1971	Apr	401.7	Sep	252.8	
1972	Nov	405.6	Sep	246.3	
1973	Oct	422.9	Jne	268.7	
1974	Oct	377.1	Jne	245.4	
1975	May	457.5	Sep	275.1	
1976	Jan	635.9	Aug	346.7	
1977	Jan	501.7	Sep	383.7	
1978	Aug	865.0	Feb	368.6	
1979	Oct	858.0	Feb	474.7	
1980	Jan	1,158.5	Apr	674.6	
1981	Mar	1,174.6	Feb	816.4	
1982	Oct	2,068.6	Jan	968.3	
1983	Jne	1,974.0	Jly	1,590.2	
1984	Aug	2,528.1	Jly	1,666.3	
1985	Dec	2,802.4	Sep	1,860.3	
1986	Dec	3,261.0	Jne	2,649.2	
1987	Oct	6,094.6	May	3,418.0	
1988	Jne	4,307.0	Nov	2,823.0	
1989	Oct	4,012.6	Sep	3,035.3	
1990	Aug	4,014.5	Sep	2,685.6	

TABLE 6-4 DAILY VOLUME RECORDS (thousands of shares)

	New York Stock Exchange			
	High		Low[a]	
Year	Shares	Date	Shares	Date
1897	878	Oct 21	83	Jan 26
1898	931	Dec 27	86	Apr 27
1899	1,603	Jan 23	169	Jly 24
1900	1,627	Nov 12	89	Aug 22
1901	3,337	May 9	183	Jly 2
1902	1,956	Apr 21	167	Jne 3
1903	1,540	Jan 9	147	Aug 27
1904	2,911	Dec 8	73	Mar 10
1905	2,042	Feb 27	132	Jne 15
1906	2,728	Aug 20	302	Oct 30
1907	2,496	Mar 14	139	Jne 24
1908	1,716	Nov 13	67	Jly 3
1909	1,650	Jne 4	294	Mar 15
1910	1,656	Feb 3	111	Dec 23
1911	1,704	Sep 27	87	Jly 14
1912	1,252	Dec 11	100	Dec 26
1913	864	Jne 10	57	Nov 24
1914	1,281	Jly 30	50	Dec 30
1915	1,673	Sep 28	114	Mar 17
1916	3,002	Dec 21	119	Aug 7
1917	2,048	Feb 1	236	Nov 24
1918	1,692	May 16	136	Aug 2
1919	2,697	Nov 12	299	Feb 7
1920	2,008	Apr 21	227	Jne 29
1921	1,290	Mar 23	280	Aug 8
1922	2,008	Apr 17	236	Jly 3
1923	1,559	Nov 22	283	Jly 16
1924	2,584	Nov 20	316	Jne 2
1925	3,391	Nov 10	790	Apr 13
1926	3,860	Mar 3	607	May 6
1927	3,214	Oct 4	1,219	Jan 28
1928	6,943	Nov 23	1,090	Jne 25
1929	16,410	Oct 29	1,996	Dec 24
1930	8,279	May 5	1,090	Aug 1
1931	5,346	Feb 24	536	Sep 1
1932	5,461	Aug 8	385	Oct 31
1933	9,572	Jly 21	477	Jan 30
1934	4,940	Feb 5	275	Aug 20
1935	3,948	Nov 14	345	Feb 4
1936	4,718	Feb 17	586	May 13
1937	7,288	Oct 19	424	Jne 21
1938	3,100	Nov 9	278	Jne 8
1939	5,934	Sep 5	235	Jly 3
1940	3,940	May 21	130	Aug 19
1941	2,925	Dec 29	224	May 19
1942	1,441	Dec 29	207	Jly 1
1943	2,805	May 4	335	Aug 30
1944	2,517	Jne 16	337	May 15

TABLE 6-4 Continued

	New York Stock Exchange			
	High		Low	
Year	Shares	Date	Shares	Date
1945	2,936	Jne 28	492	Aug 6
1946	3,624	Sep 4	487	Jly 5
1947	2,197	Apr 14	476	Aug 27
1948	3,837	May 14	465	Aug 16
1949	2,212	Dec 14	541	Jne 17
1950	4,859	Jne 27	1,061	Mar 13
1951	3,877	Jan 17	973	Jly 11
1952	2,352	Nov 19	780	May 19
1953	3,119	Mar 31	738	Sep 8
1954	4,433	Dec 29	1,215	Jan 11
1955	7,717	Sep 26	1,230	Aug 15
1956	3,921	Feb 29	1,223	Oct 9
1957	5,093	Oct 22	1,256	Sep 4
1958	5,368	Oct 17	1,566	Feb 24
1959	4,884	Mar 13	1,745	Oct 12
1960	5,303	Dec 30	1,894	Oct 12
1961	7,077	Apr 4	2,184	Jly 3
1962	14,746	May 29	1,946	Oct 8
1963	9,324	Nov 26	2,513	Jly 26
1964	6,851	Apr 2	3,051	Aug 10
1965	11,434	Dec 6	3,028	Jly 7
1966	13,121	May 6	4,268	Jne 6
1967	14,954	Dec 29	5,998	Jan 3
1968	21,351	Jne 13	6,707	Mar 25
1969	19,950	Oct 14	6,683	Aug 11
1970	21,345	Sep 24	6,660	May 11
1971	31,731	Aug 16	7,349	Oct 25
1972	27,555	Dec 29	7,945	Oct 9
1973	25,962	Sep 20	8,970	Aug 20
1974	26,365	Oct 10	7,402	Jly 5
1975	35,138	Feb 13	8,670	Sep 15
1976	44,513	Feb 20	10,301	Jan 2
1977	35,261	Nov 11	10,582	Oct 10
1978	66,370	Aug 3	7,580	Jan 20
1979	81,619	Oct 10	18,346	Jan 2
1980	84,297	Nov 5	16,132	Dec 26
1981	92,881	Jan 7	23,945	Dec 24
1982	149,385	Nov 4	36,760	Jan 4
1983	129,411	Jan 6	53,033	Aug 29
1984	236,565	Aug 3	46,364	Oct 8
1985	181,027	Dec 5	62,055	Dec 26
1986	244,293	Dec 19	48,865	Dec 26
1987	608,149	Oct 20	86,366	Nov 27
1988	343,949	Jne 17	72,088	Nov 25
1989	416,290	Oct 16	68,870	Jly 2
1990	292,360	Aug 3	92,940	Sep 4

[a]Full days only.

Sources: *New York Stock Exchange Fact Book, Dow Jones, The New York Times, Commercial & Financial Chronicle.*

TABLE 6-5 NYSE VOLUME MILESTONES

Annual	Monthly
First Volume Over 100 Million—1881	First Volume over 10 million, May 1890
Over 200 million—1901	Over 20 million—Jan 1899
Over 300 million—1919	Over 30 million—Jan 1901
Over 400 million—1925	Over 40 million—Apr 1901
Over 500 million—1927	Over 50 million—Oct 1925
Over 1 billion—1929	Over 100 million—Nov 1928
Over 2 billion—1967	Over 200 million—Jan 1967
Over 5 billion—1976	Over 500 million—Jan 1976
Over 10 billion—1980	Over 1 billion—Jan 1980
Over 25 billion—1985	Over 5 billion—Oct 1987
Series record: 47.8 billion, 1987	Series record: 6.1 billion, Oct 1987

Daily Volume Milestones	
First over 1 million—Dec 15, 1886	Over 30 million—Aug 16, 1971
Over 2 million—Jan 7, 1901	Over 40 million—Feb 20, 1976
Over 3 million—Jan 7, 1901 (3,138,000)	Over 50 million—Apr 14, 1978
Over 4 million—Mar 22, 1928	Over 100 million—Jan 7, 1981
Over 5 million—Nov 12, 1928	Over 200 million—Aug 3, 1984
Over 10 million—Oct 24, 1929	Over 300 million—Jan 23, 1987
Over 15 million—Oct 29, 1929	Over 400, 500, and 600 million
Over 20 million—Apr 10, 1968	shares—Oct 19, 1987—604 million
Series record: 608.1 million Oct 20, 1987	

Weekly volume first reached 50 million shares in the week ended April 18, 1966 at 55,457,000 shares. A 100-million milestone came about five years later, in January 1971. An unbelievable 2,299,584,000 shares were traded at the Exchange in the week ending October 23, 1987. That total exceeded the record yearly figure of 1966.

ODD-LOT VOLUME

Sixty years ago, odd-lot volume was an important sector of NYSE activity, sometimes adding up to as much as 15 percent of reported round-lot trade.

Odd-lot traders were courted. In 1929, John Muir & Co. regularly advertised in the financial press for their trade. "The uncertainty of the Stock Market makes it imperative to diversify your holdings ... Consider how much more secure you would be with 10 shares of stock in each of 10 selections than you would be with 100 shares of any one of them," read one typical solicitation.*

Odd-lot activity was closely monitored for clues to market direction. Garfield A. Drew, publisher of "Drew Odd-Lot Studies," was the best-known student of odd-lot indicators.

But if the investor in less than 100 shares was courted 60 years ago, by the 1950s such an investor was the butt of boardroom jokes and by the 1980s an unwelcome new account at most brokerage firms.

Barron's, New York, September 9, 1929, p. 2, col.1.

Starting in the mid-1960s, odd-lot traders—almost always net buyers previously—turned to the sell side. On balance, selling was heavy and persistent all through the 1980s.

TABLE 6-6   ODD-LOT VOLUME AT NYSE

	On-Balance Buying and Selling (thousands of shares)				
	Net Customer			Net Customer	
Year	Buying	Selling	Year	Buying	Selling
1920	5,122		1955	8,378	
1921	4,252		1956	14,296	
1922	1,697		1957	14,933	
1923	1,664		1958	3,668	
1924		772	1959	14,191	
1925		749	1960	9,300	
1926	801		1961		600
1927	1,747		1962	800	
1928	3,158		1963		14,900
1929	15,463		1964		2,000
1930	13,352		1965		2,900
1931	15,487		1966	13,000	
1932	4,102		1967		15,500
1933		134	1968		26,000
1934		1,078	1969		11,000
1935		4,384	1970		13,100
1936	338		1971		60,300
1937	11,834		1972		53,100
1938	1,396		1973		28,800
1939	1,367		1974		18,500
1940	1,483		1975		40,700
1941		1,287	1976		58,500
1942		199	1977		42,600
1943	2,306		1978		55,900
1944	2,010		1979		66,200
1945	5,855		1980		68,600
1946	10,707		1981		72,500
1947	3,225		1982		87,600
1948	3,147		1983		80,400
1949	622		1984		96,600
1950	708		1985		105,700
1951	7,433		1986		112,100
1952	6,298		1987		76,000
1953	3,478		1988		95,600
1954		633	1989		81,500

Source: *New York Stock Exchange Fact Book.*

VOLUME FALLACIES _____

A common fallacy has it that both bull and bear markets climax in a spectacular volume stampede. Seldom so. Most bear markets die with a whimper. And, since 1916 peak market volume at the NYSE has usually been registered months before the Dow's final bull high, as shown in Table 6-7.

This volume-price divergence in advancing markets has proven a decent indicator of approaching price peaks. In 1987, for example, monthly volume climaxed in January and the Dow in August. The lead time for the volume high has usually been a generous three to nine months.

If bear markets ordinarily expire or climax on low volume, the exceptions stand out vividly, as in 1957 and 1962. Panic moves develop enormous activity at the bottom, as in 1940, 1955 (Ike's attack), and 1987.

In the week ending July 9, 1932, the great depression low was counted on an average full-day volume of just over 711,000 shares, an extremely low level of activity. During the spring, over 40 down-days had witnessed volume of over 1 million shares. Low volume also accompanied price bottoms in 1921 and 1942. The 1974 trough was marked by restrained activity when measured against volume peaks seen earlier in the year.

VOLUME VIGNETTES _____

Lowest full-session volume in the past 100 years at the NYSE occurred on Wednesday, December 30, 1914. Only 50,000 shares changed hands. Thirteen years earlier, a hectic day on May 9, 1901, had seen 3,337,000 shares traded. That was a record which would not be broken until 1925. Last volume day below a million shares was on October 9, 1953.

TABLE 6-7   NYSE VOLUME VERSUS PRICE PEAKS

Bull market high Dow Industrials	Daily volume high	Monthly volume high	Time lag Dow high to monthly volume
Sep 1929	Mar 26, 1929	Nov 1928	10 months
Mar 1937	Jan 13, 1936	Feb 1936	13 months
May 1946	Jan 28, 1946	Jan 1946	4 months
Apr 1956	Feb 29, 1956	Mar 1956	1 month[a]
Jan 1960	Aug 10, 1959	Mar 1959	10 months
Dec 1961	Apr 4,1961	Mar 1961	9 months
Feb 1966	Dec 6, 1965	Dec 1965	2 months
Dec 1968	Jne 13, 1968	May 1968	7 months
Jan 1973	Dec 29, 1972	Nov 1972	2 months
Sep 1976	Feb 20, 1976	Jan 1976	8 months
Apr 1981	Jan 7, 1981	Nov 1980	5 months
Aug 1987	Jan 23, 1987	Jan 1987	7 months

[a]"Market" high came in August, but 15-month extended top for the Dow makes this period complex as a volume study.

Long lags between volume peaks were common until the 1980s. The daily volume record of October 29, 1929 would stand until 1968. The annual volume in 1882, 116 million shares, was not surpassed for 17 years. It was not until 1919 that the yearly trade figure of 1906 was broken.

Every volume record of the past century, however, was broken and then broken again in the 1980s. But turnover activity (shares traded divided by average shares listed) has never approached the figures seen in the first decade of this century. The flotation of U.S. Steel and the frantic railroad market of 1901 pushed the ratio to 319 percent. In 1987 the figure was only 73 percent, but that was a huge increase over the low-teen figures seen so often between 1952 and 1964.

In the years between the wars, the NYSE's annual reports lamented the low turnover rates, but the glory days of the 1900s never returned. In the black war year of 1942, volume was at the lowest full-year level since 1913 and the turnover was a pathetic 9 percent. At the Curb, turnover was below 4 percent.

Curb/AMEX

Volume at the New York Curb (the American Stock Exchange after 1953) has fluctuated more widely than at the Big Board. Between 1921 and 1929, Curb volume increased 30 times, while NYSE volume was up less than seven times. On one unique day, July 6, 1929, Curb activity exceeded that of its rival. Traders flocked to the Curb action at the end of World War II and again in the late 1960s when annual volume at the junior exchange reached its peak relative to the NYSE; activity was nearly 50 percent of that at the Exchange.

Turnover rate, as at the Big Board, has dwindled. In 1989, it was 35.1 percent; the peak since 1929 was 65.5 percent in 1968.

7

Major Stock Exchanges

--- **U.S. BOURSES** ---

THE NEW YORK STOCK EXCHANGE ────────────────────────────

The Exchange's roots go back 200 years, to the Buttonwood Agreement of 1792, which banded 24 coffee-house brokers loosely together. The sycamore tree which shaded the brokers was at 68-70 Wall.

Subscribers agreed to give each other preference in trade and to enforce a minimum commission schedule. The latter financial philosophy was so sound that it endured until Gerald Ford's first full presidential year.

In 1817, the New York Stock & Exchange Board was formed and indoor quarters were leased. The present Exchange building was completed in 1920.

New York never gained the extensive international listings of London, but by default became the world's financial center shortly after the outbreak of World War I. It remains the most famous of all exchanges, but is no longer the largest, ranking second to Tokyo.

THE AMERICAN STOCK EXCHANGE _____

In the olden days, the Wall Street Journal's standing head for New York Curb quotations was "Outside Market." Which is exactly what it was. The al fresco madness continued both summer and winter, with brokers on the street and phone clerks located in the windows of nearby office buildings.

Several locations, including uptown hotel annexes, had served the Curb players for decades but scrums for the final outdoor years blocked the street opposite 44 Broad. In 1921, the brokers finally moved indoors, despite great carping from fresh air fans.

It was about time, for Curb trading had developed a notorious reputation. The standard caveat used by the *Commercial & Financial Chronicle* in reporting prices read:

> On the "Curb" any security may be dealt in and anyone can meet there and make prices and have them included in the lists of those who make it a business to furnish daily records of the transactions.

> The possibility that fictitious transactions may creep in, or even that dealings in spurious securities may be included, should, hence, always be kept in mind . . . We give them for what it may be worth.[1]

But the addition of a Trinity Place address, ticker service, and a roaring bull market brought a respect of sorts and tremendous volume. A membership at the Curb, valued as low as $3,750 in 1921, reached $254,000 in 1929, outperforming the results of all public money managers.

Times were tough in the 1930s and early 1940s, but a revival of speculation, particularly in the Canadians, boosted business in the next decade when the Curb sought to rinse its still colorful reputation with a name change, to the American Stock Exchange.

Its best days came in the late 1960s, when volume peaked relative to the NYSE. The enormous institutional trade of the 1980s largely bypassed the AMEX, and relative activity slumped to a distressing record low.

NASDAQ STOCK MARKET _____

The National Association of Securities Dealers Automated Quotation system (NASDAQ) for unlisted stocks is an electronic stock market, but it is not a stock exchange in the physical sense.

Dealer markets for securities traded in the system are displayed on dealer NASDAQ screens and orders can be entered directly over the terminals. There are over 5,000 listings and share volume is not far below that at the NYSE, although average prices are considerably lower.

This over-the-counter (OTC) trading system was developed in 1971 and

_____

[1]The Commercial & Financial Chronicle, New York, January 24, 1920, p. 354, col. 1.

some feel that this screen-based alternative to exchange floor trading is the wave of the future. Full NASDAQ service is already available in the United Kingdom.

OTHER AMERICAN EXCHANGES

Only the Consolidated Stock Exchange and the AMEX, originally the outdoor Curb, have seriously challenged the NYSE on its own turf in the past 100 years.

But many regional exchanges flourished at one time or another. Philadelphia's brokers had organized in 1790. Boston, established in 1834, became prominent in rail and copper mine financing. The mining exchanges of San Francisco, Spokane, and Salt Lake City, among others, had exciting periods of great prosperity.

Chicago, Los Angeles, Cincinnati, Detroit, and Baltimore had regional importance at one time or another. Today, there are only seven "national regulated" exchanges, as recognized by the SEC. The regionals have consolidated with most of their volume coming from "dual trading." Shares of local and regional corporations, the former bulwark of trading at the smaller exchanges, have mostly moved to the NASDAQ system.

The C.B.O.E.

The Chicago Board Options Exchange, an offshoot of the venerable Chicago Board of Trade, was the first of its breed (1973) and has introduced millions to the intricacies and risks of listed puts and calls. Twice as much fun can be had with options on index futures. By report, Options Anonymous now has more chapters than AA.

But the options concept, first popularized over a century ago by Russell Sage, the "father" of options, is now an integral part of institutional trading and will be with us for a long time. Options are also actively traded at the AMEX, at Philadelphia, New York, and at the Pacific Coast Exchange. The basics have been widely copied in the larger foreign markets.

───────── LEADING FOREIGN BOURSES ─────────

TOKYO STOCK EXCHANGE

Japan's many stock exchanges were formally closed during the early years of the postwar occupation and it was not until 1949 that General Douglas MacArthur authorized their reopening. Tokyo would be the first, at mid-May.

Japan's economic miracle of a strong yen and astounding, if inscrutable, price-earnings ratios have pushed Tokyo into first place among the world's stock markets. Noumera Securities is the largest stock firm in the world and Japanese brokerage firms have become an enormous world presence.

Happily, the Tokyo market has been a constructive price influence. The Nikkei index climbed from below 400 to nearly 39,000 in 40 years. And it was an especially strong leader in the difficult period following the crash of 1987.

By April 1988, while U.S. pessimists were seeing a rerun of the 1929–1930 action, Tokyo was able to grind out a new all-time high. And it continued to score new records right into the end of the decade.

The vitality of the Pacific Rim should guarantee Tokyo's importance for the rest of this century, though skeptics wondered if the high multiples awarded Japanese stocks—about 55 times earnings—would bloom again after the disastrous slump of 1990. The sun also sets, they claim.

Tokyo's Nikkei 225 index, at a record 38,916 on the last day of 1989, is the most widely quoted indicator of the market's health. The oil crisis of 1990 helped drive the index down to 20,222 in early October of that year and the chilling loss of 48% matched the parameters of the great declines witnessed at New York over the past century. At the year end, the loss was still 40 percent.

LONDON INTERNATIONAL STOCK EXCHANGE

London, the world's third largest stock market, remains its most international. Even 100 years ago, Kaffirs, colonials, Indians, and American rails were actively traded there, the tides of empire and British credits having brought thousands of listings from around the world.

"How's London?" was the opening gambit for Wall Street's active traders a century ago. London quotes had an immense influence on prices and London selling could quickly topple the New York market. Communications were not as archaic as today's children might think. Arbitrage was common and practical, a round-trip telegraphic exchange to London requiring only about four minutes.

Despite the size of Tokyo and the fame of New York, the exotic listings at the London International Stock Exchange continue to excite the imagination. Securities from 35 countries fall into the tables; tea and rubber plantations, tin workings, mines from around the world, Chilean rails, the historic Penisular & Oriental Steam Navigation Co. and some curious bond antiquities of another age, defaulted paper from Bulgaria, Czechoslovakia, Montenegro, Saxony, and Yugoslavia. The best-known index at London is the Financial Times-Stock Exchange 100-share index (FT-SE 100).

CANADIAN MARKETS

Toronto ranks second in North American equity volume, after the NYSE, and Montreal has a good trade. Mining and natural resource shares get great attention at both exchanges. Penny-stock gamblers and the brave at heart take their business to Vancouver, home of some really junior mining promotions, telephone pitch-men and disappointing price executions.

OTHER WORLD BOURSES _____

International stock market competition has broadened substantially during recent years, boosted by the ease of communication and 24-hour trading.

The historic bourses of Europe in Paris, Berlin, and Zurich have seen greatly increased activity around the continent. Copenhagen, Stockholm, and Oslo have viable markets and the Baltic stock push has even reached Finland, from whence it is but a short jump to St. Petersburg, once an active European market with heavy French and German investments. The surprising political events in Eastern Europe focused attention on German stock exchanges in late 1989. Frankfurt dominates trading volume there.

Milan is the standout among the Italian exchanges, while the Madrid Stock Exchange is expected to grow rapidly as Spain's economy expands. Across the Atlantic, Mexico City's Balsa cut a few ears during the decade, despite a puny peso, and Brazil's Sao Paulo Exchange enjoyed some boisterous activity.

The great growth over the last several decades has been around the Pacific Rim. Osaka, the "other" Japanese market, does a huge business. Taiwan and Korea boomed, as did the newly consolidated Australian exchanges. Hong Kong had plenty of excitement; in fact, it was a bit too much at times and their exchange, like Brazil, was forced into unplanned closings because of stressful conditions.

Wall Street's aggressive merchandising of "national" and global funds has helped bourses around the world and the adventuresome can now invest in exotic locales without dashing off a cable. Kuala Lumpur, New Zealand, the Philippines, Thailand, Taiwan, and Korea have all attracted special attention.

Barron's regularly reports quotations from 17 world markets in addition to prices from Montreal and Toronto, but lags far behind London's *Financial Times* in foreign listings.

8

Almanacs

THE DECENNIAL PATTERNS

The "5" year in every decade for more than a century has been a market winner, usually a substantial one. This and other long-term patterns can be observed in Table 8-1, where each year's gain or loss is placed in a decennial column. All of the zero years, for example, fall into the same column and the cycle of the decades, including magic "5s" can be easily observed.

Edgar Lawrence Smith and Anthony Gaubis pioneered the decennial study 50 years ago and it continues to fascinate. Further work was done by the remarkable technician, Edson Gould, for Anametrics.

Smith and Gaubis cut market charts into ten-year segments to try and pinpoint decennial patterns and Gould developed fascinating charts of the various decade patterns.

The "5" years have been obvious perfection and the "8s" have an excellent

268

TABLE 8-1 THE DECENNIAL PATTERNS

Decades	Zero	1st	2nd	3rd	4th	5th	6th	7th	8th	9th
						% Price changes through 11 decades years of decade					
1880–1889	+	+	−	−	−	+	+	−	+	+
1890–1899	−14	+18	− 7	−25	− 0.	+ 2	− 2	+21	+23	+ 9
1900–1909	+ 7	+ 7	− 0.	−24	+42	+38	− 2	−38	+47	+15
1910–1919	−18	+ 0.	+ 8	−10	− 5	+82	− 4	−22	+11	+31
1920–1929	−33	+13	+22	− 3	+26	+30	+ 0.	+29	+48	−17
1930–1939	−34	−53	−23	+67	+ 4	+39	+25	−33	+28	− 3
1940–1949	−13	−15	+ 8	+14	+12	+27	− 8	+ 2	− 2	+13
1950–1959	+18	+14	+ 8	− 4	+44	+21	+ 2	−13	+34	+17
1960–1969	− 9	+19	−11	+17	+15	+11	−19	+15	+ 4	−15
1970–1979	+ 5	+ 6	+15	−17	−28	+38	+18	−17	− 3	+ 4
1980–1989	+15	− 9	+20	+20	− 4	+28	+23	+ 2	+12	+27
Plus years	5	8	6	4	6	11	6	5	9	8
Minus years	6	3	5	7	5	0	5	6	2	3
% change	−76%	0	+40%	+35%	+106%	+316%	+33%	−54%	+202%	—

DECENNIAL HIGHS AND LOWS

	Highs	Lows
0 year:	1930	1950
1 year:	1881	1921
2 year:		1932, 1942, 1962, 1982
3 year:	1973	
4 year:		1884, 1914, 1974
5 year:		
6 year:	1906, 1946, 1966	1896
7 year:		1907
8 year:		
9 year:	1899, 1919, 1929, 1959, 1989	

1880–1889 annual change plus or minus only. Yearly percentage changes from 1890–1899 are for the Dow Rails. The 1900–1989 changes are for the Dow Industrials.

record while the zero years have been the worst performers—bad losses in 1920 and 1930 and no big winners. Furthermore, they narrowly escaped red ink in 1900 and 1970 when the Industrials marked bear market lows in September and May, respectively. In 1990, the neagative pressure was repeated.

The 1980s closely duplicated Edson Gould's decennial charts of the previous nine decades. An important low in the second year (1982) was followed by a high in the seventh, followed by a sharp drop and then another peak in the popular ninth year.

Although a cabal of scientific types insist that the calendar for each decade ends in the "zero" year, decennial Table 8-1 opts for the populist view that the 1980s, by example, ended in 1989 and not December 31, 1990.

—— MONTHLY ALMANACS AND BOXSCORES: A 101-YEAR —— HISTORY

THE MONTHLY ALMANACS

The search for calendar secrets of the stock market was already old a century ago. And the quarrels about seasonal verities.

On January 5, 1893, the *Wall Street Journal* reported the following from a contributor. "There is a widespread belief in the street that we always have a January rise . . . There has not been in six years a continuous rise in either January or February, such as we often see in May. Only once in that time . . . did the average rise more than one per cent above the level of the early January high-water mark."[1]

Naturally, May turned into a disaster that year, and January's sharp rise must have disappointed the contributor. But the search for calendar secrets continues.

The "January barometer" begins the monthly almanacs, which measure monthly performance for the past 101 years, using the 20-Stock Average until 1896 and the Dow Industrials since that time. Tables 8-2, 8-3 and 8-4, starting on page 282, summarize monthly data. Other monthly statistics can be found in Tables 5-9 and 5-10, pages 236–239.

Note that the yearly advance-decline figures will not perfectly balance since the NYSE was closed during World War I in the months of August to November, 1914, leaving their totals one shy of the figures for the other eight months.

---

[1]The Wall Street Journal, New York, January 5, 1893, p. 2, col. 3.

THE JANUARY BAROMETER _____

January's market performance fascinates Wall Street. For as January goes, so goes the stock-market year. At least, most of the time. Since 1890, the market (the 20-Stock Average through 1896 and the Dow Industrials since then) has advanced 65 times in January and continued for a yearly gain 47 times.

Thirty six January declines have led into bearish years 23 times, giving the month's bull/bear indicator a forecasting record of 70%. Of the combined 31 month-to-year divergences, moreover, only nine have occurred since the end of World War II.

Still, investors should not assume that any seasonal trend or pattern can be followed blindly; over popularity breeds deceit. The numbers, too, can be misleading. In 1934, the Dow rushed up by nearly 13% in the last three weeks of January to post a solid monthly gain. But the year's high was but five trading days away and stubborn longs would suffer a 23% February–July slump.

The market bounced back to make the year a "barometer" winner but January's closing level would not be topped until late spring of 1935.

Carping critics claim that January's bullish forecasting success is the mindless beneficiary of the market's tendency to advance in any given year (61 ups from 1890 through 1989). The inference is that other months might handle the forecasting chores just as well in a secular bull market. January's natural calendar leadership assures its continued domination, however, among students of calendar and seasonal minutia.

January's prestige has also been enhanced by a traditional early year rally, spurred by an automatic reflex among December's battered selling victims. But the winter indicator does have a dark side. When it has failed, it has been a killer.

In 1930, a splendid rally in January lifted hopes that the 1929 debacle had ended. The year ended with the second worst loss in history. More recently, after a bad 1973 market, a healthy January push in 1974 fostered hopes for better times, but the year ended in disaster.

Investors should beware of a weak January after a strong December. It has very negative implications. Such ominous action was seen most recently in 1990 and earlier in 1960, 1962, 1973, and 1977, all bad market years. The action in the first week of January also requires special attention. Many dramatic sea changes have been recorded in that short period. Annual highs have been registered nine times since 1890 in the opening week and annual lows ten times—a rare concentration of major reversals.

The Super Bowl indicator also needs attention. This foolish, but remarkably lucky indicator, forecasts market advances in years when the National Football League wins the Super Bowl. Declines should follow victories by the American League team. Iraq blindsided the indicator in 1990, however.

JANUARY BOXSCORE

Annual Highs and Lows

Highs: 14 Since 1950: 6   Lows: 25 Since 1950: 18

Best & Worst Performances

Percent Gains	Percent Losses	Yearly Record
1976 14.4	1916 8.6	65 advances
1975 14.2	1960 8.4	36 declines
1987 13.8	1978 7.4	

Extraordinary Milestones

First Dow close over 100—January 12, 1906   First Dow over 1000 (intraday)—January 18, 1966
First Dow close over 2000—January 19, 1987

Major Tops and Bottoms

Bull Markets (3) Jan 19, 1906. Height of the copper boom.
                  Jan 5, 1960. "Soaring Sixties" ground-looped.
                  Jan 11, 1973. Institutional mania peaked.
Bear Markets (0): No bear market low recorded in January.

SUPER JANUARY 1987

Action in the first month of 1987 crowded the record book, with the Dow recording the largest monthly gain in history of 253 points. Dow 2000 was easily topped.

A buyers' panic advanced the market for 13 consecutive days. Volume exceeded 200 million on six days. On January 23, the Dow fell 100 points intraday as 302 million shares changed hands. All the figures were Wall Street records.

FEBRUARY—FEW VALENTINES

There have been few valentines for either bull or bear in Februarys of recent years. Prior to World War I, the month recorded more annual lows than any other period save December. In recent decades, however, February has been a winter dead spot, though the undertow of the great January advance of 1986 brought it modest glory. While the secular numbers favor the bears, the second-month figures have been balanced since 1970 with eleven advances and ten declines.

February action in recent years has often been a reflex, trying to reverse or consolidate an overly strong or weak January. However, February bottom picking after a weak January has been a dangerous game. Bargain hunters under these conditions were smashed in such notorious years as 1907, 1920, 1932, and 1973, among others.

The month's most dramatic action came in the 1930s. Its best ever percentage gain was in 1931 and its worst loss came just two years later as an epidemic of bank closures panicked the nation.

FEBRUARY BOXSCORE

Annual Highs and Lows		
Highs: 5 Since 1950: 1		Lows: 10 Since 1950: 3
Best & Worst Performances		
Gains (%)	Losses (%)	Yearly Record
1931 13.2	1933 15.6	48 advances
1986 8.8	1920 12.1	53 declines
1932 6.9	1946 7.1	
Major Tops and Bottoms		

Bull Markets (1): Feb 9, 1966. The top, Dow 995, would not be exceeded until 1972.
Bear Markets (1): Feb 28, 1978. Ended the third and final bear market of the 1970s.

MARCH—GAINING STRENGTH

The emergence of super first-quarter strength in the market has assisted March into a top calendar ranking. Over the past 20 years, it has a better ranking than January, with 14 gains and only seven losses.

It has done this by riding the first-quarter whirlwind, which has rushed stocks higher in January and February of such strong bull years as 1971, 1972, 1975, 1976, 1983, 1986, and 1987. In each instance, "overbought" got even more overbought as March added further gains to an explosive advance. Even in 1974, March performed strongly in the first two weeks before succumbing to a bearish tidal wave.

This recent luster comes after a so-so record between 1890 and 1940, when the month was seldom in the limelight, save in 1937 and 1938. March's record loss, in 1938, ended a short, brutal bear market which had begun exactly one year earlier.

MARCH BOXSCORE

Annual Highs and Lows		
Highs: 5 Since 1950: 1		Lows: 8 Since 1950: 1
Best & Worst Performances		
Gains (%)	Losses (%)	Yearly Record
1920 12.6	1938 23.7	60 advances
1908 11.5	1907 11.5	41 declines
1899 11.3	1939 10.5	

Major Tops and Bottoms

Bull Markets (2):	Mar 4, 1892. Minor, manipulated Rail peak. It was part of a longer-term bear move.
	Mar 10, 1937. Fed tightened and Dow's second largest advance turned quickly into severe depression.
Bear Markets (1):	Mar 31, 1938. Hitler's march into Austria rushed bear move to climax.

APRIL—NO TAXING PROBLEMS

April is the most significant month for every American taxpayer, but the market impact of income-tax worries is, paradoxically, felt more keenly in December.

Tax selling in that month and not selling for taxes in April is the important market influence. April's second half is usually weaker than the opening 14 days, when one would presume heavy stock liquidation to raise tax funds. IRA investment demand has apparently outgunned the IRS in the April 1–15 period.

The greatest monthly gain in the history of the Industrials occurred in April 1933—plus 40.2 percent—as America's confidence revived, along with the banks, following drastic economic steps by the new FDR administration.

While the 56 advances versus 45 declines for April since 1890 gives the month a slight historical nod, the figures are now somewhat deceiving. In the 1950s and 1960s, April was a strong calendar play, advancing in 15 of 20 years but since 1970, the figure has become average: 11 of 21.

APRIL BOXSCORE

Annual Highs and Lows		
Highs: 5 Since 1950: 3		Lows: 5 Since 1950: 1

Best & Worst Performances		
Gains (%)	Losses (%)	Yearly Record
1933 40.2	1932 23.4	56 advances
1915 18.0	1931 12.3	45 declines
1938 12.5	1920 9.0	

Major Tops and Bottoms

Bull Markets (2):	Apr 6, 1956. Great postwar boom paused for a "breather."
	Apr 27, 1981. Soaring interest rates finally choked off the speculative inflation boom.
Bear Markets (2):	Apr 8, 1939. Mini-bear turned quickly into a mini bull.
	Apr 28, 1942. World War II low.

MAY—TREACHEROUS _____

May has proven to be a difficult month to forecast and has a record of treacherous behavior, with last-half action usually reversing or consolidating any trend of the first few weeks. Since 1960, the month's record has been disappointing for bulls, with 18 losers including the hard hits of 1962 and 1970.

The record improved to neutral in the 1980s, at 5 to 5. Even then, the win side was difficult. In 1987, the Dow gained five points for the month. But first it suffered a collapse of nearly 200 intraday Dow points before making a miracle recovery.

Buyers of stock on any May weakness at least know that the postulated "summer rally" will within a few weeks give them a lot of lip service. More than six summer rallies of over 10 percent since World War II had their footing in May. In 1970 and 1987 the rallies amounted to over 20 percent.

The secular record is slightly negative, compared to recent action. May's three worst losses all occurred more than 50 years ago. The 1940 Dunkerque slide was the heaviest decline for any month between 1938 and 1987.

MAY BOXSCORE

Annual Highs and Lows		
Highs: 2 Since 1950: 1		Lows: 4 Since 1950: 2
Best & Worst Performances		
Gains (%)	Losses (%)	Yearly Record
1897 14.7	1940 21.7	49 advances
1919 13.6	1932 20.3	52 declines
1933 13.5	1931 15.0	
Major Tops and Bottoms		

Bull Markets (1): May 29, 1946. End of the great World War II bull market.
Bear Markets (1): May 26, 1970. A day of record panic.

JUNE—A RARE MONTH _____

June's consistency over 75 years with 13 gains and 12 losses in each 25-year segment through 1989 has been rare. The long-term equality does conceal, however, a recent strong bias to the upside.

In the harsh environment of 1974, June eked out a small advance and added reputation by then gaining in 13 of 16 years. Just when trend followers were getting the picture, June 1989 became a cropper; the last week of the month saw the Dow suffer its worst loss since March 1988. In 1990, June was a bit dicey, gaining barely four points after a late, sharp slide.

THE SUMMER RALLY

By a loose definition of summer (Wall Street places the solstice some-time in May) the "summer rally" has become a well-worn crutch of the bulls.

In the olden days, it seemed to work as hopes for a bountiful grain and cotton harvest firmed into August. Good crops meant good rail traffic.

The seasonal play got its greatest boost from patterns of the violent 1930s. In 1931, the Dow rallied 29 percent in just over four weeks within the month of June. In 1932, the lift-off was a sizzling 94 percent, July to September. In 1938, a 35 percent gain was recorded from the last day of May to early August. Gains of 22 percent and 20 percent in 1935 and 1939 helped the legend.

Best summer gain of the 1980s came in 1987. The incredible point advance of 516 points from May 20 to August 25 amounted to 23 percent, the best since the 1930s. And, along with a 21 percent increase in 1980, it helps keep the perennial dreams of a rich summer romance alive.

Buying stocks in June to sell six months later in the seasonally strong December period worked wonders in the 1950s and 1960s, but the choppy 1970s shut the game down. The same periodicity worked again in the 1980s, but then most bullish seasonals did, thanks to the long advance.

Institutional window dressing for the first half is credited for the luster June has reflected over the past 15 years.

JUNE BOXSCORE

Annual Highs and Lows		
Highs: 3 Since 1950: 0		Lows: 5 Since 1950: 2

Best & Worst Performances		
Gains (%)	Losses (%)	Yearly Record
1938 24.3	1930 17.7	49 advances
1931 16.9	1923 9.9	52 declines
1929 12.2	1962 8.5	

Major Tops and Bottoms

Bull Markets (2): Jne 4, 1890. The 20-stock advance had begun in April 1888 prior to the chronology of this volume.

Jne 17, 1901. High for Industrials. Rails diverged to the upside until 1902.

Bear Markets (2): Jne 13, 1949. Triple bottom against 1946 and 1947 lows.

Jne 26, 1962. Short but nasty Kennedy Panic recorded Dow's lowest level for the decade.

JULY—A SUMMER RALLY?

There will always be a "summer rally," even if Wall Street has to stretch the time frame over a five-month period from May to September. July thus benefits from its strategic calendar location and is a dependable part of the summer fun, though one of the great summer rallies, up 29 percent in 1931, lasted but four weeks—all in the month of June. The record hummer was in 1932: Dow up 94 percent from July 8 to September 7.

July also benefits from a sort of patriotic exuberance around the 4th, but the enthusiasm usually erodes before the month end, though 1989 was a strong exception. July's bullish record is good with 60 gains versus 41 losses since 1890. The strong odds, however, are tilted by older statistics, including 11 straight advances from 1949 through 1959.

Since 1965, the trend has changed for the worse with 15 losers against only 11 gainers. In the great bull year of 1986, July's camp followers were badly assaulted.

JULY BOXSCORE

Annual Highs and Lows		
Highs: 6 Since 1950: 3		Lows: 6 Since 1950: 1
Best & Worst Performances		
Gains (%)	Losses (%)	Yearly Record
1932 26.7	1893 18.4	60 advances
1908 10.7	1903 14.1	41 declines
1927 9.9	1914 11.4	
Major Tops and Bottoms		

Bull Markets (1): July 16, 1990. Kuwait invasion left 2999.75 as great top.
Bear Markets (3): Jly 26, 1893. Erie bankruptcy was the bad news.
Jly 30, 1914. World War I panic. The NYSE was forced to close down the next day. The "holiday" would last four months.
Jly 8, 1932. Low of the great depression.

AUGUST—STATS DECEIVING

August's bullish statistics rank second only to those in December. But its long-term 66–34 won-lost record is deceiving. The biggest part of the win side was compiled before 1950. Since 1970, the record barely favors the bulls.

Agricultural prospects were vital to the market in the olden days. Good crops meant good rail traffic. The crop outlook, good in most years, generally became clear in August and made it the best month for the Rails. But the Industrials have enjoyed some great August prosperity, also. From 1922 through 1936, the Dow advanced each August, a notable record.

In recent years, August's performance has been no better than average, possibly because the affluent and money managers are mostly off to the shore, the mountains, or Europe. Nevertheless, since World War II, the month has added a pleasant bonus to sizeable summer rallies (more than 10 percent) in 1956, 1959, 1962, 1984, and 1987.

The month became most noteworthy in 1987, when August recorded its only bull market peak. If the details of the 1987 high are already fuzzy, the 1,000-point Dow air pocket which followed will be long remembered.

AUGUST BOXSCORE

Annual Highs and Lows		
Highs: 3 Since 1950: 1		Lows: 2 Since 1950: 1

Best & Worst Performances		
Gains (%)	Losses (%)	Yearly Record
1932 34.8	1974 10.4	66 advances
1897 14.5	1990 10.0	34 declines
1891 13.0	1917 9.1	

Major Tops and Bottoms

Bull Markets (1): Aug 25, 1987. Dow still ended with gain for the month.
Bear Markets (3): Aug 8, 1896. All-time low for Dow Industrials.
                            Aug 24, 1921. Postwar crash ended.
                            Aug 12, 1982. Lower interest rates brought startling reversal.

SEPTEMBER MOURNS

September is a time for extreme caution—and not just because of memories of 1929. The month has the worst of all calendar records. The bearish season has worsened in recent years, and bulls have been forced into mourning in 17 of the past 22 years. This is the worst record in the history of the Dow Industrials. September is now regarded as a pivotal, treacherous month, more closely analyzed than any other period save January. Bearish reversals and swift acceleration of existing declines as in 1931, 1937, 1946, and 1987 have been common. While August has been a bullish month 19 times since 1960, September action has reversed that trend a surprising 15 times.

New car models, back-to-school shopping, and the vibrancy of autumn help focus attention on September's indications for fourth-quarter prosperity. The Labor Day week in particular is seen to offer important clues as to the market's direction. A decline in that holiday-shortened week is viewed as ominous.

The greatest monthly loss in history came in September 1931—not October 1929—after a post-Labor Day downer, which duplicated the performance of 1929. No indicator is perfect, to be sure. In 1987, a deceitful Labor Day weekly advance was the last chance for a decent exit from the market.

SEPTEMBER BOXSCORE

Annual Highs and Lows		
Highs: 9 Since 1950: 4		Lows: 4 Since 1950: 2

Best & Worst Performances		
Gains (%)	Losses (%)	Yearly Record
1939 13.5	1931 30.7	41 advances
1915 11.6	1930 14.8	59 declines
1916 11.5	1903 13.9	

Major Tops and Bottoms
Bull Markets (6): Sep 4, 1895. End of weak rally in longer-term decline.
Sep 5, 1899. Big spec play ended for Industrials—but not Rails.
Sep 30, 1912. End of very restrained advance, part of longer-term decline.
Sep 12, 1939. Early war-buying frenzy peaked.
Sep 3, 1929. The classic.
Sep 21, 1976. Dow had made no headway since March.
Bear Markets (2): Sep 25, 1911. Close double bottom against 1910 low.
Sep 24, 1900. Hopes for McKinley reelection turned market.

OCTOBER—A "BEAR KILLER"

October's reputation as a bear killer comes largely because it has experienced so many violent confrontations with the enraged beast. Actually, only the bear markets of 1957, 1960, and 1966 were official victims of the October reputation. But conditions of extreme panic have often been dramatically reversed or moderated during the period, as in 1937, 1946, and 1974. The market low in that last year came in October, though a pair of sullen performers in the Dow-30 dragged that index to a new low in December. And 1987? The bear may have been killed, but it was a frightful victory.

In 1914, when the NYSE was closed from August through November, the actual low for stocks (in unofficial off-board trading) came in October, so that remains an unofficial tally for the bear-killer reputation.

Other nasty October encounters came with the Cuban missile crisis in 1962 and the twin "October massacres" of 1978–1979.

Despite the month's reputation, the secular advance/decline ratio of 53 to 47 is not impressive. October 1929 and 1987 are paired as frightening bear legends, but both September 1931 and March 1938 caused more Dow damage.

OCTOBER BOXSCORE

Annual Highs and Lows		
Highs: 5 Since 1950: 3		Lows: 6 Since 1950: 4

Best & Worst Performances		
Gains (%)	Losses (%)	Yearly Record
1982 10.7	1987 23.2	53 advances
1974 9.5	1929 20.3	47 declines
1931 9.1	1907 14.8	

Major Tops and Bottoms

Bull Markets (0): No bull market has ended in October.
Bear Markets (4): Oct 22, 1957. High-volume end to the Sputnik I shock.
Oct 24, 1960. Mini-bear discounted Kennedy victory.
Oct 6, 1966. Another mini-bear finished after nine months.
Oct 19, 1987. End of a classic panic. Dow down 508 points with NYSE volume of 604 million shares.

NOVEMBER'S ELECTION QUIRKS

November has great historical strength and, additionally, ushers in a three-month period of supurb market performance—the strongest off-bias "quarter" of the year. But the month has often suffered from extreme quirkiness in years when the GOP counted a White House victory.

Even George Bush's victory, a strong upset after the late summer polls, saw the market droop after the election. Republican presidential victories have been well discounted since Herbert Hoover's win in 1928. Ike's second election saw November as a down-month, a disappointment repeated for Ronald Reagan in 1984. Nixon escaped the quirkiness, but only by weeks. In-place bull markets ended shortly after both his presidential election victories.

Otherwise, November boasts a solid record of 27 advances versus 14 losses since 1950. In the period, its record is almost the equal of December and January, and it is the superior buying month, given the strong early winter seasonals. Tax-selling victims, however, will become even cheaper in December.

NOVEMBER BOXSCORE

Annual Highs and Lows		
Highs: 12 Since 1950: 4		Lows: 7 Since 1950: 3

Best & Worst Performances		
Gains (%)	Losses (%)	Yearly Record
1928 16.3	1904 14.3	59 advances
1904 14.3	1973 14.0	41 declines
1900 12.8	1937 10.6	

Major Tops and Bottoms

Bull Markets (4):	Nov 19, 1909. Five years of market apathy and low volume would follow.
	Nov 21, 1916. "Peace scare" ended war boom.
	Nov 3, 1919. Tight money torched World War I victory celebration.
	Nov 12, 1938. "Peace in our time" euphoria topped.
Bear Markets (2):	Nov 9, 1903. End of "Rich Man's Panic."
	Nov 15, 1907. J. P. Morgan calmed last of the old-time panics.

DECEMBER—"YES, VIRGINIA . . ."

"Yes, Virginia, there is a Santa Claus" at the NYSE. Since 1890, records show 71 advances for the Dow against but 30 losses in the month of December.

December is the most jolly month at the Exchange. Since 1940, the Dow has scored 18 annual highs during the period, 26 in the past 100 years.

The post-Christmas sessions are reliably bullish, influenced by a relief from tax selling. In 16 years of this century, the Dow has closed on its absolute yearly high in the period between Christmas and New Year's.

Despite a deserved reputation for reliable gains, large trading profits have been scarce. December has never enjoyed a double-digit percentage gain. A skein of advances—19 in 21 years—at mid-century realized average profits of just over 3 percent.

Only twice since 1924 has December brought the best advance of the year for the DJIA, despite the month's impressive statistics. The Rail-Transports index, over the same period, has recorded its best yearly gain in eight Decembers.

Part of the cause is the great attention attracted to "tax bargains," fallen market favorites being sacrificed on the IRS altar. Some trading strategies call for a switch from large gainers into these battered tax victims.

December's party is not just for the month, but helps celebrate the yearly trend—61 advancing years since 1890, including eight in the 1980s. Institutional window dressing is yet another spur to December's progress.

DECEMBER BOXSCORE

Annual Highs and Lows		
Highs: 26 Since 1950: 14		Lows: 11 Since 1950: 3

Best & Worst Performances		
Gains (%)	Losses (%)	Yearly Record
1924 8.2	1931 17.0	71 advances
1971 7.1	1899 12.5	30 declines
1905 7.0	1916 10.4	

Major Tops and Bottoms	
Bull Markets (2):	Dec 13, 1961. Speculators ran out of shove.
	Dec 3, 1968. Ratcheting interest rates killed the "sizzle market."
Bear Markets (3):	Dec 8, 1890. Baring crisis climaxed intrayear bear move.
	Dec 19, 1917. War instigated selling finally at end.
	Dec 6, 1974. Market low came in October, but Dow persisted.

ALMANAC OF ANNUAL HIGHS AND LOWS

TABLE 8-2 DOW JONES INDUSTRIALS MONTHLY ALMANAC OF CLOSING HIGHS AND LOWS

	Highs						Lows					
January:	1906 1940 1977	1907 1941 1984	1910 1953	1913 1960	1917 1962	1920 1973 (14)	1905 1945 1961 1976	1918 1950 1963 1983	1922 1951 1964 1985	1927 1954 1967 1986	1936 1955 1972 1988	1943 1956 1975 1989 (24)
February:	1903	1931	1934	1966		(4)	1908 1933	1909 1944	1912 1958	1915 1959	1919 1978	1928 (11)
March:	1914	1923	1932	1937	1974	(5)	1898 1948	1904 1968	1925	1926	1935	1938 (8)
April:	1902	1930	1956	1971	1981	(5)	1897	1916	1939	1942	1980	(5)
May:	1946	1969				(2)	1924	1947	1952	1970		(4)
June:	1901	1911	1948			(3)	1913	1940	1949	1962	1965	(5)
July:	1933	1943	1947	1957	1975	1990 (6)	1906	1910 1914	1932	1934	1984	(6)
August:	1898	1926	1987			(3)	1921	1982				(2)
September:	1897 1967	1899 1976	1912 1978	1929	1939	1951 (9)	1900	1911	1953	1981		(4)
October:	1918	1922	1979	1988	1989	(5)	1923 1990	1946	1957	1960	1966	1987 (7)
November:	1908 1936	1909 1938	1916 1950	1919 1964	1925 1980	1935 1983 (12)	1903 1979	1907	1929	1937	1971	1977 (7)
December:	1900 1927 1952 1963 1985	1904 1928 1954 1965 1986	1905 1942 1955 1968	1915 1944 1958 1970	1921 1945 1959 1972	1924 1949 1961 1982 (26) (94)	1899 1931	1901 1941	1902 1969	1917 1973	1920 1974	1930 (11) (94)

TABLE 8-3   DOW JONES RAIL-TRANSPORTS[a] MONTHLY ALMANAC OF CLOSING HIGHS AND LOWS

Month	Highs						Lows					
January	1893 1914 1953 1984	1903 1917 1957	1906 1921 1960	1907 1932 1970	1910 1940 1973	1913 1949 1974 (19)	1894 1936 1955 1971 1988	1901 1943 1958 1975 1989	1902 1944 1961 1976	1918 1945 1963 1983	1922 1952 1964 1985	1927 1954 1967 1986 (26)
February	1896 1966	1931 1969	1934	1947	1951	1962 (8)	1908 1928	1909 1933	1912 1948	1915 1979	1920	1924 (10)
March	1892	1923	1930	1937		(4)	1904 1978	1925 1980	1926	1935	1938	1968 (8)
April	1899	1972	1981			(3)	1897	1898	1916	1939		(4)
May	1901	1919	1956	1977		(4)	1905	1906	1940	1947		(4)
June	1890	1946	1990			(3)	1900 1951	1913 1965	1921	1942	1949	1950 (8)
July	1911	1933	1943	1948	1959	(5)	1891	1893	1910	1932	1970	1984 (6)
August	1894	1909	1941	1967	1979	1987 (6)	1896	1923	1973	1982		(4)
September	1895 1939	1897 1971	1902 1978	1922 1989	1926	1929 (10)	1903	1911	1934	1953	1960	1981 (6)
October	1912	1916	1927	1936	1961	1964 (6)	1946 1990	1962	1966	1972	1974	1977 (7)
November	1915 1958	1918 1975	1920 1980	1928 1983	1942	1955 (10)	1907	1929	1956	1959		(4)
December	1891 1924 1950 1976	1898 1925 1952 1982	1900 1935 1954 1985	1904 1938 1963 1986	1905 1944 1965 1988	1908 1945 1968 (23) (101)	1890 1919 1969	1892 1930 1987	1895 1931	1899 1937	1914 1941	1917 1957 (14) (101)

[a]20-Stock Average, 1890–1896

TABLE 8-4 DOW JONES UTILITIES[a] MONTHLY ALMANAC OF CLOSING HIGHS AND LOWS

Month	Highs						Lows					
January	1937	1940	1941	1942	1966	1969	1943	1944	1945	1949	1951	1952
	1971	1974	1978	1981	1987	1988	1954	1956	1958	1961	1963	1975
	1990					(13)	1983	1985	1986			(15)
February	1934	1947				(2)	1948	1960	1977	1989		(4)
March	1931	1953	1959	1962	1973	(5)	1933	1935	1938	1964	1968	1980
												(6)
April	1930	1965	1967			(3)	1936	1939	1942			(3)
May	1946	1950	1957			(3)	1947	1976	1988			(3)
June	1948	1975				(2)	1940	1953	1962	1970	1972	1984
												(6)
July	1933	1943	1955	1977		(4)	1932	1950	1982			(3)
August	1939	1956	1963	1986		(4)	1966	1990				(2)
September	1929	1932				(2)	1959	1974	1981			(3)
October	1936	1938	1982	1983		(4)	1937	1946	1955	1957	1979	1987
												(6)
November	1961	1964	1968	1972	1980	(5)	1929	1967	1971	1978		(4)
December	1935	1944	1945	1949	1951	1952	1930	1931	1934	1941	1965	1969
	1954	1958	1960	1970	1976	1979	1973					(7)
	1984	1985	1989			(15)						
						(62)						(62)

[a]Utility index first calculated in 1929.

DAILY AND SHORT-TERM ALMANAC

SHORT TERM PATTERNS

Best Day to Sell Stocks: Friday

The catchy title of Yale Hirsch's recent book, "Don't Sell Stocks on Monday," perfectly summarizes the short term pattern of the stock market. The veteran chronicler details scores of market oddities and influences in the volume and points out that Monday is the only day of the week with a long-term negative market record. Stocks tend to favor the downside on Monday and the upside on every other day of the week. Hirsch's study is supported by figures from the S&P Composite Index.

The Dow Industrials, not surprisingly, display the same pattern. Monday is the worst day to sell. Friday is the best day. Saturday had even better odds for a favorable execution on the plus-side until the five-day week caught up with the NYSE in 1952.

Bull markets, however, favor Tuesday as the top day; the most infamous ending came in the post-Labor Day session of 1929. Monday and Wednesday cluster just behind Tuesday.

Important market lows have also favored a Monday or Tuesday climax; the dramatic 1987 finish came on Monday. In 1932 and 1974, however, the bear's reign ended on a Friday.

During the last 101 years, annual highs have been evenly divided between Monday, Tuesday, and Friday—23, 21, and 23 peaks, respectively. Tuesday and Monday have both marked annual lows 23 times. Since 1970, Monday has scored the year's high nine times, possibly reflecting a weekend global build-up of sell orders. Wednesday has become the most common annual-low day.

Thursday, both in the short span and over the past century, has been the least likely day to write its name on either the high or low readings.

Intra-month, historical studies show that the most positive investment returns are earned during the first half of the month. On a cumulative basis, all of the market's gains have occured in that period. Strongest upward pressure has been counted in the month's first four trading days though recent records indicate that the last trading day of the month has been gaining strength. Institutional investment of month-end funds is believed responsible for this calendar phenomenon.

Yale Hirsch, Don't Sell Stocks On Monday, New York, New York, Oxford, England, © 1986, Facts on File Publications.

9

The D.C. Connection

FEDERAL RESERVE RATE CHANGES AND RESULTS

Wall Street's most direct connection with Washington, D.C. is to the Securities & Exchange Commission. But the most closely watched agency in the Capitol is the Federal Reserve Board (FRB). "Fed watching" is a well-paid trade on the Street.

Rumors and speculations about FRB action, or lack of action, are a daily force in the market. Tight money is seen as the enemy of upward progress while Fed easing is welcomed by the bulls.

The President and Congress, of course, both have even greater market impact with their posturing, actions, and threats of action, but such influences do not lend themselves to tidy tables.

In addition to its power over government interest rates and bank reserve requirements, the FRB also sets margin requirements, though the last change came in 1974. Such changes have usually been well discounted and are of little importance as compared with changes in the discount rate.

Discount Rate—Notable Sequences of Change

A single change in the Fed's discount rate, up or down, has seldom had great influence on stock prices. Cheaper money does not automatically reverse a bear episode and dear money alone will not summarily choke off a bull market. Perceptions of longer term trends are important. A chain of rate increases or decreases does build inverse market pressure, although the history of the early 1930s offers a stubborn exception. No matter how low the discount rate sank in that period, stocks fell even lower.

Two notable and nearly identical sequences came in 1921 and 1982. In both instances, a lightning series of summer rate cuts led to important market reversals in August, to be followed by bull markets of historic dimensions.

Major Discount Rate Changes: 1914–1980 Federal Reserve Bank of New York

Initial 6% rate set at New York Federal Reserve Bank in November 1914 as the reserve system began formal operations.

Dec 23, 1914–December 21, 1917—Three cuts, to 4% by late February 1915, spurred war-frightened credit and confidence, and helped Dow to record 1915 advance. A further cut to 3% was made September 26, 1916.

December 21, 1917–May 5, 1921—Fed fought inflation with higher rates, 3.5% in December 1917 and 4% in April 1917. The boiling post war boom forced the rate to 4.75% on November 3, 1919 and a further increase to 6% was made in January 1920 with a hike to 7% on June 1 of the same year.

May 5, 1921–February 23, 1923—Deflation and depression allowed the Fed to relent in May 1921 with a rate cut to 6.5%. It would be followed by four more downward revisions, to 4.5% by the year end. A further cut was made in June 1922, when the discount figure dropped to 4%.

February 23, 1923–May 1, 1924—Rate 4.5%.

May 1, 1924–February 27, 1925—Discount fell to 3% by August 1924 and helped spark the beginning of the "Coolidge Market."

February 27, 1925–May 18, 1928—Rate remained remarkably stable, up to 3.5% in February 1925 and then locked at that figure or 4% until May 1928.

May 18, 1928–Nov 1, 1929—Three increases, the last to 6% on August 9, 1929 were too little, too late to halt the market frenzy.

November 1, 1929–May 8, 1931—Panic in October 1929, took the rate down to 5% and, when depression deepened, the figure slid steadily down to 1.5% in the summer of 1931. A record eight consecutive cuts were of no help to market bulls.

October 9, 1931–February 26, 1932—Sterling and gold crisis pushed rate to 2.5% on October 9, 1931 and to 3.5% later in the month.

February 26, 1932–Apr 25, 1946—With the exception of a brief hike during the crisis days of March–April 1933, the rate then moved lower for years. It was 1½% from 1934 until August 1937, when it was cut to 1% in an effort to halt the looming industrial collapse. The 1% rate would become a split rate, 0.5–1% in October 1942, and that figure would remain in effect until pushed higher by the hustling post war boom in 1946.

Apr 25, 1946–Jan 16, 1953—Four increases had only modest impact on the stock market, for the final figure was but 2%.

Apr 15, 1955–Nov 19, 1957—Seven consecutive increases, the last to 4% finally put a forceful top on the market in summer of 1957.

Nov 15, 1957–Sep 12, 1958—Recession quickly pulled rates down to 2.25%. That low figure, set in April 1958 has not been equalled since.

Sep 12, 1958–Nov 13, 1970—Rates moved irregularly higher, from 2.25% to the 6.5 figure set in April 1969. A cut from 4% to 3.5% in August 1960 reflects the recession problems of that year. Another brief decline was seen in the winter months of 1966–1967 and a token .25% cut to 5.75% was made shortly before the 1968 election. It lasted but four months.

Nov 13, 1970–Jan 15, 1973—Four cuts in less than three months gave the stock market a huge lift. Rate dropped from 6.5% to 4.75%. A slight increase in July was short-lived, to be followed by two more reductions, leaving the rate at 4.5%.

Jan 15, 1973–Dec 9, 1974—A stock market beset by inflation, OPEC, soaring gold prices, and Watergate couldn't get a break. Eight increases hiked

TABLE 9-1 DISCOUNT RATE CHANGES, 1980–1989 (FRB of New York)

Year	Date	Rate (%)	Year	Date	Rate (%)
1980	Feb 15	13[a]	1984	Apr 9	9
	May 30	12		Nov 21	8.5
	Jne 13	11		Dec 24	8
	Jly 28	10			
	Sep 26	11	1985	May 24	7.5
	Nov 17	12			
	Dec 5	13	1986	Mar 10	7
	Dec 15	14		Apr 23	6.5
				Jly 11	6
1981	Nov 2	13		Aug 22	5.5
	Dec 4	12			
			1987	Sep 11	6
1982	Jly 20	11.5			
	Aug 2	10.5	1988	Aug 24	6.5
	Aug 27	10			
	Oct 12	9.5	1989	Feb 24	7
	Nov 22	9			
	Dec 15	8.5	1990	Dec 18	6.5

[a]From 12% set October 8, 1979.

Series records: Most consecutive increases: 14, Aug 21, 1977 to Feb 15, 1980
Most consecutive declines: 8, Nov 2,1981 to Dec 15, 1983 and Nov 1, 1929 to May 8, 1931
High Rate: 14%, Dec 15, 1980 to Nov 2, 1981
Low Rate: Split .5 to 1%, Oct 30, 1942 to Apr 25, 1946

the discount rate to a frightening 8%, which was set in April 1974. The interest rate tide and the Dow both reversed course in early December 1974.

Dec 9, 1974–Aug 31, 1977—Depression and the worst market slump since the 1930s made 8% an overkill. Multiple cuts pushed a huge stock rally ending in September 1976. One more cut in November, to 5.5 percent, couldn't help the Dow, but the rate stayed there for nine months.

August 31, 1977–Feb 15, 1980—The steam roller. Fourteen consecutive increases, the last to 13%, frightened the world. The DJIA actually gained over 40 points during the period, but earnings were severely discounted and the inflation-adjusted Dow also lost ground.

MARGIN REQUIREMENTS AND CHANGES

Initial Margin Requirements

Minimum federal margin requirements are set by the Board of Governors of the Federal Reserve Board, but only since 1934. During the 1980s, the requirement was 50 percent. An investor wishing to purchase $10,000 in approved securities had to put up at least $5,000 in cash or $10,000 in marginable stocks. The latter category has come to include many unlisted issues, but they were excluded until 1969.

The NYSE upon occasion has established higher margins than the Fed for certain stocks. In the late 1960s, frenzied speculation put scores of stocks under special requirements at the Exchange; many were at 100 percent.

Prior to 1934, there was no federal regulation of margins and while a 10 percent requirement was not all that common, that low figure has been widely blamed for part of the 1929 troubles. References can be found to "5-point" margins in the early 1900s. In such cases, the customer put up only $500, generally on popular stocks selling for $100 or less.

TABLE 9-2   CHANGES IN INITIAL MARGIN REQUIREMENT INITIAL RATE 10/15/34: 45%

Change effective	Rate (%)	Change	Rate (%)	Change	Rate (%)
Feb 1, 1936	55	Jan 17, 1951	75	Jly 10, 1962	50
Nov 1, 1937	40	Feb 20, 1953	50	Nov 6, 1963	70
Feb 5, 1945	50	Jan 4, 1955	60	Jne 8, 1968	80
Jly 5, 1945	75	Apr 23, 1955	70	May 6, 1970	65
Jan 21, 1946	100	Jan 16, 1958	50	Dec 6, 1971	55
Feb 1,1947	75	Aug 5, 1958	70	Nov 24, 1972	65
Mar 30, 1949	50	Oct 16, 1958	90	Jan 3, 1974	50
		Jly 28, 1960	70		

───────────── **THE PRESIDENTIAL ELECTION CYCLE** ─────────────

If Wall Street psychosomatics had nothing else to worry about, they would fret full time about the political cycles. When ambitious men spend millions to win offices which pay but a pittance, there is need for worry.

Political worries run an endless chain from candidacy to nomination to the opinion polls to a possible postelection slump. The most serious concerns involve the four-year presidential cycle. Table 9-3 breaks down the yearly Dow changes for each White House administration of the past 100 years and indicates the timing for the cycle's highs and lows.

Presidential cycle lows are extensive in the first or second year following election, though President Bush escaped the first-year pattern in 1989. Since 1916, every low of the presidential sequence has come in either the first or second year of the administration, with the exception of Herbert Hoover's term of office when the 1932 depression low was recorded in his final year.

Interestingly, every bear market low since John F. Kennedy's presidency has been recorded in the election mid-years, 1962, 1966, 1970, 1974, 1978, and 1982.

Presidential cycle highs predominate in the fourth year since Wilson's first administration, and since 1948, only 1968, 1976 and 1988 failed to make a grand finish. The first two were narrow misses, barely failing the respective peaks of 1966 and 1973. But 1988 never approached the 1987 top.

Few on the Street have given the stock market's political cycle more attention than Yale Hirsch. In his 1988 *Stock Trader's Almanac,* he summarized the political cycle since the time of Andrew Johnson and presented the flip side of early cycle weakness.

His most important finding: "The last two . . . years of the 39 administrations since 1832 produced a total market gain of 515%, dwarfing the 54% gain of the first two years of those administrations."[1] The second Reagan term added to the luster of the number.

When election year comes, the election worries of the spring–summer period usually provide a decent buying opportunity, as in 1988. Election year highs have come in the final quarter in 16 of 25 presidential cycles since 1888. And two other peaks were recorded in September.

Such a preelection bull strategy, however, fell victim to bear market years in 1892, 1920, and 1960.

---

[1] Yale Hirsch, Stock Trader's Almanac, Old Tappan, New Jersey, ©1977, The Hirsch Organization Inc., p. 125.

TABLE 9-3   THE POLITICAL CYCLE AND THE DOW

Winner & Party	Dates—election year high/low		1st Year (%)	2nd Year (%)	3rd Year (%)	Election 4th year (%)	
	High	Low					
1888 Harrison (R)	Oct	Apr	+10	H −14 L	+18	− 7	1892
1892 Cleveland (D)	Mar	Dec	H −25	− 1	+ 2	− 2 L	1896
1896 McKinley (R)	Nov	Aug	+21 L	+22	H + 9	+ 7	1900
1900 McKinley (R)	Dec	Sep	H − 9	− 0	−24 L	+42	1904
1904 Roosevelt (R)	Dec	Mar	+38	H − 2	−38 L	+47	1908
1908 Taft (R)	Nov	Feb	H +15	−18	+ 0 L	+ 8	1912
1912 Wilson (D)	Sep	Feb	−10	− 5 L	+82	H − 4	1916
1916 Wilson (D)	Nov	Apr	−22 L	+11	H +31	−33	1920
1920 Harding (R)	Jan	Dec	+13 L	+22	− 3	H +26	1924
1924 Coolidge (R)	Dec	Mar	+30 L	+ 0	+29	H +48	1928
1928 Hoover (R)	Dec	Feb	H −17	−34	−53	−23 L	1932
1932 Roosevelt (D)	Mar	Jly	+67 L	+ 4	+39	H +25	1936
1936 Roosevelt (D)	Nov	Apr	H −33	+28 L	− 3	−13	1940
1940 Roosevelt (D)	Jan	Jne	−15	+ 8	+14	H +12	1944
1944 Roosevelt (D)	Dec	Feb	+27	H − 8 L	+ 2	− 2	1948
1948 Truman (D)	Jne	Mar	+13 L	+18	+14	H + 8	1952
1952 Eisenhower (R)	Dec	May	− 4 L	+44	+21	H + 2	1956
1956 Eisenhower (R)	Apr	Jan	−13 L	+34	+16	H − 9	1960
1960 Kennedy (D)	Jan	Oct	+19	−11 L	+17	H +15	1964
1964 Johnson (D)	Nov	Jan	+11	H −19 L	+15	+ 4	1968
1968 Nixon (R)	Dec	Mar	−15	+ 5 L	+ 6	H +15	1972
1972 Nixon (R)	Dec	Jan	H −17	−28 L	+38	+18	1976
1976 Carter (D)	Sep	Jan	−17	− 3 L	+ 4	H +15	1980
1980 Reagan (R)	Nov	Apr	− 9	+20 L	+20	H − 4	1984
1984 Reagan (R)	Jan	Aug	+28 L	+23	+20	H +12	1988
1988 Bush (R)	Oct	Jly	+27	− 4	+ 2		1992

Yearly Percentage Change for Dow

High and low for each four-year presidential cycle designated by *H* and *L*.

291

───────────────── **WAR AND THE THREAT OF WAR** ─────────────────

When Washington Sounds the Bugle

War and the threat of war are not always the making of those on the Potomac. Often, the events are thrust upon them. But it is Washington that sounds the bugle. There has never been a popular vote on this dominant market force.

Every important war threat—save that of World War II—has brought selling into the market. The response has ranged from uneasiness to panic and the duration of liquidation has lasted from a few days to several years.

After the initial news impact, the market has tended to align itself with the course of battle. But even success has had a flip side. Every major conflict has at one time or another developed a "peace scare" as investors worried about the adjustment to peace from a war-boosted economy.

Foreign conflicts, as well as domestic wars, have pressured the market. Stock exchange prices collapsed in December 1899, when the British forces suffered severe reverses in the Boer War. Japan's invasion of Manchuria and China, Mussolini's adventure in Ethiopia, Hitler's demands in Central Europe, the Suez crisis, and the recurrent Middle Eastern wars have all served as an excuse, at least for a few days, for excited selling of stocks in New York.

Table 9-4 tabulates the most serious war events and threats of the past century, showing the market's short-term response as well as changes over the next three, six, and twelve months. The short-term drive to lower prices has usually lasted for two to three weeks; panic selling after Pearl Harbor was over in three weeks. After the U.S. battleship *Maine* was blown in Havana Harbor on February 15, 1898, however, the urgent selling continued for over five weeks.

In 1990, soaring crude oil prices and inflation fears conspired to push stocks lower for over two months following Iraq's invasion of Kuwait. Panic selling, however, was over by the end of August.

TABLE 9-4   WAR AND THE THREAT OF WAR
Market Reaction to Hostilities[a]

Event and Date	Short-term Dow change	Dow three months later	Dow six months later	Dow one year later	Comments
War threat with England December 1895	−14.7%	—	—	—	President Cleveland seen to threaten war over Monroe Doctrine violation.
	England, Venezuela in bitter border dispute. Crisis was not a market factor after January 1.				
Battleship *Maine* sunk in Havana February 1898	−14.8%	−6.6%	Plus	—	War on Spain declared on April 25. By then, it had been discounted.
	Peace treaty signed less than six months after Maine loss.				
United Kingdom suffered heavy reverses, Boer War December 1899	−12.7%	−5.4%	−3.7%	Plus	London big seller. United States feared U.K. credits would be called.
	Industrials hurt worse than Rails—down 23% in December selling. Loss on 18th would be worst for next 30 years.				
World War I July 1914	−11.6%	Lower	−3.5%	Plus	Unofficial Dow level of late October was World War I low.
	NYSE closed Jly 30 to Dec 12, 1914.				
United States and Germany broke relations February 1917	−8.8%	−2.3%	−3.9%	−19.3%	President Wilson's war request cost Dow 6.6% in three-week April period.
	Unrestricted U-boat campaign, break with Berlin took Industrials down 8.8% in two days.				
World War II September 1939	+16.0	+8.4%	+4.0%	−5.5%	Market held gain until May 1940 "blitz."
	Exception to the rule that first war news is bearish.				
Pearl Harbor December 1941	−8.8%	−10.3%	−10.5%	−1.2%	Pearl Harbor Dow level not crested until January, 1943.
	World War II low came in April 1942.				
Korea June 1950	−12.0%	Plus	Plus	Plus	Dow at record high by December 1950.
	June 24 NYSE volume largest since September 1939.				
Cuban Missile Crisis September–October 1962	−8.2%	Plus	Plus	Plus	Dangerous October confrontation over in few days.
	November reflex made it best Dow month since 1939.				
Gulf of Tonkin August 1964	−2.1%	Plus	Plus	Plus	LBJ: PT boats attacked two U.S. destroyers.
	This was start of "official" United States war in Vietnam, but that involvement was already in the market.				
Iraq invaded Kuwait August 1990	−14.5%	−14.2%	−5.8%	—	American troops arrived in Saudi Arabia August 8.
	Oil prices, oil stocks soared early on.				

[a]20-Stock or Dow Rail Average in 1895, 1898, and 1899. Dow Industrials thereafter.

Glossary

Advance-decline ratio. A technical measurement of market breadth. Number of advances versus declines can be accumulated and charted as a line. Other important technical aids are derived from the figures.

American depository receipts. These receipts represent shares of a foreign corporation held in vaults of a foreign branch of U.S. banks. They make foreign investing easier and are quoted in dollars.

AMEX. American Stock Exchange.

American Stock Exchange. Also known as AMEX or ASE. Formerly New York Curb Exchange.

Arbitrage. To buy and sell same or nearly identical securities in two different markets to take advantage of price disparities. Merger arbitrage has same basis, but is usually in same market.

Bear. One who thinks or wishes market will go down.

Bear raid. Organized assault by bears to drive market lower. Easier in old days when short sales did not require an uptick. But modern program traders have found loopholes not available to individual speculators.

Big Board. New York Stock Exchange.

Blue chip. Classy security with solid background of earnings and dividends.

Blue sky. State laws to protect investor rights and insure that underwritings are fairly presented are called blue sky laws. Kansas was first to pass such legislation in 1911.

Bond. A debt security which does not represent ownership interest. Usually issued in $1,000 par denominations or multiples thereof, but there are some "baby bonds" of $100 denomination. *Bond funds* are mutual funds that invest in bonds.

Bucket shop. Illegal brokerage scam of the old days. Operators obtained a Western Union "drop" for stock quotations and "bucketed" or took the other side of customer orders, betting that the mini-margined clients would be wrong. It was the "house" against the speculator.

Call money. Money borrowed by brokers to finance their inventory and margin accounts. Loan has no term and can be called at any time. Interest rate charged to customer margin accounts fluctuates with call loan rate. In old days rate was very volatile, even on a daily basis. Funds were brokered at the Money Desk on floor of the NYSE. Rates were seen as gauge of market sentiment.

Clearing house certificates. Bank clearing houses issued these in periods of financial crisis. The clearing house took in bank assets, such as commercial paper and bonds, and issued certificates against the paper. They were guaranteed by the clearing house and used to settle interbank differences in lieu of cash. Widely used in panics from 1860s until 1914. They were briefly resurrected during 1933 bank holidays.

Closed-end fund. A mutual fund with a set number of shares. Underwriter does not redeem stock, which trades on open market, frequently at NYSE. Shares often trade at discount to net asset value, unlike open-ended funds.

Conglomerate. A "go-go" business combination form popular in the late 1960s. Often a dozen or more wildly divergent industries were gathered under the conglomerate's control.

Corner. A form of manipulation which attempts to punish the shorts, or bears on a stock. A consequence of a condition where most of the issued shares, or most of the floating supply, are in hands of a group turning the vise on the shorts, who must "cover" the stock they have sold short.

Curb. The Curb was the old outdoor market, but got in out of the weather in 1921 and in 1953 became the American Stock Exchange.

Customer's man. Popular title in the 1920s for stock and bond salesmen. More recently known as: registered representative, broker, investment executive, account executive, and so on.

Cyclic stocks. Like autos, steels, and papers. Earnings tend to rise and fall directly with the business cycle.

Discount rate. Interest rate charged by the Federal Reserve Banks to member banks for loans. Rate varied widely in the 1980s from 6 to 14 percent.

Dividends. Payment to stockholders. Does not have to be from earnings. Cash is usually preferred, but stock dividends are common and there have even been dividend payments in kind—gold, whiskey receipts, and so on.

Double top. Menacing chart formation with two clearly defined and well-separated peaks. Important double tops were seen in the Dow in 1937 and 1946. A *double bottom* is a reverse formation and promises higher prices.

Dow Jones Averages. See Chapter 5.

Dow theory. A controversial theory of market forecasting based on confirming action by both the Industrials and Transports (Rails prior to 1970).

Fancy stocks. New and untried stocks quoted at high prices.

Green Mail. Premium buy-out of a hostile shareholder or group.

Head & shoulders. No rinse, but a chart formation of great reliability. It resembles a line drawing of head and shoulders. Is also reliable in inverse formation.

Holding company. A firm whose primary business is holding a controlling interest in the securities of other companies. Northern Securities was the Morgan-designed holding company for Northern Pacific and the Great Northern Railroad (1901–1904).

Index Futures. These provide a way to gamble on the direction of several stock indices, and are just as lively as those other futures—like pork bellies and soybeans—that mother warned against.

Industrial trust. Popular business combination form at the turn of the century. A large number of firms in the same line of business—a horizontal combination—would be consolidated into a trust, which held the shares as trustee for the individual concerns. U.S. Steel was the largest; it was, however, a "vertical" trust controlling ore, coke, railroads, lake steamers, steel mills, and fabricators of wire, rods, tin plate, bridge forms, and so on.

Institutions. They now dominate the action in all financial markets, whereas until the mid-1960s individual investors were the biggest players. Pension funds continue to grow enormously, but mutual funds, life insurance companies, casualty companies, and banks, among others, have been big investors for decades.

Investment banker. No deposits, please. Investment bankers deal in mergers, acquisitions, reorganizations, underwritings, private placements, and expensive advice. A major profit center for brokerage firms for over a century.

Investment trust. It pools funds and invests the capital in other companies. A mutual fund is an investment trust.

Irish dividend. A dividend in reverse—an assessment against stockholders. Decades ago, many stocks were assessable and the device was popular among bankruptcy judges as a means of raising cash for strapped railroads.

Junk bonds. Some were designed that way, as in the late 1980s. Some good bonds just deteriorated into junk, because of bad management or changed industry conditions. They are high-yield, high-risk debt securities with a poor credit rating—double-B or lower.

Leveraged buy-out. Ideally, a buy-out group leverages its equity with heavy borrowing and then takes a target company private with a fat bid to shareholders. Then, hopefully, the new owners repay the debt by peeling off assets to sell, or draining the privatized company's cash flow to pay down the takeover debt.

Margin. In popular usage, this is the amount put up by an investor using credit to buy securities. FRB sets minimum requirements.

Margin account. As opposed to a cash account. Documents need to be signed for a margin account and interest is charged on the debit balance.

Margin call. Initial margin calls, for new purchases, are expected. But maintenance calls are bad news. They come when the investor equity has dropped far below the original 50 percent requirement. "House calls" come when that level approaches 30 percent (house minimums vary); the NYSE minimum requirement is 25%.

Money market funds. No-load mutual funds that invest in the short-term money market. They favor commercial paper, but also buy CDs, Treasury bills, and so on.

Mutual fund. An investment company which is "open end," in most common usage. More stock can be issued at prices related to net asset value (NAV). Shares do not trade publicly but will be redeemed by company at NAV.

Options. Stock options are contracts giving the owner a right to buy (or sell) a specific security at a specific price any time up to and including the expiration date of the option. Calls give the right to purchase; puts grant the right to sell. Both are based on 100-share units.

Over the counter. Unlisted stocks are over-the-counter stocks (OTC).

Par value. Meant more in the old days. Now, there are plenty of $100 stocks with a no-par or $1 par value. But "par" is essential knowledge for preferred stocks and bonds since it is on that value that dividends and interest are calculated. A 6 percent $50 par preferred would pay $3 annually, by example.

Pegged. A "pegged" price is fixed or stabilized, as for an underwriting offering, when the SEC allows stabilization. Pools usually pegged prices while they worked off their manipulations.

Pink sheets. National Quotation Bureau publishes these pink-colored sheets daily, listing thousands of OTC stocks and the brokers who "make a market" in them. Prices are subject to further negotiation.

Pool. Not nice now but legal until 1934. A pool was initiated with a legal agreement to pool speculators' funds and manipulate a certain security. A pool manager was in charge of day-to-day operations which involved a great churning of the selected stock. Pool activity peaked in 1929, but bear and other pools continued until SEC legislation.

Price earnings ratio. Stock price divided by annual earnings equals the PE ratio. If earnings are $2 for a 24 dollar stock, the PE ratio is 12X.

Prime rate. A "best customer" loan rate charged by commercial banks to large clients. Much more volatile than the FRB discount rate.

Preferred stock. Preferred because it has a senior claim on earnings and also on assets (in event of liquidation) as compared with common stock. It carries a fixed dividend which is usually cumulative.

Program trading. This multimillion dollar computer game was not *designed* to sap the small investor. It was engineered to capitalize on market anomalies between stocks and index futures. But the innocent had more chance with a 1931 bear pool than with a giant computer blindly bulldozing a half-hundred popular favorites.

Puts and calls. *See* Options.

Regulation T. FRB regulation governing extension of credit by broker-dealers to margin accounts.

REITs. Spelled sorrow in 1974. The acronym stands for Real Estate Investment Trust, which is a closed-end mutual fund investing in real estate equities, mortgages on office buildings, and the like.

Sell short. Short sellers sell a stock which is not in their possession to deliver; they borrow the shares to deliver to the buyer. Sellers will profit if the shares fall in price. They must pay any dividend declared since they have "created" extra shares.

Short interest. The total number of shares short in the market or in a specific stock.

Specialists. Every stock at the NYSE has registered specialists who usually are specialists in many other issues. Their duty is to maintain a "fair and orderly" market in their issues and they will buy or sell for their own account when there is a disparity of price and orders. Thus, they fade or take the other side of the orders. This is not always economically sane and stocks can become alarmingly disorderly.

Syndicate. *See* Underwriting syndicate.

Treasuries. U.S. government debt, usually long-term bonds. But short-term treasuries refer to government bills (91 days) and notes.

Triple top. A chart formation with three widely separated peaks. Rare for a market average, but a triple top for the Dow stretched out for 15 months in 1956–1957.

Triplewitch. Slang for the day, once each quarter, when equity and index futures options expire along with index futures. Usually, there is great volatility in the final hour or minutes.

Trust. *See* Industrial trust.

Underwriting syndicate. Group of investment houses who undertake and guarantee an underwriting of stocks or bonds.

Yield. For stocks, yield is the dividend divided by market price. For bonds, a coupon yield is expressed as a percent of par value, while current yield is the coupon rate divided by the market price. The yield to maturity is calculated from market price to maturity date. If the bond price is below par, the yield to maturity will exceed the coupon rate. A premium (over par) bond will yield less than the coupon rate to maturity.

Abbreviations

A-D Advance-decline (usually a ratio)
ADR American Depository Receipt
AMEX American Stock Exchange
AMR American Airlines
ASE American Stock Exchange
AT&T American Telephone & Telegraph
B&O Baltimore & Ohio Railroad
CBOE Chicago Board Option Exchange
CBOT Chicago Board of Trade
CD Certificate of Deposit
CIO Congress of Industrial Organization
CFTC Commodity Futures Trading Commission
CME Chicago Mercantile Exchange
C&O Chesapeake & Ohio Railroad
CPI Consumer Price Index
DJIA Dow Jones Industrial Average
DJRA Dow Jones Rail Average
DJTA Dow Jones Transportation Average
DJUA Dow Jones Utility Average

DOW DJIA unless otherwise noted
FDR Franklin Delano Roosevelt
Fed Federal Reserve Board
FNMA Federal National Mortgage Association (Fannie Mae)
FRB Federal Reserve Board/Bank
GM General Motors
GMO Gulf Mobile & Ohio Railroad
GN Great Northern Railroad
GNP Gross National Product
IBM International Business Machines
ICC Interstate Commerce Commission
IPO Initial public offering
IRA Individual retirement account
JFK John Fitzgerald Kennedy
JPM J. Pierpont Morgan
LBJ Lyndon Baines Johnson
LBO Leveraged buyout
L&N Louisville & Nashville Railroad
LSE London Stock Exchange
LTV Ling-Temco-Vought
ML Merrill Lynch
M-K-T Missouri Kansas Texas Railroad
MOP Missouri & Pacific Railroad
NASD National Association of Security Dealers
NASDAQ NASD Automated Quotation System. An electronic market
   for OTC stocks.
NAV Net asset value (investment trust)
NP Northern Pacific Railroad
NRA National Recovery Act (1933)
NYSE New York Stock Exchange
OTC Over-the-counter (unlisted)
PE Price-earnings (usually a ratio or multiple)
RCA Radio Corporation of America
REG T Regulation T
REIT Real estate investment trust
RFC Reconstruction Finance Corporation
SBIC Small Business Investment Company
SEC Securities and Exchange Commission
SIPC Securities Investor Protection Corporation
SOO Minneapolis, St. Paul & Sault Ste. Marie Railroad
S&P Standard & Poor's
SP Southern Pacific Railroad
TWA Trans-World Airlines
UAL United Airlines
UAW United Auto Workers

UMW United Mine Workers
UP Union Pacific Railroad
WI When issued
WSJ *The Wall Street Journal*

Index